The Rigoberta Menchú Controversy

p.61

The Rigoberta Menchú Controversy

Arturo Arias, Editor

With a Response by David Stoll

University of Minnesota Press

Minneapolis

London

Published by the University of Minnesota Press
111 Third Avenue South, Suite 290
Minneapolis, MN 55401-2520
http://www.upress.umn.edu

Library of Congress Cataloging-in-Publication Data

The Rigoberta Menchú controversy / Arturo Arias, editor; with a
response by David Stoll.
       p.   cm.
    Includes bibliographical references and index.
    ISBN 0-8166-3625-7 (HC : acid-free paper) — ISBN 0-8166-3626-5 (PB :
acid-free paper)
    1. Menchú, Rigoberta. Me llamo Rigoberta Menchú y así me nació la
conciencia.   2. Menchú, Rigoberta.   3. Stoll, David, Rigoberta Menchú
and the story of all poor Guatemalans.   4. Quiché women—Biography.
5. Mayas—Guatemala—Government relations.   6. Women human
rights workers—Guatemala—Biography.   7. Mayas—Civil rights.
8. Arias, Arturo, 1950–   II. Stoll, David, 1952–
F1465.2.Q5 M387 2001
972.81004'97415—dc21   00-012083

12 11 10 09 08 07 06 05 04 03 02 01   10 9 8 7 6 5 4 3 2

Contents

Acknowledgments

This book came together as a result of the cooperation of many people. I would like to thank Professor Marc Zimmerman from the Center for Latin American Studies, University of Illinois at Chicago. It was he who urged me to embrace this project, despite my initial reluctance to take on such a task: I was partially burned out by the bitter, drawn-out Guatemalan political process and wanted to focus more on specifically literary matters. Professor Zimmerman's belief in me and his insistence that these efforts ought to be led by a Guatemalan intellectual familiar with the different sides of the issues, and not by a gringo, ultimately convinced me of the need for me to steer this enterprise. I will remain eternally grateful for his persistence.

Jennifer Moore, acquisitions editor at the University of Minnesota Press, shared the same interest and enthusiasm. From the very start, she was supportive, energetic, and determined to bring this project to fruition. Whenever I needed any kind of support, from someone's E-mail address to typesetting guidelines, she was there offering her knowledge, her contacts, her words of wisdom. It is doubtful that this book would have seen the light of day two years after the controversy first began without her decisive intervention.

Jill Robbins, my beloved wife, was equally instrumental in the success of this project, especially within the narrow time parameters allotted. She gracefully ceded vital amounts of time and energy from her own research project to help me with the translations of original documents from the Spanish, general editing, and a most welcome reworking of my own "Spanglish." Indeed, I dedicate this entire effort to her *estímulo y amor.*

Jamie Davidson, the best graduate student I have ever had, happily prepared most of the manuscript for production in record time, a thankless task, but one without which the book might not have been published.

Professor John Beverley became a closer friend during this entire experience, as he reworked his own contribution to fit the volume's needs, dialogued constantly with me, and visited San Francisco State University, where he enlightened his audience with a powerful talk on some of the issues at stake.

Finally, I want to thank all the contributors. Regardless of what side of the issue they were on, they all gladly collaborated with the project, focused on it during a time when most had other obligations, returned their articles to me in record time, and were gracious when cuts and modifications were suggested. I thank all of them for the ease of working with them, and for their happy, friendly dialogue and cooperation.

Abbreviations

AGNU	Asociación Guatemalteca Pro Naciones Unidas (Guatemalan Association for the United Nations)
ANN	Alianza Nueva Nación (New Nation Alliance)
ASIES	Asociación de Investigación y Estudios Sociales (Social Studies Research Association)
AVANCSO	Asociación para el Avance de las Ciencias Sociales en Guatemala (Association for the Advancement of the Social Sciences in Guatemala)
CACIF	Cámara de Agricultura, Comercio, Industria y Finanzas (Chamber of Agriculture, Commerce, Industry, and Finance)
CEH	Comisión para el Esclarecimiento Histórico (Commission for Historical Clarification)
CEIDEC	Centro Integral de Desarrollo Comunal (Integral Center for Communal Development)
CETRAL	Catholic Center for Latin American Relief
CGUP	Comité Guatemalteco de Unidad Patriótica (Guatemalan Committee for Patriotic Unity)
CNEM	Consejo Nacional de Educación Maya (National Council of Maya Education)
CONAVIGUA	Confederación Nacional de Viudas de Guatemala (National Confederation of Guatemalan Widows)

COPMAGUA	Coordinadora de los Pueblos Mayas de Guatemala (Coordination of the Mayan People of Guatemala)
CPRs	Comités de Poblaciones en Resistencia (Civilian Resistance Committees)
CUC	Comité de Unidad Campesina (Committee for Peasant Unity)
EGP	Ejército Guerrillero de los Pobres (Guerrilla Army of the Poor)
FAR	Fuerzas Armadas Rebeldes (Rebel Armed Forces)
FDNG	Frente Democrático Nueva Guatemala (Democratic Front for a New Guatemala)
FP31	Frente Popular 31 de enero (Popular Front of the 31st of January)
FRG	Frente Republicano Guatemalteco (Guatemalan Republican Front)
FUNDAPI	Fundación de Ayuda al Pueblo Indígena (Foundation for the Aid of Indigenous Peoples)
GAM	Grupo de Apoyo Mutuo (Mutual Support Group)
GSN	Guatemalan Scholars Network
IGE	Iglesia Guatemalteca en el Exilio (Guatemalan Church in Exile)
INC	Instancia Nacional de Consenso (National Instance for Consensus)
INTA	Instituto Nacional de Transformación Agraria (National Institute for Agrarian Transformation)
MINUGUA	Misión de Naciones Unidas para Guatemala (United Nations Verification Commission in Guatemala)
MRP-Ixim	Movimiento Revolucionario del Pueblo-Ixim (People's Revolutionary Movement-Ixim)
ORPA	Organización del Pueblo en Armas (Revolutionary Organization of the People in Arms)
PACs	Patrullas Autodefensa Civil (Civil Self-Defense Patrols)

REMHI	Recuperación de Memoria Histórica (Recovery of Historical Memory)
RUOG	Representación Unitaria de la Oposición Guatemalteca (Unitary Representation of the Guatemalan Opposition)
TIMACH	Tijolb'al Mayab' Adrián Inés Chávez (Adrián Inés Chávez Mayan Studies Center)
TSE	Tribunal Supremo Electoral (Supreme Electoral Court)
UCN	Unión de Centro Nacional (National Unity of the Center)
URNG	Unidad Revolucionaria Nacional Guatemalteca (Guatemalan National Revolutionary Unity)

I
Background

Rigoberta Menchú's History within the Guatemalan Context

Arturo Arias

Guatemala, the largest and richest country in Central America, borders the southernmost Mexican state of Chiapas on the west, the Yucatán peninsula to the north, El Salvador, Honduras, and Belize to the east, and the Pacific Ocean to the south. Approximately the size of Ohio or Tennessee, it has a population of about eleven million people, half of them Maya. Most Mayas live in the central and western highlands of the country, called the Sierra Madre here as in neighboring Mexico. The Sierra Madre, the southern continuation of the Rocky Mountains, gives Guatemala its mountainous landscape.

When the Spaniards conquered Guatemala in the early sixteenth century, they burned and looted Maya cities, and they executed the entire Maya elite. In one of history's first holocausts, it is estimated that as many as two and a half million Mayas died in the fifty years following the Conquest. Since then, Mayas have been enslaved, oppressed, and discriminated against. During Spanish colonialism, they were virtual slaves, despite the fact that, according to the Laws of the Indies, indigenous peoples technically could not be enslaved. Independence from Spain in the early nineteenth century did not improve their lot. The *criollos* fundamentally ignored Mayas in the early part of the nineteenth century and granted them a degree of autonomy by default. However, Mayas were forced by Ladinos to work against their will in the coffee plantations after 1871, and they were treated as subhumans, barely subsisting. The so-called liberal regimes that succeeded each other throughout the twentieth century never worried about improving the Mayas' lot, nor

3

about ending rampant discrimination from Ladinos. Despite this continuous abuse, Maya patience prevented any explosions until the Alliance for Progress introduced the rudiments of modernity into Maya communities in the 1960s. The prospect of finally being enfranchised, followed by the disillusionment after the Arana Osorio dictatorship in the early 1970s, coupled with the devastation of the 1976 earthquake, which killed twenty thousand people and destroyed hundreds of highland villages, created the conditions for political organizing, initially in a clandestine manner. This long struggle led to the formation of an organization called the Committee for Peasant Unity (CUC) in 1973. (It still remains a matter of contention whether Vicente Menchú, Rigoberta's father and an activist of Catholic Action,[1] was one of its founding members, or even a member at all. Indeed, David Stoll dwells quite a lot on this ambiguity in his book.) Given the brutally oppressive nature of the Guatemalan military dictatorship and the endemic racism in the country, CUC and analogous organizations had to operate underground. This factor, coupled with the increasing radicalization within the country itself and within the Central American area as a whole, led to an eventual absorption of CUC by the Guerrilla Army of the Poor (EGP). Although it was originally the EGP's intention to implement an orthodox *foco* guerrilla strategy,[2] the leaders' prerogatives changed with the Sandinista victory, which implied that it was possible to achieve a quick triumph against the military dictatorship. Here they grossly underestimated the Reagan administration's response to the Central American crisis: a dramatic increase in military aid to the "pro-American" governments fighting against "Marxist guerrillas." It was as part of this unfortunate strategic shift that the EGP absorbed CUC and other radicalized mass organizations, which were eventually to become the "popular army" of the revolution, guided by the theology of liberation as its de facto ideology. Of course, the EGP's vision of a quick victory never came to pass. Recognizing the guerrillas' strategy, the army seized the initiative with a series of attacks on the guerrillas' safe houses in Guatemala City in 1981, followed by the systematic destruction of Maya villages, primarily in 1982, an action that brutally suppressed any further spontaneous insurrection in the highlands. Even prior to the more detailed report provided by the United Nations Commission for Historical Clarification (Comisión para el Esclarecimiento Histórico, CEH) in 1999, both the human rights organizations and the army itself often spoke of the destruction of more than 450 Maya villages, more than a hundred thousand deaths, and more than a million refugees. Rigoberta Menchú Tum survived this massacre by fleeing to neighboring Mexico. She first told her story at the peak of the genocidal campaign against her people, when some experts wondered if Maya culture would ever be able to recover from what seemed like a fatal blow.

Rigoberta the Unknown

When Rigoberta Menchú Tum fled Guatemala for the safety of Mexico, she was virtually unknown in her own country or even among the Maya peoples. In Guatemala, the name of her father, Vicente Menchú, had gained symbolic notoriety among progressive sectors after the destruction of the Spanish embassy by the Guatemalan army on January 31, 1980. On that date Vicente Menchú and thirty-eight others protesting human rights violations in the Ixil area of the country were burned to death in the embassy by the Guatemalan army along with the ambassadorial staff and some individuals who happened to be doing business at the embassy on that day. A year later, an organization called "Vicente Menchú's Christian Revolutionaries" was created in his memory. It became part of the January 31st Popular Front, an umbrella group that included the Committee for Peasant Unity (CUC), labor groups, and other popular organizations representing different segments of Guatemalan society. However, starting in the summer of 1981, most of these organizations were crushed in the military's urban offensive, whose purpose was to destroy the rearguard of the revolutionary movement and its safe houses in the city. By the end of 1983 there was no trace left of the January 31st Popular Front, and, of the organizations that were its members, the only one that survives to this day is the CUC. "Vicente Menchú's Christian Revolutionaries" disappeared without a trace, although some of its members did regroup in a new organization called the Guatemalan Church in Exile (IGE).

Rigoberta Menchú Tum's public visibility at the end of 1981 was limited to circles close to the Guatemalan opposition and its solidarity groups in Mexico. They principally saw her as the daughter of a Maya grassroots activist and a martyr of the Spanish embassy, whose name had become emblematic of that particular misadventure. Vicente Menchú himself, however, had not been a national public figure, and for "mainstream" Guatemalans—that is, urbanized Ladinos of both the upper and middle classes who simply refused to believe that an actual war was taking place in their country—he was simply "another Indian" burned to death in the Spanish embassy tragedy. Rigoberta Menchú Tum was herself a member of the CUC and worked on its behalf in Mexico City. However, the nature of exile itself implied that "political work" done outside of the country had inevitably to focus on international solidarity and/or diplomatic work. Therefore, it was only natural that, in its desire to gain international recognition, the Guatemalan opposition to the military dictatorship should launch a media campaign during the course of 1981 in which several representatives of different organizations then residing in Mexico toured the United States and Europe in order to alert the world to the ruthlessness and viciousness of the Guatemalan regime, which was implementing a process of "ethnic cleansing." International support, especially from the Reagan administration in the United States, flowed to the aid of the regime implementing the ethnic cleansing, under the guise that those being killed were "Communist agitators" and not activist Mayas, radicalized Catholics, or simply antidictatorial democrats.

It was during this tour that Menchú Tum began to be recognized as a particularly articulate spokesperson for the movement. Cécile Rousseau, a French-Canadian working then with the Revolutionary Organization of the People in Arms (ORPA), first noticed her innate ability to tell a good story and seduce her audience. She told Arturo Taracena, the Guatemalan representative of the EGP in France, that Elisabeth Burgos-Debray was looking for someone with her characteristics to do an interview, and Taracena arranged for a meeting between Menchú Tum and Burgos-Debray, an ethnologist of Venezuelan origin, very well connected to publishing houses in France through her ex-husband, Régis Debray, then a minister of state in the Mitterrand administration. Eventually, the decision to tape Menchú Tum's story was made, a process that went forward during the first weeks of 1982 at Burgos-Debray's house. Many aspects of this process remain points of contention to this day. Arturo Taracena claims that he participated in part of the interviewing itself, something Burgos-Debray denies. David Stoll sides with Burgos-Debray on this issue, as well as on other controversial ones, such as just how many people actually edited the manuscript itself. Arturo Taracena claims that the majority of the transcription work was performed by Paquita Rivas, a young woman of Cuban origin who was the secretary of Gonzalo Arroyo, a Chilean Jesuit exiled in France who headed CETRAL

(Catholic Center for Latin American Relief). Taracena also claims that he himself did most of the editing. Stoll, on the other hand, endorses Burgos-Debray's claim that she was the sole editor. Stoll also endorses Burgos-Debray's position that the manuscript was inspected by Rolando Morán, commander in chief of the EGP, whereas Taracena claims that it was Gustavo Meoño, past president of the Menchú Foundation, who read it and suggested minor modifications in order to protect the identity of EGP members, but that the EGP was not really interested in the project. What everyone agrees is that the edited manuscript was presented by Burgos-Debray to the Casa de las Américas Annual Contest, where it won the award as best testimonial narrative for 1983. However, disagreements resume immediately after that. Menchú Tum claims that, when she did not receive any of the prize money, she found out that Burgos-Debray had registered all the copyrights in her own name. Stoll endorses Burgos-Debray's contention that she paid the royalties to the organization that Menchú Tum and Taracena indicated, and that she has in her possession the receipts for those sums of money. Whatever actually happened, it was this prestigious international award that marked the beginning of Menchú Tum's international notoriety. Still, because of the nature of the political situation inside Guatemala, she remained unknown in her country of origin. For that to change, the gradual opening in Guatemalan politics that began in 1986 would be necessary.

Rigoberta's Slow Entrance into Guatemalan Consciousness

The small political opening that began in Guatemala in 1986 allowed for the first time a freer circulation of Rigoberta Menchú's book within the country.[3] The timid opening also enabled many members of the democratic left who were not linked directly to armed struggle to return to the country and begin to participate in its political affairs. Most of those who returned at this time were "Ladinos," non-Maya Guatemalans, whose ethnic consciousness had been raised by their nearly seven-year exile in Mexico, where they personally met Menchú Tum, as well as other Maya *popular* leaders such as Pablo Ceto, Antonio Calel, Gabriel Ixmatá, Francisca Álvarez, or Domingo Hernández Ixcoy.[4] In many instances, these Ladino political activists who returned were the first to start speaking publicly about Menchú Tum herself, at the same time as the Pan-Maya movement began its own struggle for Maya rights with "issues of cultural origin and self-definition" (Warren 1998, 37). Both efforts, however paternalistic the first one might have been, began to open up a debate inside the country that had remained bottled up during the years of the insurrection in the highlands. Many of the Ladino activists were appalled to hear the terms still used in Guatemala to address Mayas, especially the offensive and pejorative words *indios* or *inditos*. It was, even to someone only partially sensitized to ethnic issues, a grossly discriminatory, racist, and offensive language that connoted quite explicitly the semifeudal mentality that was dominant among the great majority of Ladinos from all walks of life. It symbolized the racism institutionalized and "naturalized" in Guatemala at a level seldom seen in contemporary times.

This gross bias and outright racism concerned many of the Ladino returnees and led to a rise in public activities around the problematics of ethnicity. Many of the former exiles formed new nongovernmental organizations (NGOs) or grouped themselves in centers for social research, and out of these new institutions they began a vigorous campaign to air issues of ethnicity and racism in the city, albeit from a Ladino point of view. However, in a society unaccustomed to such criticism, their presence was as confrontational as the participation of white activists in the South of the United States during the civil rights movement in the early 1960s. For the most part, in those years (1986–90) ethnic issues came linked to human rights and to broader political topics such as democratization, the opening of the political system, and peace negotiations with the insurgents. However, the problem of ethnicity was dealt with in specific terms within that larger framework.[5]

Guatemalan views also became increasingly influenced by international trends in the social sciences. Foreign anthropologists and social scientists developed a keen interest in ethnic issues. Furthermore, Maya cadres who had studied in universities in the United States and Europe during the years of the conflict returned to the country and contributed to a broadening awareness of ethnic issues as they swelled the ranks of the pan-Maya movement and began to steer ethnicity in a new direction (García-Ruiz 1991).

Many anthropologists who had done fieldwork in the 1970s were concerned with the fate of the areas they had studied and of their close personal friends, who were officially designated in anthropological lingo as their "informants." During the years of insurrection, many of these social scientists formed part of a loose network called the Guatemalan Scholars Network (GSN), and they regularly presented papers dealing

with Maya issues and concerns at meetings such as the American Anthropology Association (AAA) and the Latin American Studies Association (LASA). In these forums, they met exiled Maya leaders, including
Menchú Tum, whose book most of them had read as soon as it came
out, when the solidarity network in both the United States and Europe
made sure that it came to their attention. They themselves returned to
the country when it became viable and continued their fieldwork with
a more politicized consciousness. As such, they became channels for communication between the outside world and the Maya communities, and
in many cases they informed the communities about Rigoberta Menchú's
book and her own rising international fame (Carmack 1988).

Maya scholars who had spent the war years abroad had originally
been labeled *etnicistas*[6] by the Maya *popular* sector. They did not believe
that a class-based alliance between Mayas and "poor Ladinos" under the
Ladino leadership of Guatemala's revolutionary organizations was the
soundest way to further a Maya agenda. Instead, they favored a movement led by Mayas themselves, centered on the elimination of racism
and the conformation of identity politics, celebrating and asserting a
distinctive community allegiance along ethnic lines that could serve "to
create a social movement focused on the cultural revitalization and unifi-
cation across language divides of indigenous Guatemalans" (Warren
1998, 36). Or, as Edward F. Fischer and R. McKenna Brown explain:

> The Maya had long been denied a voice in academic representations of
> their culture and history, and Maya scholars are resentful of the manner
> in which their culture and history have been appropriated by the non-
> Maya academy, noting that much "objective" and seemingly apolitical
> scholarship has had dire political consequences for the Maya people.
> (1996, 2–3)

Kay Warren argues in her book that the "movement rejects Guatemala's melting pot ideology, which has compelled indigenous people
'to pass' as nonindigenous Ladinos if they seek employment outside
their home communities and pursue education and economic mobility" (1998, 10).

For this "Maya *cultural*" group, Rigoberta Menchú Tum was not a natural ally at first, given her original membership in the CUC and her alleged links with the Guerrilla Army of the Poor (EGP). Yet this same
sector recognized the symbolic status that she had achieved internationally and felt that she could very well become a useful icon for articulat-

ing Maya demands in opposition to Ladino society within the new constitutional spaces that were beginning to open up.[7]

Finally, the revolutionary organizations themselves, grouped around
the Guatemalan National Revolutionary Unity (URNG), championed
her cause internationally as a means of validating their own agenda and
demands at a time when they had suffered major military setbacks and
were having to negotiate with the Guatemalan military from a position
of weakness. Therefore, the clandestine agents inside Guatemala of some
of the organizations comprising the URNG exalted the figure of Menchú
Tum in order to further awareness of their own demands.

As a result, by 1986 there was a confluence of factors, not the last of
which were Menchú Tum's energy, intelligence, and dedication, which
all contributed to make the name of Rigoberta Menchú known within
Guatemala. We will skip over some of the details chronicling her rise to
international prominence, for the sake of explaining to a primarily American audience her own ascendancy within Guatemala itself.

Rigoberta Finally Returns to Guatemala

After her name had begun to spread inside Guatemala, and various international advisers felt that conditions in the country were safe enough,
Rigoberta Menchú Tum ventured back into the country. As we have explained, she was already well known by both left- and right-wing political
sectors (the so-called political class). Upon her return to Guatemala, however, it was the military's own mismanagement of the situation that possibly had the greatest hand in transforming Menchú Tum, still a relatively
obscure figure for the majority of Guatemalans, into a national heroine.

In an attempt to prove to the world that Guatemala was now a democracy, President Vinicio Cerezo (1986–91) had been courting exiled leaders
and personalities to return to the country. The son of President Cerezo
personally invited Menchú Tum to return to the country in 1986. Then,
in March of 1988, the Guatemalan ambassador to Switzerland, José Luis
Chea, invited the RUOG delegation attending the United Nations Geneva
meetings that spring to return to their country. The RUOG (Unitary
Representation of the Guatemalan Opposition) was a civilian, international diplomatic branch of the Guatemalan opposition, operating within
the confines of the United Nations. Linked informally to the URNG
through some of its members, it was founded by prominent Guate-

malans in exile, all of them members of the Guatemalan Committee for Patriotic Unity (CGUP), at the height of the massacres committed against the Maya population. Founded in 1982, it operated primarily out of New York City with the primary function of lobbying the United Nations. Menchú Tum was invited to be part of RUOG from its inception, and, as its representative, she participated every year at the spring meetings in Geneva, Switzerland, where the UN Subcommittee for Ethnic Issues met.

Menchú Tum flew into Guatemala on April 18, 1988, as part of an RUOG delegation that included three other prominent exiled figures.[8] Given the violent and treacherous nature of the Guatemalan military, and the accusation that all members of RUOG were members of the revolutionary armed opposition, the URNG, an international delegation was formed to escort RUOG, thus offering some degree of protection to its members. Included in this delegation were members of the European Parliament, the German Bundestag, the Mexican Parliament, the Roman Catholic Church, and human rights organizations. The delegation also included aides to several U.S. congressmen. The purpose of the trip was to meet with Guatemala's National Reconciliation Commission and, in the words of Menchú Tum herself, "to observe if indeed there is a political opening in the country."[9]

Divided by contradictions between its diplomatic efforts and an internal hard-line policy still dictated by its military, the Guatemalan government accused the members of this delegation of being militant subversives themselves and required that they apply for political amnesty. Otherwise, they would be arrested or not allowed to enter the country. No one complied with this dictate.

The day of their scheduled arrival, the Guatemalan government sealed off the airport and surrounded it with hundreds of armed security forces. Local press trying to enter the airport grounds to cover the event were accosted by secret service agents, who destroyed their equipment.[10] What is more, some two hundred people who had assembled outside to welcome RUOG members were not able to get inside the airport. However, the attitude of the security forces so outraged the press and the media that it turned the event into a front-page news item in which all members of the RUOG delegation were uniformly portrayed in a positive light.

Shortly after their arrival at La Aurora International Airport on a Mexicana flight originating in Costa Rica, Rigoberta Menchú Tum and Dr. Rolando Castillo Montalvo were seized by government agents, arrested, and charged with "attacks against the internal security of the state."

Their detention lasted only a few hours and became for the government a carnivalesque fiasco. They were taken to the Supreme Court building in the Civic Center with a parade of sympathizers and well-wishers trailing the grotesque display of police force. Once inside the Supreme Court, after some bureaucratic maneuvering, Judge Oscar Sagastume declared that he was releasing Menchú Tum and Castillo Montalvo for "lack of proof."[11]

While the ordeal lasted, thousands of university students and members of the Mutual Support Group (GAM, a group that organized the relatives of those who had "disappeared," that is, citizens who had been arrested, tortured, killed and buried in unmarked graves) congregated in front of the Supreme Court. After Menchú Tum and Castillo Montalvo were released, they held an impromptu meeting in the Civic Center, something that had never happened before under the repressive military rule, and then their sympathizers followed the released members of RUOG to the El Dorado Hotel, where they held another informal meeting.

The arrest and subsequent release of the RUOG members was front-page news in the Guatemalan press for several days, provoking a nationwide debate. The spectacular show of force at the airport, followed by the rapid backdown, was widely depicted as an embarrassment for the government. For the first time, Menchú Tum's face appeared not only in all the newspapers, but on television as well. It was on that day that her name became for the first time a household word for average Guatemalans, even if for some she still represented the image of a subversive, a *guerrillera,* or simply a Maya woman, which, for a society unaccustomed to problematizing ethnic or gender issues, signified that she did not deserve her lofty status. Nonetheless, among progressive citizens, copies of her book began to circulate from hand to hand, and, since that moment, Menchú Tum remained constantly in the public eye inside Guatemala.

The Path toward the Nobel

Three weeks after this incident, a coup attempt took place in Guatemala. Among the elements cited by the coup plotters as triggering their intentions was the government's capitulation to the RUOG delegation. In political terms, the failed coup attempt had consequences for the democratic process in the country. For Menchú Tum, it created an opening for her to assert her own particular agenda of resistance, which had quietly become more "ethnic" and less "revolutionary," though she still had not broken any alliances at that time with members of either RUOG or the URNG. The fact that her presence in the country was perceived by the hard-line sector of the army as threatening enough to justify a coup attempt gave her a measure of power. From that moment on, Menchú Tum remained prominent in the pages of local newspapers as well as on television screens, even if she left the country right after the meeting in the El Dorado Hotel and still had no political base of her own among the Mayas themselves. Nonetheless, in the capital city especially, these events established a context in which to recognize her as a symbol of broader resistance to oppression, primarily among the large, politicized sector of poor, urban Ladinos who still saw the URNG as a sign of hope in ending military control of the country. Her dignity in confronting Judge Sagastume demonstrated to this group her moral fiber, which impressed even some Guatemalans who did not share her political agenda, including middle-of-the-road Ladinos who otherwise behaved in an unconsciously racist manner.

From that moment on, the terms of the national political discourse began to change. Menchú Tum gradually became a symbol of all those who had put their lives on the line for democracy and had lost everything except their dignity and their will to continue the struggle against the military. For progressive Ladinos she was a symbol of democracy and freedom of expression. By 1990, many of them were finally buying and reading *I, Rigoberta Menchú*, though the text never became a bestseller outside the university campuses.[12]

This "new look" was already evident in Menchú Tum's next major visit to the country, the second week of October 1991, to celebrate the Second Continental Meeting to commemorate five hundred years of indigenous popular resistance.[13] As the first international forum of representatives from indigenous and popular movement groups from throughout the hemisphere to gather in Guatemala (the first forum of these groups was held in Bogotá, Colombia, in 1989), the conference was a historic achievement. It was also the perfect setting to launch Menchú Tum's candidacy for the Nobel Peace Prize because rumors already existed that

1992 would be a propitious year for an indigenous laureate. The forum was held at the fairgrounds just outside Quezaltenango, Guatemala's second largest city and the largest urban center in the northwestern highlands. Given the international nature of the event, the Serrano Elías government (1990–93) did not interfere with its proceedings and even tried to gain diplomatic credibility by presenting an image of openness and tranquillity.[14] Indigenous groups linked to the Maya *popular* sector took advantage of this stance to make this meeting the most public display ever of their cause within Guatemala's borders. Michael Willis, himself a sympathizer of the Maya *popular* sector and writing primarily from their perspective, described its public impact as follows:

> After an inaugural event and press conference at the Ritz Hotel in Guatemala City, the delegates and guests left for Xela (Quetzaltenango) in a caravan of vehicles which were decorated with streamers and banners. Each bus was a moving billboard that stated demands of indigenous Guatemalans such as "Stop the displacement of Indians from our lands of origin."
>
> The buses with their colorful decorations grabbed attention as they passed pedestrians and vehicles. Yet, people were cautious about their signs of support. Waving and applause came only in areas where little traffic was passing. On the highway to Xela and in town the visible presence of military or other security forces was minimal.[15]

In that congress, all Guatemalan indigenous groups controlled by either Maya *popular* organizations or the URNG participated in huge numbers alongside international delegations. Maya *culturales,* as indicated previously, complained of being either excluded from the event or marginalized (Warren 1998, 35). Nonetheless, the event was large and important enough that they still chose to participate when included. Kay Warren quotes Demetrio Cojtí's critique about Maya *populares* not being part of the pan-Maya movement because they "did not demand indigenous rights," but she herself quotes Charles Hale's statement arguing that

> Indians who identify as *populares* generally have chosen to emphasize the demands that unify them with subordinate Mestizos. This does not imply a "loss" of Indian identity ("culture loss" is a problematic term in any case) but it does tend to involve either a shift in priorities away from demands specific to Indian cultural roots, or to a difficult commitment to struggle for those demands from within a predominately non-Indian political movement. (Warren 1998, 36)

Thus, it became the first time that groups of a broad ideological range, from *culturales* to neo-Marxist *populares* closely allied to the URNG, participated jointly in an indigenous event. Despite the anger, resentment, and fear of co-optation, it did open up horizontal lines of dialogue among Mayas themselves.

On October 12, Majawil Q'ij organized a march as the closing event of the conference.[16] More than twenty-five thousand people joined, making it one of the largest indigenous marches in Guatemalan history. It was also Menchú Tum's first march in Guatemalan territory since 1980, and the very first in which the respect and affection of the masses of Maya peoples for her became palpably evident. Michael Willis claims:

> For the people of Guatemala, the return of exiled indigenous leader
> Rigoberta Menchú was a highlight of the week. Two previous attempts
> to return for visits, in 1988 and 1989, had been cut short by government
> intervention and death threats. This visit was Rigoberta Menchú's
> triumphal return. Throughout the week she was accompanied by
> Danielle Mitterrand, the wife of the President of France, and an
> entourage of reporters. Guatemalan press accounts of the conference
> featured photographs of Menchú. All the news media carried interviews
> with her in which she spoke candidly about the impunity of human
> rights violators in Guatemala, the negotiations between the government
> and guerrillas, and the demands of indigenous peoples in Guatemala
> and the Americas. The evening after the October 12 march, Guatemalan
> television carried a 15-minute interview with her. Over Menchú's voice
> the camera showed the thousands of Mayans marching through the
> streets of Xela and under the shadow of the volcano on the way to the
> fairground.[17]

Willis's account is somewhat hagiographic, given his sympathy for Menchú Tum. Nonetheless, the facts he mentions are correct, and he does go on to mention that throughout the march indigenous women brought their small children to Menchú Tum to receive her blessing. We have to understand this uncanny phenomenon more within the Maya cultural context than within the more traditional Western notion of transformation of Menchú Tum into a sort of lay saint. Nonetheless, that gesture, more than anything, signified the degree of recognition that she had finally achieved among at least a sector of her own people, and the fact that this particular sector had begun to see her as an icon, as a symbolic representative of Maya peoples over political or ideological differences. Some Maya *culturales* disagree with this particular element of the analysis, and Demetrio Cojtí has written against it. However, this perception was later confirmed by another well-known Maya leader who kept herself at a distance from both Maya *culturales* and Maya *populares,* Gloria Tujab.[18] At this stage, Menchú Tum had achieved a high enough degree of recognition that even those groups that opposed her position on ethnic issues felt compelled to support her when the Continental Campaign announced that she was being nominated for the Nobel Peace Prize. Moreover, her political clout was manifested when even Ladino politicians went out of their way to get their pictures taken with the person they themselves had once reviled as a "subversive."

The Nobel Peace Prize

When Menchú Tum returned to Guatemala in July 1992, she was already an official Nobel Peace Prize candidate and a well-established national and international celebrity. The moment she arrived at Guatemala City's Aurora International Airport, she was greeted by cheers and applause from hundreds of Guatemalans who had crowded the airport to await her arrival. Cynics argue that this enthusiastic welcome was staged by either Maya *populares* or URNG supporters. At other moments of her visit, that could be the case. Susan Poff, an extremely sympathetic observer of Menchú Tum but nonetheless a reliable witness, accompanied her on this trip. She describes the scene as follows: "Members of the press besieged her in their eagerness to speak with her. Outside the airport, a large crowd waited to welcome her; people pressed in on all sides to exchange a few words, give her flowers or shake her hand."[19] Also, Santiago Bastos and Manuela Camús (who, if they have any bias at all, favor Maya *culturales* against the *populares*) state in their book that, during her July 1992 trip to Guatemala, Menchú Tum had a much more sophisticated discourse about ethnic issues and identity politics than any other member of the Maya *populares* (1996, 182). In fact, they even quote Demetrio Cojtí, the most important leader of the Maya *culturales,* as stating that "before it was harder to expect something . . . [from Menchú, because of her alleged links to the Maya *populares*], but now changes are taking place, so it is possible to expect something from Rigoberta Menchú" (ibid., 183).

The public reception of her during this trip indicated that a symbolic mantle now covered Menchú Tum. What it meant, like all symbols, could very well be polysemic. For some, she symbolized the URNG's return to Guatemala; for others, the possible dawning of peace; for still others, an affirmation of the Maya movement. Whatever people read into her presence, her growing international recognition gave her the power to publicly articulate critical perspectives on the rights of the indigenous population, the continuing violation of human rights in the country, the lack of social or economic justice, and the need for a new consciousness to confront the nation's crises, without being harmed or silenced. In fact, she could now be treated as an honored dignitary for verbalizing such views.

Menchú Tum used this power—both the symbolic and the real—as a means of redesigning her own identity so as to appear more and more the Maya leader as opposed to the previous image of a "radical, leftist" popular leader, without Maya or gender attributes, that had mainly defined her identity ten years earlier. She also used it as a means of attempting to redefine the indigenous movement as a whole, as well as distancing herself from both the URNG and the Maya *populares* so that she could begin to exercise leadership in her own right. As Susanne Jonas points out:

> This issue—a continuing discussion of "new ways of being Indian"—takes on added significance in the context of the 1992 "500th Anniversary" of the Spanish Conquest.... In the words of CUC activist Rigoberta Menchú, 1992 could be the occasion for a genuine encounter among all of the cultures of Latin America (certainly Guatemala), "a moment of self-discovery, in which we all listen to each other." (1991, 239)

Menchú Tum had become a de facto spokesperson for all Maya peoples because she could speak out and utter a discourse in which most Mayas recognized themselves yet could not utter themselves for fear of reprisals. She began to reconceptualize her role as that of unifying the different tendencies among the Maya peoples, whose positions about what needed to be done to further their own cause remained plural and contradictory. In voicing their support for her Nobel candidacy, representatives of different Maya groups declared:

> Her voice is the symbol of the struggle of our Maya people of Guatemala for peace and development.... Her work has shown the way to restoring the dignity of our peoples and the remembrance of our history.... Rigoberta Menchú's struggle is an expression of the resistance of all Mayans, and is a contribution to the construction of a new society in which neither Mayans nor any other peoples will be marginalized or neglected. (Poff 1992, 11)

By this point, only right-wing elements dared attack her, accusing her of "living a life of luxury with intellectual Marxist Europeans" or of "being utilized by all those *señores* who hate Guatemala and have harmed her so much" (ibid.). However, on the whole, the tide had turned even among significant numbers of mainstream Ladinos, who might still harbor unconscious racist attitudes but were expressing pride in the international achievement of a compatriot.

Menchú left the country on July 16 after a meeting with several indigenous organizations in Chimaltenango organized by Rosalina Tuyuc of CONAVIGUA,[20] promising to return for October 12, 1992, the date of the celebration of the five hundredth year of indigenous resistance to Western occupation of the Americas. This date would mark the beginning of the commemoration of the International Year of Indigenous Peoples. As a result, Menchú Tum was in Guatemala, in the department of San Marcos, when the announcement of her winning the Nobel Peace Prize was made on October 15, 1992, an event she describes in her second book, *Crossing Borders*. When the news of her victory hit the airwaves, the bells of all the Catholic churches in the highlands began to ring, as well as those of the popular neighborhoods in Guatemala City. She was flown by helicopter to the capital, where a demonstration took place the next day to celebrate her victory.

The government responded with equanimity in public, and President Serrano Elías even praised Menchú Tum and sent his congratulations. However, officials were privately shocked by the political implications of the award. They had never believed that a Guatemalan indigenous woman could actually win such a coveted prize and were not prepared for such a turn of events.[21] Only the foreign affairs minister, Gonzalo Menéndez Park, was undiplomatic enough to verbalize what many inside the government felt in private: that the prize was undeserved because Menchú Tum was a subversive element. Menéndez's remarks so infuriated both public opinion, swollen by nationalist and patriotic pride, and the international community that had celebrated the award and extended honors of their own to Menchú Tum, that he was forced to resign within a short period.

Menchú Tum's award changed the configuration of Guatemalan politics. If repressive elements of the state apparatus had the upper hand up until the Nobel Peace Prize announcement, from that point on momentum began to build in favor of the liberal sector. Other factors, such as Helen Mack's winning the Right Livelihood Award—the alternative Nobel Prize—at about the same time for her struggle to bring her sister's assassins to justice, and Serrano Elías's own missteps, would contribute to this momentum. However, the turning point was without question Menchú Tum's Nobel Prize victory. It was read as such by both the majority of Guatemalans, who then recognized her as a national leader and the Maya peoples' most charismatic figure, and by the international community that had lobbied for the Nobel Peace Prize as a means of triggering peace negotiations in Guatemala and settling the Central American conflict once and for all. As Susan Berger points out:

> Political configurations were also shaken by the recent awarding of the Nobel Peace Prize to Rigoberta Menchú Tum. While some members of the government were quick to congratulate Menchú, others were obviously frightened by the significance of the event. For the first time, indigenous Guatemalans—more than 55% of the population—had an internationally respected leader who could use her prominence to fight for political recognition for the indigenous majority. Indicative of the seriousness of this challenge, after Menchú's award, political violence against popular sectors increased in the form of threats against union and human rights activists, as well as disappearances and assassinations.[22]

Precisely because of the implications of the prize, the Ladino "political class" (professional political sector) for the most part ignored the Nobel ceremony. Exceptions to this were the National Unity of the Center (UCN), which published a newspaper ad congratulating Menchú Tum for her award, and the Social Democrats and other opposition politicians, who scrambled to be seen with her. Coverage of the event itself, however, was front-page news in all of the country's newspapers, and the major news event in all TV news broadcasts. Although President Serrano Elías's comments were muted, he did add that "Guatemalans were sick and tired of being accused of violating human rights."[23] By "Guatemalans" he meant the Ladino elites, the army, and the government.

Menchú Tum in the Midst of the Serrano Crisis

After the Nobel Prize ceremonies in Oslo, Norway, Menchú Tum settled back in Mexico City. However, she wanted to get the Vicente Menchú

Foundation off the ground as soon as possible and to capitalize on the aura of the award by forging ahead with Maya unity. First, she lead an impressive display of power: a world council of native peoples against racism. This World Summit of Native Peoples took place May 24–28, 1993, in Chimaltenango. The idea was to come up with a manifesto that would then be presented to the United Nations in order to declare not only a year but an entire decade in commemoration of indigenous peoples.[24] Other demands included a UN High Commissioner for Indigenous Peoples and a Universal Declaration of Indigenous Rights.[25]

However, the World Summit was clearly overshadowed by President Serrano Elías's self-generated coup launched in the early morning hours of May 25. Embassy personnel from the different countries represented at the summit rushed to Chimaltenango to ensure the safety of the delegates, and Menchú Tum herself was escorted back and forth between the capital and the conference every day until the end of the summit, at which time she headed immediately for Guatemala City. Once in the capital, she immediately led the popular sectors in their public demands for a return to a constitutional regime. She also led marches through the streets of the capital against censorship and against the coup.[26]

Menchú Tum and other members of the popular sectors had at first demanded the resignation of the entire Congress and the creation of a Constitutional Assembly that would write a new constitution for the country. However, when it became evident that their demands could not carry the day, they joined other sectors of Guatemalan society in signing the petition that called for the resignation of the president, the vice president, and the executive committee of Congress, and for the arrest and prosecution of corrupt officials.[27]

Recognized as both a popular and a Maya leader, Menchú Tum was also invited to join the ad hoc commission that grouped sectors from all of Guatemalan society, including for the first time members of Guatemala's elite who ran the Chamber of Industry and Commerce (CACIF).[28] Susan Berger observes: "In fact, even Rigoberta Menchú was asked to participate in the negotiations, though she ultimately walked out, claiming that representatives were not interested in her real participation but hoped to use her presence to legitimize the process" (1993, 6).

However, after Menchú Tum and others walked away from any compromise that might allow President Serrano Elías to save face, something unprecedented in Guatemala happened: Menchú Tum and the heads of other popular sectors actually collaborated, however guardedly, with members of CACIF, if not with the political class. The ad hoc commission that brought them together was labeled the National Instance for Consensus (INC). It was this body that eventually selected for Congress the candidates who would replace Serrano Elías as president: Arturo Herbruger, president of the Supreme Electoral Court (TSE), and Ramiro de León Carpio, Human Rights Ombudsman, who was eventually chosen by Congress as president on the evening of June 5.

As a result of these negotiations, Menchú Tum had a voice and a vote in selecting the man who would run the affairs of the nation and attempt to settle the constitutional crisis. This crisis marked the first time ever she had actually exercised a national leadership role within Guatemala's borders, and it earned her the recognition of all sectors of Guatemalan society, including CACIF, which had labeled her a "subversive element" only months before. Some Guatemalan newspapers quoted by Stoll in his book, however, ran accusations that her entire participation was manipulated by the URNG (1999, 223). One account even had her calling up her "handlers" during an interview to be told what to say. In fact, Menchú Tum had been distancing herself rapidly from any contact with the EGP or the URNG since receiving the Nobel Prize in December 1992, and, by 1993, when these events happened, she was on the verge of a complete political rupture with them. However, she was careful not to make her criticisms of the URNG public, to prevent their own loss of political capital at a time of political negotiations. The people she often called were those trusted political associates that she hired to work in both the Vicente Menchú Foundation and later the Rigoberta Menchú Tum Foundation. It is true that some of them, including the foundations' first president, Gustavo Meoño, are ex-EGP members, but by 1993 they had already broken their links with the EGP, and part of what united them as a group was their past militancy, their shared criticism of the EGP, and the bonds of trust that some of them had developed at a personal level despite their paranoia about the organization's mishandling of militants' lives and political strategy. Determined to be independent, Menchú Tum was, at this stage of her life, more adamant than ever about calling her own shots. Whereas she certainly had, and still has, a group of trusted advisers whom she consults constantly, it is ludicrous to refer to them as "handlers," any more than the advisers of any U.S. president are his "handlers."

On June 4, 1993, when the INC was meeting in order to propose to Congress a successor to President Serrano Elías after the latter had resigned, and his vice president, Gustavo Espina, had been prevented from illegally taking office, it was Dionisio Gutiérrez, a businessman and a member of CACIF, who threw into the pool the name of Menchú Tum.[29] His proposal was not wholehearted, and it was a way of paying her a backhanded compliment for having joined them the previous day in signing the compromise petition. However, the enormity of actually having a member of CACIF propose her for president of the Republic, even if only as a symbolic gesture, cannot be overlooked. Menchú Tum had indeed become a symbol of both Guatemalan nationalism and Maya identity in the eyes of certain members of the Ladino elite. At the grassroots level, the cry of excitement was even more audible. Several enthusiastic supporters confirmed both publicly and privately that "Rigoberta es presidenciable" (Rigoberta is presidential timber). After this episode was settled, Menchú Tum returned to Mexico briefly, only to move permanently to Guatemala in 1994.

As Victor Perera points out,[30] the new Maya opposition made its influence felt in the low turnout for a referendum called by President de León Carpio on January 30, 1994. The Mayas called for nonparticipation because the referendum did not address issues embodied in Maya demands: the abolition of civil-defense patrols, the end of forced military recruitment, the appointment of an independent truth commission to investigate human rights violations and agrarian reform, and other economic incentives for Guatemala's indigenous majority. Only 18 percent of eligible voters turned out to vote on the referendum.

In 1995, the Vicente Menchú Foundation headquartered in Mexico City was dissolved, and in its place was created the Rigoberta Menchú Tum Foundation, with headquarters in Guatemala City. Some have tried to read sinister meanings into the name change, but it primarily had to do with the transfer of capital from one country to the other, as well as the rigid requirements for creating nonprofit institutions in both countries. It enabled Menchú Tum, however, to make a clean break from any remnants of URNG- or EGP-controlled organizations, such as the CUC, and to position herself for a public political role in Guatemala, cashing in on her own name recognition. The foundation carries out projects directed at education, health care, and human rights, with an emphasis on citizens' civil rights. Its projects also involve housing and urban planning, as well as agricultural production. The foundation makes efforts to strengthen the unity between different Maya sectors, so as to promote their mutual cooperation on their rights and values.

Among Menchú Tum's 1996 projects, linked to the foundation's work inside Guatemala, was her effort to mobilize Mayas to vote. She did this in a nonpartisan way, as a mechanism to enfranchise as many Maya voters as possible. This was to empower them, not so much in the arena of national politics, as to become actors in local politics, allowimg them to gradually gain control of their own town halls, as the XEL-HUH Maya coalition did in Guatemala's second-largest city, by surprisingly helping Rigoberto K'emé Chay win the mayoral election.

When the peace accords were finally signed in the old National Palace of Guatemala City on December 29, 1996, Menchú Tum was a prominent guest and a sought-after figure by all the heads of state in attendance at the ceremony. Her second book, *Crossing Borders,* was published in 1998. In it, Menchú Tum begins with her being awarded the Nobel Peace Prize in 1992, then proceeds to her subsequent return to Guatemala in 1994. Shortly upon her return, her nephew was kidnapped by a family member. She describes the implications of this act on her political career, and she also narrates how, weeks before the country's elections, the army carried out yet another massacre, this time in the village of Xamán. Menchú Tum went to visit the site immediately afterward and became involved in the village's plight by playing the role of a *"querellante adhesiva,"* a person who takes the initiative to bring about a criminal prosecution against the perpetrators of a crime, despite not being a direct victim of it, but only a nonlegal representative of the victims. In the book she also mentions her difficulties with the United Nations, where the simple recognition of the existence of indigenous peoples was a major struggle. Finally, she speaks of the Mayas' worldview, as well as of the courage of her mother.

The English edition of the book, published by Verso, itself became controversial because it did not indicate that Guatemalan writer Dante Liano—one of Menchú Tum's closest friends—and Italian journalist Gianni Minà had been the text's compilers, thus creating the illusion of its having been compiled by translator Ann Wright. The case is still in court. Menchú Tum was not involved in this fiasco, which arose from a problem between the Italian agent and the English editors, and she has publicly supported Liano and Minà's role in the text.

The Present State of Affairs

A new Maya opposition is emerging in Guatemala—however fragmented it may look at times—that increasingly uses its political clout. The insurrection of 1979–82 paved the way for Menchú Tum to emerge as one of the spokespersons for Maya peoples, and she became the most recognized figure among them both inside Guatemala and internationally. This role, however symbolic, given her lack of a political base, has facilitated the under-the-table negotiations among a heterogeneous ethnic group, and it has contributed to making them authentic political players. Despite their different origins and tendencies, they all share in common the platform of strengthening a distinct Maya identity, and they benefit from Menchú Tum's achievements.

Menchú Tum, as a result, is now playing as significant a political role inside Guatemala as she previously did in the international arena. In her transition from international symbol of oppression and racism to political actor, she has succeeded in reinventing herself.[31] She has undergone a transition from the peripheral silence to which all Mayas have been condemned by virtue of racism, to a prominent role as national leader and internationally recognized personality.

Notes

The format of the present article follows the basic outline of a previous article, "Rigoberta Menchú: From Peasant to National Symbol," in *Teaching and Testimony: Rigoberta Menchú and the North American Classroom,* ed. Allen Carey-Webb and Stephen Benz (Albany: State University of New York Press, 1996). However, it has been updated and significantly altered, to reflect the material that has come to light since that date, as well as the changes that have taken place both in Guatemala and in Rigoberta Menchú Tum's life.

1. Catholic Action was an organization founded by Spanish missionaries in the 1930s and consolidated after the coup in 1954 to foment the creation of Maya lay preachers capable of rendering "the word of God" in villages where permanent priests were not available. Although it began as a fervently anti-Communist group of primarily Spanish missionaries of the Order of the Sacred Heart, it became more linked during the 1960s to the progressive wing of the Democratic Christian Party. Catholic Action members were trained to exercise communal leadership, and they were empowered to become village political leaders by the missionaries. The most

radical among them became founders of the Committee for Peasant Unity (CUC) in 1973, although the existence of this organization was not disclosed until shortly before May 1, 1978.

2. The *foco* strategy was theorized by Ernesto "Che" Guevara in his book *Passages of the Cuban Revolutionary War* and revisited by Régis Debray in *Revolution in the Revolution?* It basically consisted of focusing on a specific area of the countryside with weak military defenses as the starting point of guerrilla struggle. In that area, guerrillas would build solid bases and support from the rural population, and then gradually expand into the rest of the countryside like ripples after a stone is thrown into the water. The theory called, therefore, for a war meant to last a long period of time, and in which the guerrillas only very gradually moved from one step to the next. However, as Mario Payeras argued in *Los fusiles de octubre*, the *foco* strategy was not even applied in Cuba itself, contrary to what Guevara himself believed; it was a disaster in Bolivia, leading to Guevara's own death; and it was the wrong theory to apply in Guatemala as well.

3. It must be noted that Menchú Tum's book was sold only in a couple of bookstores in the country, those frequented by a small number of "intellectual" customers, and in very limited quantities. Most of the copies that circulated prior to the Nobel Prize were passed from hand to hand and were read almost exclusively by the political class.

4. All of these Mayas had been founders or leaders of CUC, and most had been members of the Guatemalan Committee for Patriotic Unity (CGUP), formed in Mexico in 1982. This committee, modeled along the lines of El Salvador's Frente Democrático Revolucionario (FDR, Revolutionary Democratic Front), which grouped prominent personalities of different political tendencies opposing the Salvadoran military regime, (FDR), included mostly Ladino personalities among its members. As their own ethnic consciousness grew, some of these original "Maya *popular*" leaders chose, later in the 1980s, to distance themselves from their own revolutionary roots, and they gradually built a closer relationship with the "Maya *culturales.*"

5. For the Ladino side of the returnee picture, we rely on the personal testimony of Luis Alberto Padilla. Padilla had been president of the Guatemalan Commission for Human Rights in Mexico during his exile in that country. Upon his return, he founded the Guatemalan Association for the United Nations (AGNU). Under this mantle, the Institute for International Relations and Peace Research was created. In August 1988, this institute organized the first broad Ladino conference held on ethnic issues in Guatemala City since the intensification of the civil war.

6. As an organized movement, this position, which would evolve into the "Maya *cultural*" sector and be the main artificer of the Pan-Maya movement, had not been significant prior to 1982. However, its ideas succeeded early on in mobilizing some Maya sectors prone to "reverse racism" against Ladinos, a natural response by some Mayas fed up with the system's racism. The Pan-Maya movement, however, found its real base in the communities that correctly blamed the EGP and its Ladino leadership for the army's genocidal offensive in 1982. The EGP's armed units withdrew to the safety of the jungle, thus abandoning the exposed highland villages to their fate. The Guatemalan army, on the other hand, sought a massive destruction of Maya ethnic identity, precisely to prevent ethnicity from becoming a focal point for political transgression against the regime. As a result, unarmed Mayas suffered the brunt

of the gruesome brutality originally aimed at the "Communist" or "subversive" movement, as it was normally called by the army and its supporters.

7. Gloria Tujab, personal communication, summer 1992.

8. The other three were labor lawyers Frank LaRue and Marta Gloria de Torres, and the former dean of the School of Medicine of the University of San Carlos, Dr. Rolando Castillo Montalvo.

9. *Report on Guatemala* 9.3 (1988): 2.

10. The government later claimed that the purpose of this show of force was to protect the exiles against threats by groups of the extreme right. See *Report on Guatemala* 2.

11. Menchú Tum was accused of belonging to a fictitious guerrilla organization named the Committee for Campesino Action. It is unclear why she was not accused of being a member of CUC or of the EGP itself.

12. Personal communication from Sagrario Castellanos, Guatemalan cultural critic (February 19, 1994).

13. As they themselves defined it, *popular* referred to groups, such as workers, peasants, women, and shantytown dwellers, who had been marginalized and oppressed by the same forces responsible for five centuries of indigenous suffering and who also had a significant history of organized resistance. See *Report on Guatemala* 12.4 (1991): 2. However, the name itself (Second Continental Meeting) is indicative of the fact that this event was organized by the Maya *popular* sector, with logistical support from the URNG. Indeed, Maya *"culturales"* complained that they were either not allowed to participate in this event, or were placed in marginal positions within it, so that Maya *populares,* and especially Menchú Tum, could play a preferential role in it.

14. Jorge Serrano Elías was elected president in 1990 for the term beginning in January 1991 and ending in January 1996. He thus became the second constitutionally elected president of this new period, following Vinicio Cerezo (1986–91). However, as we will chronicle later, Serrano Elías violated the constitution in 1993 and attempted to garner dictatorial powers. As a result, he was removed from office, an incident in which Menchú Tum participated.

15. *Report on Guatemala* 12.4 (1991): 2.

16. Majawil Q'ij is the coordinating body for Guatemalan indigenous organizations involved in the popular movement, that is, the Maya *populares.* Founded in July 1990, it consists primarily of nine peasant, human rights, and indigenous rights groups. The name means "New Dawn" in the Mam language.

17. *Report on Guatemala* 12.4 (1991): 2.

18. Personal communication, summer 1992.

19. Susan Poff, "Rigoberta Menchú Visits Guatemala," *Report on Guatemala* 13.3 (1992): 11.

20. *Crónica* 6.256, December 18, 1992, 17. CONAVIGUA stands for National Confederation of Guatemalan Widows.

21. *Crónica* 6.256, December 18, 1992, 16.

22. Susan Berger, "Guatemala: Coup and Countercoup," *NACLA Report on the Americas* 27.1 (1993): 4–5.

23. *La Jornada,* Mexico City, December 1992, 46.

24. *Crónica* 7.276, May 21, 1993, 31.

25. *Crónica* 7.278, June 4, 1993, 48.

26. Ibid., 15.

27. Ibid., 17.

28. The next day, the Constitutional Court made the final arrangements for Serrano Elías's departure, and Menchú Tum found herself in the National Palace, sharing the spotlight with the Guatemalan political class. However, when it was rumored that the army endorsed their position, Menchú Tum chose to abandon the palace rather than give the impression that she shared the same position as the army, or that she accepted their endorsement of the proceedings.

29. *Crónica* 7.279, June 11, 1993, 30.

30. Victor Perera, "The Mayans: A New Force in Guatemalan Politics," *Los Angeles Times*, February 6, 1994, M1.

31. Whether this is actually possible is a question raised by Antonella Fabri, "Memories of Violence, Monuments of History," paper presented at the American Anthropological Association meeting, San Francisco, December 2–7, 1992, 8.

Bibliography

Arias, Arturo. 1990. "Changing Indian Identity: Guatemala's Violent Transition to Modernity." In *Guatemalan Indians and the State, 1540–1988*, ed. Carol Smith. Austin: University of Texas Press: 230–57.

Bastos, Santiago, and Marcela Camús. 1996. *Quebrando el silencio: Organizaciones del pueblo maya y sus demandas 1986–1992*. Guatemala: FLACSO.

Berger, Susan. 1993. "Guatemala: Coup and Countercoup," *NACLA Report on the Americas* 27.1: 4–5.

Carmack, Robert, ed. 1988. *Guatemala: Harvest of Violence*. Norman: University of Oklahoma Press.

Casaus Arzú, Marta Elena. 1992. *Guatemala: Linaje y Racismo*. San José: FLACSO.

Cojtí Cuxil, Demetrio. *Configuración del Pensamiento Político del Pueblo Maya*. Vol. 1. Quetzaltenango: AEMG, 1991.

———. 1995. *Ub' aniik Ri Una'ooj Uchomab'aal Ri Maya' Tinamit: Configuración del Pensamiento Político del Pueblo Maya*. Vol. 2. Guatemala City: Seminario Permanente de Estudios Mayas and Cholsamaj.

Esquit Choy, Alberto, and Víctor Gálvez Borrel. 1997. *The Mayan Movement Today: Issues of Indigenous Culture and Development in Guatemala*. Guatemala City: FLACSO.

Fischer, Edward F., and R. McKenna Brown, eds. 1996. *Maya Cultural Activism in Guatemala*. Austin: University of Texas Press.

García-Ruiz, Jesús. 1991. Untitled manuscript.

Jonas, Susanne. 1991. *The Battle for Guatemala*. Boulder, Colo.: Westview Press.

Menchú, Rigoberta. 1998a. *Crossing Borders*. Trans. Ann Wright. London: Verso.

———. 1998b. *Rigoberta: La nieta de los mayas*. Ed. Dante Liano and Gianni Minà. Madrid: El País/Aguilar.

Menchú, Rigoberta, with Elisabeth Burgos-Debray. 1984. *I, Rigoberta Menchú: An Indian Woman in Guatemala*. Trans. Ann Wright. London: Verso.

Payeras, Mario. 1997. *Los pueblos indígenas y la revolución guatemalteca: Ensayos étnicos 1982–1992*. Guatemala City: Luna y Sol.

Poff, Susan. 1992. "Rigoberta Menchú Visits Guatemala." *Report on Guatemala* 13.3.

Stoll, David. 1999. *Rigoberta Menchú and the Story of All Poor Guatemalans.* Boulder, Colo.: Westview Press.

Warren, Kay B. 1998. *Indigenous Movements and Their Critics: Pan-Maya Activism in Guatemala.* Princeton, N.J.: Princeton University Press.

I, Rigoberta Menchú and the "Culture Wars"

Mary Louise Pratt

Rigoberta Menchú is the most famous indigenous leader in the world. She received the Nobel Peace Prize in 1992 for a decade of international work to end a campaign of military terror in her native Guatemala that cost some two hundred thousand indigenous lives.[1] Her powerful testimonial text, *Me llamo Rigoberta Menchú y así me nació la conciencia* (*I, Rigoberta Menchú*, 1983), achieved a worldwide reception that undoubtedly saved many Guatemalan lives, including Menchú's own. It also made her powerful enemies.

The latter were undoubtedly pleased when in December 1998, the global press was gripped by a sensational front-page report in the *New York Times:* an American anthropologist, professor at a prestigious college, claimed on the basis of nearly ten years of research, that *I, Rigoberta Menchú* was a tissue of lies, inventions, and distortions. So dramatic were the revelations that the *New York Times* had sent a reporter to Guatemala to verify sources used by the researcher. Not coincidentally, the latter's book on the subject was about to appear in bookstores.[2] If Menchú's testimony embarked her on a road to the Nobel, these new writings appeared aimed toward the Pulitzers.

It is not my purpose here to review the frenetic and impassioned media barrage that was unleashed, less by David Stoll's book than by the newspaper scoop that launched it on the market. Despite its sorry origins in an act of great and unjustified aggression, the episode can be the occasion for a deepened reflection on what Fernando Coronil has called the "geopolitics of truth." Scholars face an opportunity and a responsiblity

29

to work through the issues the controversy raises, which include a series of important epistemological, methodological, and ethical questions.

The pages that follow attempt first to situate the controversy in its American (that is, U.S.) context. In part for anecdotal reasons, *I, Rigoberta Menchú* played a conspicuous role in the ideological conflicts that burst out in the field of education in the United States, especially under Reaganism. These conflicts, and the iconization of *I, Rigoberta Menchú* within them, form the context for the book's reception in North America. They also explain the high profile the attacks on the book and Menchú received in the press, and the triumph these represent for the political right. For American readers of my own generation, some of what follows may be familiar. But a review seems worthwhile, especially given the international dimensions of the controversy and the serious stakes for Menchú, the Guatemalan peace process, indigenous movements worldwide, and the future of critical scholarship in the American university. The final section of the essay offers some ideas for approaching Menchú's testimony and the recent questioning of its credibility.

Reaganism and the "Culture Wars"

What have come to be known as the "culture wars" in the United States were the result of a fatal collision between two historical processes: on the one hand, the arrival on university faculties of the "children of the '60s," and, on the other, the arrival at the White House of Ronald Reagan along with a dogmatic political right hungry for power. Beginning in about 1975, veterans of the student movements and the counterculture, doctorates freshly in hand, began joining university faculties as young colleagues of the professors whose classes they had once boycotted and whose values they had rejected. Antiracist and feminist struggles opened the doors of American higher education to the most diverse student bodies in the history of the country. Many disciplines, most dramatically law, history, literary studies, and anthropology, developed critical wings that questioned their ideological and historical underpinnings. At the same time, a conservative movement humiliated by the defeats of Watergate, Vietnam, and others, gathered strength and began promoting an ideological, religious, and cultural agenda, along with a political one. Since the 1980s, most universities in the United States have been thrown into upheaval by these ideological and generational conflicts.

The "culture wars" acquired particular visibility at Stanford University, where David Stoll did his doctoral studies in anthropology and began the investigation that resulted in *Rigoberta Menchú and the Story of All Poor Guatemalans*. At a number of points, Stanford wound up on the front lines of the debate in part because of its prestige, but mainly because it was at one and the same time the intellectual seat of the Reagan revolution, and the site of a significant effort for educational reform, in which the present writer participated. In many ways, however, developments there were typical.

The intellectual seat of the Reagan revolution was Stanford's well-known Hoover Institution of War, Revolution, and Peace, founded in 1919 by Herbert Hoover, prior to his presidency. For many years, the Hoover has been one of the chief research centers of the right in the United States and a nucleus of Republican Party activism.[3] It was an important force in the promotion of Reagan's presidential candidacy and held great influence in his administration. Stanford's departments and teaching programs, on the other hand, had a liberal profile. In the 1970s, Stanford was one of the universities that most conspicuously altered their demographics in response to pressures to create more diverse and inclusive institutions. Under a progressive president, a former official of the Carter administration, affirmative action was implemented seriously at Stanford. African American, Chicano, and Native American students were actively recruited; the new faculty hired in the 1970s included the first Latino and African American professors, along with the first critical mass of women. The curriculum opened up. As in universities across the country, programs in feminist studies and African/Afro-American studies appeared, along with a Center for Chicano Research. Traditional course requirements were eliminated.

Reactions swiftly followed. In 1980, on the recommendation of a group of faculty concerned about the erosion of traditional humanistic knowledge, the university adopted a yearlong course in Western culture as a requirement for all entering first-year students. The course was based not on an articulated pedagogical project, but on a corpus of readings that, it was felt, would provide all students with "knowledge of the roots of their culture" (as if all the students had European "roots") and a "common intellectual experience." I reproduce this reading list below not as a curiosity, but because, strange as it may seem, it had a great deal to do with the fate of *I, Rigoberta Menchú* in the years that followed. The list is divided between required (above) and recommended (below) texts.

FALL	WINTER	SPRING
Bible	Augustine	Voltaire
Plato	Dante	Marx/Engels
Homer	Thomas More	Freud
a Greek tragedy	Machiavelli	Darwin
	Luther	
	Galileo	
Thucydides	Boethius	Rousseau
Aristotle	Aquinas	Hume
Cicero	a Shakespearean tragedy	Goethe
Virgil	Cervantes	Mill
Tacitus	Descartes	Nietzsche
	Hobbes	a nineteenth-century novel
	Locke	

The predominance of classical and northern European philosophical materials is obvious, as is the absence of American writers and thinkers, of women, twentieth-century materials, nonelite expressions. Stanford's student body in 1980 was quite diverse—nearly half the entering classes consisted of Asian American, Latin, African American, and Native American students. Nearly half were women. Half the Anglo-American student body was from California and the U.S. West. It was incongruous to such a student body that this corpus in any way represented "the roots of their culture," and impossible to produce the impression of a common intellectual experience at a moment when students were learning above all from their differences. From the beginning, the Western culture course appeared to many not only an anachronism but the exemplar of everything that needed to change in the new university. In 1984–86, demands for change gave rise to a multiethnic student movement inspired by Jesse Jackson's Rainbow Coalition, and in fact mentored personally by Jackson. A network of faculty also formed, some identified with emergent paradigms of cultural studies. Two years of furious debate followed, culminating in a full-fledged institutional crisis that lasted for nearly two years.[4]

Of greater consequence for Rigoberta Menchú was the fact that the Stanford debate was launched onto the national media scene by Reagan's secretary of education, William Bennett, who latched onto Stanford's internal discussion as an ideological platform. On national television and newspapers he forcefully took sides in favor of the traditional curriculum and the Occidental civilizing mission in general. His intervention touched a nerve in a society confused and anxious about its identity and its values. Beginning in the *Wall Street Journal,* the Stanford debate became the subject of editorial pages across the country. When the conflict was resolved in 1988, in a new program that, among other things, eliminated the notorious reading list and required the inclusion of non-European materials, the story was front-page news. (In 1987, at the height of Stanford's internal debate, David Stoll entered the doctoral program of its Department of Anthropology. Unlike most of his peers, he was a mature student with an established career in journalism.[5] It was while doing thesis research in the summer of 1989 in El Quiché that he encountered discrepant versions of the events narrated in *I, Rigoberta Menchú* and began actively seeking informants whose accounts contradicted the book. Stoll received his doctorate from Stanford in 1992.)

A Battle of Books instead of Ideas

The debate at Stanford, and others like it across the country, had the positive effect of opening spaces for new optics on culture and history. In the long run, however, one of the great successes of the right was that of defining the issue as a debate over books rather than ideas. In the media, the confrontation came to be known as "the battle of the books," and this is the form it took in universities and secondary schools across the country. Opponents represented new curricular proposals as acts of substitution (or murder) in which the great books written by European men were displaced by inferior books written by unknown and marginal figures.[6] Lists of authors and titles like Stanford's came metonymically to represent Western culture itself, besieged by barbarism in the form of such books as *The Autobiography of Frederick Douglass,* or Frantz Fanon's *Wretched of the Earth* or Jean Rhys's *Wide Sargasso Sea,* or Juan Rulfo's *Pedro Páramo* or *I, Rigoberta Menchú.* Whereas the classics were studied for their implicit merit and importance, the new books, it was said, were prescribed for ideological reasons. Among advocates of curricular reform as well, discussion all too readily reduced to a question of changing the readings.

Having taken this form, the debate inspired many stupidities, in large part because opponents of change were arguing from ignorance. After all, they were not about to sit down and read the intruding, barbarian books. Even respected conservative intellectuals, such as C. Vann Woodward or George Will, freely discarded writers and books simply on the basis of their non-European authorship. In the pages of *Newsweek*, Will insisted that Shakespeare's *Tempest* had nothing to do with colonialism or slavery, and Saul Bellow pronounced in a Chicago newspaper that "when the Zulus have a Tolstoy, we will read him." (The key term here is undoubtedly "we.") Armed by ignorance, the battle of the books thwarted the possibility of serious dialogue over what was really at stake: how to transform cultural capital in a society of the Americas that has decided to recognize and develop itself as multiethnic, heterogeneous, democratic, and postcolonial.

As many readers will recall, the debates tended to be impassioned. Critiques of the status quo created uncomfortable and often intensely painful situations for mainstream scholars passionately committed to their work and convinced of its human value. Because of the demographics of the university, these were overwhelmingly white men, many of whom considered themselves politically progressive. Even those most disposed to change faced the loss of interpretative monopolies and the displacement of things prized for their truth, goodness, and beauty. Nor were they likely to find sympathy for the painful existential circumstances they faced. Echoes of their pain and rage often resonate, for example, in the rejection of subaltern perspectives as "narratives of victimization" or as instances of an unjustified "epistemological privilege." From the beginning, such responses characterized the debate around *I, Rigoberta Menchú*.

Even before Rigoberta Menchú won the Nobel Prize, her *testimonio* was caught up in the battle of the books. Her text appeared often in courses aimed at decentering the Eurocentric cultural and geographic panorama, or teaching critical analysis of the West. Stanford's curricular reform, for example, gave rise to a course called "Europe and the Americas" based on a relational approach to culture and a historical vision centered on the Americas. One of its strategies was to teach European classics and materials from the Americas in dialogue with each other (Augustine's *Confessions* with a Navajo life story; Shakespeare's *Tempest* with Aimé Césaire's 1968 rewrite, *A Tempest;* Caribbean vodun with Greek ecstatic cults, for example). The course included many readings on the legacy of colonialism in Europe and the Americas, from Columbus's letters and the chronicles of the Andean Guamán Poma de Ayala, to Juan Rulfo and Zora Neale Hurston. *I, Rigoberta Menchú* was assigned in dialogue with the *Popul Vuh* and other texts, and every year was the text students described as having had the greatest impact on them.

Those of us teaching this course found ourselves enmeshed in one of the most interesting and fruitful experiences in our teaching careers, but we were surprised by attacks in the media, based on the authors and titles we assigned. One critic called them "obscure authors with chips on their shoulders or knives in their teeth."[7] In December 1989, to our surprise, the *Wall Street Journal* dedicated its editorial page to the course ("I always knew you'd amount to something," said my mother), publishing the syllabus, appropriately edited, and a sarcastic editorial titled "The Stanford Mind." The presence of Fanon, Rulfo, Césaire, and Menchú "in place of" Locke and Hobbes (but not Rousseau—he was on the syllabus) provoked particular indignation. "Mr. Fanon," it said, quoting the conservative Alan Bloom, "is a demonstrably inferior and derivative thinker to whom no one would pay any attention if he were not currently the ideologue of popular movements and if as a black Algerian [*sic*—Fanon was Martinican] he did not fit Stanford's job description" (December 22, 1989).

In 1991, the polemic produced the book that definitively established *I, Rigoberta Menchú* as a political target, Dinesh D'Souza's *Illiberal Education: The Politics of Race and Sex on Campus*, a passionate and intensely ideological attack on the educational reforms of the 1980s written by a young disciple of the Republican right.[8] In part reacting to the Stanford course, D'Souza dedicates an entire chapter to the Menchú *testimonio*. Titled "Travels with Rigoberta," it attacked Menchú on two opposing fronts: as an ignorant and uneducated Indian woman from whom we have nothing to learn, and as an Indian woman whose experience and life choices make her insufficiently typical to represent an indigenous view of the world. D'Souza's book was written under conservative foundation support, and had the benefit of a national advertising campaign. For critics of his book, however, there was no analogous path by which analyses of its distortions and errors could make their way into national debate. It was at this point that many of us began receiving calls from magazines such as *U.S. News and World Report* and *Forbes* (yes, really!)

checking "facts": "Is it true that you teach *I, Rigoberta Menchú* in your course? Why do you teach it? How do you justify including a communist in your curriculum? Do you really believe it is a great book?" We tried to learn about sound bites, but we weren't very good at it.

On one front, in the 1990s, then, *I, Rigoberta Menchú* was demonized by the right as an icon of a destructive and promiscuous multiculturalism. On another, it generated reflection and debate around important questions such as the "representation" of subalterns in academic inquiry, and the forms the decolonization of knowledge should take. More broadly, its English translation came to be a reading of choice in social science and humanities courses seeking to develop critical and non-hegemonic perspectives and began to appear frequently in the freshman composition courses required of nearly all first-year college students. In these interdisciplinary contexts, there is no doubt that the book was sometimes taught in a decontextualized and reified manner. In 1996, its impact was attested by a volume of essays, *Teaching and Testimony: Rigoberta Menchú in the North American Classroom*, dedicated to disseminating the pedagogical approaches to the book.[9] In these years, Menchú made fairly frequent personal appearances on American campuses, where audiences admired her eloquence, wisdom, and courage. At the same time, Stoll began appearing at conferences (beginning with the Latin American Studies Association in 1991) raising his concerns about the veracity of her text.

In Good Company

The author of *Rigoberta Menchú and the Story of All Poor Guatemalans* acknowledges in his prologue that his investigation and its published results were intended as interventions in the debates outlined in the preceding section. Of the book's three objectives, Stoll says, one is to oppose a "new orthodoxy" in the academy whose premise, according to Stoll, is that

> Western forms of knowledge, such as the empirical approach adopted
> here, are fatally compromised by racism and other forms of domination.
> Responsible scholars must therefore identify with the oppressed,
> relegating much of what we think we know about them to the dustbin of
> colonialism. The new basis of authority consists in letting subalterns
> speak for themselves and agonizing over any hint of complicity with the

system that oppresses them, and situating oneself in relation to fashionable theorists. (xv)

The statement is a caricature of the critical optics developed since the late 1970s, but it makes clear that the exposé of Menchú was viewed by its author as a taking of sides in the national debate. The aggressive questioning of Menchú's *testimonio* and her personal trajectory was undertaken with the awareness that it would be received by the right as a splendid vindication not only against Menchú and her *testimonio,* but also against multiculturalism, social movements, and the efforts to decolonize higher education in the United States. I underscore this point because it is obvious that the project could have taken other forms— reading *Rigoberta Menchú and the Story of All Poor Guatemalans* one often finds oneself imagining the other (and better) books it could have been. With relation to the national debates, the book tells an emancipatory tale: its protagonist-hero is the metropolitan researcher who stops agonizing about his complicity and reassumes the authority to discover truth in the chaos of the world (in this case, the historical chaos Guatemalans have produced in their country). D'Souza was quick to enter the scene, publishing a sarcastic article, while, from the conservative Center for Popular Culture in Los Angeles, David Horowitz bought newspaper ads condemning *I, Rigoberta Menchú* as a fraud, and criticizing academics who defended it. Given the timing, analogies with the investigation of Bill Clinton were unavoidable: for accusers, if Menchú had lied, she and her book should be impeached.

In point of fact, it is inaccurate to attribute these responses to the book itself, for, as others in this collection have observed, they were the product of the international media blitz it set in motion. Many journalistic commentaries appear to be based not on a reading of the book at all but on media reports, or a look at the early chapters. To a great extent, this was predictable. For one thing, even for a motivated reader, *Rigoberta Menchú and the Story of All Poor Guatemalans* makes for unrewarding reading. The first two hundred pages review in detail those aspects of Menchú's *testimonio* that Stoll has found reason to doubt, and argue for alternative accounts or interpretations; the last hundred pages comment on Menchú's personal and political trajectory since 1983. The text is composed as a dizzying labyrinth of voices, judgments, details, and possibilities. Few general readers will last past the opening chapters. For those whose aim is to expunge *I, Rigoberta Menchú* and books like it from reading lists and libraries, however, the particulars of Stoll's argument are not important because the history and inhabitants of Guatemala are of no importance. Nor are they what is at stake in the argument. In this sense, oddly enough, Stoll perhaps wrote a book for a nonexistent readership. It is also, of course, a book aimed at unleashing the kind of media coverage without which, as we know, books rarely reach mainstream awareness.

At one level, then, what is at stake in the United States is neither Menchú nor Guatemala, but academic authority. The entry of new subjects and intellectual agents into the field of academic knowledge-production has always been resisted. In this sense, though not in others, the current controversy is academic business as usual, and the attacks on Menchú were predictable. Certainly they have antecedents. David Horowitz, for instance, recently launched an attack on feminist Betty Friedan, whom he accuses of falsely presenting herself in her classic *The Feminine Mystique* as a housewife radicalized by the experience of domestic claustrophobia in the 1950s. Based on his research, Horowitz says, she was the daughter of a family with long-standing Communist sympathies and had a record of political activism long before her entry into feminism. The project, then (the parallels with Menchú are unmistakable), is to unmask Friedan's book as a lie, Friedan as a liar, and feminism as the fruit of Marxist subversion.[10]

Better known, perhaps, is the attack some years ago by the sociobiologist Derek Freeman on cultural anthropologist Margaret Mead. Like Menchú and Friedan, Mead was an international public figure and a respected iconoclast whose strengths and weaknesses were well known within her field. Freeman's attack was directed less at Mead's work than at her status as an icon (on whose back, paradoxically, Freeman built his own reputation). The aggressive discrediting of Mead was part of a campaign to establish a new hegemony in the field of anthropological knowledge, that of sociobiology (a terrain still occupied almost entirely by white men). The humanistic Mead had to be destroyed as the image of the anthropologist; in similar fashion, it appears, the highly autonomous Menchú has to be destroyed as the image of the subaltern, restoring the Occidental academic subject as the normative producer of knowledge, especially knowledge of the other. The drama confirms the analysis made years ago by cultural critic Jean Franco, that the *testimonio* represented "a struggle for interpretative power."[11]

"I Had No Idea!"

From the perspective of their ideological commitments, educational conservatives have not been wrong in singling out *I, Rigoberta Menchú* for attack. Its significance in American classrooms has everything to do with the powerful impact the text tends to have on the young readers who encounter it on their reading lists when they arrive at colleges and universities. As many of us have discovered in the classroom, most students have never read anything of the kind, and the book tends to have dramatic and sometimes transformative effects. Its construction as a personal, experiential narrative has the power to break down the distancing strategies that normally govern young Americans' encounters with their racial and economic others. The extraordinary specificity and vividness of the narrative and its elaborate emotive dimension overcome the dehumanizing reflexes that tend to insulate young Americans from the suffering of others, limiting their capacity for empathetic response. On reading the book, many students encounter for the first time the notion that the rich are rich because the poor are poor, and vice versa. For many, the book destabilizes for the first time their relation with their nation and their government. In the midst of the pious rhetoric of national foreign policy, they are shocked to find that a few short years ago genocidal violence occurred in a neighboring country with the tacit collaboration of their government. "I had no idea!" is a general response to the book, often followed by "What can I do?"

For students of privileged backgrounds, *I, Rigoberta Menchú* often creates a dramatic first engagement with the realities of poverty, insecurity, and the absence of choice. The reactions, invariably intense, vary from aggressive rejection to illumination, from guilt to mobilization. For students from poor backgrounds, or who have lived everyday violence, the book is a vindication of their historical consciousness and social experience, which their studies otherwise rarely engage. The book's American reception is shaped in advance by the historic role that autobiographical writing plays in North American culture, as an expressive vehicle both of individualism and of an egalitarian notion of the subject. From Benjamin Franklin and Frederick Douglass to Helen Keller and Hank Aaron, new and emergent subjects in American culture enter the social imaginary through the doorway of autobiography or what has come to be called "self-writing."

In university classrooms, *I, Rigoberta Menchú* generates difficult, painful, passionate, and revealing dialogues. As Stanford anthropologist Renato Rosaldo commented, after teaching the book for many years in the "Europe and the Americas" course:

> In the classroom, Menchú's work has made vivid both Mayan traditions and the more recent trials of Mayan peoples in the face of genocidal military incursions. The work can be read next to the classic Mayan telling of the creation, the *Popol Vuh*, a narrative whose echoes appear in her life story. Her narrative, not unlike the classic confessions of Saint Augustine and Jean-Jacques Rousseau, provides readers with a compelling worldview and an impassioned articulation of a historical crisis. Such works engage students with significant cultural and historical issues by combining fine elements of historical writing with compelling personal narrative. Menchú's work engages students in rich discussions that range from the character of cultural traditions, the impact of military incursions against indigenous peoples, the factors that transform rural, agricultural ways of life, to the struggles of social groups to live their lives with dignity and self-respect. The book brings cultural and social issues to life in a way that is realistic and humanly engaging; it is a gift to the classroom.[12]

However problematic their work relation may have been, Debray and Menchú made a powerful book. Its capacity to enlighten and move metropolitan subjects does not derive from the fact that the book is the *testimonio* of a young Guatemalan indigenous woman who has suffered many painful experiences. It derives from the manner in which the text is made, its expressive power, its coarticulation of aesthetic, narrative, ethical, and emotional dimensions, its ability to evoke a history and a country, and also a cosmos. To some degree, this force derives from the aspects of the text for which Menchú is now under fire: the strong ethical-political commitment, the interpretation of local events through national paradigms, the consciousness of metropolitan expectations and stereotypes in her presentation of herself, the representation of experiences of her fellows as her own, the eyewitness reporting of things heard at second hand.

Of these aspects, only the last two are news; that is, until now, North American readers have for the most part believed that Menchú herself did the things she says she did and saw what she says she saw. On these points the new revelations have been startling and disconcerting. At the same time, these same readers have never doubted for a minute that the book is a politically partial account, that other participants would tell the story very differently, that the book involves selection and idealization. These are standard aspects of *testimonio*, regularly recognized in readings (and teachings) of the text. To find fault with them is to misapprehend the genre. The logic of the *testimonio* dictates that the testimonial subject decides what to tell and how to tell it. Within these parameters, *I, Rigoberta Menchú* has been trusted in terms of what one might call the historical fidelity of the book, that is, its capacity to reflect richly and plausibly the historical reality it addresses. This recognition of the book's overall accuracy has been and continues to be shared by area specialists on Guatemala, and is reaffirmed by Stoll himself. Nevertheless, historical fidelity or no, *I, Rigoberta Menchú* is likely now to disappear from many American classrooms, reading lists, and libraries, and when it is taught, Stoll will be on the course list too.

Testimonio, Transculturation, and the "Personal"

Were it not for its polemical bent, Stoll's research could have provided the occasion for a valuable and fascinating reflection on the composition of *I, Rigoberta Menchú* and the nature of its expressive power. Perhaps such a reflection is still within reach. Certainly it is not too late to consider more fully the epistemology of *testimonio* in general. Historically, the university has always privileged lettered knowledge over narrated experience as a source of understanding. The communications revolution, from which the *testimonio* arises, has undermined this hierarchy, yet the process of constructing corresponding models of authority and meaning-making has barely begun. From academic standpoints, experiential knowledge is often dismissed as anecdote or unreflected spontaneity. At the same time, on a global scale, marginalized groups are insisting on entering into dialogue with lettered knowledge, from alternative epistemological grounds. Metropolitan academies quite likely have the power to repress or dismiss these interlocutors, or to intimidate them into silence. But if they succeed, we all lose.

The "literary" treatment of *testimonio* has been much criticized from a cultural-studies perspective. Yet current debate on *testimonio* suffers from confusion with respect to the question of genre. Excellent studies exist, several by writers in this volume, but we still lack well-developed theoretical frameworks for specifying what *testimonio* is, how it should be read, produced, taught. The lack of such interpretative and ethical frameworks has left the field open to the application of norms that are irrelevant or arbitrary. For example, in a number of instances the accusations of falsehood, distortion, and partisanship against Menchú apply norms from legal testimony. But, of course, the *testimonio* is not legal testimony at all. Is it more like autobiography? Impartiality is never asked or expected of autobiographers. Who would fault Frederick Douglass for lacking a more balanced attitude toward slavery, or Winston Churchill (or Hitler, for that matter) toward Nazism? Nor is selectiveness considered deviant. Rousseau and Benjamin Franklin were not expected to report in their autobiographies their catastrophic conduct as spouses or parents, which surely compromised them as the civic moralists they wanted to be. The omissions are registered by scholars on the reception end, but not as expectations on the production end. The autobiographical contract (between writer and reader) presupposes on the part of the producer a will to truthfulness qualified by self-interest, partisanship, and the fragility of memory.

But the *testimonio* is not autobiography either, though the two have much in common. Other generic relatives include the "life story," often used by anthropologists doing qualitative research; "oral history," that is, historical reconstruction by means of interviews with multiple participants in a process; and "as told to" autobiography, in which the autobiographical subject relates her memories to a writer who converts them into a book. In this generic field, *testimonio* stands out as a genre produced transculturally, across the division between center and periphery, the West and the non-West, modernity and its others. For this reason, *testimonio* exists in a state of permanent, and often productive, contradiction. For instance, though the testimonial subject is asked to narrate her or his individual experience, the "testimonial contract" defines that subject as a member of a group that is living an important historical transition. The category of "experience" is thus ruled simultaneously by paradigms of individualism (uniqueness) and of collectivity (exemplarity). According to the testimonial contract, the subject who is other to the metropolitan self voluntarily narrates its personal experience to the metropolitan subject. But, of course, "personal experience" here is a modern Western existential category that presupposes a subjectivity that the testimonial speaker is understood not to possess. This is not at all to say that the idea of personal experience and the genre of personal narrative do not exist outside the West. That is palpably false. The claim is that the coproducers of *testimonios* locate themselves in a process of transculturation or cultural reconversion in which they seek to align Western concepts of life, experience, subjectivity, and the person with the experiential and verbal repertory of the non-Western or subaltern subject.[13] What binds the two together is an ethical commitment to the project of communicating the subaltern's individual and collective reality to metropolitan audiences who are ignorant of it, in a discourse those audiences can decipher and with which they will identify. It involves irremediably what Jürgen Habermas would call "systematically distorted communication," as does all transcultural communicative action.

This context of production obliges testimonial subjects to make decisions as to what to relate and how to relate it, most likely on the basis of only partial understanding of the category of personal narrative as it operates in metropolitan culture. However partial or complete her understanding, Menchú appears to have made a series of strategic, though not necessarily conscious, decisions to present as her own experiences that happened to others, and collective processes. Her reconversions, on the one hand, overcome the limits of the metropolitan "personal," and at the same time they violate its norms.

It is easy to imagine arguments in favor of or against these moves, and ways of producing testimony that avoids—or authorizes—them. The important challenge, in my view, is finding ways to grasp transcultural communication situations and the epistemological and ethical aspects of reconversions. How do testimonial subjects evaluate their communicative situations and make their decisions? How should the results be assessed? Despite the metropolitan cult of the fact, for instance, it is common in everyday practice that verisimilitude counts as veracity. Under what conditions, as in the case of Menchú now (but not before), does that equivalence break down? When does it not? Questions like these help situate *testimonio* as a rich and problematic form of communication and source of transcultural knowledge. The current controversy obliges scholars to address them.

Hubris

I close with a few observations related specifically to Stoll's exposé. It is a disconcerting text that often seems an act of hubris. It questions point for point the veracity of Menchú's account, but raises many doubts as to its own reliability. It proposes to vindicate empirical research (247), but deploys an intensely partisan rhetoric and hermeneutics. It proposes interpretations and arguments, and then sets them aside without explaining why.

It is up to Guatemala specialists to assess the empirical precision of Stoll's conclusions and research methods. As the essays here attest, there seem to be many discrepancies. Most specialists, for instance, reject outright the claim that there was no justification for a guerrilla presence in the area where Menchú lived because the highland peasants had not suffered an economic decline in the 1970s (64). The interpretation of the CUC as originally a guerrilla organization is also rejected by other researchers. Scholars who have done fieldwork in the same communities doubt that the manner and circumstances in which Stoll's interviews were carried out permit a reliable reconstruction of what happened. For some, the failure to identify informants consistently violates the norms of this kind of research. Often the choice between one interpretation and another is not explained, and patently false versions are included without comment. On these points and others, the reflections of area experts are critical.

One does not have to be an expert, however, to notice the way in which some facts invent themselves in the course of Stoll's highly rhetorical account. At times, what appears initially as one possibility among others later reappears as an empirical claim. In chapter 8, for instance, two eyewitnesses affirm that Menchú's father, Vicente, was not present when the guerrilla first entered his town of Chimel. Two other informants say the opposite, one of whom appears to be speaking at second hand (110–11). In chapters 12 and 17, however, it has become a fact that Vicente Menchú personally received the guerrilla in Chimel (172, 240). In reverse fashion, other facts turn themselves into fictions. Early on, the author affirms that Menchú's account of the capture, rape, torture, and death of her mother is "basically true," and gives reasons for this conclusion (125). Nevertheless, in chapter 14 we read that Menchú "imagined" the death of her mother (194), and chapter 17 offers a perverse metaphor, speaking of "the calvaries through which Menchú [textually, we suppose] puts her mother and brother" (308).

Frequent incongruencies arise between the author's conclusions and the facts cited to support them. One of Stoll's main points is that the guerrilla movement never had massive support among indigenous peasants, from which he deduces that anyone who did support the guerrilla cannot speak reliably about the experience of the peasants during the war. At the same time, we read of the "inundation of recruits from religious, peasant and labor organizations" in 1981 (174); of an expansion in Santa Cruz del Quiché so massive that it overwhelmed the guerrilla's capacity for growth; that the Guatemalan guerrilla was the first in Latin America to attract significant numbers of indigenous adherents (208). The racial factor is constantly downplayed, especially in land disputes, and at the same time we are told that Ladino landholders collaborated unanimously and violently with the army, and that the lands of Chimel wound up during the war in the hands of a Ladino who was able to gain title despite prior indigenous ownership. Menchú's school is depicted as a cloister "isolated from the outside world," leading to the claim that her political education began only after she left Guatemala. At the same time, however, the school is described as "under siege" by the military during the 1980s, and surrounded by soldiers threatening the nuns, who were reporting human rights violations (164) and trying to "protect their pupils from reprisals" (191). The suggestion is made that Menchú could not have traveled as a child to pick coffee with her family because she was at school, yet Stoll's reconstruction of her education indicates a gap of several years at the very age Menchú says she went to the *fincas*. The book is supposed to correct the naive and harmful support given to the guerrilla by the North American left, but states that by 1990 this support had ceased to exist. Menchú's public appearances are described as "political meetings aimed at consolidating support for the Guatemalan Left" (they are not), yet Menchú is quoted remarking that the labels left and right have not meant anything to her for a long time (266). Again, one senses an act of hubris.

But obviously the most difficult thing for Stoll's readers to accept is what might be called the ethical scale of his argument. By this I mean that however significant the discrepancies between Menchú's narrated testimony and the reconstructible facts of her life, it remains incongruous to equate these ethically with the monstrosities of the army, the enormity of indigenous suffering and loss, the immensity of the inequalities and injustices of Guatemalan society, the courage and stamina of those who survived, the legitimacy of the demands for peace and justice, the other facts for which truth commissioners have lost their lives, the infinity of the despair and pain, including that inflicted by the book itself, the corrupt complicity of the American government, the benefit the book affords to the Guatemalan army and paramilitary. It is not easy to imagine an ethical compass whose point of orientation is not these truths but the truth that Menchú was not present when they killed her brother or that she does not discuss her family's internal quarrels. To the extent that Stoll's book asks its readers to make that ethical choice, it subverts itself, and impedes reflection on the serious issues it raises. Again, hubris.

Those issues are not simply empirical. Far from bearing us upward into the realm of truth, the whirlwind of voices, details, innuendos, questions, possibilities, and judgments that make up the book creates a truth seeker's purgatory from which it does not propose an exit. Written subjectively, it could have been a masterpiece. All of which suggests, perhaps, a testimonial reading of *Rigoberta Menchú and the Story of All Poor Guatemalans,* as the personal account of the trajectory of a partisan subject whose people are undergoing a painful historical transition.

Postscript USA: In 1998, the states of California and Texas abolished their programs of affirmative action in the public sector, and in Stanford the course program housing the Europe and the Americas course was replaced. In April 1999, a hunger strike by students in ethnic studies at the University of California, Berkeley, won a series of demands.

Postscript Guatemala: On May 12, 1999, Roberto Belarmino González, leader of the Frente Democrático Nueva Guatemala, the only left party currently in the Guatemalan congress, was gunned down while leaving his house. Two days later, in a national referendum, more than 70 percent of voters rejected a constitutional reform that guaranteed certain indigenous rights, recognized Guatemala as a multiethnic state, and limited the power of the military, but failed to finalize the peace accords between army and guerrilla. Rigoberta Menchú, along with the Guatemalan government, campaigned for the yes vote. In November 1999 in national elections, Alfonso Portillo Cabrera was elected president of Guatemala. Portillo represented the Frente Republicano Guatemalteco (FRG), a Christian right party headed by former president General Ríos Montt, the leader held responsible for the worst campaigns against the indigenous population in the 1980s. General Ríos Montt remains secretary-general of the FRG, and president of the Congress. Ineligible by law for reelection, he is generally understood to be running the country. More than 62 percent of the electorate abstained and 6 percent cast blank or annulled ballots.

Notes

1. These were the conclusions of the United Nations-appointed truth commission, whose report was presented by its director, the German Christian Tomuschat, in February of 1999. The commission was established as part of the peace negotiations between the Guatemalan army and the URNG in 1996. The commission concluded that 93 percent of the killings were the work of the army, which responded to a guerrilla uprising with a campaign of genocide. The death toll reflects only a fraction of the violence, which included the widespread use of torture, forced conscription into the army and civilian patrols, and forced displacement of tens of thousands of people.

2. David Stoll, *Rigoberta Menchú and the Story of All Poor Guatemalans* (Boulder, Colo.: Westview Press, 1999).

3. Host of one of the best library collections in the world on the history of leftist movements, the Hoover today counts among its senior fellows such cold war heroes as Edward Teller, inventor of the atomic bomb; Peter Duignan, defender of European colonialism; and the architects of neoliberalism, Milton Friedman, Michael Boskin, George Shultz, and William Perry; and the Afro-American conservative activist Thomas Sowell.

4. For a fuller discussion of this debate, see Mary Louise Pratt, "Humanities for the Future: Reflections on the Stanford Western Culture Debate," in *The Politics of Liberal Education*, ed. Darryl Gless and Barbara Herrnstein Smith (Durham, N.C.: Duke University Press, 1990).

5. He had already published one book on Protestant missionaries in the third world, *Fishers of Men or Founders of Empire?: The Wycliffe Bible Translators in Latin America* (London: Zed Press, and Cambridge, Mass.: Cultural Survival, 1982), and he was preparing a second on evangelical movements, *Is Latin America Turning Protestant?* (Berkeley: University of California Press: 1990). Stoll's doctoral thesis, published as *Between Two Armies in the Ixil Towns of Guatemala* (New York: Columbia University Press, 1993), advanced the argument that reappears in the most recent book, that *(a)* most *campesinos* during the war saw themselves as caught between two forces, the army and the guerrilla struggle, neither of which they genuinely supported, and *(b)* the guerrilla struggle is heavily responsible for the suffering and loss of life because it initiated the confrontation with the army and was able neither to defend the *campesinos* nor to arm them in their own defense.

6. Empirical studies by the Modern Language Association showed that this impression was false. Canonical texts continued to dominate in university curricula, but they no longer monopolized it completely.

7. Letter to the *Stanford Daily*, December 7, 1988. The phrase alludes to the title of one of the readings in the course, *With a Pistol in His Hand*, the classic study of the Mexican American *corrido* by the Chicano scholar Américo Paredes.

8. Dinesh D'Souza, *Illiberal Education: The Politics of Race and Sex on Campus* (New York: Free Press, 1991). Today a fellow of the American Enterprise Institute, D'Souza got his start at Dartmouth College in a chain of conservative student news-

papers founded by the Republican right in the 1980s as a seed ground for young activists and ideologues, who received internships, salaries, and training in how to harass left-wing, minority, and gay faculty members. Five years after *Illiberal Education,* the Free Press published another right-wing blockbuster, Richard Herrnstein and Charles Murray's *The Bell Curve: Intelligence and Class Structure in American Life* (New York: Free Press, 1996), which attempted to revive older debates about a genetically based racial hierarchy, demonstrated by standardized tests.

9. Allen Carey-Webb and Stephen Benz, eds., *Teaching and Testimony: Rigoberta Menchú and the North American Classroom* (New York: State University of New York Press, 1996).

10. Friedan's career has an interesting point of intersection with the history of the *testimonio.* In 1975 she presided at the first UN International Conference on Women that inaugurated the UN Decade for Women, where the Bolivian activist Domitila Barrios de Chungara made her dramatic speech pointing out the abysses that separated first- and third-world women. On the basis of that encounter, Barrios de Chungara with Moema Viezzier went on to produce *¡Si me permiten hablar!,* the best-known *testimonio* after *I, Rigoberta Menchú* (Mexico City: Siglo XXI, 1977); English translation, *Let Me Speak!,* trans. Victoria Ortiz; *testimonio* coproduced with Moema Viezzer (New York: Monthly Review Press, 1978).

11. Jean Franco, "Si me permiten hablar: La lucha por el poder interpretativo," *Casa de las Américas* 29.171 (1988).

12. Renato Rosaldo, Public statement, January 20, 1999.

13. The concept of cultural reconversion is developed by Néstor García Canclini in *Culturas híbridas: estrategias para entrar y salir de la modernidad* (Mexico City: Grijalbo, 1990); English translation, *Hybrid Cultures: Strategies for Entering and Leaving Modernity,* trans. Christopher L. Chiappari and Silvia L. López (Minneapolis: University of Minnesota Press, 1995). The concept of transculturation is developed by Ángel Rama, *Transculturación narrativa en América Latina* (Mexico City: Siglo XXI, 1982).

II
Documents
The Public Speaks

Documents
The Public Speaks

The new controversy surrounding Rigoberta Menchú Tum's first book, *I, Rigoberta Menchú*, began on December 15, 1998, when the *New York Times* gave front-page coverage to Larry Rohter's article "Tarnished Laureate," which questioned the authenticity of the biographical facts in her famous *testimonio*. The prominence of this article came as a surprise, because the daily had downplayed other significant events that took place in Central America during 1998, including the assassination in Guatemala of Bishop Juan Gerardi, the head of the Recovery of Historical Memory commission (REMHI), forty-eight hours after he presented the printed version of the commission's human rights document, *Guatemala, Never Again*.

Rohter's article reopened a polemic that seemed to have closed at the end of the cold war. The narrower and more categorical way in which Rohter framed Stoll's allegations made Menchú Tum appear as a "liar," something of which Stoll never accused her, and that is how Stoll's book came to be perceived internationally, as the *Times* article traveled around the world. Rohter's views were reproduced in newspapers, as well as in partisan attacks against Menchú Tum, such as those launched by David Horowitz's Center for the Study of Popular Culture in Los Angeles, or the Hoover Institution at Stanford University. However, even Stoll's more nuanced indictments have broader implications because *I, Rigoberta Menchú* is currently used throughout academia and in many high schools in the United States as a means of furthering multicultural debates and issues of identity politics in the classroom. Stoll's argument, as a result, forced not only postcolonial theorists, but also all professors and teachers interested in multicultural issues, to rethink the nature of history, narrative, and truth. Outside of the United States, of course, Menchú Tum is a publicly recognized celebrity and acknowledged leader of native and subaltern peoples' human rights, on friendly terms with the president of France, who has given her the highest medal in his country, the king of Spain, the prime minister of Sweden, and the secretary-general of the United Nations. She is also a heroine to most progressive people in Latin America. Thus, Stoll's accusations became front-page news in all of those countries, and a source of concern not only to obscure academics, but also to heads of state themselves.

Although the debate was picked up in both Europe and Latin America, it became most intense in Guatemala, Rigoberta Menchú Tum's native country, and in Spain. The leading daily in Spain, *El País,* one of the most important European newspapers along with France's *Le Monde* and England's *The Times,* had copublished Rigoberta Menchú Tum's second book—titled *Crossing Borders* in its controversial English version in which the credits of coeditors Dante Liano and Gianni Minà were mysteriously left out—in the summer of 1998. *El País* reproduced Rohter's *New York Times* article almost in its entirety on December 16, 1998, and subsequently published a series of articles on the issue, starting with Rosa Montero's column, titled "Her," on December 29, 1998. On Sunday, January 3, 1999, *El País* published an interview conducted by its Paris correspondent, Octavio Martí, with Elisabeth Burgos-Debray, the problematic compiler or alleged author of Menchú Tum's first book, *I, Rigoberta Menchú.* This interview, titled "The Pitiful Lies of Rigoberta Menchú," created the impression among international observers that the powerful *El País* was distancing itself from Menchú Tum. However, on Monday, January 11, 1999, the well-known Spanish writer and journalist Manuel Vásquez Montalbán published a defense of her in *El País* as well, called simply "Rigoberta," and finally, on Sunday, January 24, 1999, the Spanish newspaper published a long interview with Rigoberta Menchú Tum herself, conducted by its Mexico correspondent Juan Jesús Aznárez. This interview became Menchú Tum's clearest response to David Stoll to that point, and its publication in *El País* indicated the prestigious Spanish paper's support for her. We include all of these documents in the present volume.

In Mexico, one of the leading newspapers, *La Jornada*, also reprinted Rohter's article nearly in its entirety on December 16, 1998, and backed Menchú Tum throughout the controversy, flexing its own nationalist sentiments against what its editors perceived as a new U.S. intervention in Latin America. *La Jornada* first granted space to the Rigoberta Menchú Tum Foundation to publish its official response to Stoll's book, "The Truth That Challenges the Future." The paper then allowed Menchú Tum to meet with its editorial board during her visit to Mexico City in January 1999 and reproduced the Aznárez interview a day after it was published as an exclusive in *El País*.

In Guatemala, Rohter's article generated front-page headlines in all major newspapers, which were followed shortly afterwards by myriad strong "opinion pieces." Whereas Guatemalan journalism emerged from nearly forty years of repression and censorship looking more like British tabloids than serious, analytical journals like *Le Monde* or *El País*, the return of political exiles to the country in the 1990s has improved the intellectual level of debate. At the same time, the signing of the peace treaty has created a new openness in which virtually all positions, from the extreme right to a passionate defense of "guerrilla" strategy, are now routinely published and commented upon by readers, with little fear of lawsuits—virtually nonexistent in Guatemala—or political assassinations, a much more common censorship of opinionated commentators until very recently. The Guatemalan articles succeeded in gathering positions from nearly the entire cast of major players in this affair: David Stoll and Rigoberta Menchú Tum, of course, but also Elisabeth Burgos-Debray and Arturo Taracena. Elisabeth Burgos-Debray, of Venezuelan origin and trained in ethnology, achieved notoriety and a French nationality when she became the wife of Régis Debray, a French scholar and author of *Revolution in the Revolution?*, an underground revolutionary classic in the 1960s that theorized guerrilla strategy. Caught aiding Che Guevara's failed campaign in Bolivia in 1967, Debray was judged and imprisoned in that country. While in prison, he married Elisabeth Burgos. After his sentence was commuted as a result of pressures from France's Gaullist government, the couple returned to Paris. Although separated later from Debray, Burgos-Debray remained on friendly terms with her ex-husband, who became a minister of state when François Mitterrand's Socialists came to power in 1980. It was because of both her ethnographic background and her political connections that Arturo Taracena first introduced Burgos-Debray to Menchú Tum. The Venezuelan was so taken with the Mayan woman's charisma that she proceeded to record a book-length interview that became *I, Rigoberta Menchú*. Burgos-Debray acknowledges reorganizing the material "to give the text a thread, to give it the sense of a life, to make it a story, so that it could reach the general public" (185). The difficulties between her and Menchú Tum began in 1983, when the book won the Casa de las Américas Award for *testimonio*. Menchú Tum expected half the prize money and was surprised to discover that it all went to Burgos-Debray. It was only then that she discovered that Burgos-Debray owned the copyright to the book. It remains a point of contention just how much of the book's profits Burgos-Debray has shared with Menchú Tum and the means by which these payments have been made, but the issue has created a rift impossible to heal between the two of them.

Arturo Taracena, a noted Guatemalan historian and scholar, was the representative of the Guerrilla Army of the Poor (EGP) in France during the early 1980s. As such, he helped organize and program the visit that first brought Menchú Tum to France. Taken as well by her charisma, Taracena conceived the idea of recording Menchú Tum's life story as a way of furthering the solidarity work with the Guatemalan opposition in Europe, and it was he who introduced her to Burgos-Debray and arranged for the interview to take place. It also remains a point of contention just how much of the work was done by Taracena himself and how much by Burgos-Debray. Taracena claims that he was responsible for the bulk of the transcription and editing and that Burgos-Debray has done her best to take all credit away from him. She retorts that he did not want any public recognition of his role at the time, given the sensitivity of his political post, and she claims that he is now inflating his role in the elaboration of the book.

The three major Guatemalan dailies adopted different positions that, nonetheless, were less polarized than they were in the United States. The neoconservative *Siglo XXI* took advantage of the news to distance itself from Menchú Tum, yet it gave progressive columnist Danilo Rodríguez the freedom to publish an article questioning Stoll on December 20, "About Rigoberta's Lies." *Prensa Libre,* the oldest and most traditionally right-wing paper in the country, also adopted a moderate tone, in keeping with its new role as supporter of the peace treaty. The editors first interviewed David Stoll through E-mail and then, on December 18, 1998, published the interview, conducted by Dina Fernández García, the grand-daughter of one of the paper's founders, with the title "Stoll: I Don't Seek to Destroy Menchú." After maintaining a moderate position for two weeks, the newspaper allowed one of its leading columnists, Carolina Escobar Sarti, to come out openly against Stoll in its editorial pages, with the ironic title "A Hamburger in Rigoberta's Black Beans." The editors also kept their hands off when well-known writer Margarita Carrera, one of the country's leading feminist poets, published a column on January 22, "Against Gerardi and Against Rigoberta, Attacks Are Continually Made to Make Them Lose Some of Their Luster," in which she vehemently defended Menchú Tum, making a parallel between the attacks against her and those launched against Bishop Gerardi, the slain head of the Recovery of Historical Memory Commission (REMHI). The liberal *El Periódico de Guatemala* adopted from the first a judicious defense of her, while at the same time allowing Jorge Palmieri, one of its best-known conservative and virulently anticommunist columnists, to publish a column nastily attacking Menchú Tum, titled "Lies by the Nobel Prize Winner."

After Christmas 1998, Pablo Rodas Martini, the conservative commentator of *Siglo XXI*, challenged Arturo Taracena to come clean and tell the truth about the book. Taracena answered the challenge and, for the first time, granted an interview about the compilation of *I, Rigoberta Menchú*. This interview was conducted by the cultural editor of *El Periódico de Guatemala*, Luis Aceituno, and it was published on Sunday, January 10, 1999, with the title "Arturo Taracena Breaks His Silence." The interview revealed previously undisclosed information regarding the details of the proceedings with Menchú Tum, the decision to publish her material as a book, the editing process, and the very limited role of Guatemalan guerrilla organizations in any phase of the book's creation. This interview created a sensation in Guatemala. It was later circulated, via the Internet, around the globe, in both the Spanish version and the English translation by Jill Robbins. To the surprise of many, this interview was backed ten days later by conservative Congressman Jorge Skinner-Kleé, longtime ideologue of the moderate right. Skinner-Kleé sided with Taracena in a column published by *Siglo XXI*, arguing that Stoll's book was more like journalistic muckraking than scientific anthropology.

On the Sunday following the appearance of the Taracena interview, *El Periódico de Guatemala* published my article "Point of View From San Francisco," in which I discussed the journalistic methods of anthropologist David Stoll and the history of his attacks on the left in Central America. This article, which mistakenly accused Stoll of working on behalf of fundamentalist Christians, also circulated widely on the Internet and was later misquoted without my permission or consent in a negative article in the academic journal *Linguafranca*. A week later, Dante Liano's "The Anthropologist with the Old Hat," published as well by *El Periódico de Guatemala* on Sunday, January 31, 1999, followed the same path. *El Periódico de Guatemala* also reproduced Menchú Tum's interview with *El País*, and the official response to Stoll from the Rigoberta Menchú Tum Foundation and a declaration by the National Council of Mayan Education (CNEM), "The National Council of Mayan Education and Its Twenty-two Member Organizations Publicly Declare." Meanwhile, *Siglo XXI* scored a coup with the first newspaper article on the subject written by David Stoll himself, his first public declaration since his interview in *Prensa Libre* on December 18, 1998, when the controversy first erupted. Published on Wednesday, January 27, 1999, and titled "David Stoll Breaks His Silence" to echo Taracena's interview seventeen days earlier in *El Periódico de Guatemala,* this article attempted to show that Taracena's account of the composition of *I, Rigoberta Menchú* was as full of contradictions as Menchú Tum's earlier account of her life story. Stoll also chastised Taracena for not responding when he originally sent him a draft of chapter 17 of *I, Rigoberta Menchú and the Story of All Poor Guatemalans.* Then, on Sunday, February 7, Stoll published a "Letter to the Editor" in *Siglo XXI* attacking both Dante Liano and me for our previous articles in *El Periódico de Guatemala.* It is interesting that all of Stoll's responses have been in Spanish and published exclusively in Guatemala, whereas one would have assumed that he would seek more understanding and a sympathetic audience in the United States, especially given that his name now appears in nearly every conservative article put out on the World Wide Web, but it is likely that the academic reaction against him has tempered the latter option. Stoll has not, until this moment, explained why his responses have been limited to the Guatemalan press, but informal sources claim that he has been frustrated in his attempts to respond in English.

On February 14, 1999, *El Periódico de Guatemala* published an article in which I deconstructed the preface to Stoll's book, followed by a second one at the beginning of March. I argued that Stoll's allegedly neutral language is in fact ideologically charged and biased against granting any veracity to Menchú Tum's accounts. This was followed by a fourth and last article in early April. All of the Guatemalan articles except my own and one published by Mario Roberto Morales, who has written a new article for this volume, appear in the present book.

Tarnished Laureate

Larry Rohter

New York Times, Sunday, December 15, 1998

For Rigoberta Menchú, the painful road to world prominence began in this impoverished and isolated tangle of mountains, cloud forest, and peasant hamlets. As winner of the 1992 Nobel Peace Prize, she has become an internationally acclaimed spokeswoman for—and symbol of—the rights of indigenous peoples, based largely on her best-selling account of growing up here as an uneducated and oppressed member of the Quiche people.

In the autobiography *I, Rigoberta Menchú,* first published in Spanish in 1983 at the height of Guatemala's brutal civil war, Ms. Menchú, now thirty-nine, tells a wrenching tale of violence, destruction, misery, and exploitation as moving and disturbing as a Victor Hugo novel. So powerful was the book's impact that it immediately transformed her into a celebrated and much-sought-after human rights campaigner and paved the way for her being awarded the Nobel Prize.

Key details of that story, though, are untrue, according to a new book written by an American anthropologist, *Rigoberta Menchú and the Story of All Poor Guatemalans.* Based on nearly a decade of interviews with more than 120 people and archival research, the anthropologist, David Stoll, concludes that Ms. Menchú's book "cannot be the eyewitness account it purports to be" because the Nobel laureate repeatedly describes "experiences she never had herself."

Using contacts provided by Dr. Stoll and others found independently, a reporter for the *New York Times* conducted several interviews here in early December that contradict Ms. Menchú's account. Relatives, neighbors, friends, and former classmates of Rigoberta Menchú, including an older brother and half sister and four Roman Catholic nuns who educated and sheltered her, indicated that many of the main episodes related by Ms. Menchú have either been fabricated or seriously exaggerated. This is the way they recall it:

The land dispute central to the book was a long and bitter family feud that pitted her father against his in-laws, and not a battle against wealthy landowners of European descent who manipulated government agencies into trying to drive her father and other Indian peasants off unclaimed land that they had cleared and farmed.

A younger brother whom Ms. Menchú says she saw die of starvation never existed, while a second, whose suffering she says she and her parents were forced to watch as he was being burned alive by army troops, was killed in entirely different circumstances when the family was not present.

Contrary to Ms. Menchú's assertion in the first page of her book that "I never went to school" and could not speak Spanish or read or write until shortly before she dictated the text of *I, Rigoberta Menchú,* she in fact received the equivalent of a middle-school education as a scholarship student at two prestigious private boarding schools operated by Roman Catholic nuns. Because she spent much of her youth in the boarding schools, it is extremely unlikely that she could have worked as an underground political organizer and spent up to eight months a year laboring on coffee and cotton plantations, as she describes in great detail in her book.

Her Defense: Racist Politics to Blame, She Says

In an interview in September, Ms. Menchú repeatedly declined to respond to the discrepancies the Stoll manuscript raises. "I'm proud of the book," she said, describing it as "part of the historical memory and patrimony of Guatemala" and dismissing any criticism as part of a racist political agenda intended to gain attention and publicity.

"There have been fifteen thousand theses written about me all over the world by people who have read the book and made commentaries about it," she continued, referring to her autobiography, which has been translated into at least a dozen languages. "I don't dedicate myself to checking this, and I don't deny or contradict what is said in books about me. That's not my job." Ms. Menchú declined repeated recent requests for comment.

Aside from one person, those interviewed in Guatemala have not read her book and were sympathetic to Ms. Menchú and the trials she and her family underwent during Guatemala's thirty-six-year civil war, which ended in 1996. Between 1979 and 1983, Rigoberta Menchú's father, mother, and two brothers all died at the hands of government security forces, everyone here acknowledges.

"She suffered greatly, seeing her whole family dispersed by the violence," said Clemente Díaz Cano, a neighbor and contemporary of Ms. Menchú. "The truth may be distinct from how she has told it, but that does not mean Rigoberta did not suffer greatly in those years." The exception is Alfonso Rivera, one of the few people here who has actually read Ms. Menchú's autobiography. As the clerk for the municipal government for thirty years, he kept all official records. "The book is one lie after another, and she knows it," Mr. Rivera said. "When she visited here, I asked her how she could say such things, and she could not give me a satisfactory answer."

At the time she wrote her autobiography, which has since been added to the reading lists of universities around the world, Ms. Menchú was an anonymous exile seeking to focus international attention on the suffering of Guatemala's predominantly Indian peasantry. The success of the book led human rights advocates to treat her as the embodiment of the indigenous cause, and in 1992 she was awarded the Nobel Peace Prize "in recognition of her work for social justice and ethno-cultural reconciliation."

The Nobel Panel: "No Question" of Revoking Prize

Geir Lundestad, director of the Norwegian Nobel Institute and permanent secretary of the Norwegian Nobel Committee, said in a telephone interview from Oslo that he was aware of the Stoll manuscript and had no reason to doubt its veracity. Nevertheless, he said, "there is no question of revoking the prize" to Ms. Menchú. "All autobiographies embellish to a greater or lesser extent," he continued. He added that the decision to award the prize to Ms. Menchú "was not based exclusively or primarily on the autobiography" and that while "the details of the family history are not without relevance, they are not particularly important, and so this will lead to no reconsideration on our part."

During the last year, Ms. Menchú has sought to distance herself from her autobiography. Any problems with the text, she suggested, are the responsibility of Elisabeth Burgos, the Venezuelan anthropologist who interviewed Ms. Menchú, transcribed and edited the resulting twenty-six hours of tapes, and secured a publishing contract.

"I am the protagonist of the book, and it was my testimony, but I am not the author," Ms. Menchú maintained during the September interview, describing her current relationship with Ms. Burgos as "nonexistent" because of a disagreement over publishing royalties. "She gave the book its final form, so she is officially the author of the book and has the commercial rights to it."

But in a new book published in Spanish this spring and in English in October as *Crossing Borders* (New York: Verso Books), Ms. Menchú asserts precisely the opposite. She maintains there that she had full and final authority over her book. "I censored various parts that seemed imprudent to me," Ms. Menchú writes in the new book. "I removed the parts that referred to our village, a lot of detail about my little brothers, many details about names."

In a telephone interview from her home in Paris, Ms. Burgos said that "every phrase in the book comes from what Rigoberta Menchú said on the tapes." She said she still has the original recordings, some of which Dr. Stoll was able to listen to, and is willing to make them available to a university so that other researchers can have access to them.

The Neighbors: Local People Tell a Different Story

As published, *I, Rigoberta Menchú* portrays Vicente Menchú Pérez, his wife Juana Tum Cotojá, and their nine children, of whom Rigoberta was the sixth, as devout Christians forced by poverty, Indian blood, and lack of education to endure unending misery and exploitation. In the end, the entire family becomes involved in a left-wing peasant movement, but are cruelly killed or driven into exile by Guatemalan security forces.

The unifying thread of the tale is the twenty-two-year struggle by Vicente Menchú to gain title to fertile land that he cleared and tilled himself, but that was coveted by wealthy ranchers who harassed him with bureaucrats and gunmen. But that is not how people here, including close relatives, remember the situation. As they tell it, Vicente Menchú was locked in a battle with Antonio Tum Castro, his wife's uncle, and his sons.

"The Tums were our enemies," Rosa Menchú Calam, the Nobel laureate's fifty-eight-year-old half sister, said in an interview here. "They were always cutting the barbed wire on our fences, and they would send their animals into my late father's fields to eat our corn so that we would not have enough to eat."

Rosa Menchú's recollections were echoed by other residents of this remote town of 5,500 people. Their account is also supported by more than six hundred pages of government records on file at the headquarters of the National Agrarian Transformation Institute in the Guatemalan capital.

The records cover more than thirty years, and indicate that the Menchú and Tum families repeatedly challenged each other's claims to a fertile parcel of 373 acres that both wanted, and frequently filed complaints about each other's behavior. There is virtually no mention of the Brol, Garciá, or Martínez families, the Spanish-speaking landowning elite that Rigoberta Menchú asserts sought to drive her father off his land.

"No, it was a family quarrel that went on for years and years," said Efraín Galindo, who was mayor of Uspantán from 1970 through 1972. "I wanted peace, but none of us could get them to negotiate a settlement."

Her Brothers: Account of Deaths Said to Be Untrue

People interviewed here also expressed skepticism about Ms. Menchú's account of the deaths of two of her brothers. In one of the most heartbreaking episodes of the book, Ms. Menchú tells how in 1967 she watched her youngest brother, Nicolás, die of malnutrition while the family was working for slave wages on a coffee plantation in southern Guatemala.

But Nicolás Menchú turns out to be alive and well, the owner of a well-kept homestead here. He is forty-nine, a full decade older than his famous sister, and said in an interview that he had no recollection of a younger brother who died in the fashion described in the book, an affirmation repeated by Rosa Menchú.

"I had two brothers who died of hunger and disease, one named Felipe and another whose name escapes me," Mr. Menchú said. "But I never knew them, because they both passed away before I was even born, and I was born in 1949."

Family members and residents expressed similar doubts about Ms. Menchú's account of the death of another brother, Petrocinio. In her book, she describes how she, the rest of her family, and fellow residents of Uspantán are summoned to the nearby town of Chajul, where her younger brother and other prisoners are lined up. Gasoline is poured over them, and "then the soldiers set fire to each one of them."

Residents here have many grievances against the army and were quick to recount other abuses. But they could not recall an incident anywhere in the region of a mass public execution by burning.

"Around here, nobody was ever burned alive that way," said Mr. Díaz, the neighbor of the Menchú family. "It was a dirty war here. They kidnapped you from your home, and nobody knew where you were killed. That's how Petrocinio and a whole lot of other people died."

"I don't know exactly what happened to Petrocinio," said Nicolás Menchú. "I know that he was kidnapped and handed over to the army. After that, I heard that they kept him in a hole, and that then they shot him."

According to family members and residents, Petrocinio's body was dressed in the olive green uniform of the guerrillas and dumped, along with the bodies of several other youths suspected by the army of sympathizing with insurgents, in the town square in Chajul. "Some acquaintances of my father recognized his body and sent news that he had been killed," Nicolás Menchú said.

Family members, neighbors, and the nuns who educated her were even more emphatic that Rigoberta Menchú received a level of education unusual at the time for an Indian girl. In her autobiography, Ms. Menchú maintains that she never received any formal schooling, in part because her family labored on the plantations, but also because her father did not want it.

But "my father thought that life was hard and that there was nothing here for us, no school at all," Nicolás Menchú said. "He had a lot of ideas, and since he couldn't read or write a letter himself, he believed it was necessary for us to get as much instruction as we could."

Her Schooling: Nuns Recall a Gifted Pupil

Nicolás and Rosa Menchú, who with their other siblings received only a rudimentary education, said that Rigoberta was singled out for special treatment because Belgian nuns who were friends of the family thought her unusually bright and promising. They recalled their little sister correcting their imperfect Spanish and proudly showing off her ability to read and write when she visited home on vacation from boarding school.

"Rigoberta was about five years old when my father enrolled her in school," Nicolás Menchú said. "She went off to boarding school in Chichicastenango and stayed there for about three years before returning."

According to Rosa Menchú, Rigoberta had to come back because the family was experiencing money problems. But as she and the family's friends and neighbors tell it, the Belgian nuns again came to the rescue, arranging for Rigoberta to live in their convent here while she attended school for a year.

"Our congregation had a very close relationship with the Menchú family," said Sister Magdalena van Meerhaeghe, a sixty-year-old Belgian nun from the Order of the Sacred Family who confirmed the arrangement. "Her father was a catechist, and when we went up to do work in their area, her mother fed us."

In separate interviews, Sister Magdalena and three other nuns, all affiliated with the Order of the Sacred Family and the private school they operated, the Belgian-Guatemalan Institute, clearly recollected Rigoberta as a gifted pupil. They said she studied at their school in the capital and a branch in the province of Huehuetenango, completing the equivalent of the first year of junior high school.

"I can't tell you for certain what years those were, because we no longer have the records," Sister Magdalena said. "But I do know that when her father was killed in January 1980, Rigoberta had just enrolled in her second year of middle school" and thus was not working as an underground political organizer, as she maintains in her autobiography.

Because the Guatemalan school year runs from mid-January to the end of October, classmates and relatives said, it would have been virtually impossible for Rigoberta Menchú to have spent up to eight months a year as a farm laborer, as she maintains in her book. "Since she was studying, she couldn't go to work on the plantations," said Rosa Menchú.

In his book, Dr. Stoll concludes that Ms. Menchú drew on experience common to others in Guatemala and "drastically revised the prewar experience of her village to suit the needs of the revolutionary organization she had joined" and on whose behalf she was touring Europe when she dictated her life story to Ms. Burgos.

"By presenting herself as an everywoman, she has tried to be all things
to all people in a way no individual can be," Dr. Stoll writes. As a result,
it is necessary for readers "to distinguish between what can be corroborated and what cannot, what is probable and what is highly improbable."

Stoll: "I Don't Seek to Destroy Menchú"

Interview by Dina Fernández García

Prensa Libre, Guatemala City, Friday, December 18, 1998

This week, his name has been in the headlines, including in the prestigious *New York Times*. This is an important change for an anthropologist like David Stoll, whose criticism of Nobel Peace Prize winner Rigoberta Menchú kept him for years on the margins of the academic world, where ideological loyalties and political correctness prevail. Professor of anthropology at Middlebury College, Stoll has written and documented a book that very few Guatemalans have read, but many have already demonized. By way of the Internet, Stoll answered *Prensa Libre*'s questions:

Rigoberta Menchú maintains that the testimonio *published in* I, Rigoberta Menchú *is true, and that she will order a scientific investigation to prove it. What do you think about that?*

Rigoberta should do it. I am confident that the results will corroborate my own research.

Do you believe that her book is a lie invented by the Guerrilla Army of the Poor (EGP)?

No. The narrative is so convincing that it could not have been programmed by anybody, especially by a group as dogmatic as the EGP. The fact is that in 1982 Rigoberta was a militant of the EGP. Having joined the movement not long before and being profoundly affected by the murder of three members of her family, she believed in the ideology and used it to frame the experience of her family and people. I've never said that her testimonial is a lie or a fraud. In fact, one can argue that it was good that Rigoberta told this story in 1982, because it attracted the world's attention to the crimes committed by the Guatemalan army, and in the end that contributed to the signing of the peace agreement.

Rigoberta says that you don't know her, nor have you ever spoken to her.

Rigoberta knows many gringos and we all look alike. Possibly because of this she doesn't remember me. But we did talk at an academic conference near Washington, D.C., in April 1991.

Later, she recognized me at a press conference in July 1992 because she took the occasion to complain about anthropologists, arguing that they don't let indigenous people speak for themselves. A bit later, she claimed I was a racist. I asked her for an interview and, in response, in June 1997 her Foundation requested a copy of my manuscript. I sent it to them. For a year and a half, Rigoberta had access to my research, and she could very well have answered.

She says you want to profit from her to become rich. "He did not put his elegant face on the book cover because it would not sell," she said.

It's true that my face is not as elegant as Rigoberta's, and that it would not sell as many copies.

But my book will never come close to selling the half million copies that hers has sold. Besides, anybody who knows how the class structure works in the United States knows that I could make much more money in another line of work. Gringos like myself don't go to Guatemala to make a fortune. For that, they stay in New York.

Was it hard to find a publisher?

I solicited thirty publishing houses in the United States, more than half of them academic publishers, before finding someone willing to send out the manuscript for review. The aura of sanctity around Rigoberta is very strong. I can't say what editors were afraid of, but they were afraid of something.

What has been the academic community's response to your book?

Very divided. I've received moral support from colleagues who think that issues have to be faced, but I have also faced considerable opposition.

What are the three main arguments in your book?

Rigoberta said that her story was the story of all poor Guatemalans, but the story of a single individual cannot be the story of everybody else, except in a literary sense. I didn't write this book to prove that a Nobel laureate had embellished part of her biography. There are more important issues. First, it is not an accurate account of the problems that her family and village faced before the violence, nor of how the violence reached Uspantán. Second, I wanted to challenge preconceived and romantic ideas about indigenous peoples and guerrilla warfare. Based on my interviews with peasants, I don't believe they were the revolutionary avant-garde that others claim they were. In the third place, when a book becomes almost sacred, it is a sign that it hides contradictions that ought to see the light of day. In the case of Rigoberta's foreign admirers, I think that they have chosen to listen to voices that gratify their own needs, instead of facing Guatemala's complexity.

Rigoberta says that your book is a racist attack sponsored by a group of anthropologists that lives off indigenous peoples and does not allow them to have their own voice.

It is not racist to gather different versions of events and compare them. No other anthropologist has conducted systematic interviews in Uspantán. No other anthropologist has contested Rigoberta's 1982 story. She's not being attacked by a group of anthropologists. Anthropologists have taken too long in questioning the EGP's version of events. Rigoberta has a problem with only one anthropologist: me.

They say that your book will either sink Rigoberta or else make her more famous. Did you think of that when you were writing it?

I don't believe my book will sink Rigoberta. Guatemala needs a symbol like her to think through what happened during the era of violence and to make sure it doesn't happen again. The only person that could sink Rigoberta is herself. I regret that it wasn't possible to publish a Spanish version at the same time, but it's still difficult to publish academic critiques of the EGP's version of events, even when they are based on peasant testimonies. To argue that the war was not inevitable and that it did not emerge from the struggle of poor people, that instead it was a tragedy that arose from the confrontation between Guatemalan patriots of both the left and the right, is still perceived as an apology for the Guatemalan army. But it is not.

In your book, you claim that Mayan don't care if the events described in Rigoberta's testimonial really happened to her or not. What do you think about that?

The accuracy of Rigoberta's testimonial might not be significant to many Guatemalans because it is obviously the truth, in a national sense if not a personal one.

Criticisms

Stoll's book goes beyond the refutation of historical inaccuracies. In his investigation the anthropologist tries: to analyze how political violence reached Uspantán; to defy romantic prejudices about indigenous communities and guerrilla warfare; to prove that rebel movements originated in the urban middle class; to explain why they did not develop roots among indigenous peoples; and to analyze how the academic world constructs the sacred, to the detriment of the scientific spirit.

Translated by Arturo Arias

About Rigoberta's Lies

Danilo Rodríguez

Siglo XXI, Guatemala City, Sunday, December 20, 1998

It is surprising what has been published concerning the allegedly wrong facts that, according to the research of anthropologist David Stoll, appear in Rigoberta Menchú's testimonial, gathered by Elisabeth Burgos and published in the book *I, Rigoberta Menchú.*

There are some who, using the alleged lies (Rigoberta reaffirms that the contents of her testimonial are true), try to deny the bloody past and the suffering of Guatemalan citizens under state terrorism, as well as the dantesque episodes of the "scorched-earth" policy, the physical disappearance of 460 villages from the country's geography, and the restructuring attempts suffered by indigenous communities under the poles of development policy.

The argument: because it is a lie that one brother died from malnutrition, and that the other one was actually burned in front of his family, dying in different circumstances (but still at the hands of the army), that she never went to school, and that the great majority of indigenous peoples supported the guerrillas, then the entire criticism of the army in the book is not true; many episodes in the book are pure invention.

Three considerations: [1] The poles of development were also a project to break down traditionally resistant communities, an attempt to break the reproductive mechanisms of traditional indigenous societies (Jesús García in *Guatemala: Poles of Development* [Centro Integral de Desarrollo Comunal]), by marginalizing them from the rest of the country and subjecting them to direct military control. [2] This project required a series of anthropological, sociological, and psychological studies. [3] The poles of development were established in areas of strong political resistance (loyalty to the guerrillas) and where original inhabitants were displaced by state terrorism: in the Ixil area, it includes the towns of Nebaj, Chajul, and Cotzal, in El Quiché, as well as Playa Grande, also in El Quiché; others were established in Laguna Perdida, El Petén, in Chisec, Alta Verapaz, where three model villages were also created: Acamal, Saraxoch, and Chituj, just outside of Cobán; and, in Chajac, county of Nentón, Huehuetenango.

According to accusations stemming from that time, anthropologist David Stoll was involved in the research leading to the poles of development. His previous book, *Between Two Armies,* has a clear mistake: that there were two armies involved in the first place, as well as his suggesting that the guerrilla also massacred the civilian population, something that did not happen (the EGP made mistakes when confronting civil patrols; these actions were later forbidden, and Rolando Morán, commander in chief of the EGP, admitted the error of those actions). Up to the time Stoll documents, the guerrilla had limited its operatives to armed propaganda. The only clear combat happened in Tres Aguadas (Petén), where guerrillas from FAR [Rebel Armed Forces] defended the displaced population that was being chased by the army. It is only after 1984 that guerrillas actually become an irregular army. If they already had been one in 1982, they would have overthrown the government and come to power. What, then, is the purpose of researching the allegedly false data in Rigoberta's book?

We live in an age when the power of a financial oligarchy is being consolidated. This domination is being built on the basis of delegitimating both the left and the popular movement. Therefore, there is a need to portray everything that both the left and the popular movement did as either bad, ugly, or both. This attitude has become even more evident after the Guatemalan National Revolutionary Unity (URNG) was left militarily ineffective through a process of either co-optation or neutralization by way of granting privileges to ex-combatants. Mistakes made by ex-guerrillas have also played into this strategy. Has Rigoberta now become an objective of this campaign?

The problem of truth: to attempt to behave according to one's own truth is a human trait, a need for human coexistence, and a condition for credibility among politicians and public personalities. Lies, on the contrary, and hiding information, always turn against those who practice that behavior. The truth is slow, but it always comes out. The situation of those who lie and persist in lying leads to further difficulties. We have Clinton's case as an example. We live in a political world where lying or hiding the truth is a way of life. In Guatemala, the privatization of the telephone company, Guatel, is the biggest example of this. Should we all become liars then?

In Rigoberta's case, if her testimonial has equivocal data or falsehoods, this should be admitted publicly. It will only make her bigger than she already is. Could she ever stop being the person deserving of the 1992 Nobel Peace Prize?

Translated by Arturo Arias

Lies by the Nobel Prize Winner

Jorge Palmieri

El Periódico de Guatemala, Guatemala City, Monday, December 21, 1998

One has to be extremely careful when touching a topic like this one. One is exposed to accusations of being racist, *machista,* an extreme right-winger, a McCarthyite, and a whole series of other silly adjectives of the same sort that, frankly, blow in from the north.

There is a saying that "lies shine until the truth emerges." This popular expression has acquired new validity during the last few days. Articles are coming out about the recent publication in the United States of the book *Rigoberta Menchú and the Story of All Poor Guatemalans,* written by anthropologist David Stoll after ten years of careful research in Guatemala. Stoll affirms that the famous Nobel Prize winner of 1992, who has gathered many *honoris causa* honorary Ph.D.s and has been a UNESCO ambassador, "exaggerated the truth" in the narration of her alleged testimonial *I, Rigoberta Menchú,* according to an article published a few days ago on the front page of the *New York Times.* Stoll points out some imprecisions (so as to say not that they are outright lies) that Rigoberta Menchú told Venezuelan anthropologist Elisabeth Burgos, the author of Menchú's book.

A colleague of ours, Conrado Alonso, pointed out yesterday in *Prensa Libre* that, among the many falsehoods that the book contains, on page 59 of the sixth edition (1991) it tells the story of the death of an alleged brother of hers as a consequence of contamination from pesticides sprayed from the air onto the coffee plantations where she said they worked, but in reality that brother never existed. Besides, she forgot or else ignored the small detail that in Guatemala coffee trees are not sprayed from the air. And that is not the only falsehood Menchú states in the book and that she has then repeated everywhere.

For example, without in any way honoring the Nobel Prize, she recently participated in one of those stupid television programs of that abominable Cuban woman, "Cristina," and said on the air that her father died in the company of other people when they peacefully went to request political asylum at the Spanish embassy, but when they had already obtained said asylum, the soldiers arrived and burned down the entire building just to burn them alive. She cynically lied before millions of unaware TV watchers who waste their time watching those incredibly stupid programs. Because the truth is that her father and those in his company participated in what was called "Operation Climbing." They arrived at the diplomatic installations of the Spanish embassy armed with machetes and Molotov cocktails, and took as prisoners outstanding personalities from this country that had been called to the embassy under false pretenses by the disgusting and Communist-oriented ambassador Máximo Cajal, and they also died in the terrible tragedy when one of the invaders tried to throw a Molotov cocktail through the window. It fell on a plastic rug that caught fire immediately, igniting the other Molotov cocktails, which started the fatal fire in which not only the invaders died, but also the entire diplomatic and administrative personnel, with the exception of the damned nosy ambassador.

One has to be very clear and very precise when it comes to giving personal testimony about the historical events in our country. One should not employ fantasy so that the end result reads like a dramatic novel or a sensationalist story, even if it is an outright lie. The personal story of Ms. Menchú is full of attitudes and facts that make her stand out from other winners of the Peace Prize or any other type of award. One cannot blame her for being a militant in the Guerrilla Army of the Poor (EGP) until just shortly before she won the Nobel prize (with its cool million dollars), because we have to admit that during many centuries our indigenous compatriots have stoically suffered many abuses and injustices committed by powerful elements, and it was fair and necessary that they try to employ whatever means necessary to struggle for their rights. Sincerely, I cannot blame her for that, nor for spending all her time pro-

moting the solidarity of the international community—especially in so-
cialist countries—in favor of subversive struggle and against the various authoritarian governments that came and went. But it is not right
that one repeats forever lies such as those pointed out by anthropologist
Stoll in his book. By the way, he is not identified as being a reactionary
right-winger, a racist, or anything like that, but as a militant of the left.

Finally, Merry Christmas!

Translated by Arturo Arias

Her

Rosa Montero

El País, Madrid, Sunday, December 27, 1998

I met Rigoberta Menchú a couple of years ago. We coincided by chance in the same place, had a drink, and chatted for a while. As a journalist, I've had to deal with thousands of famous personalities, which has cured me from being overly impressed with anybody. It is usually a disdainful gesture. Menchú, however, impressed me. She has an uncanny authenticity. Of course, one has to be truly someone to walk around Madrid's yuppie bar scene dressed like an Indian without looking pathetic.

Now some Americans are saying that she lied in her autobiography. They claim it wasn't true that Rigoberta saw a brother die of malnutrition (although it is true that he died before she was born). It is not true that another brother was burned alive before her very eyes (although it is true that the same brother and her father were murdered and probably tortured). It would seem that those who denounce Menchú, obsessed by small details, have lost sight of the big picture. The end result is plain nonsense, because they do not want to see the substantial truth about Rigoberta, nor the fact that the mind is also a product of one's own myths; it is a novel that one more or less writes about one's own existence. To say that Rigoberta lies seems to me a much bigger lie than the imprecisions in her autobiography.

But all things being equal, the worst thing about this entire episode is all those who immediately jumped in to beat her, when nobody has ever said anything about many other Nobel Peace Prize winners who

were infinitely more questionable, like that ridiculous Walesa, the opaque
Arafat, or the very disgusting Henry Kissinger, who, among his many
other accomplishments, protected the CIA's criminal doings in Chile;
now, that's a lie for you. But, of course, all of those are men, powerful
men, and Rigoberta is nothing but a poor Indian woman in her forties
with braids.

Translated by Arturo Arias

The Pitiful Lies of Rigoberta Menchú

Octavio Martí

El País, Madrid, Sunday, January 3, 1999

"The book's purpose has been to let people know what has been happening in Guatemala," claims Elisabeth Burgos, coauthor of the first autobiography of 1992's Nobel Prize winner.

A book recently published in the United States, *Rigoberta Menchú and the Story of All Poor Guatemalans* by American anthropologist David Stoll, has caused a major scandal. In this book, the biographical details that made the Guatemalan indigenous woman the winner of the Nobel Peace Prize in 1992 are questioned. According to Stoll, Rigoberta Menchú makes herself a spectator of tragedies at which she was not present, and attributes to herself vital dramas that she did not live. Immediately, some have voiced certain concerns regarding Stoll's empiricist approach in his research, reproaching him for getting lost in details and not seeing the big picture of the truly tragic destiny of many of Latin America's indigenous peoples. It is a repetition of the old debate about the means and the ends in the context of suspicion that accompanies all public personalities.

Elisabeth Burgos, a Venezuelan anthropologist living in Paris and coauthor of the first autobiography of the Nobel Prize winner, *I, Rigoberta Menchú* (1984), plays an important role in the reigning confusion about Menchú's life. Even though she has since had a falling out with Menchú, Burgos interviewed her in 1982 so that her words could become a biographical narrative. "The point of departure," explains Burgos, was a work of a journalistic nature that was supposed to help the movement in solidarity with Guatemala's guerrillas. I myself, as well as many other people, felt involved and could see that Guatemala's drama was hardly known outside the country because no Guatemalan wanted to bear witness to what was happening. Those who still lived in the country did not do it for obvious reasons, but those already living in exile did not do so because they feared that the army would retaliate against the family members they had left behind. It was at this point that a Canadian doctor who was a friend of mine introduced me to Rigoberta Menchú. She had a decisive need to talk. I was with her for an entire day, and the whole scene seemed to me so impressive that we agreed to meet again when she returned from a trip to Holland. Later she moved in with me, and from nineteen hours of our taped conversations the book was born.

To the extent that it was "much more a militant than an anthropological" work, another element in a "strategy of resistance" against dictatorship, Elisabeth Burgos did not question the veracity of the facts provided by her interviewee.

> I must say that Rigoberta expresses herself with great assurance and she provided many telling details. A little while later, when I did a film about her for French television, she repeated before the cameras everything dealing with her brother's death, how the army had stripped him so other Indians could see his torture wounds, and this would teach them a lesson. While she explained all this, tears came to her eyes. It was impossible not to believe her.

In 1982, Elisabeth Burgos could not visit Guatemala and attempt to corroborate the facts. "I limited myself to sending the manuscript to Ricardo Ramírez, the guerrilla leader, who sent it back with a congratulatory note. He only asked me to modify a couple of details, one dealing with the participation of children in guerrilla operations, and another one dealing with the burning of the Spanish embassy (in Guatemala City on January 31, 1980, where Rigoberta's father, Vicente, died), because there were in that episode some confusing elements about the origin of the fire. That was all," claims the anthropologist.

Now, fifteen years have passed since all of this happened, and things look different. It has not been necessary for Stoll's book to appear for Burgos to realize that she participated in a mystification effort.

> At the end of the 1980s, I began to receive information that did not corroborate my book. I understood to what extent the guerrillas' strategy

was a Jacobin effort, willful and dangerous. It was then that Rigoberta's campaign for the Nobel Prize began, and they no longer wanted to associate me with her because I had said that I didn't approve of certain things. Stoll's book, which is very well documented, not a pamphlet at all, proves that it isn't true that Rigoberta never went to school, that it isn't true that her brother Nicolás died of hunger—in fact, he's still alive—that it is even less exact that Rigoberta worked as a maid in the capital, and, therefore, she could not have suffered the racist humiliations that she talked about, that she didn't witness the murder of her other brother, Patrocinio, at the hands of the military that burned him alive, and that her idealized image of her father is not true either.

All this false information does not offend either Stoll or Burgos.

One cannot say that Rigoberta lies. She's a person that belongs to a different cultural tradition, a preliterary tradition, an oral tradition, in which history has a collective nature, facts are stored in a common memory and belong to the entire community. Everything she told has happened, even if it didn't happen to her personally. Her family does know what poverty is, even if her own village is not as miserable as she painted it. There are people whose children were indeed burned alive, fathers that were executed by the army, and that's what Rigoberta has said.

Criticism of the Guerrillas

The major criticism that Burgos makes of Rigoberta "is the same one Stoll makes: to keep hidden how guerrillas have benefited from violence." It is not, of course, a matter of denying the responsibility of the army nor the crimes that it has committed, but to admit "that the guerrillas also have violated human rights, that they also killed indigenous peoples to radicalize the situation and attract Indians to their cause." In this sense, the book by Stoll, a specialist in issues of violence, also puts the theology of liberation on the spot.

The oral tradition, the mythical nature of historical explanations proposed by sympathizers of Castro, collective memory, the influence of a theology sympathetic with armed struggle, and a historical context in which the United States is always the great menace—in 1954 Guatemala suffered a bloody coup d'état sponsored by the United Fruit Company, and during the 1980s there were many U.S. attempts to end violently the Sandinista experiment—are not enough to free Rigoberta Menchú from all responsibility. The explanation given by Geir Lundestad, permanent secretary of the Norwegian Nobel Committee, is not very convincing either: he said that "all autobiographies embellish to a greater or lesser extent the role of the protagonist, and the details about her family are of secondary importance. The prize was not based exclusively or primarily on her autobiography."

For Elisabeth Burgos there is no doubt that

> Rigoberta's and my book has been useful so that people could know what was happening in Guatemala. Until that time, there was only curiosity in Europe about Argentina and Chile, by a white left that spoke French. And, we should not forget that when you fight a war of resistance, you employ methods that in a different context would not be acceptable.

The bad thing is that today, those mistakes, half-truths, or full lies uttered by Rigoberta Menchú can discredit not only her own person but an entire movement, or color all the information that addresses the suffering of Central America's Indians.

A Prisoner of Her Own Image

The indigenous peasant who today travels around the world representing mistreated ethnic minorities is very conscious of her own image. When Elisabeth Burgos started to doubt the efficiency of guerrilla warfare or its democratic contents, Rigoberta Menchú tried to reappropriate her own life.

> Then, she denied that I had written the book, she pretended that she had written it in Mexico with help from her comrades, and that I had only attended the interviews. Undoubtedly, she didn't think that I had saved all the tapes of our nineteen hours of conversations. I let Stoll hear them. From that point on, Rigoberta adopted a different strategy: accusing anthropologists of racism.

Transformed into a political character, a fabulous heroine with an unimaginable destiny, a survivor of tragedy, Menchú is today a prisoner of her own image, and of the image of a movement that has never admitted the slightest mistake or crime. "The most pathetic thing of all is that the guerrilla has had no impact on the institutionalization of democracy in many countries. We wasted our time for forty years."

Translated by Arturo Arias

Arturo Taracena Breaks His Silence

Interview by Luis Aceituno

El Periódico de Guatemala, Guatemala City, Sunday, January 3, 1999

Mentioned some time back as one of the key players in assembling the book *I, Rigoberta Menchú* (1983), Arturo Taracena Arriola has remained silent for sixteen years regarding his role in the matter. Following the polemic generated in Guatemala and other countries by the book *Rigoberta Menchú and the Story of All Poor Guatemalans* (1999) by the American anthropologist David Stoll, Taracena has finally decided to discuss the role he played in the conception of the book by Nobel Peace Prize winner Menchú. A writer and Ph.D. in history, Arturo Taracena was the representative in Europe of the URNG (Guatemalan National Revolutionary Unity) and an adviser to Rigoberta Menchú for several years. After abandoning political militancy in the early 1990s, he has dedicated himself exclusively to his profession. His book *Invención criolla, sueño Ladino, pesadilla indígena: Los Altos de Guatemala, de región a Estado, 1740–1850* (Creole invention, Ladino dream, Indian nightmare: The Guatemalan highlands, from region to state, 1740–1850) was published in 1997.

What was the origin of the book I, Rigoberta Menchú?

In January of 1982, I was approached by the representative in Paris of ORPA (Revolutionary Organization of the People in Arms), a woman then known as Marie Tremblay, a Canadian psychiatrist whose real name is Cécile Rousseau. She told me that Elisabeth Burgos, whom I had met in Paris in 1975, was interested in publishing a testimony by a Guatemalan Mayan woman. Marie told Elisabeth that there was a very interesting young woman named Rigoberta Menchú Tum in Paris at that moment giving her testimony, and that if she wanted to contact her she should do so through me because she was staying at my house.

What was Rigoberta doing in Paris?

She was with a delegation of the CUC (Committee for Peasant Unity) raising consciousness, not only about what happened in the Spanish embassy (which was burned to the ground by the Guatemalan army on January 31, 1980, with members of the CUC, including Rigoberta's father, Vicente Menchú, and Spanish diplomats still inside), but also about what was happening in Guatemala at the time, during the military dictatorship of General Lucas García. She had just come to France from Mexico, where she was selected to do this European tour because of her great ability to express herself.

And how was the encounter between Elisabeth Burgos and Rigoberta Menchú arranged?

Well, I called Elisabeth, we agreed on a meeting time, and the following Sunday I went to see her, accompanied by Rigoberta. It was not at all as Elisabeth led David Stoll to believe, that is, that Rigoberta arrived on her own at the house. That would have been impossible. Rigoberta didn't speak French and didn't know how to get around on the *métro,* since it was her first time in Paris. During that first conversation on Sunday we came to an agreement about how the interview would be handled. On Monday, Rigoberta and I arrived very early at Elisabeth's house and began to map it out. Elisabeth's interest in Guatemala came from her friendship years before with Ricardo Ramírez, alias Rolando Morán, and Aura Marina Arriola [Ramirez's ex-wife], but she didn't know the country itself or what was going on there, so we spent the first part of the day setting up the primary topics of the interview together. Then we spent the rest of the day interviewing Rigoberta. I think that if Elisabeth actually releases the original tapes of those twenty-six recorded hours, as she has promised to do, you will see that the first part of the interview was done by both her and me, following an outline that had been drafted by the three of us, and in which Rigoberta and I played a very important role because we were the ones who knew the country and were aware of what was going on there.

What happened next?

On Tuesday we continued the interview, but at one point we had to go back and rethink the outline because Rigoberta's narrative capacity, as well as the subject matter itself, began to go beyond what we had originally conceived. I also participated in the interview on Tuesday, but on Wednesday I decided not to participate anymore. I made that decision because I was at that moment the representative in Europe of the EGP (Guerrilla Army of the Poor), and I felt that Rigoberta might feel inhibited by my presence. It was also suggested that a conversation between two women might flow more easily. For those reasons, they spoke alone on Thursday and Friday, and Rigoberta decided to sleep at Elisabeth's house. On Friday night I picked her up and brought her to my house, where, on Saturday, we recorded the last tape of the interview, this one only between Rigoberta and me, in which we talked primarily about death. In the introduction to her book, Elisabeth refers to this tape, saying something like, "At the last minute a friend dropped by to leave me a tape of Rigoberta." She reduces all mention of my work on the project to that. The truth is that, from the beginning, she planned to eliminate any mention of me in the text so that there would remain no trace of my participation, and I agreed to it.

Because of your role as representative of the EGP?

That was one reason. I agreed not to participate so as not to politicize the book. So it wouldn't look like a teleprompted work, which is more or less how certain sectors in Guatemala think it was done.

Did you conceive of the interview as a book from the very start?

No, it was just a regular interview, and, as Elisabeth herself says, the idea of the book came up afterward. It was when we were reviewing the twenty-six hours of tape, where we heard this voice with such strength and narrative capacity, that we realized that there was enough rich material for a book. That is to say that, beyond the testimony itself, there was a profound literary quality to Rigoberta Menchú's voice. On the other hand, and I wish to be most emphatic about this, once Rigoberta left Paris on the following Sunday, after a week of working on the interview, she never saw the material again. She never had the opportunity to see how Elisabeth Burgos and I were editing the book.

How was the editing process carried out?

Well, Elisabeth claims that she did the work of transcribing the text, but that is completely false. She tried, but she couldn't do it, so I looked for donations to pay for the transcription. I negotiated with Marlise Strasser, who was in charge of the Latin American branch of the Catholic Committee against Hunger and for Development, for around thirty thousand francs to put together a publication for the CUC, since the CUC was the movement most supported by French solidarity groups. With that money I paid Paquita Rivas, a young woman of Cuban origin, to do the transcription. Paquita was the secretary of Gonzalo Arroyo, a Chilean Jesuit exiled in France who headed CETRAL (the Catholic Center for Latin American Relief). The complete transcription is Paquita's work. Once the material was transcribed, Elisabeth and I sat down to do the editing, but I did most of the dirty work, the work of hard editing. It's interesting how the Guatemalan press has insisted that Elisabeth Burgos was the one who wrote the book, because Elisabeth Burgos never wrote the book; she edited it, and she edited with my help. What I mean to say is that the book is a narration only by Rigoberta, with her own rhythm, with her own inventions, if there are any, with her own emotions, with her own truths. What we did afterward was the work of editing.

What did the editing entail?

My job was to work on the grammatical coherence, everything having to do with syntax, gender, number, and tenses, which Rigoberta did not dominate very well then. I am shocked now by this polemic about how Rigoberta finished high school. The truth is that Rigoberta spoke Spanish very poorly; she was fluent in her expression, but her grammar was very poor. You could tell that her studies, to the extent that she had completed any, were very limited, and she could not possibly have finished high school. It was also my task to eliminate all repetitions, to take out the questions, and to compile a list of all the local Guatemalan words and expressions. Not only that, the glossary in the book was done completely by me. And then I presented Elisabeth with a document already divided into major themes: father, mother, death, this and that. Once that was done, Elisabeth started to divide it up by chapters. I also helped her with that task because it was just too much. Once the narrative had taken form, we gave it back to Paquita Rivas, who made a clean copy.

Unfortunately, I didn't keep that first document; it never occurred to me that this whole copyright issue would come up.

Did you have some model you followed in setting up the book?

The model was Domitila Chungara's book.[1] There it's perfectly clear that the author is Domitila, and the person who did the interview, the introduction, the notes, explains her role very well. In our case, two of us did the interviewing, although by common agreement, my credits disappeared because of the role I played in the EGP and because of our desire that the book not be seen as hard-line propaganda, but rather as an attempt to present a testimony with literary quality. Rigoberta's material and the quality of her narration gave us the possibility of putting together a really exceptional book.

Why have you remained silent about your role for such a long time?

For sixteen years, I remained silent out of respect for Rigoberta and even out of respect for Elisabeth Burgos herself, but everything has a limit. What's more, I wasn't looking for recognition or royalties. I participated in the book in my capacity as historian and revolutionary. And I did so because I believed, and I still believe, that the book played an important role, not only in the denunciation of the government, but also in the rise of the Maya and other indigenous movements in Latin America. On the other hand, it's true that the agreement with Elisabeth was that my name would disappear from the credits because of my political participation in the EGP. But it's another thing altogether for her to refer to me as a mere spectator and to insist on that for all these years. Rigoberta doesn't know about these issues because she didn't witness them. It was just the three of us, as I said: Paquita Rivas transcribing, and Elisabeth and I editing the book.

Is it true that the material was inspected by the EGP?

Well, once we had the clean copy, the one Elisabeth refers to, we sent it to Nicaragua, not to Mexico as she claims, by way of Vicente, the alias of Víctor López, who had arrived in Paris in May 1982, accompanied by José Luis Balcárcel and Héctor Nuila, to proclaim the creation of the URNG. He was the one who carried the manuscript, and he was the one who returned it to me with a letter. Later, I always believed that the person who inspected the document was Mario Payeras. He did read it, but about a year ago I found out that the one who had really decided which passages had to be suppressed was Gustavo Meoño, the current president of the Menchú Foundation.[2] Within the EGP, Gustavo was the liaison between the leadership and the mass movement, and so he was in direct contact with the CUC. He asked us to take out three passages (which I'll talk about later because they're related to what Stoll says) for a very specific reason. There was never a process of censorship; the passages were suppressed because they could have had implications for the security of members of the CUC. We knew Rigoberta as a member of the CUC, and as the daughter of the Mr. Menchú of the CUC who had been killed in the Spanish embassy. People forget what those years were like, 1982, 1983, the years of [General] Lucas García, [General] Ríos Montt, what was going on at that time. For us, the only way to keep people alive in the popular movement was through exactly this type of emphasis on security. Elisabeth says that she recognized the handwriting of Ricardo Ramírez in the letter sent to Paris with the manuscript, but that's just not true. The letter was written by Vicente.

And then what happened to the materials?

Once the document had been read over and revised, we gave it to Elisabeth and then we lost track of it. It was a manuscript with several chapters completed; it was as grammatically correct as possible; it had a glossary; it had repetitions eliminated, and so on. From that moment on, Elisabeth continued working on it and showed it to Ugné Karvelis (a reader for the French publisher Gallimard and ex-wife of Argentine novelist Julio Cortázar), to the Argentine poet Juan Gelman, and to other people who gave her their opinions and their suggestions, while she worked on the final structure. And she had a very positive attitude, in my opinion. For example, when the French translator insisted that the rhythm and the voice gave the impression of a *petit nègre,* as the French say, she defended the syntax and the narrative voice of Rigoberta. When she told me about that, I thought it was fantastic.

It's been said that you corrected the proofs.

I could not have corrected the proofs for a very simple reason: the first edition of the book was in French, and I don't know French well enough to do that kind of work. I'd like to clarify something else: when Elisabeth refers to me, she says I opposed her idea of including epigraphs by Nobel laureate Miguel Ángel Asturias because to include them would make people think Rigoberta was in ORPA (Revolutionary Organization of the People in Arms) instead of the EGP [because Asturias's eldest son Rodrigo was commander in chief of ORPA]. That really insults my intelligence and my sensibility. It's worth mentioning that in November 1982, which is when she finished the editing and was in the process of translating the book, I defended my doctoral dissertation at the École des Hautes Études en Sciences Sociales in Paris on the topic of the origins of the workers' movement in Guatemala. One of the chapters of that dissertation is devoted to Miguel Ángel Asturias and the generation of 1920, and that chapter is the foundation of my essay in the book about Asturias's journalistic writing in Guatemala, which was published by the Archivos Collection [Miguel Ángel Asturias, *París: 1924–1933. Periodismo y creación literaria*, 1988]. According to Ms. Burgos's parameters, I would never have been able to include that chapter in my dissertation because people would think I was in ORPA rather than the EGP. But that assertion reveals Elisabeth's need to present me solely in the role of the perfect political commissar, and to deny that I helped her put the book together, a need to erase every trace of me, and to say, as she said in an interview here in Guatemala, "I'm the author, I own the copyright, and that's that."

But how did you negotiate the rights to the book?

Elisabeth is the one who signed a contract with Gallimard, for the first edition of the book, which appeared in French. I don't know if the publisher gave her the money to translate the manuscript into French, but it's the translation that Elisabeth and Gallimard used to draw up the contract. I understand that Elisabeth kept the rights to the editions in Portuguese and Spanish, and Gallimard kept the rights for the editions in French and all other languages. The book has been translated into twenty or thirty languages. It is my understanding that, over all these years, Elisabeth has never given Rigoberta the royalties for the different editions. This quantity has kept growing, and Elisabeth has always kept the author's royalties. What she has done is make certain donations to Rigoberta, but I am not familiar with the quantities or the details because I've never gotten involved in that issue.

Did you know about the negotiations between Gallimard and Elisabeth Burgos?

No. What's more, I went to Nicaragua at the end of 1982, and, when I returned to Paris in January 1983, the book had already come out. The book presentation took place at the Maison de l'Amérique Latine, in the presence of the Guatemalan playwright Manuel José Arce, the representatives of ORPA in Paris, Marie Tremblay, Isabel Romero, and Jorge Rosal, as well as some other Guatemalans. I was not present.

And were you satisfied with that first edition?
I had a major disagreement with her about it, not only because Rigoberta did not appear as the author, but also because she didn't even mention the other people who had participated. Later she included those acknowledgments in the Spanish edition, but they don't appear in the editions that have come out in French, German, English, and so on. Then I had another run-in with her because in November Marie Tremblay let me know that, in her introduction to the book, Elisabeth had removed all references to Rigoberta's role as a militant for the CUC and presented her as an indigenous feminist. I quarreled with her about this issue, and then she corrected the introduction to make Rigoberta look like a militant girl from some indigenous peasant movement in Guatemala. I think that in all of this, Marie's testimony is crucial. I've tried to reach her, but in vain. I know she lives in Canada.

How did Rigoberta react to these problems?
There was a lot of bitterness between Rigoberta and me. She didn't understand why, after she had trusted in me, I let her testimony be taken away from her. But the truth is that I was as naive as she was about these matters. Neither of us could foresee anything like what happened. But it overpowered us. When, through me, we appealed to the leadership of the EGP, saying, "Look, help us, let's go to court to settle these issues," several members refused to do so because of the role that Elisabeth played at that time. I'm talking about 1984, which is when we started figuring out all these problems. The French attorneys Philippe Texier, Louis Joinet, and Leo Matarasso are familiar with all the details.

It's always been said that the book was a project of the EGP.
Not at all. As I told you, the interview came up on the spur of the moment and, if it later became a book, it was because of the sensibility of the four of us who participated in it. The truth is that the EGP never thought the book would have the success it has had. They were only concerned at that moment that there wouldn't be any security problems (that's why we sent the book to them in Nicaragua), and then they let it

take its own path. Not only that, their silence about it up until now shows beyond a doubt that there was no Communist conspiracy behind the book. Now, all of this about the alleged conspiracy and my alleged role as political commissar is where Stoll's investigation takes off regarding the origins of the book.

What do you think of the polemic caused by the book Rigoberta Menchú and the Story of All Poor Guatemalans *by the anthropologist David Stoll?*

To start with, I don't agree with Stoll's argument in chapter 13 of his book, titled "The Construction of the Book by Rigoberta Menchú," which is the only one with which I'm familiar and in which I play an important role. I should say that Stoll has a skewed vision of what a testimony is, beginning with the question of who is the author—the interviewee, the interviewer, the editor, the transcriber. If we use anthropological criteria, the interviewer and the editor are as much authors as the narrator is. In this case, there were four of us involved. What I'm getting at is that it is a collective construction, and the errors and horrors that may exist in the text are part of that construction. At any rate, in any biography there are inaccuracies, there are lies, voluntary or involuntary. But you have to ask in this case whose lies they are, if there are any. Are they Rigoberta's, or do they go far beyond her? Stoll says, "All I want to do is clear up the truth." But Robert Carmack, in an interview that has just come out, makes a very important observation, reminding Stoll that "anthropologists are not journalists; what they do is represent facts from the point of view of different peoples, and the focus is not on veracity but on significance." That is exactly the problem; Stoll's first profession was journalism, and that's what betrays him. What interests him are the lies of Rigoberta versus the truths of the testimonies he has collected that contradict her. What's more, he doesn't even attempt to question the affirmations of those other testimonies, only those made by Rigoberta.

According to his own statements, David Stoll says that he has nothing against Rigoberta.

Yes, he says he has nothing against Rigoberta, but he has spent the past ten years trying to catch her in a lie. The problem is that Stoll's book is a product of the cold war. It was put together with that logic because, although he admits that Rigoberta's narration has a certain spontaneity, he sees her primarily as a product of the ideological vision of the EGP, and therefore, for him, the book must be the product of a

Communist conspiracy. The implication is that indigenous people are incapable of transmitting their own experience; there has to be a political machine as "doctrinaire as the EGP" behind all of it.

Speaking now of the matter of lies...

He says that Rigoberta lied about the death of her little brother, and to clarify this issue he interviewed only a sister of her father. You have to ask yourself if this version of her brother's death was Rigoberta's invention or a family myth. Rigoberta was about twenty years old when she gave her testimony, and this story can only have come from a tradition based on family memories. Stoll says that Rigoberta's brother did not die in the way that she says. Again, whose invention is this—is it Rigoberta's, the CUC members', the family's? That is to say, who invented this version of her brother's death? At that moment, in 1982, nobody knew how Patrocinio had died. What Stoll really doesn't understand is the narrative voice of the book, that an indigenous person considers both the individual context and the collective context, and that these two become intertwined. He, as an anthropologist, is incapable of seeing the dimension Carmack mentions, because what he did was a journalistic poll, as if he were working for a truth commission, rather than an anthropological analysis. He says that what he wants to do is break down the myth that the left created about Rigoberta, but part of the myth was created by the right and books like Mr. Stoll's.

What do you mean when you say that part of the Rigoberta myth was created by the right?

What I mean to say is that Rigoberta is disturbing because she represents the two great contradictions of this country, even aside from the gender issue, which goes beyond national issues. One is the confrontation between the indigenous and the Ladino ["Western" people of mixed indigenous and European origin], and the other is the confrontation between the left and the right. Rigoberta combines the indigenous with the ultraleft, the "Communist." The other thing is that, within Stoll's system of logic, which has been a constant of U.S. anthropology, indigenous people are infinitely manipulable, always under the influence of a modernity foreign to them. This view coincides with the historical logic of the elite in Guatemala. When Guatemala was a Spanish colony, the elite saw indigenous people as children, and during the republic they saw them as second-class citizens. Stoll's view is that behind everything

Rigoberta said was the EGP's version of historical events. But the book is not Rigoberta's version of historical events; it is the testimony of a twenty-year-old girl, an indigenous militant, who speaks of her life, her family, her brothers and sisters, her childhood, her memories, her own experience, in which there are of course influences of the CUC, of family traditions, of the left, of the EGP. But you can't ignore the fact that this is a person who lived through the war, whose father, mother, sister, brothers, and so on were killed.

What are your disagreements with this chapter 13 of which you speak?

Stoll sent me this chapter, "The Construction of the Book by Rigoberta Menchú," in February 1998, asking for my comments. I'd like to clarify that I'm referring to the first manuscript version that he sent to me, which appeared in volume 57 of the literary journal *Brick,* published in Toronto, Canada. This chapter was modified before the book was published. The essential part of the chapter is what Elisabeth Burgos tells him about which passages were removed from the book (passages and not "parts," as the press put it, that I had asked to be taken out). One was supposedly that children were used to gather unexploded bombs. The passage really said that children were used to relay messages between the population at large and the guerrillas. The second one purportedly talked about the links between the FP31 [Popular Front of the 31st of January] and ORPA. That is completely absurd because there never were any links between the FP31 and ORPA. Everyone knows that the FP31 was a mass movement that had links with the EGP and not with ORPA. Here is a real error of fact, and if Elisabeth Burgos really said that, he as a scholar could have cleared it up. But, no, he does not question at all the versions that are related to him. The third passage that was suppressed, always according to Elisabeth, was where Rigoberta supposedly affirmed that the testimony by Máximo Cajal [Spain's ambassador in Guatemala at the time of the bombing of the embassy] regarding the burning of the Spanish embassy was that the CUC threw the Molotov cocktail that destroyed the embassy, making Rigoberta's father partially responsible for the disaster.[3] There is one passage, however, that really was suppressed, but that Elisabeth forgot to mention, and it is where Rigoberta said that the person who taught her to read and write was Romeo Cartagena. It was not included so they wouldn't kill him. But the army ended up killing him anyway.

And in the published version of the book are there any modifications of these statements?

In the book version, Stoll, without mentioning the misinformation provided by Elisabeth Burgos, whom he interviewed in 1995, softens that version of the suppressed passages by noting: first, that, regarding the use of children in the war, the people were acting in self-defense, that is, they didn't really collect bombs, as he had claimed in the earlier version. Second, that the relation of the FP31 was with the guerrilla movement in general. And third, attributing Cajal's supposed statements more generally to the members of the CUC. In regard to this last point, what Vicente [the EGP member who read the book] said in his letter was that the version that the members of the CUC had performed a suicide bombing was not Cajal's version of events, but rather the version circulated in the Guatemalan press at the time.[4] At any rate, Stoll makes no mention of these contradictions in his book because it would discredit one of his principal interviewees.

What has your relationship with Rigoberta been like in recent years?

I first met Rigoberta when she passed through Paris in 1982 and asked me to put her up in my house, and we have been friends ever since. We did the book; I supported her; I took an interest, as she says, in her formation; I was her adviser; I coordinated her campaign for the Nobel Peace Prize. After she won the prize, I dedicated myself fundamentally to my profession. I don't agree with her about some things, but I do agree with her about many others. That is to be expected. I don't think, as Pablo Rodas Martini says in one of his columns [in the Guatemalan newspaper *Siglo XXI*], that Rigoberta's "great lies" have delegitimized the civil rights movement of Guatemalan indigenous people for the next ten years. That's absurd and merely part of the campaign against Rigoberta. It's as if one said that Democrats would have no political ground for the next twenty years because of President Clinton's problems.

What do you think about the rumors that, after Stoll's book, Rigoberta's right to the Nobel Peace Prize becomes questionable?

Rigoberta did not win the prize, as Elisabeth would have us believe, only because of the book. It was because of her political organizing, her leadership role, and her political capacity. Rigoberta won the Nobel Prize for an entire trajectory. She was where she had to be at the right time. She was in the United Nations, in Geneva, she campaigned for human rights and for indigenous rights, not only in Guatemala, but throughout the Continent; she managed and maintained a leadership role at a global level. She came back to Guatemala, and she was captured. The Nobel wasn't given to her as a writer; besides, the book came out ten years before she won the prize. The Nobel Prize was a message to all of Latin America from Europe regarding the question of indigenous peoples and the construction of democracy and peace, but many people refuse to see that.

Translated by Jill Robbins

Notes

1. [Domitila Barrios de Chungara, *Si me permiten hablar* (Let me speak), published in 1975 by Moema Vezzier, chronicles the life of Bolivian tin miners' labor organizer Domitila Chungara. The book made Domitila a well-known Latin American public figure, and it became a classic text for *testimonios* about women. It was latter superseded and overshadowed by *I, Rigoberta Menchú.—Ed.*]

2. [Meoño has since resigned as president of the Menchú Foundation, to keep it from being tarnished after unsubstantiated accusations were made against him that he committed atrocities during the war.—*Ed.*]

3. [Máximo Cajal has since published a book of his own memoirs of the burning of the Spanish embassy (*¡Saber quién puso fuego ahí! Masacre en la Embajada de España* [Madrid: Siddhartha Mehta Ediciones, 2000]). In it he claims that he, as well as other witnesses, saw a member of Guatemala's armed forces carrying what looked like a flamethrower, and that scientific evidence from the corpses indicated that they had been burned by white phosphorus and not gasoline, the ingredient used in a Molotov cocktail. Cajal mailed a copy of his manuscript to Stoll in 1995, but Stoll disregarded it for his own book.—*Ed.*]

4. [Cajal confirms this in his own book.—*Ed.*]

Rigoberta

Manuel Vásquez Montalbán

El País, Madrid, Monday, January 11, 1999

The campaign to discredit political indigenism in Latin America has operated from different platforms. First, Monsignor Gerardi, author of a report about military repression that dared to name names, was assassinated; then, there was an attempt to tarnish Samuel Ruiz, bishop of San Cristóbal de las Casas, Chiapas, and Subcommander Marcos, by way of innuendo or hearsay, or else through writings at the service of an alleged modernity under attack or challenged by indigenism. Now it's Rigoberta Menchú's turn. There was already an attempt to lower her moral and political stature with the argument that her book *I, Rigoberta Menchú* owed more to the promotional skills of compiler Elisabeth Burgos than to Rigoberta's dramatic biography. Now the *New York Times* comes out behind the research of anthropologist David Stoll, who points out the exaggerations or omissions in the autobiographical confessions of Rigoberta. For example, it is true that her father was burned alive in the Spanish embassy, that she herself had to go into exile while very young, and that her brother was murdered by the military, ah! but not burned alive, just shot.

This offensive against the guerrilla movement aims at disqualifying the conversion of the guerrillas into a valid political movement with a good chance of winning the elections in Guatemala because the Nobel prize winner is accused of not being hard enough in her denunciations of the guerrilla's own crimes. Dante Liano, Guatemalan writer, and collaborator of both Gianni Minà and Rigoberta in writing *Crossing Borders* (Rigoberta Menchú's second book) has launched from Italy a strong denunciation of the anti-indigenous liberal yuppie anthropological front that will be heard around the world. When I interviewed Rigoberta for *And God Entered Havana,* I was completely convinced that I was in the presence of a formidable political analyst who learned almost everything she knows by defending herself from the military forces, the paramilitary forces, the anthropologists, and those intellectuals from the left who are now begging forgiveness for having been leftists.

Translated by Arturo Arias

About David Stoll's Book *Rigoberta Menchú and the Story of All Poor Guatemalans*

Jorge Skinner-Kleé

Siglo XXI, Guatemala City, Friday, January 15, 1999

This book was launched with a large publicity apparatus, which claimed that it questioned the veracity of what Ms. Menchú said in her own book. After reading Stoll's book, I do not find such questioning, although I do perceive a certain prejudice on Stoll's part concerning what Ms. Menchú did say. This would be clarified perfectly in an interview recently conducted with Dr. Arturo Taracena, a brilliant historian.

It is evident that many of the facts narrated by Ms. Menchú, some of which she did not witness personally or see with her own eyes, were gathered by what we could call a communal memory if not an ideational one, so that it is my opinion that it is not worth it to try to question her, because it is impossible to separate what Ms. Menchú saw and what people in the community, including her own family, told her, and that she feels as if it were something she lived personally and to which she can therefore bear witness. It seems as if Dr. Arturo Taracena's judgment that Stoll is more of a journalist than an anthropologist is correct. His style of research is a journalistic one, something that is easier to see in his first book, *Between Two Armies*.

Without a question, there are a series of studies and books about indigenous communities in this country that in some way complement each other or intermingle with each other, instead of proving the others wrong. We should mention among these Carmack's studies on Totonicapán, Sandra Orellana's work about the Zutujil Mayas, and, of course,

Richard Adams, the pioneer in this field. One cannot fail to mention either the brilliant work done by Alain Breton about the Rabinal Achí and Jan Piel's about Sajcabacjá. I believe that the most serious study done about the Ixils is Horst Nachtingall's *Die Ixil,* possibly less likely to be read because it was written in German. However, the notable intellectual Julia Vela, when she was director of the Institute of Fine Arts, had a translation of that book done, which must still be lying somewhere in the archives of that institution. The translation is still somewhat raw, it needs polishing, but it is an effort that should not die in the basement of Fine Arts. I believe that there is still much that can be written about Guatemala, and that can be said about Ms. Menchú and her book, and I believe that it is a good and constructive thing.

Translated by Arturo Arias

Let's Shoot Rigoberta

Eduardo Galeano

La Jornada, Mexico City, January 16, 1999

Guatemala? Central America? Kansas is in the center of America. Guatemala does not appear on most maps available to the general public, the ones that manufacture the world's public opinion. However, by way of a small miracle, a Guatemalan woman, Rigoberta Menchú, is occupying plenty of space lately. Not because of what she has voiced from her own country, which is just coming out of one of the longest and most ferocious holocausts in the Americas in the twentieth century. Rigoberta is not the one making the accusations but the one being accused. Once again, as it should be, the victims sit in the chair of the accused.

The Gases of Infamy

From the United States, as would very well be expected, a new chemical warfare has been launched that has poisoned many. It all began when a North American anthropologist spent ten years of his life trying to catch Rigoberta in a contradiction and to uncover the guerrillas' share of blame for the repression that indigenous peoples have suffered. "He came to Guatemala to study us as if we were insects," claims writer Dante Liano. "In his own book he invokes witnesses and archives. What archives can there possibly be about the recently concluded war? Did the Guatemalan army open their archives to him?" Not too long ago, Congressman Barrios Kleé tried to consult those same archives, and he was later found with a bullet hole in his head. Bishop Juan Gerardi, who had tried the same thing, ended up with his own head smashed to smithereens.

The *New York Times* offered its front page for this business. The newspaper confirmed and published the anthropologist's conclusions: the testimonial *I, Rigoberta Menchú,* published some twenty years back, contains "imprecisions and falsehoods." For example, Rigoberta's brother Patrocinio was not burned alive: he was shot and thrown into a common ditch. Or, for example, "She attended a boarding school for three years," which makes it sound as if she had gone to a Swiss finishing school, rather than a marginal little school for native peoples in Huehuetenango. And it goes on like that, finding other specks in the milk.

Smoke Screen

From that point on, the powder keg exploded, and the fire caught on internationally. All of a sudden, the voices that speak of a scandal have multiplied, the voices that call Rigoberta a liar and that, in passing, repudiate the indigenous resistance movement that she represents and symbolizes. With suspicious celerity, a smoke screen is rising to hide forty years of tragedy in Guatemala, magically reduced to a guerrilla provocation and to family quarrels, those typical "Indian things."

It goes without saying that the voluminous and well-documented report put together by the church, a committee presided over by Bishop Gerardi and published just last year, two days before his murder, did not enjoy the same publicity. There was no front page in the *New York Times.* Thousands of testimonials gathered throughout the entire country came together as small pieces of a gigantic jigsaw puzzle that recorded the memory of pain: 150,000 Guatemalans dead, 150,000 disappeared, a million exiles or refugees, 200,000 orphans, 40,000 widows. Nine out of ten victims were unarmed civilians, Maya in their majority, and in eight out of ten cases, it was the fault of the army or its paramilitary bands. The report writes of a direct responsibility, the responsibility of paid puppets. About the others, about the paying puppet masters, it would be well worth it if the United States would send all its anthropologists and if the *New York Times* mobilized all of its foreign correspondents to investigate the matter. But the White House and the Pentagon can whistle and look the other way. Most Americans don't have a clue where this country, Guatemala, with its exotic name so hard to pronounce, is located.

The Nobel and Her

The campaign against Rigoberta even reached Oslo. There are those who demand that she return the Nobel Prize or that it be taken away from her. The prize has already been given, and properly given, ratified the Norwegian Committee: "the details invoked are not essential," said their spokesperson.

Imagine if they had not reacted this way. The Nobel Peace Prize that Rigoberta won in 1992 was not only the one decent and fair commemoration of those five hundred years called the "Discovery of the Americas," but it turned out to be a good thing for the prize itself, which needed some cleansing of its own. The Nobel Peace Prize had picked up a lot of dirt along the way since 1906, when it was given to Teddy Roosevelt, who claimed to whomever cared to hear him that war purified men, and it got even dirtier when other warmongers won it, such as Henry Kissinger, who gave the world a lot of deaths, and fathered [Chilean dictator Augusto] Pinochet and other smaller monsters. The world is upside down if it is discussing now whether Rigoberta deserves the prize, when it should be debating whether the prize deserves her.

The Country and Her

Indigenous peoples are a majority in Guatemala. But the dominant minority treats them, in dictatorship or in democracy, as South Africa used to treat its blacks during the times of apartheid. Out of every six adult Guatemalans, only one votes. Mayas are good for attracting tourism, for picking cotton and coffee, and for playing the role of beasts of burden in the national economy, and as target practice for the army. "You act like an Indian," say the bosses, who think they are white, to their own children when they misbehave. "Guatemalan society" was not amused when the news of the Nobel Prize reached them. "Filthy Indian," they call Rigoberta since then, voices of rancor, and also "uppity Indian." Now they can also say, "lying Indian."

She has stepped out of her place, and that offends people who think they're white. That Rigoberta is a Maya and a woman is her problem, a double disgrace for her to bear. But that this Maya woman turned out not to accept her lot and then sinned by becoming a universal symbol of human dignity, oh my God. Powerful men in Guatemala and in the world hate that.

Time and Her

Rigoberta comes from a family that was annihilated, a village that was razed, a memory burned. She spent the first twenty years of her life closing the eyes of the dead that opened her own eyes. Basque writer Bernardo Atxaga asked her:

"How can you possibly be so happy?"

"Time," she answered. "Ever since we were children, we were raised to understand time as something that never ends, even if our transit through this world is very brief."

It is written in the sacred Maya books: "What is a person on the road? Time."

Rigoberta is a daughter of time. As all Mayas, she has been woven by the threads of time. And she often says:

"Time weaves slowly."

In the long run, slowly, time will decide what will be worth remembering from all of this. The passage of the days and the years will separate the wheat from the chaff. Maybe time will forget that Rigoberta Menchú received a Nobel Prize, but certainly time will not forget that she receives, day in and day out, in the Maya highlands of Guatemala and in so many other places, a prize much more important than all the Nobels in the world: the love of the oppressed and the hatred of the oppressors. Those who stone Rigoberta ignore what they are praising. After all, as the old proverb says, it is the tree that gives fruit that receives all the stones.

Translated by Arturo Arias

Rigoberta Menchú Tum

The Truth That Challenges the Future

The Rigoberta Menchú Tum Foundation

Official document from the Rigoberta Menchú Tum Foundation, originally distributed to all media on Thursday, January 21, 1999, at the foundation's headquarters in Guatemala City.

In recent weeks, publications that have appeared in the media in different countries have sought to call into question the testimony of Rigoberta Menchú Tum, starting with the publication of the work of a North American researcher who attempts to refute the recent history of Guatemala—that today is recognized by both the world and the parties to the internal conflict—a history that is dealt with as an ideological invention of the left, which he accuses, at the same time, of manipulating the person and fabricating the myth that is personified by the Nobel Peace Prize winner.

Just when the commemorations of the five hundredth anniversary appeared to have left behind the arrogance and the superiority complexes of those who have, until now, written history since the Conquest, now we see how some people celebrate with unconcealed enthusiasm the appearance of these new chroniclers who attempt to return to their place—the same old place—those who had the audacity to add to the Official Story that which it was lacking: the vision of the conquered. And they do so protected by the presumably scientific rigor conferred upon them by the fact that they speak in the name of the North American academy.

Nevertheless, ten years of idle pursuits to assemble a version made up of bits and pieces of interviews of dubious seriousness are no longer sufficient to modify this new history, nor much less to take us back to the myth that saw indigenous people as juvenile, ignorant, and incapable of making their own decisions. One cannot keep appealing to that paternalistic vision according to which it was always others who decided their fate, be they the Iberians who came to "make America" five hundred years ago, or those who cannot bear the fact that the legitimate revolts of yesterday and today might be genuine expressions of those desirous of freedom and redemption for those peoples to whom the right to be themselves had been denied.

The public opinion campaign unleashed by this work has emerged in a moment in which it has become fashionable to lie and in which it seems necessary to validate the right to lie with impunity, inverting the values of honesty that up until now public personalities have had to practice. Neither does its coincidence with the recipe of punishment—even annihilation, to be precise—of those who work to defend the right to be different appear to be casual.

The testimony of Rigoberta Menchú has the value of representing not just the story of a witness, but rather the personal experience of a protagonist and the interpretation of that which her own eyes saw and wept over, that which her own ears heard, and that which they were told. No testimony can be viewed as journalistic reporting, nor as a neutral description of the reality of others. The testimony of Rigoberta Menchú has the bias and the courage of a victim who, in addition to what she personally suffered, had a right to assume as her own personal story the atrocities that her people lived through. Their dead are still dead, and that is denied neither by the researcher, nor his sources, nor the signers of the peace accords that ended the Guatemalan tragedy. It is not important whether they were burned alive or if they were already dead, either by kerosene or white phosphorous, and no one has the right or the authority to deny the pain that her heart has felt and continues to feel.

None of the alleged imprecisions, exaggerations, or omissions that are purported in the mentioned text either detract from or weaken the truth of the testimony of Rigoberta Menchú. Moreover, in 1983, her testimony contributed not only to the denunciation of those aberrant crimes that were committed in this part of the world, but also saved the life of many of the protagonists and those of their families, whether it was her own, those of the nuns that protected her, those of the indigenous peoples or peasants who shared their fate with her, or those of the combatants who understood the path of the guerrillas to be their only way out of the shameful situation that her people had confronted for more than four decades.

The path for which Rigoberta Menchú opted, in contrast to that which her detractors now claim, was that of involving the conscience of the international community—which was up until then very distant from that reality—in the drama of her people; that of uniting her voice with those who demanded a just, democratic, and peaceful solution to the Guatemalan conflict and the recognition of the neocolonial reality to which, even today, the majority of indigenous peoples in the Americas and in the rest of the world continue to be subjected; and that of seeking to bring down the wall of impunity and silence with which the powerful have hidden that reality.

That path took Rigoberta Menchú to the Nobel Peace Prize, and this contributed, in an effective way, to the opening of the road to peace in Guatemala, and the recognition of the situation and the indigenous demands expressed in the declaration of the International Year and Decade of Indigenous Peoples. This path is, moreover, eloquent as to the personality, moral stature, and leadership of Ms. Menchú, and amply belies the image that this slanderous publication and the campaign of those who have echoed it now seek to transmit.

At this stage, and now far from the dazzling celebrations and commemorations of 1992, we can find evidence of the weakening of the commitments that were assumed at that time and that of the political will of many of the actors for moving it forward. The agenda that the struggle of the indigenous peoples bequeathed to the Decade has gradually been emptied of its promising content, its negotiation is threatened by the indifference of governments and international institutions, and in addition there is an increasing demobilization of some indigenous organizations.

It is cause for concern to state that in many circles of power throughout the world there is an increasing sense that indigenous peoples are an obstacle to the stability of the prevailing order and a potential danger, given the accumulation of discontent and frustrations. It would seem that, with the end of the cold war, some people need to find new enemies in order to prolong the confrontation.

In this setting, the attacks against those to whom we refer today broaden their meaning and seek to place into question not only this or that testimony, but rather the truth about the colonial history that all of the world's States recognized in naming Rigoberta Menchú as an Ambassador of Good Will for the International Year of Indigenous Peoples, and seek to deliberately forget the commitments acquired.

At the end of the millennium, we note the worrisome broadening of the conditions of poverty, inequity, intolerance, and marginalization that affect the majorities in our nations, making it incomprehensible that the progress of science and technology and the advances of modernity are not translated into solutions for these problems. To the contrary, that reality in which individualism and shortsightedness increase injustices leaves open the path for the emergence and deepening of the conflicts that threaten peace.

As this year begins with one that ends a decade marked by wars and fratricidal confrontation, we wish to emphasize the demand for a new civilizing order, based on the recognition of pluralism and respect for differences, on tolerance and dialogue, on development that leads to equity, and on the truth that leads to justice, all of which are values that summarize the ethic of peace to which Rigoberta Menchú has given testimony with her life.

This pronouncement is a call to public awareness, to social organizations, governments, and institutions of the international system to revive critical reflection, to reaffirm commitments, and to renew the decision and the will to face up to the debts incurred by humanity with the history that, until a few years ago, it refused to recognize.

Against Gerardi and Against Rigoberta, Attacks Are Continually Made to Make Them Lose Some of Their Luster

Margarita Carrera

Prensa Libre, Guatemala City, Friday, January 22, 1999

There is no doubt whatsoever that those enemies of human rights that stick close to the army and to parties with overt fascist sympathies and clear racist attitudes are determined to declare war on our two greatest humanitarians, Bishop Gerardi and Rigoberta Menchú.

The first was assassinated for publicizing around the world one of the most moving documents in the human history of the twentieth century: his famous "Never Again" or "REMHI" [Recovery of Historical Memory], and the second, for having written the book *I, Rigoberta Menchú.* In both documents one confirms how the Guatemalan government ment was at the service of capitalist interests and defended by the army (which received its orders from the Pentagon) and committed crimes against humanity impossible to either forgive or forget.

Both books have gone around the world, pointing fingers and detailing the most horrifying crimes and tortures committed against unarmed, defenseless civilians. Two well-known personalities who deal with the same subject describe in detail the four hundred thousand and some massacres, which can only be compared to the Nazi Holocaust. Against Bishop Gerardi, and against Rigoberta, continual attacks, innuendo, and hearsay are made on a daily basis so that they lose some of their luster because they have both committed the same sin: they have revealed what is forbidden by those forces who benefit from power and have done so for the last five hundred years. They have both revealed the truth about the Guatemalan civil war.

After incarcerating Vielman and then Father Orantes [a homeless person and a priest originally accused of Bishop Gerardi's murder], they now launch other accusations to make those who defend human rights lose their prestige. In what seems to be the worst of them, they name a relative of [army captain Byron Lima] Oliva, an army man himself accused of human rights violations, to investigate the crime. I am speaking, of course, of Juan Carlos Solís Silva, who continues the campaign to end the Gerardi case with the cynical theory that a band of drug traffickers was responsible for his murder. The next victim's name has already been announced: it is Father Efraín Hernández.[1] All this to preserve impunity and protect the military.

The campaign against Rigoberta is an international one. A gringo, suspiciously claiming to be an academic, writes a dissertation with the only goal of discrediting our Nobel Prize winner. Even if he claims he does not mean to destroy Menchú, his effort to evidence details where he claims she altered the truth is highly suspicious, as is his claim that he is not racist. Besides the Guatemalan military and its backers, who else but North American politicians that followed the guidelines of those who overthrew President Arbenz [in 1954] and supported military dictatorships in our country during the entire civil war could be interested in this work of tarring and feathering?

And why does the North American press give so much space to the findings made by this book, as if these insignificant little facts were truly an uncanny piece of news that affected the security of the entire world? All these are questions whose answers undoubtedly would unveil ideological kinships between those who killed here and those who ordered the killings there.

Translated by Arturo Arias

Note

1. [It was suggested in the press that Father Orantes was involved in a homosexual relationship with the bishop so that the crime could be attributed to a gay lover's rage or jealousy and Monsignor Gerardi's name besmirched. Later, Father Efraín Hernández, who first reported the crime, was accused of fathering two members of a notorious street gang, so as to discredit his testimony regarding the murder. At present, army captain Byron Lima Oliva and his father Byron Lima Estrada, a retired army officer, have been accused of the crime, but no trial date has been set. Lima Oliva claims that he is innocent and that he is willing to name the real perpetrators of the crime if his safety can be guaranteed.—Ed.]

Rigoberta Menchú

Those Who Attack Me Humiliate the Victims

Interview by Juan Jesús Aznárez

El País, Madrid, Sunday, January 24, 1999

Only a few weeks ago a scandal broke out that affects the image of the 1992 Nobel Peace Prize winner. Anthropologist David Stoll, and a report in the *New York Times* using Stoll's book as a script, imputed to the book *I, Rigoberta Menchú,* written in 1984, exaggerations, inventions, or falsehoods. Stoll, in November, and *Times* reporter Larry Rohter, on December 15, affirmed that Menchú's text is not a testimonial text, as it pretends to be, and that its recounting of events does not correspond to reality. The disputed episodes took place during the thirty-six years of internal war in Guatemala, whose final numbers are horrific: 100,000 people dead, 40,000 disappeared, 200,000 orphans, and a wandering legion of 100,000 widows.

According to anthropologist Stoll and the *Times,* the territorial dispute that the Nobel Prize winner attributes to a battle against landowners with Spanish surnames, one of the foundations of her book, was, in reality, a family battle between her father and some relatives; there was no younger brother who died of malnutrition because Nicolás Tum, Rigoberta Menchú's brother, is alive and well in San Miguel Uspatán; and it does not seem certain that another of her brothers, Petrocinio, was really burned alive by soldiers while family members were forced to watch.

What is more, they write, it is not true that the Nobel Prize winner scarcely attended school nor that she barely knew how to read because she studied in a parochial school run by Belgian nuns of the Order of the Holy Family. She is accused as well of representing other people's experiences as her own. "She tried to be all things to all people," the authors conclude.

The Rigoberta Menchú Foundation reacted Wednesday afternoon, underscoring that none of the imputations attributed to the Nobel Prize winner by the author of *Rigoberta Menchú and the Story of All Poor Guatemalans* (Stoll) has merit nor does it weaken a testimony that "has the bias and the courage of a victim who, in addition to what she personally suffered, had a right to assume as her own personal history the atrocities that her people lived through."

She defends the right to her own historical memory, to narrate the events in function of what she herself lived or what they told her and her own perception of them. "Should I beg forgiveness because they killed my father? Should I beg forgiveness because they killed my brother? Or should I beg forgiveness because they massacred the entire village where I lived? *I, Rigoberta Menchú* was a testimonial, not an autobiography," she clarifies. "I have my truth of what I lived for twenty years. The history of the community is my own history."

Is it true that your book omits events and invents or exaggerates others?
I recognize, because I do not say so in the book, that I was a servant in the Belgian school. I did not say so then in order to protect my relationship with the sisters in those years. How I would have loved to tell all the experiences I had, not only with the Sisters of the Holy Family of the Belgian convent, but in my pastoral work, my work as a catechist with religious communities!

Were you a student of that school?
They forgot to ask what I did there. I was a servant. I earned twelve quetzales a month (twelve dollars at that time) working in the school. We paid one quetzal in Social Security, so I received eleven quetzales in cash. That is another part of my life that I did not include in my book because the last thing I would have wanted during those years was to associate the Belgian school with me, because one program of the sisters took the young ladies (the students), who were of course from well-to-do families, to do some work in the countryside, which meant that they lived in a rural community for two or three days, met the people there, got the sense of being in a small village on the outskirts of the capital, and thereby completed their education. Many of those young ladies have

died. The nuns had other convents that were completely destroyed during the war. Why would I want to associate the Belgian school with me publicly when it was said that I was subversive, communist, and so on? If I had stayed in Guatemala, I would have been killed, too.

Did you take classes there?

We had two classes per week, three hours per day, after 3 P.M. We didn't study with the rest of the students; we had our own teacher who taught us reading and writing, then sewing and cooking, on Saturdays and Sundays. They called it home economics. Our duty was to clean before class, and afterwards, to clean until 11 P.M.

You didn't participate in the normal course of study?

No, no. What I would have given to have that grand opportunity! Later, I won a scholarship for an adult education program.

How did your brother Petrocinio die?

For many years I couldn't even say that my mother told the truth about my brother Petrocinio, and admit it to myself, because I never wanted my mother to be in anyone else's mouth. We should let the dead rest in peace. What most offends me is that they say: "Well, Rigoberta's brother wasn't burned alive there; he went to a common grave." That is true of so many victims in Guatemala, where the uncertainty is demonstrated by the existence of common graves.

Did you see his murder?

My mother saw it. And she can no longer speak about it. And how could I possibly have presented my mother as the number one witness, when they have killed so many witnesses so they can't speak? That was a common practice in Guatemala. That [account] is one truth, my mother's truth. And if you ask me if I believe Stoll or my mother, it is obvious that I believe my mother.

Your mother told you how Petrocinio died?

Of course. She went to look at all the faces of the cadavers that were produced in the region, still trying to doubt it, that her boy had died. She didn't want to believe it, and she had to go see each dead body in case there was the slightest hope that it hadn't been him. I can say that if my brother was not that boy, and if it was just the fantasy of a crazy mother looking for her son in every tomb, that it was my mother's fantasy. Let them show me the common grave where my brother is buried. If someone hands over his corpse to me, I will change my mind. My truth is that Petrocinio was burned alive.

Territorial Disputes

And the territorial disputes? Were they against landowners or were they a family quarrel?

This is a fifty-year-old problem. We have recovered my father's records from 1952 in order to gain lawful rights to those lands. All his life my father struggled there. It is said that my grandfather, Nicolás Tum, who died in the 1980s, long before the problems began, supposedly sold the land to another Ladino who lives in another village. And in 1996, we had to negotiate with that Ladino so he would sell back to us the land where my father made his life, where I was born, where I grew up. I bought back this land that was my father's. My grandfather never would have sold those lands, and he (Stoll) reduces it all to a simple family dispute. Everyone knows that the issue of land was one of the most debated issues in the peace accord.

Why?

Because it had an extremely high budget, much higher than any other issue of the peace accords. First, because they had to do a census of the lands. The World Bank had to promise a million-dollar contribution. The land only has the heritage of conflict, there are always many owners, and the wiliest becomes the owner of the land. There was a need for a political negotiation between all the parties concerned. In this process entire communities, big landowners, woodcutters, and other businessmen are involved. There is a lot of speculation.

They say that your brother Nicolás did not die.

I want to be very frank with you. I have a brother, Nicolás I, the one who died, and another, Nicolás II, who is still alive. That is very normal in Guatemala, that names are repeated in families.

And in yours?

He [Stoll] is supposedly an anthropologist who has studied the indigenous worldview. And that, the repetition of names, is commonplace in the so-called Maya world and in all indigenous communities in Latin America. That repetition is a theme that has been much discussed in the classification of the reports done by the REMHI [acronym in Spanish for "Recovery of Historical Memory"], where names are also repeated. An investigator has to understand that logic and say that in any given family there are three or four members with the same name. In my family, there were only two, not three or four. I have two brothers named Nicolás. If both were alive, we would have to talk about Big Nicolás and Little Nicolás. Big Nicolás died, the older one, my mother's first son.

Is it true that he died of malnutrition?

Yes, exactly. The incoherence in this is that in the book, it seems that they are talking about Little Nicolás, my younger brother. It was so easy to erase with the stroke of a pen the history of two Indians [her brothers] who, if they had been alive, would have been indignant to be used in that way! When they have nothing to do with my own convictions, nor with my struggle, nor with the decisions that I make because I am an adult.

They criticize you for representing other people's experiences as your own.

I can't force them to understand. Everything, for me, that was the story of my community is also my own story. I did not come from the air, I am not a little bird who came alone from the mountains, from parents who were isolated from the world. I am the product of a community, and not only the Guatemalan community. And, in response to whether my brothers, my father, were rich, go to Chimel and you will see for yourself that there is no electricity, that this year could see the opening of its first school.

There are those who are asking that they take away your Nobel Prize.

They are confusing things. The Nobel Peace Prize is not the Nobel Prize for Literature. That one they give to someone who writes books. They did not give it to me for a single book. The Peace Prize is a symbolic prize given for the role one played in the peace process.

Venezuelan anthropologist Elisabeth Burgos, coauthor of your book, is hurt that you covered up the atrocities committed by the guerrillas.

First, you have to imagine yourself in the Guatemala of the mid-1980s. Anyone who even seemed to be part of the opposition, not even of the guerrilla movement, would certainly be persecuted immediately. It has been a dreadful story. There were no spaces, there were no intermediaries. I have never said this before, but I am going to say it to you: the truth is that simply belonging to the CUC [Committee for Peasant Unity] was interpreted as if one were part of the Guatemalan guerrilla. There were links to the guerrilla movement. Many exiles had links to the guerrilla. The current Guatemalan vice minister of external affairs [Gabriel Aguilera Peralta, vice-minister of external affairs, 1996–98] was the delegate that I met from the Guatemalan Workers Party, which was the Communist Party, the best known of them. They introduced the chancellor to me as an expert on the close relationship between the insurgent movement in Guatemala and Central America. And I could go on. I met the private secretary of President Arzú when he was a high commander in the guerrilla. There is no hidden agenda. Some people think that I have a hidden agenda, a hidden truth, and that therefore they must bring out that truth. Today I can tell you all these things because nobody will be assassinated tomorrow because of it.

Some people affirm that "Rigoberta lies."

Not even Mr. Stoll's book says I am a liar. What a coincidence that they should say that now, that Rigoberta lies, just like that. In that case, the twenty-five thousand witnesses that Monsignor Gerardi interviewed before his death also lied because they affirm and reaffirm and super-re-affirm the same thing and more that I said in my testimonial *I, Rigoberta Menchú* [Juan Gerardi, the assistant bishop of Guatemala, was assassinated April 26, 1998, two days after presenting the report *Guatemala, Never Again*]. What a coincidence that they say that Rigoberta lies when the Commission for Historical Clarification [CEH] has gone to all the communities and has found not only this truth, but has been able to find all kinds of other crimes against humanity.

But Stoll questions your biography, he doesn't deny the atrocities that took place in Guatemala.

Of course. All of us victims lie. He has already reached a conclusion ahead of time, and he adorns everything to reach that particular conclusion. And the most aberrant of all is that not only are we all ignorant, as Mr. Stoll says, so that both communism and liberation theology were able to manipulate our minds, and they created us and made us myths, of me in particular they made a barbarous myth, a mysterious phantasm; he is also saying that we are liars, not just ignorant and savage. That is something that I will not accept for anything in the world.

Stoll, the CIA, and the *New York Times*

Would you be willing to confront him face-to-face?

My problem is not with an individual or two. It is not a lie that I'm anxiously awaiting a photograph to form for myself a picture of how a rival looks that I do not know. I am not rancorous. The day I took a picture with the Guatemalan armed forces and with their commanders I knew it was a message sent to the rest of the world because they were no less than the perpetrators of the murder of my own people, my village, my family. And the day I planted a tree together with the minister of defense and a guerrilla commander I felt that through our lives passed a categorical message. My reasons and my cause amply justify that.

What do you know about David Stoll's work?

It is the first book that holds truly aberrant theses about Guatemala. He claims that the internal armed conflict never existed as such, that it was an exaggerated creation of communists, and they succeeded in convincing a lot of people. He says that Efraín Ríos Montt [a general, dictatorial ruler of Guatemala during 1982–83] was never responsible for any massacres, but was actually someone who was outside of power without any control over security forces or over repression. He tries to beautify the story of Ríos Montt.

Has all this scandal hurt you much?

Yes, very much, because it humiliates the victims. It wasn't enough to kill them, to leave them dead. It wasn't enough that my mother was killed, my father, my brothers, but they even want to build a polemic around the dead.

Do you think someone is trying to get something by hurting you?

I hate to speculate unless I have evidence. We are not going to say it was the CIA, but we cannot believe that someone wasn't behind this, either.

What interest did the New York Times *have in manipulating your story? Larry Rohter is considered a professional with years of experience in Central America.*

It is too early to reach a conclusion. I have no elements. We are trying to work over the various points of view of our own friends in the United

States. I only know that it was an article by the *New York Times*. That's what I know. I have no elements. What hurts so much is that the article does not even include the nuances of Mr. Stoll's own book. It is something very strange for me.

Do you have ways to prove the truth of your own narrative?

Read the report on the Recovery of Historical Memory, which gathered the truth about twenty-five thousand victims in Guatemala. It is also enough to go to Guatemala and stand in an agro-exporting *finca* [plantation] to see just how many children work in them cutting cane. They are horrible realities that do not belong to the past. It is not a question of you believing in my own truth or someone else's; I'm simply saying that I have the right to my memory, as do my people.

The Voice of Indigenous Peoples in Latin America

Rigoberta Menchú Tum, forty years old, is a K'iché Mayan, one of the twenty-three indigenous groups that constitute 60 percent of the Guatemalan population. Since 1981, she has been denouncing the oppression suffered by indigenous peoples and the internal situation in her country, which suffered the longest and bloodiest conflict in Central America. The signing of the peace accords on December 29, 1996, opened a new process in a nation exploited for many decades by the arbitrariness of right-wing military dictatorships, excepting the democratic periods of presidents Juan José Arévalo and Jacobo Arbenz, the latter overthrown in 1954 in a coup supported by the CIA.

Rigoberta Menchú was the sixth of nine children of Vicente Menchú, a communal leader, and Juana Tum, a midwife and healer. Her family worked on coffee plantations. Her father died during the occupation of the Spanish embassy in Guatemala, on January 31, 1980. Rigoberta Menchú fled to Mexico, where she spent twelve years and where she met Bishop Samuel Ruiz of the dioceses of San Cristóbal de las Casas, Chiapas.

On a trip to Paris, she narrated the story of her life, *I, Rigoberta Menchú*, published in Spanish sixteen years ago, then in English, and translated afterwards into other languages. After her return to Guatemala, in 1988, she was detained at the airport and later freed, thanks to international pressure. Four years later, her name became known globally when she was granted the Nobel Peace Prize. For two decades she has been the principal figure leading indigenous struggles in Latin America, she has participated in many international forums in their defense, and her biography, now embroiled in controversy, contributed to attracting the world's attention to the bestial behavior taking place in this small Central American country.

"Guatemala's history is impossible to change one way or the other," she claims, "because the crimes committed have sealed the memories of our people. There were thousands and thousands of disappearances, tortures, assassinations, people burned alive." Her primary objective is the promotion of indigenous peoples.

Translated by Jill Robbins

David Stoll Breaks the Silence

David Stoll

Siglo XXI, Guatemala City, Wednesday, January 27, 1999

With my book *Rigoberta Menchú and the Story of All Poor Guatemalans* (Westview Press, 1998), I wanted to encourage more survivors to share their experiences of violence. That is why I am pleased that historian Arturo Taracena has given his own point of view in an interview published in *El Periódico de Guatemala* on January 10.

As a representative of the Guerrilla Army of the Poor (EGP) in Paris, in 1982, it was Taracena who introduced Rigoberta Menchú to Elisabeth Burgos. He also participated in the editorial work entrusted to Burgos and served as an adviser to the future Nobel Peace Prize winner, giving him an honorable place in Guatemalan history.

In 1997–98, I requested an interview with Taracena on two occasions. He did not respond. That did not surprise me because it was evident that the Nobel laureate had placed him in a difficult position. Because of her differences with Burgos, Menchú was downplaying the role played by the editor of *I, Rigoberta Menchú* and playing up that of Taracena.

Because the veracity of the laureate's *testimonio* was becoming problematic, her turn toward Taracena gave the impression that the former EGP liaison could share responsibility for the historical imprecisions in Menchú's text. And while the Nobel laureate hailed the ex–EGP representative, she simultaneously denied any link with his organization. Worse, Menchú began to claim an important role in the editing of her own *testimonio*, another impossibility in a web of contradictions.

From all this confusion, Taracena emerges with a certain gentility in his interview with *El Periódico*, correcting the Nobel laureate without seeming to. At the same time, Taracena feels that he has never received proper acknowledgment for his own contribution and argues that Burgos committed various injustices.

On this point I should linger for a moment. According to Taracena, in 1982 he himself was in agreement with suppressing his role, for the good of an underground organization. If Burgos had really kept the royalties, as Taracena claims, this would be a true injustice. But here Taracena and the Nobel laureate have erred, because Burgos has the receipts to prove that she sent the royalties to a solidarity committee in Paris approved by Menchú. In the end, it seems as if Burgos's alleged transgressions are limited to the issue of who is and is not mentioned in the acknowledgments.

This is no surprise because the Nobel laureate has been denouncing Burgos for the past year, for alleged crimes that change from one interview to the next. What surprises me is that Taracena feels free to condemn my book when, as he himself admits, he has read only one of the twenty chapters, a draft that I sent him and to which he never responded.

In reference to chapter 13 of my book, Taracena holds that I have committed a misdeed by eliminating small mistakes from the final product. If Taracena is a professional historian, he must know that there is nothing unusual in making corrections between drafts.

Contrary to what Taracena says, I never painted him as a political commissar, nor did I represent Menchú's story as a communist plot, least of all as a lie. But it is evident that Menchú interpreted her experience according to the ideological vision of the EGP, of which she was a member. That is not a crime, least of all under General Lucas García's regime. Actually, my own position is close to that of Taracena and Burgos, namely, that the power of Menchú's narrative cannot be explained apart from the evident capacity of the narrator herself. A puppet would not have been able to tell the story of *I, Rigoberta Menchú.*

Because he rejects a book that he has not read, Taracena ignores a wealth of data that enriches our understanding of an archetypal case. Contrary to his statements, Menchú's testimony that the Guatemalan army burned her brother alive in Chajul's plaza cannot come from her family because in 1980 they had a different view of the facts, the same one expressed by residents of Chajul and human rights reports. What everyone agrees (except Menchú two years later in Paris) is that the army shot Petrocinio and six other victims from Uspantán. What is important is not that she dramatized the way in which her brother died; the responsibility still lies with the military. What matters is that Menchú was not the eyewitness to the event that she claims to be.

Taracena is right that anthropologists try to go beyond mere journalism, that is, focusing on facts at the cost of understanding the context. We are more interested in the issue of different perspectives than in the facts themselves. However, in a case in which there is a strong tendency to idolize a preferred source of information, it has to be demonstrated that this is a partial version before proceeding to deeper issues. For example, how is it that Menchú became a cultural hero, a scapegoat, and a political saint for her various audiences inside Guatemala and internationally? In the end what has to be unmasked is not Menchú's *testimonio,* which will hold its own in history and literature, but the wish to create quasi–religious cults around it.

Translated by Arturo Arias

The Anthropologist with the Old Hat

Dante Liano

El Periódico de Guatemala, Guatemala City, Sunday, January 31, 1999

In late December 1998, some American and European newspapers saw as controversial news the publication of Stanford-trained anthropologist David Stoll's *Rigoberta Menchú and the Story of All Poor Guatemalans.* The volume argued that much of Rigoberta's personal odyssey, as contained in her well-known 1982 memoir *I, Rigoberta Menchú: An Indian Woman in Guatemala,* was the result of deliberate distortions. Soon after, Rigoberta's defenders, among them the Spanish novelist Manuel Vázquez Montalbán and the Uruguayan essayist Eduardo Galeano, began to respond to Stoll's allegations, thus upgrading the controversy to a full-blown scandal. Another defender was Arturo Taracena Arriola, who had kept silent for sixteen years about mediating in Paris between Rigoberta and Elisabeth Burgos-Debray, the editor of Rigoberta's autobiography.

Stoll's interest in the Guatemalan poor is actually old hat. His work on the subject goes back to the early 1990s, when he published his doctoral dissertation as a book, *Between Two Armies in the Ixil Towns of Guatemala.* There he put forth the thesis, taken as explosive today, that the forty years of war in the Central American nation, defined by ferocious massacres against indigenous peoples, were the result, to a large extent, of opposition to military dictatorships. According to him, the guerrillas did not peacefully enlist, but rather forced, the Indians to fight against the army; as a result, the latter simply performed its duty of defending the country against Communism. If thousands of people were disappeared, tortured, and murdered, it was the fault of those who rebelled, not of those who followed orders. The latter were just complying with their homicidal and torturous duties.

This paradoxical thesis was confirmed by Stoll in an interview he granted to the Guatemalan daily *Prensa Libre*. In it he stated that "to argue that the guerrilla was not inevitable and did not come from the poor's struggles, and that, on the contrary, it was a tragedy born of the confrontation among Guatemalan patriots from the right and the left, is still interpreted as an apology for the Guatemalan army. But it is not so."

Obviously, we shall always need an American anthropologist to explain what our lives are really about. Nicolás Guillén once said to his native Cuba: "There was always someone who found you!" and his words are true of the rest of the Americas too. We in Guatemala always had someone who came to study us like insects, to write a thesis, to draft a book explaining what we have been and will be forever. Then the *New York Times*, the *Washington Post*, and other American and European newspapers, and similar journalistic sources, simply spread the word around the globe.

Among the best books I know about Guatemala is *La patria del Criollo* [The Creole's country] by Severo Martínez. Did the *New York Times* ever devote a single line to it? But Stoll's latest effort has deserved full coverage. Some time ago, he announced its publication by stating that the "liar" Rigoberta Menchú would finally be unmasked. The announcement reminds me of a secretary Pablo Neruda once had who, upon being fired, devoted his life to persecuting the poet. A day before the Chilean author was to be awarded the Nobel Prize for Literature, the secretary sent a letter to the Swedish Academy accusing him of stealing the funds of refugees of the Spanish Civil War. The academy decided not to award Neruda the prize then, and another year had to pass before he received it. Every celebrity has a private Jabert.

In a lengthy article in the *New York Times*, Larry Rohter states that Dr. Stoll interviewed a total of 120 persons. He then opposed the memory of one interviewee to another, but obviously chose only those who were in agreement with his argument. Rohter also states that Stoll consulted archives thoroughly. Which archives, it is hard to know. Are there actual files on the war in Guatemala? If there are and they were opened for an American, it might be useful to ask why the army has denied access to them to the Commission for Historical Clarification, as well as to Guatemalan congressman Héctor Barrios Kleé, who, by the way, was recently killed by a shot to the head.

Inspired by Stoll, Rohter also went to Guatemala. He interviewed Rigoberta's relatives, friends, neighbors, and purported former classmates, and came to the conclusion that, indeed, "many of the main episodes related by Ms. Menchú have either been fabricated or seriously exaggerated." His list of inaccuracies makes up the bulk of the article "Tarnished Laureate." But, as is the case with Stoll, his facts need to be taken with a grain—or better yet, a bucket—of salt.

A couple of examples shall suffice. It is not true, for instance, affirm Stoll and Rohter, that one of Rigoberta's brothers was burned alive by the army; Patrocinio was murdered with bullets and his body thrown into a common grave. Or: Rigoberta lies when she says she was illiterate when she dictated her book; in truth, from the ages of five to eight she attended a boarding school in Chichicastenango. Something may have been lost in translation, for the term "boarding school" does not have the same connotation in Latin America as it does in the United States. At any rate, is a death by bullets better than one by burning? Is partial illiteracy better than total ignorance? From these falsehoods readers ought to surmise that Rigoberta's heightened moral teachings have been discredited, diminished.

Rohter and the *New York Times* are not entirely to blame, though. What we have is a classic campaign to rewrite history. It calls to mind the technique used to attack the veracity of the Holocaust survivors: "but you just said you were in that camp, whereas the documents prove you were in another camp; and if that concentration camp did not exist, perhaps no concentration camps ever existed at all." The strategy is simple: humiliate the witness, make him stammer, cast the shadow of doubt on his testimony, so shame itself can be questioned.

Is the suffering of Maya Indians less painful because Rigoberta embellished her life story? In vain has the philosopher and Christian activist Paul Ricoeur written many large volumes about the relation between historical narrative and fictitious narrative. In vain have American academics produced one volume after another on *testimonio*, particularly on the question of veracity. Stoll summarily dismisses the issue. For him, Rigoberta's lies are the lies of all poor Guatemalans.

Rohter might be forgiven for confusing "autobiography," the term he uses exclusively to refer to Rigoberta's edited statements and "*testimonio*."

But not the right-minded Stoll. With 120 interviews and "archival research," he reinvents, in a single stroke, the essential problems at the heart of testimonial literature: the painter and the model are obviously one and the same. The echoes of this reinvention combined with a defamation campaign are astonishingly predictable. A major newspaper publishes the story as a piece of news. Another paper picks it up quoting an "authorized source" and "so-and-so's opinion." Then a third paper, or better yet a press agency, recycles the whole affair by pointing out that "the international press has highlighted. . . ." In the global media world, repetition begets truth. This, by the way, was the same method used in 1954 against Guatemala's ill-fated democratic government.

The act of discrediting Rigoberta is part of a larger campaign led by Guatemala's oligarchy and its foreign supporters. In this context, the murder of Monsignor Juan Gerardi in his home in April 1998 acquires greater meaning. Monsignor Gerardi, it is a well-known fact, had gathered crushing evidence against the military. He was ready to name names in the genocide of indigenous peoples. The answer was instantaneous and brutal: first his death, then his defamation. Rigoberta is undergoing a similar punishment for damaging the government's image. Because her strength lies in her international public image, nothing better than to unleash a smear campaign, not only against her but against what she represents. To say that she lied means that no genocide ever occurred in Guatemala, troops never went into villages, gathering women in schools and men in churches, and then systematically killing them to "raze the land" around the guerrillas.

To say that Rigoberta Menchú lied is taken to mean that no social injustice takes place in Guatemala. It means that children don't die of malnutrition, that their worm-filled bellies don't explode. It means that most people are not illiterate. To say that she lied is taken to mean that everybody lied: the church, Amnesty International, the UN, various human rights commissions. It means that it was all a mistake by the usual suspects designed to stain the good name of that marvelous tourist paradise "Guatemala" in which peace and order shall always reign.

Translated by Will Corral

The National Council of Mayan Education and Its Twenty-two Member Organizations Publicly Declare

Originally published in all Guatemalan newspapers on Friday, February 5, 1999

First

Its rejection of the campaign, based on a series of partial affirmations in the book by the North American anthropologist and journalist David Stoll, orchestrated to tarnish the 1992 Nobel Peace Prize winner and Guatemalan indigenous leader Rigoberta Menchú Tum, given that it is not only an attack against her personally, but an attack to demerit and question the recent history of our country, especially its darker and more painful side, full of human tragedy, that we have recently lived. Also, because of its clear intentions to minimize and exclude from history the truth about the victims.

Second

Its deep concern because the campaign against Rigoberta Menchú is not directed exclusively against her person, but also against the emerging Guatemalan indigenous movement. The idea is to wrest any credibility and reduce the possible role that indigenous peoples can play in their struggle to become subjects of their own and true history, as well as builders and participants, within the boundaries of legal rights, of a national and global future where the dignity of human beings is their only bastion.

Therefore

They manifest their deepest solidarity with their sister Rigoberta Menchú, as once again she is forced to remember and relive the pain suffered by her family, by the people of Guatemala, and, especially, by Guatemala's indigenous peoples during the last five hundred years. We also say to Rigoberta: Courage! This is another battle that will be won by history. We wish to remind her what Eduardo Galeano said: "it is the tree that gives fruit that receives all the stones."

Translated by Arturo Arias

A Hamburger in Rigoberta's Black Beans

Carolina Escobar Sarti

Prensa Libre, Guatemala City, Thursday, February 11, 1999

Academic David Stoll dedicated ten long years of his life to try to find "irrefutable proof" about the alleged lies to be found in the book *I, Rigoberta Menchú,* whose author's name we don't even have to spell out. Trying to find the straw that breaks the camel's back, he finally reached conclusions that he thinks are very serious and professional. To what purpose?

Based on archives that only the army could have provided him (because no other institution has those kinds of archives), and after interviewing 120 persons, he reached "professional" conclusions, such as that she had studied in a private boarding school of "wealthy señoritas" from the city, and that some of her relatives had not died in the way she described, but in other ways, among other things.

Of the 120 interviews, Stoll chose only the few he thought would be useful for his purposes and discarded many others that did not support his argument. Rigoberta worked with the nuns from the Belgian School, and she stood out enough so that they cared about teaching her how to read and write. Stoll used this information to argue that she was a regular student there. So her brother Petrocinio did not die as she said he did? Anyway, he ended his days in a common ditch, just like other members of her family.

Without a doubt, there are some incorrect facts in Rigoberta's testimonial, as in all biographies. These are obviously due to the circumstances in which it was written, the type of life she lived, and the point of view of the person telling the story. As a consequence, any text that comes out of an oral narration would have to be questioned, even the *Popol Vuh* [sacred book of the K'iché Maya], as well as the Bible. Any student of texts knows this. The important thing is not the small details, but the big themes revealed by the text, which undoubtedly form part of a real history. Clandestine cemeteries, secret "archives," and the testimonials compiled by REMHI are more than enough proof that the facts she talks about in her book are real.

That any person should choose to cast a pall on Rigoberta's words because of their racial and ethnic prejudice, or because of their social and economic status, can be understood (even if not accepted), but that an academic should spend ten long years of his life researching, without scientific rigor, a case in which he reaches conclusions of so little value is more than regrettable.

Obviously, the ideology of the author, as well as considerable economic help, supported this effort against Rigoberta. This ideology is evident in a previous book by Stoll, in which he blames the guerrilla for forcing Mayas to fight against the army. Regretfully, Stoll did not see the other side of the tortilla, because the army was composed of Mayas recruited against their will and forced to fight against people of their same ethnic group. Stoll also points out in his book that the thirty-six years of internal armed conflict were the responsibility of those who opposed military dictatorship, because the fault rests with those who disobey, who do not do what they are told by dictators. Without attempting to analyze what he claims, it goes without saying that any research that is not based on a rigorous, nonideologized method is no more than gossip or innuendo disguised in a scientific discourse.

As a person, Rigoberta is a survivor of pain, and the voice of the great majority of Guatemalans that never were able to speak out. As an image, she is what has allowed people to appreciate Mayas as people of flesh and blood, and not as tourist attractions, dolls in a window, or museum pieces. In a society in which many Ladinos still call all Mayas "my son" or "my daughter," "boy" or "girl," she has opened up new spaces, new opportunities unthinkable before her time.

When she was proposed for the Nobel prize, the opposition from traditional sectors of power was felt quite overtly. Throughout her trajectory, many have never even asked themselves why; they simply cannot accept that an "Indian" has won such an award, and they have tried to either devalue her or ignore her. But she gains more and more strength all the time and becomes one of those people who change history in a positive way, by moving the story of an entire nation toward more fair and just relations.

Anyway, it is not reasonable that a foreigner can just come in like that and try to tell us that he knows better how our history was made, and that hamburgers are better than black beans.

Translated by Arturo Arias

III
Responses and Implications

Responses and Implications

Menchú Tum's first book has been at the center of a major U.S. academic controversy ever since the start of the so-called cultural wars in the late 1980s, when Stanford University first included *I, Rigoberta Menchú* in its major revision of the "Great Books" canon that all incoming freshmen had to study, as Mary Louise Pratt explains in her essay. The asperity of that debate, abetted by the support that Stanford's own Hoover Institution threw behind the conservative cause, led to a chapter on this issue in Dinesh D'Souza's neoconservative text *Illiberal Education* (1991), titled "Travels with Rigoberta" to evoke the cold war rhetoric of "Communist fellow travelers." D'Souza's book was as controversial in 1991 as Stoll's became in late 1998. The polarization generated by the "cultural wars" seemed to exhaust itself, recede, or die down in the early 1990s, perhaps even weighted down by the downright silliness of many of the debates waged at the time by specialists on both sides of the divide. It appears now, however, that these issues never actually died, but merely remained dormant during the Clinton years, awaiting some new controversy to reawaken them.

This became even more evident on March 5, 1999, when the *Chronicle of Higher Education* published an article by Denise K. Prager revealing that David Horowitz's right-wing think tank, the Center for the Study of Popular Culture, was running advertisements in student newspapers at six universities (Brandeis, Columbia, Harvard, Yale, Illinois at Champaign-Urbana, and North Carolina at Chapel Hill) attacking professors who defended Menchú Tum's first book even though, according to Horowitz, it "has been labeled a fraud." The advertisement called Menchú Tum a "Marxist terrorist" who had been "exposed by Stoll as an intellectual hoax" and added that "this fraud was originally perpetrated and is still defended by your professors and by the Nobel Prize Committee."

The present essays are a response to these larger issues.

In Part III, we present fourteen academic essays analyzing the various angles of the relationship between Rigoberta Menchú Tum's first book, David Stoll's criticism of it, and the implications of their textual strategies in identity politics and Central America's struggle for affirmation, from a U.S. point of view as well as from a Guatemalan Ladino and Maya one.

In the first essay, "Why Write an Exposé of Rigoberta Menchú?", Carol A. Smith argues that few paid much attention to Stoll's previous efforts to make a general point about guerrillas being as dangerous to innocent peasants as the army in his first book on Guatemala. According to Stoll, this was in part because Menchú Tum's book played a major role in mythologizing the popular roots of Guatemala's revolutionary movement, displacing authentic indigenous perspectives about the violence. Stoll also claims that most of the conflicts over land were among Maya smallholders (254). Finally, Stoll argues that, in the world of human rights activism, journalism and scholarship are forcing Westerners to cede authority to non-Western peoples. As a consequence, truthful reportage and "objective" portrayals of complex situations have been discredited. Smith argues that Stoll is wrong on all these points. In her eyes, Stoll produced a polemic that comes less from scholarly conviction than from personal frustration.

In "Textual Truth, Historical Truth, and Media Truth: Everybody Speaks about the Menchús," Claudia Ferman affirms that although Stoll argues that "[h]uman rights is a legal discourse, but what propels its application around the world is solidarity—political identification with victims, dissidents, and opposition movements" (235), the argument unravels under the media rules of the press. It was Larry Rohter's article on the *New York Times*'s front page that put the controversy in motion, and not Stoll's articles or his book. Without Rohter's article, Stoll's book would have achieved only a very limited notoriety. Rohter's story purports to encompass its own independent journalistic research, creating a simulacrum of objective authentication for Stoll's book. The article, however, is in fact based largely on interviews conducted only a few days prior to its publication, and the majority of Rohter's sources are those provided by Stoll himself. Stoll's book is presented as a point of departure—a trigger—that motivates an investigation by the Central American and Caribbean correspondent for the newspaper.

The third article is "The Primacy of Larger Truths: Rigoberta Menchú and the Tradition of Native Testimony in Guatemala," by W. George Lovell and Christopher H. Lutz. The authors are "perplexed that Stoll's dissection of the debatable details of one individual's life serves to divert attention from the undeniable deaths of thousands of others." They go back to the times of the Conquest to establish a relationship between the documents that emerged during the sixteenth century and Menchú Tum's first book. They discover that some of the features that Stoll identifies as problematical in Menchú Tum's testimony have antecedents in Maya texts extant from the sixteenth century. Like Oliver LaFarge, they view the Conquest not as a distant, historical experience, but as a discernible, present condition. Conquest as a *way* of life lingers on as the central *fact* of life for the Maya half of Guatemala's national population. Menchú Tum cried out in the early 1980s when facing even worse violence, but because she could not appeal to an allegedly impartial Spanish king, her only outlet was to appeal to the international community.

In "Telling Truths: Taking David Stoll and the Rigoberta Menchú Exposé Seriously," Kay B. Warren argues that what seems to be at stake is the integrity of a public intellectual and human rights leader. She frames this within the context of the transformation of anthropology in the last decades of the twentieth century. Anthropologists will increasingly engage public intellectuals and other peers from the countries they study. With his empiricist approach, Stoll appears less aware that his work is marked by a set of unspoken narrative conventions. She then suggests that one way of understanding the Stoll–Menchú controversy is to see it as a clash of genres or paradigms for political expression. She concludes that David Stoll has not escaped the dilemma of being political any more than Menchú Tum has in her quest for justice. For Warren, this is an indication of the need to study multidimensional realities that, in their diversity and dynamism, call for multifaceted understandings.

In the fifth essay, "What Happens When the Subaltern Speaks: Rigoberta Menchú, Multiculturalism, and the Presumption of Equal Worth," John Beverley argues that it is important to recognize that Stoll is not saying that Menchú Tum is making up her story. But, says Beverley, he does argue that the inaccuracies, omissions, or misrepresentations undermine her ethical authority. This seems to him Stoll's underlying ideological agenda. By undermining Maya agency, Stoll is able to condemn the guerrilla struggle. But because Menchú Tum's book argues that armed struggle grew *necessarily* out of the conditions of repression in the indigenous communities, Stoll needs to prove those elements of her book wrong. Beverley then compares Stoll's positions with those of Guatemalan critic Mario Roberto Morales and argues that both participate in the logic of neutralization and containment of Maya agency; thus both texts frame subaltern agency and insurgency through the cultural assumptions and practices of the elites against which that particular agency is directed.

Doris Sommer's "Las Casas's Lies and Other Language Games" addresses David Stoll's language game of gathering information and shows how it slips into the game of giving advice. She claims that language games are about much more than telling facts and falsehoods. According to her, his language slips into playing games with policy considerations, and she wonders why he wants to shift public attention from the war to a struggle between disempowered groups. "What is his purpose in foregrounding current peasant conflicts while the country is urgently debating how to develop public institutions that acknowledge indigenous rights? Why are the competitions between peasants made so weighty in Stoll's story? . . . Does he pursue the truth?" She argues that any careful reader will note that Menchú Tum's book does not proselytize to potential comrades. According to Sommer, Menchú Tum's *testimonio* is ultimately an appeal for international support, and it is a lesson in the distinction between giving support and giving orders.

In "The Poetics of Remembering, the Politics of Forgetting: Rereading *I, Rigoberta Menchú*," Elzbieta Sklodowska focuses on the role of memory in the mediation of telling, writing, reading, and critical interpretation. In an era that has redirected its critical energy from investigating "the truth" toward the study "of inventing, making, creating or . . . constructing," Sklodowska finds the recent debate surrounding the "truthfulness" of Rigoberta Menchú's testimony oddly out of place. After all, she claims, recent studies across a broad range of disciplines in the humanities and social sciences focus on the "constructed" or "invented" nature of such notions as ethnicity, sexuality, nationality, and gender. If all these fit the category of "created objects," then it is logical to assume that Menchú Tum's testimonial narrative, too, should be approached with "a self-conscious acknowledgment of [its] artifactual nature." For her, the lesson from the current polemic is that the interpretation of *testimonio* is still relative both to ideological purpose and to disciplinary focus. Thus, where Stoll sees lies and fabrications, Sklodowska sees allegories and metaphors.

The eighth essay, "Whose Truth? Iconicity and Accuracy in the World of Testimonial Literature," is a defense of David Stoll's position by Daphne Patai. She believes that the hostile responses that have greeted David Stoll's critique of Menchú Tum's story reveal a depth of commitment on many readers both to Menchú Tum personally and to the book that is akin to hagiography. She then proceeds to compare Menchú Tum's testimonial to medieval lives of saints, which embody a higher kind of truth to which their hero is the witness. Patai is convinced that if the object of this controversy were not a figure revered by leftist "faithfuls," the reaction to the half-truths, misrepresentations, and outright falsehoods would be very different. For her, this implies that truth is being made subservient to politics, and it exposes the political corruption that exists at the heart of what she calls "the prolific academic industry on *testimonios*." Patai feels that we should not rush to give willing credence to stories just because they fit our preconceived ideas, while insisting on sound evidence for those that do not.

In "Menchú Tales and Maya Social Landscapes: The Silencing of Words and Worlds," Duncan Earle affirms that conditions in the Quiché province of Guatemala were even worse than the way Menchú Tum describes them in her book. For anthropologists like him, the religious split and the frequent animosities among Mayas were just part of the normal social landscape. The problem Earle sees with her book is that, though Menchú Tum is a Catholic Action affiliate, she often talks about issues that border on *costumbre* practices (traditional Maya religion), on the one hand, and paints a social scene of communalist unity among the Maya, on the other, thus flirting with an essentialist attitude. Still, he values the book for drawing world attention to an invisible holocaust. He feels that it should be situated in a context, that is, the divide between Catholicism and Maya religion that splits most Maya communities. He also feels that the book silenced the local internal conflicts for the sake of disclosing the horror lived in the country. Thus, he concludes with the need to consider other Maya voices without dismissing the position represented by Menchú Tum.

Allen Carey-Webb tells us in "Teaching, Testimony, and Truth: Menchú's Credibility in the North American Classroom" that most American high school and college students know very little about Guatemala. Considering the long history of American intervention in Central America, the general lack of knowledge about the region is disturbing. He argues that we need to recognize that most U.S. classrooms have only one cliché about Central America: poverty. Thus, reading Menchú Tum's testimonial can create a "cultural shock," to which a frequent response is rejection and retreat. Teachers of Menchú Tum's *testimonio* thus consider it vital that students connect critical understanding to personal and ethical responses. North American students do not understand why Menchú Tum does not portray indigenous Guatemalans as more assertive, more ready to fight back, and even more eager to join armed revolutionary movements. Carey-Webb concludes that teachers bringing Menchú Tum's text into the classroom should be lauded and supported, not publicly attacked.

"Between Silence and Lies: Rigoberta Va" by Ileana Rodríguez argues that David Stoll's book is situated within a long tradition. This begins with the arrival in 1524 of Spanish conquistador Pedro de Alvarado to the same area Stoll is researching. In Alvarado's attempt to describe his route to Hernán Cortés, he initiates a tradition characterized by obfuscation, approximation, and invention. According to Rodríguez, Stoll uses this same measure to prove step-by-step that the testimonial rendered by Menchú Tum is a kind of "red book" or "guerrilla communist manifesto" of the EGP, which therefore does not speak for "all" poor Guatemalans. Thus, Stoll's aim falls squarely within a tradition that tries to prove that the testimonials rendered by members of indigenous populations are not accurate. What is most important to her, however, is how Stoll repeats a five-hundred-year-old theme: that of being unable to discern between misunderstandings (that which translations are unable to account for), silences (that which informants are not ready to tell), and lies (that which informants believe the interrogator wants to hear). Rodríguez concludes that Stoll ends up blaming the victims.

"Menchú after Stoll and the Truth Commission," by Guatemalan Ladino scholar and writer Mario Roberto Morales, begins by stating that a new battle in the ongoing cultural war between "leftist" and "rightist" scholars about the subaltern subject and his/her struggles was launched by the "corroboration" of Stoll's facts by Rohter. It also reactivated, according to him, the ongoing cultural war in the "academic left" over the issues related to political correctness and identity politics, which allowed "leftist" scholars to avoid the academic debate that deals with the validity of only selected truth standards—their own. Menchú Tum was reframed and put in a different perspective by Stoll. Morales feels that, after Stoll and the truth commission, Menchú will never be the same because she has been humanized. He also believes that the debate will benefit the left, in the United States as well as in Guatemala, by retiring certain kinds of idealism that have outlived their usefulness. This suggests major new responsibilities for representatives of the subaltern such as Menchú and for intellectuals who want to support them.

A Maya point of view appears in the thirteenth essay, "Truth, Human Rights and Representation: The Case of Rigoberta Menchú," by Jak'alteko scholar Victor D. Montejo. He believes that anthropologists have imposed their own views on indigenous people, not respecting their truth in their own terms. He also recognizes the difficulties of "presenting" the facts of such a violent and genocidal war to the general public. Montejo feels that for those who, like himself, lived those moments of despair and massacres, the need to add details to ensure that the full magnitude of the event is actually portrayed in words is done to assure that one's voice is heard effectively. After stressing also the similarity between Menchú Tum's book and the accounts of those Maya who denounced the atrocities of the Conquest during the early sixteenth century, Montejo argues that to imagine the recent Guatemalan holocaust as a fictional epic would be to remove ourselves from the reality of a genocide that left two hundred thousand dead during the thirty-six years of armed conflict. He therefore concludes that what needs to be done is to reconstruct history with multiple voices and not with a single voice or truth.

Finally, in "The Battle of Rigoberta" David Stoll replies to his academic colleagues. Stoll remains adamantly convinced that Menchú Tum's story is not her own, but rather the version of events of the Guerrilla Army of the Poor (EGP). He then asks whether Menchú Tum's version was an inevitable response by the poor to oppression. In other words, Stoll's primary concern is not so much in unmasking Menchú Tum as in undermining the EGP's narrative, which claims that violence in Guatemala was the inevitable outcome of decades of military dictatorship, exploitation, oppression, and discrimination against the majority of its citizens. For Stoll, unless this story is questioned, the Guatemalan left will be on the moral high ground, and he is invested in fully discrediting not only the Guatemalan revolutionary left itself, but also the academic left in the United States. Stoll believes that Menchú Tum's book should still be read in the classroom, but it should not be assumed that everything it says is true.

Why Write an Exposé of Rigoberta Menchú?

Carol A. Smith

Originally published in *Latin American Perspectives*, November 1999

In the preface and first chapter of his book, David Stoll notes the following about Rigoberta Menchú's book. "There is no doubt about [her] most important points: that a dictatorship massacred thousands of indigenous peasants, that the victims included half of Rigoberta's immediate family, that she fled to Mexico to save her life, and that she joined a revolutionary movement to liberate her country" (1999, vii). She is only misleading or wrong about the "situation of her family and village life before the war" (ibid.), as well as about her presence at some of the situations she describes. He adds, "most of the pressure that forced the army and the government to negotiate [with the guerrilla, leading to a peace accord at the end of 1996] came from abroad, and it was generated by human rights imagery" (8) in which Rigoberta's book played an extremely important role (11). After these concessions, Stoll asks, "if Rigoberta is fundamentally right about what the army did, if her story expresses a larger truth about the violence, why dissect a personal account that is inevitably selective?" (xiv). He answers his question with the following four points.

First, the catastrophes that befell Rigoberta's family, her village, and other indigenous villages in western Guatemala were brought on by the revolutionary guerrilla as much as by the army. In the particular case of Rigoberta's village, Rigoberta's father, Vicente, appears to have invited the guerrilla there—or at least to have received them warmly.[1] Hence the targeting of him and his family by the army was quite natural. In the case of Vicente Menchú's death through conflagration at the Spanish embassy, it may be that the victims (who were protesting army murders of their relatives) immolated themselves.[2] More generally, guerrillas pursue "a high-risk strategy that usually ends in defeat and disillusion, after sacrificing peasants to romantic images of resistance" (10). Despite Stoll's previous efforts to make this general point about guerrilla warfare in his first book on Guatemala (Stoll 1993), few seem to have paid much attention—because of the influence of Rigoberta's book, according to Stoll (10).

Second, Rigoberta's testimony suggests that there was powerful support among indigenous people for the guerrilla, when in fact support was very weak. In this way Rigoberta played a major role in mythologizing the popular roots of Guatemala's revolutionary movement (xv). Although dissecting the legacy of guerrilla warfare may require "beating a dead horse" (x)—since even leftists no longer support a guerrilla strategy—Stoll feels it must still be done because Che Guevara and the third-world guerrilla continue to provide a romantic legacy to Western solidarity types and to the middle-class urbanites of the third world—giving them the illusion that they could wield real political power in an unjust world. More important, Rigoberta has displaced authentic indigenous perspectives about the violence—most of which equate the guerrilla with the army. "Rigoberta's version [of events] was so attractive to so many foreigners that Mayas who repudiated the guerrillas were often ignored or discounted" (xiv).

Third, Rigoberta's story depicts "noble Indians [being dispossessed by] evil [Ladino] landlords ... [which has] encouraged the Guatemalan Left and its foreign supporters to continue viewing the countryside as a contest among social classes, ethnic blocs, and structural forces" (xii). But the real problems of peasant villages are not these. Most contestation over land is not between Indians and large Ladino landholders but *among* Indian smallholders (254). The poverty of those peasant villages is brought on by the indigenous livelihood practices, which involve

> a degenerative process of population growth, slash-and-burn
> agriculture, and migration [to frontier areas] that is complicated, but
> not altered in any fundamental sense, by the Ladino-indígena conflict
> and inequitable land tenure to which Rigoberta gives so much attention.
> Romanticizing peasants is a hoary tradition that has the virtue of
> dramatizing their right to their land. (19)

Fourth, in the world of human rights activism, journalism, and scholarship, a "new standard of truth" (xv) is forcing Westerners to cede authority to the non-Western subaltern and to local witnesses—that is, to people such as Rigoberta—and thus to support those who are invariably apologists for one side or another in situations that cannot be reduced to two sides. Created under the influence of multiculturalism, postmodernism, and postcolonialism, this new criterion for veracity has discredited "objective" portrayals of complex situations. "The underlying problem [with Rigoberta's book] is not how Rigoberta told her story, but how well-intentioned foreigners have chosen to interpret it" (xiv). She is taken as the only authentic voice on "all poor Guatemalans" because as an Indian, a woman, and a poor Guatemalan, she (unlike Stoll) represents the "new standard of truth."

Given that Rigoberta and her story on the violence in Guatemala have been granted more authority in the West than David Stoll and his story, Stoll had to discredit her if he was to make his point. So I will take Stoll's arguments seriously and evaluate exactly what Stoll wants to assert in contradistinction to Rigoberta: that is, about guerrilla warfare, indigenous support for revolution in Guatemala, the extent of and reasons for indigenous poverty, and the impact of multiculturalism and the "new standards of truth" on the nature of reportage. We will also have to consider what exists in the way of evidence for the two positions. We cannot go to the same eyewitness (or hearsay) accounts Stoll used. But we can go to other accounts—not on the truthfulness of Rigoberta's testimony (which Stoll concedes "expresses a larger truth about the violence"), but on Stoll's points about the economic and political situation in Guatemala—the reasons he gives for writing his exposé of Rigoberta Menchú.

1. Did Guatemala's guerrillas recklessly target those indigenous areas least able to defend themselves? Were the guerrillas responsible for the brutal massacres carried out by the Guatemalan military governments? Can one equate the guerrilla and the army as two similar sources of violence affecting peasants? Stoll documents two guerrilla killings to nearly one thousand army killings in the *municipio* where he interviewed Rigoberta's neighbors and family members (Uspantán), which would lead most of us to wonder about the disparity. Stoll also wonders about it. After rejecting the argument of racism (which many specialists on Guatemala consider a powerful factor influencing Guatemalan violence

over the years [see Palma and Arenas 1999]), he argues that the "fanatical anti-communism of Guatemala's government that allowed it to slaughter so many men, women, and children could not have happened without the spectre of foreign communism as provided by the revolutionary theatrics from Cuba" (279). And because insurgents muddy the distinction between themselves and noncombatants, according to Stoll, "brutality toward civilians is the predictable result" (155). He does not ask why civilian massacres by armies were *much* less common everywhere else in Latin America where guerrilla warfare was waged—as in El Salvador and Nicaragua.

In the context of Cuba it is important to make several points that weaken Stoll's argument. First, the period when Guatemala's guerrilla "went public" was when insurgents in Nicaragua and El Salvador seemed likely to take power. The revolutionaries took power in Nicaragua in 1979. In El Salvador, there was ultimately a "brokered compromise" between the guerrilla and the army—but virtually all experts agree that the insurgents (strongly supported in the countryside) would almost certainly have won had the United States not poured billions of dollars into El Salvador's army (Dunkerley 1988). The strength of these two other revolutionary movements in Central America certainly affected guerrilla strategy in Guatemala. Guatemala had always been considered a more questionable revolutionary theater because of the time it would take to recruit the indigenous population to a mixed-ethnic revolutionary strategy. When revolution seemed imminent in Nicaragua and El Salvador, Guatemalan revolutionaries—a large middle-class group since mid-century because of Guatemala's murderous dictatorships—felt they could not hold back. Much more significant than this, however, is that the Guatemalan insurgents were not supplied with the arms they expected from the Cubans, unlike the insurgents in Nicaragua and El Salvador. That fact was enormously important to the fate of Guatemala's revolutionary movement, especially its ability to "protect" its peasant recruits.

I argue later in this essay that the guerrillas appear to have been relatively successful in recruiting Indians to their cause. But they were unable to arm them, which left the peasant population extremely vulnerable to the army. Of course, at the time the guerrilla announced their presence, they had no reason to expect that they would be unable to arm their recruits. The area in which the EGP (Guerrilla Army of the Poor—

the only guerrilla group really discussed by Stoll) worked, moreover, was a frontier area, close to the Mexican border, over which civilians as well as the guerrilla could presumably escape. The other peasant-recruiting group (ORPA), worked in a more vulnerable area but took far fewer public actions—though it did charge a war tax on the large plantations of the south coast.[3] It is difficult, then, to blame the EGP for being reckless. It was more successful than it expected and it did not get the arms it had been promised.

So who is at fault for the murders and exile of more than 150,000 Mayan peasants in Guatemala? Most experts on Guatemala consider the army responsible, especially because it showed a consistent tendency to avoid encounters with the guerrilla, preferring to attack unarmed civilians. I can think of no one other than Stoll who would blame persons like Vicente Menchú, even if he were a "guerrilla collaborator." Many solidarity types blame the Cubans as much as Stoll does, but for reasons quite different from Stoll's—the Cuban failure to arm the Guatemalans. Those who know Guatemalan politics well blame the United States for replacing one of Guatemala's first democratically elected governments with a lawless military government in 1954, instilling Guatemalan elites with an enormous fear of "communism" together with the certainty that the United States would do whatever needed to support them against communism, that is, helping to arm, train, and provide intelligence to what had formerly been a poorly organized army, and advising that army about guerrilla counterinsurgency techniques—such as drying up the ocean (killing civilians) to eliminate the fish (the guerrilla). (Stoll occasionally mentions U.S. guilt in the situation, but invariably undercuts it.) There are, it would seem, a surplus of people and groups to blame. I personally see the situation as a national tragedy that had been brewing ever since a military government took power in 1954. Military dictatorships motivated various forms of leftist protest, nonviolent as well as violent, and mark the period when death squads began to eliminate political activists, union leaders, indigenous leaders, and Christian Democrats. Many such murders occurred before there was a guerrilla presence. Racism accounts for the nature of the "final solution" in the 1980s— the huge massacres of indigenous people.

2. Let us now consider how much the peasants blame the guerrilla for what happened to them. Stoll bases his entire analysis of indigenous response to the guerrilla and army on information from four

municipios—three in the Ixil area plus neighboring Uspantán, where Rigoberta's family lived. Hence I cannot use information I have about the impact of and support for guerrilla warfare in other parts of Guatemala (mainly Quezaltenango, Chimaltenango, and San Marcos), where circumstances were quite different. Instead, I use a recent Ph.D. study undertaken by Paul Kobrak (1997) in a *municipio* neighboring the Ixil, Aguacatán, to discuss changes in support for the guerrilla there. In some respects Paul Kobrak, whom Stoll seems to admire, is no more flattering to the guerrilla operating in Aguacatán (also the EGP) than Stoll is of those in the areas he covers. But he makes two extremely important points that Stoll fails to make. First, he observes that support for the guerrilla in the remote and very poor K'iché-speaking hamlets[4] was initially quite strong, even though the guerrilla spent relatively little time in the area. Locals told him that the entire population could have gone either way (Kobrak 1997, 142)—that is, with the guerrilla or with the army in mid-1982—but after careful consideration, as a group decided that it was much more dangerous to go with the guerrilla because of the greater army brutality. Nonetheless, a large number of them joined the CPRs (civilian resistance communities) in the Ixil area (191).

Second, and most important, Kobrak provides a historical context for the period when he was interviewing survivors in Aguacatán (roughly the same time Stoll was working in the nearby Ixil area). As Kobrak describes it, the male civilian population had been so militarized and exposed to army propaganda under the civil patrols (groups of village men made responsible for "protecting" their communities under the direction and control of the army) that they had significantly reconstructed their local history. Like Stoll, Kobrak notes the common use by villagers of the phrase "[we were] between two armies" (130), but he observes that this local construction was a way for peasants in the patrols to "neutralize" their own position in the war:

> In the 1990s context in which I collected these reconstructions of the violence, the army was the preeminent power in Guatemala, having decisively defeated the guerrilla movement and established their civil patrols throughout the countryside. The army had committed far more abuse against the civilian population, but the army's victory made it easy (and satisfying) to vilify the rebels. With their participation in the civil patrol system [which involved carrying out many brutalities ordered by the army] villagers had a strategic and psychic need to justify collaboration with the army. Residents of civil patrol villages [and this included

virtually all villages in the five *municipios* discussed here] are most comfortable with rhetoric that equates the two sides, putting them in the middle as unwilling participants in the war, as spectators to the repression, rather than as participants. (132)

The point here is that in the late 1980s and 1990s it was virtually impossible to obtain a clear view of how villagers in the affected regions (where village civil patrols operated twenty-four hours a day from 1982 to 1996) viewed the guerrilla or the army. Historical memory in a time of extreme violence is volatile, all the more so when the victorious side takes direct control of village life. (See Hale [1997], who critiques Stoll's first book on exactly this point.) Almost certainly the victims of army brutality, who then had to become directly *complicit* in army brutality, are going to put a different construction on their history, on the army, and on the guerrilla—who are blamed by the army for all of their suffering. I do not question that support for the guerrilla dropped off dramatically everywhere (including the less affected areas I know best) after it became clear that the guerrilla were unable to protect the people exposed to army retaliation. Even the redoubtable EGP guerrilla comandante Mario Payeras—who in 1984 broke away from the EGP to cofound a noncombative group—thought the EGP strategy was a disastrous failure (Payeras 1991). But that does not mean there was never support for the guerrilla in Guatemala—or that Guatemalans blamed the guerrilla as much as the army.

What most differentiates Kobrak from Stoll is that Kobrak makes it clear that indigenous peasants were not the dupes of either the army or the guerrilla. Many Indians supported the guerrilla, but changed their position when they saw what happened to guerrilla supporters and sought army protection. Others decided to flee the country under guerrilla protection. Obviously, not all succeeded in finding protection. But according to Kobrak, the peasants had a fairly clear idea of what they were doing—they were not, as Stoll would have it, "lured into confronting the state" (xii) in the absence of knowledge about the state, which they had confronted in various ways for more than two hundred years. From what I know of indigenous peasants in western Guatemala, very few were completely ignorant of Guatemala's violent political history in the 1970s and early 1980s.

3. The question now becomes, How intolerable was the poverty of Guatemalan Indians in the early 1980s and what were its causes? This is

something on which institutions such as the World Bank have information and comparative statistics; the World Bank is also a good source for an evaluation of Guatemala's land distribution and its significance, because it rarely makes revolutionary recommendations. The World Bank reports in a study done just before the peace accords were signed (1995), that on virtually every indicator of poverty (income, malnutrition, infant death, life expectancy, literacy) Guatemala was close to or the most poor of all Latin American countries in both time periods. In 1995, the poverty rate of all Indians was 93 percent, whereas the poverty rate of urban Ladinos was 40 percent. Even when they controlled for all the poverty indicators—such as rural locality and education—Indians had a 15 percent higher chance of being poor than Ladinos did. More than three-quarters of the indigenous population (81 percent) lived in "extreme poverty," defined as lacking the income needed to purchase sufficient food.

My own work before the violence showed (as Stoll notes)[5] that many fewer indigenous people in the western highlands were migrating to the south coast to work seasonally for wages on plantations than before. But that does not mean that they were prospering. My work has always emphasized the significant differences between peasants in the periphery (most of highland San Marcos, Huehuetenango, and El Quiché, which includes the area covered by Stoll and Kobrak) and peasants in the core (the area near Quezaltenango). (See, e.g., Smith 1978, 1989.) Virtually no peasants from the core had migrated to plantations since the 1960s, only peasants from the periphery. Commercial diversification occurred in both parts of western Guatemala in the 1970s, but large numbers of people from the periphery still worked on the plantations and many in the core were becoming increasingly indebted. The statistics on poverty from the World Bank, which covers both the previolence and postviolence periods, speak for themselves—*the majority of indigenous people were not getting enough food to eat!*

What about the causes of poverty? Was it limited indigenous access to economic and political power, caused by Ladino monopolies, which is what I argued (Smith 1978)? Was it the extremely unequal distribution of land, as Rigoberta argued? Or was it uncontrolled population growth among the Maya and their destructive farming practices, as Stoll argues? My data on 124 *municipios* in western Guatemala from 1976 showed a higher correlation between indigenous poverty and Ladino monopolies than with any other municipal variable (e.g., population density, place in region, average indigenous landholding, economic specialty). But Stoll could dismiss these data with the argument that I am simply another scholar who "views the countryside as a contest among social classes, ethnic blocs, and structural forces" (vii)—thus supporting the leftist interpretation of economic reality.

The World Bank highlights land distribution—which puts it in the same "structuralist" category Rigoberta is in. In Guatemala's 1979 agricultural census, the Gini Index for land distribution was calculated to be 85.9, higher than any other Latin American case. In fact, it rivals land distribution in prereform (1969) Peru. In all land-size groupings, Indians held significantly smaller amounts of land than Ladinos. The section of the report on land distribution concludes:

> The dissatisfaction with poverty and inequality precipitated an armed conflict that has lasted, with varying degrees of intensity, for 40 years and has been estimated to have cost the lives of approximately 100,000 people and displaced many more. Now that negotiations are underway to end the conflict, Guatemala must search for alternatives to violence and repression to deal with problems and inequality that, in many respects, are as severe as they were at the start of the conflict. (World Bank 1995, v–vi)

The World Bank's three main recommendations for dealing with poverty and inequality include providing greater access to land for the poor and supporting an increase in tax revenue to improve education (human capital) and infrastructure in the rural areas. There is no mention of introducing new ("less destructive") farming practices or population control measures, policy issues with which the World Bank is quite familiar.

If land distribution is as important as the World Bank (and Rigoberta) think, why do peasants fight each other over small amounts of it rather than fight the few major landowners in the country (only 2.5 percent of the farm owners own more than 65 percent of the land)? This is Stoll's question. By implication, the countless squabbles over small amounts of land waste time, energy, and resources that could be better spent in a more "rational" attack on the big landlords. Stoll apparently does not know what happens to peasants who attack major landlords in Latin America. Almost everywhere they end up in jail—if they are lucky; as often they end up dead. Robert Williams (1986) has a brilliant description of political relations between *latifundistas* and *minifundistas* for all of Central America, including Costa Rica. Even without the guerrilla menace, large landlords in Latin America viciously attack peasants who compete for their land, usually with state support. In peasant battles, by contrast, a persistent smallholder (such as Vicente Menchú) has at least a 50 percent chance of winning against his neighbor.[6] Most of us who work with peasants do not assume, as Stoll believes we do, that peasants are noble. But we have discovered that they are relatively rational. I find it very odd that Stoll asks the question he does about struggles between smallholders. Does he believe that his (weakly supported) argument that these struggles are more common than struggles against major landlords will prove that land inequality is not a major problem in Guatemala?

Stoll's claim that the real development issues in Guatemala are uncontrolled population growth and ecologically destructive farming practices is much more serious. He is quite right that Guatemala's (especially its rural, indigenous) population has a high rate of population growth. But what he appears not to appreciate is the difference between cause and effect. Most population experts believe that the underlying *cause* of high population growth is poverty and a primitive economy—where most income is made through expenditures of raw, unskilled labor. It is now well known that in economies where the rates of infant mortality, income inequality, *and land inequality* are low, where most children are sent to secondary school (true of a very small minority in Guatemala), and where most women work outside of the home (again, Guatemala's rate is very low), birthrates fall dramatically. In other words, transforming a country with a high population growth rate calls for a "revolutionary" economic reform that Guatemala may well never see—for the only political sector that has supported such an economic policy has been the left. Such a radical economic reform in Central America has been most fully achieved in Costa Rica (through land reform, high taxation, and high educational achievement), where the birthrate has significantly fallen. High birthrates are not a church or cultural problem, as Stoll implies. Catholic Italy currently has the lowest birthrate in the world, well below national reproduction.

A similar relationship exists, with some differences, between wealth and ecologically sound farming practices. Farmers have to be rich enough to be able to afford ecologically sound farming. Or they have to have

been pushed out of full-time farming. The farmers of San Miguel Totonicapán, where no one has had enough land to be a full-time farmer
for more than fifty years, are the only Guatemalan farmers I know who
have the time to terrace, rotate trees over their fields, and use organic
fertilizer. Those who are clearing new land in frontier areas (the situation of Vicente Menchú and others in areas that Stoll knows) are probably in the worst possible situation in this regard.[7] They have insufficient labor, very little infrastructural support, and a pressing need to
produce enough to keep their families alive each year. Under such circumstances, clear-cutting is typical—whether undertaken by a small-
holding peasant or by a larger plantation. Regardless of whether peasants
or plantations are the worst offenders in this situation, it seems rather
bizarre to blame Guatemalan peasants for their poverty by noting their
"destructive" farming practices (not to mention uncontrolled population
growth). Stoll gives no review of the literature on either issue, and I very
much doubt that his analysis of Guatemala's poverty would be accepted
as it stands for an M.A. or Ph.D. by any social-science department em-
phasizing development issues. Blaming the victims for their poverty in
the case of Guatemala also seems utterly gratuitous.

4. Objective reportage, according to Stoll, is no longer appreciated
in the social sciences, heavily influenced by literary theory, postmoder-
nity, and a general postcolonial or multicultural uncertainty about the
trustworthiness of white first-world men. Witnesses who represent the
subaltern—people like Rigoberta, who are from oppressed classes in
third-world countries—are better sources on the oppressed and on the
meaning of their lives than are outside reporters. This has given Rigoberta an "unfair" advantage over Stoll—the objective reporter, just trying to get at the truth. Perhaps the best response to this charge would
be a brief synopsis of the discussion and debate around "situated knowledges" in feminist theory. This literature pointed out that men could not
be trusted to represent women, that white women could not be trusted
to represent black women, that anthropologists from the imperial centers could not be trusted to represent the "natives"—not because they
were less "objective," but because everyone is positioned and situated in
the world with bias so that they cannot fully see the reality of another
world. The subaltern herself sees the world through a distinct positionality or bias and thus needs to be in dialogue with people and scholars
who represent other positions and positionalities. Hence the encourage-

ment by most contemporary scholars to bring new and different voices into the canon that have not previously been represented—not just Marx, Weber, and Durkheim on oppression and exploitation, for example, but Marx, Weber, Durkheim, and Rigoberta.

Most scholars consider the argument about new voices, new ways of representing the world, new ways of seeing such things as truth and responsibility to be a very progressive move. There may have been excesses. And it is not always a sure bet that the representative from the third world will have a more useful take on its problems than a representative from the first world. But David Stoll's very positionality in the debate he has set up between himself and Rigoberta Menchú makes it seem all the more important that Rigoberta exists as one (not the only) voice for "all poor Guatemalans," and that Stoll exists to represent the illusory truth of "objective" reportage.

I have used Rigoberta's book for many years in my classes and have always emphasized the phrase she uses on her first page: "[T]his is my testimony... [but] I'd like to stress that it's not only *my* life, it's also the testimony of my people.... My story is the story of all poor Guatemalans. My personal experience is the reality of a whole people" (Burgos 1983, 1). I tell my students to read the book as if it is a general rather than particular depiction of life in Guatemala, noting that in *testimonios* it is typical for a person to present the experience of a whole people as if it happened to a single individual—because that may be the only way outsiders can understand and empathize with another way of life. Even though I do not teach—and I doubt many students go away with—the literalist reading that Stoll feels compelled to refute, my students learn a great deal about a life of poverty, politicization, and struggle in Guatemala by reading Rigoberta's book.

We read many other things, many different kinds of analyses, at the same time. On the issues of poverty and revolution we read World Bank statistics, a David Stoll article, and Robert Williams (1986). We also read articles by one of the first and most important critics of guerrilla strategy in Latin America, Timothy Wickham-Crawley (1991, 1992) and Mario Payeras (1983), who provides a frank account of guerrilla brutality.[8] I include a wonderful selection from Barrington Moore (1966) on the costs of peasant revolutions postponed. Hardly a radical, Moore describes the high costs of *any kind* of peasant struggle, and then compares those costs to the costs of unfulfilled revolution—in terms of deaths by starvation, malnutrition, class and state murder and oppression, and delay in achieving political and economic "modernity." The point is that in most courses where various new subaltern or postcolonial voices are introduced, they are almost always introduced in dialogue with very different perspectives. In the future I will probably even introduce chapters from Stoll's exposé. The "postmodern and/or postcolonial" move to add new voices to our experience is not an attempt to *restrict* the repertoire of perspectives, it is an attempt to expand it to include voices never before represented. Only reactionaries in the academy object to this move.

One reason we now emphasize the complexity of truth and the need to hear many voices rather than a single "objective" source is that facts do not speak for themselves, they always have to be interpreted. Let me illustrate this point with one simple example from Stoll's book. Stoll asserts that Guatemala's conservatives immediately recognized the falsehoods in Rigoberta's testimony (198), and it is almost certainly "factually true" that most did reject her depiction of indigenous life in Guatemala from the beginning. But on what basis did they recognize falsehoods? What do Guatemala's conservatives know about Rigoberta's or Guatemalan peasant life? I was always shocked at how very little they knew. What makes Stoll think that their rejection of Rigoberta's testimony was anything other than a statement of their political convictions? To present conservative knowledge as some kind of bolstering "factual" evidence for his own position without any interpretation of who the characters are and why they believe what they do is quite ludicrous. It seems to be little more than a rhetorical device—of which there are a great many in Stoll's book. It nonetheless rests on an absurd kind of "truth."

For this reason, then, I have to conclude that if forced to take out one of the perspectives listed above from a course on Central America, it is more likely to be Stoll than any of the others. The reason is that he is the least clearly positioned of all the authors. He *is* positioned—having at least an antileft, antipostmodern, antistructuralist, and antisolidarity position—but he claims not to be positioned and then tries to bolster weak scholarship on the larger issues (Guatemala's guerrillas, historical memory, poverty and its causes, and multiculturalism) with spurious claims of objectivity on unrelated phenomena (who Rigoberta's father battled over land). Stoll basically produces a polemic about Rigoberta and his four issues, which comes less from scholarly conviction and more from personal frustration about losing a monopoly on authority. This,

I think, explains why Stoll wrote an exposé of Rigoberta Menchú. One wonders if he will try to topple all the alternative voices on Guatemala with exposés.

Notes

1. Stoll argues that Vicente Menchú had little connection to CUC, a civilian front of the EGP, but may have been directly connected to the EGP. Although the chapter treating Vicente and the EGP makes it clear that the evidence supporting this allegation is very thin (a few neighbors' accusations versus denials by many others), this does not prevent Stoll from describing Vicente as a guerrilla collaborator without qualification later in the book (277). This is not atypical of the way Stoll argues.

2. This is only Stoll's speculation, for which there is little to no evidence—though Stoll devotes a chapter to it. Stoll's evidence is not always so weak, but the mixture of arguments on which there is some, none, and a great deal of evidence makes his case seem much stronger than it actually is.

3. According to Stoll, any army is likely to treat with brutality any population whose loyalty is uncertain (154). Yet the army carried out no massacres of the plantation populations, certainly not of plantation owners, even though their revolutionary "taxes" were much more substantial than the small amounts of subsistence goods peasants provided the guerrilla. In other words, it is far too simplistic to see army brutality against civilians as a mere effect of their uncertainty about the enemy.

4. These K'iché speakers were the poorest people in Aguacatán, unlike the situation of K'iché speakers in Uspantán, thus contradicting Stoll's essentialist image of the K'iché (17), Rigoberta's ethnic-language group. The people living near the pueblo in Aguacatán had very little contact with the EGP, though some of them were still heavily attacked by the army.

5. This is about all Stoll uses in the way of evidence for his claim that the economic situation of Indians was improving right before the revolutionary attempt. He essentially has no data on indigenous poverty.

6. Stoll makes an enormous point of the fact that Vicente Menchú mainly fought his indigenous in-laws over land rather than large Ladino-owned estates in Uspantán, as Rigoberta suggests in her book. Although this might very well be the case, it is quite likely that Rigoberta's father spoke often and critically of the large estate owners in the vicinity, several of whom were known to pay extremely low wages to their indigenous workers.

7. Throughout his book, Stoll describes Vicente Menchú as the owner (holder of a title) of 2,753 hectares—an enormous amount of land in the context of Guatemala—and continuing to fight for 151 hectares with his in-laws. It appears, however, from Stoll's own discussion, that Menchú is holding the title for at least forty-five families, if not more, as is typical in an INTA (National Institute for Agrarian Transformation) land-settling operation; that most of the land except the disputed piece is poorly watered; and that making this land productive will take decades of hard labor.

8. On the logic and negative features of guerrilla warfare, Wickham-Crawley develops a much stronger and more reasoned argument than Stoll by presenting a fuller picture of variation. He notes, for example, that Guatemala's record of peas-

ant massacre and murder by the government in both the 1960s and the 1980s went well beyond the records established in any other case of guerrilla warfare. Stoll uses Wickham-Crawley to support his argument that guerrilla warfare is costly to peasants, but never mentions this caveat about the case of Guatemala.

Bibliography

Dunkerley, James. 1988. *Power in the Isthmus: A Political History of Modern Central America*. New York: Verso.

Hale, Charles R. 1997. "Consciousness, Violence, and the Politics of Memory in Guatemala." *Current Anthropology* 18: 817–38.

Kobrak, Paul. 1997. "Village Troubles: The Civil Patrols in Aguacatán, Guatemala." Ph.D. diss., University of Michigan.

Menchú, Rigoberta, with Elisabeth Burgos-Debray. 1984. *I, Rigoberta Menchú: An Indian Woman in Guatemala*. Trans. Ann Wright. London: Verso.

Moore, Barrington. 1966. "Revolutions of the Oppressed: A Case Made." In *Social Origins of Dictatorship and Democracy*. Boston: Beacon Press.

Palma Murga, Gustavo, Charles R. Hale, and Clara Arenas Bianchi, eds. 1999. *Identidades y racismo en Guatemala*. Guatemala City: AVANCSO.

Payeras, Mario. 1983. *Days of the Jungle*. New York: Monthly Review Press.

———. 1991. *Los fusiles de octubre*. Mexico City: Juan Pablos.

Smith, Carol A. 1978. "Beyond Dependency Theory: National and Regional Patterns of Underdevelopment in Guatemala." *American Ethnologist* 5: 574–617.

———. 1989. "Survival Strategies among Petty Commodity Producers in Guatemala." *International Labour Review* 128: 791–813.

Stoll, David. 1993. *Between Two Armies in the Ixil Towns of Guatemala*. New York: Columbia University Press.

———. 1999. *Rigoberta Menchú and the Story of All Poor Guatemalans*. Boulder, Colo.: Westview Press.

Wickham-Crawley, Timothy P. 1991. *Exploring Revolution: Essays in Latin American Insurgency and Revolutionary Theory*. Armonk, N.Y.: M. E. Sharpe.

———. 1992. *Guerrillas and Revolution in Latin America*. Princeton, N.J.: Princeton University Press.

Williams, Robert. 1986. *Export Agriculture and the Crisis in Central America*. Chapel Hill: University of North Carolina Press.

World Bank. 1995. *Guatemala: An Assessment of Poverty*. Report no. 12313. Washington, D.C.

Textual Truth, Historical Truth, and Media Truth

Everybody Speaks about the Menchús

Claudia Ferman

> They go so far as to accept a man who is not affected at all by some
> particular moment in the past as the right man to describe it.
>
> —Friedrich Nietzsche

On December 15, 1998, the *New York Times* published a front-page story
titled "Tarnished Laureate: Nobel Winner Finds Her Story Challenged."
Authored by Larry Rohter, the article vigorously reactivated a series of
debates that extend far beyond Rigoberta Menchú, though this celebrated
Guatemalan remains central to them. The debates raise two pivotal issues:
first, the manner in which "truth" is constructed in the various discursive practices involved in the controversy; and second, the way in which
this controversy illuminates the complex reading contract presupposed
by texts that we now classify as *testimonio*. In essence this controversy
asks us to revisit the very definition of *testimonio*.

Inquiring about the truth or truthfulness of a *testimonio* is a valid response to it. In previous work, I argue that testimonial texts are characterized by the particular "reading contract" that lies implicitly embedded in the very act of receiving the text.[1] In what Algirdas Julien Greimas
calls "a veridiction contract," the reader "has to be persuaded to interpret the discourse as truth" (Sklodowska 1996, 88). *Testimonio* controls
the communicative conditions in which the reading act is performed,
involving the reader in continuous "acts of faith," through a series of devices that I term "conditions of authentication." These conditions (or
the "protocol system," to use Gérard Genette's category) include (1) the

introductions written by the mediator/interlocutor and presented at the beginning of the book; (2) the fact that the testimonial subject presents herself as a "plural subject," a part of the whole, and thus presupposes the sense of historical representation;[2] (3) the particular data that ascribes historical weight to the text—for example, the Nobel Peace Prize for Menchú rather than the prize in literature; (4) the presence in these texts of pictures of the *testimoniantes* on the cover, the back cover, or inside the text; and (5) the context in which these texts are presented, such as the university classroom. These conditions of authentication guarantee that the reader, who is aware of the specific reading act in which he/she is involved, cannot escape facing the "long-suffering" (pathos) presented in the text because it comes without the comforting alibi of fiction, the place of the imagined. Both the extent and the limitations of these conditions of authentication have been discussed thoroughly by Sklodowska. Of particular concern here are the response mechanisms triggered in the reader by these conditions and their implications for the interpretation of a text.

Fiction does not ask the reader to make these continuous "acts of faith"; it calls, instead, for the suspension of disbelief—the Aristotelian "deception" necessary for catharsis. Such suspension of disbelief is inherently associated with the reader's processes of identification with the narrative voice. As Sommer and many others have noted, the textuality of women's *testimonio* rejects the reader's "imperialist substitution" of himself/herself with the protagonist, through the process of "*estar con la hablante* [being with the speaker]" and not "*ser ella* [being the speaker]" (142). In other words, *testimonio* makes us marginal observers whether we feel linked in solidarity with its message or we regard it from a removed, distant, even antagonistic viewpoint.[3] Thus, unlike a fictive text that presupposes various processes of identification, the positioning of the reader is absolutely central to the very act of reading *testimonio*.[4]

As many others have noted, *testimonio* may also operate as a mirror to the reader. Reading a *testimonio* may compel the reader to reexamine his/her approach to issues beyond those presented in the text. In his introduction to *The Real Thing*, Gugelberger summarizes, "While not necessarily making the subaltern 'visible,' *testimonio* has helped to make ourselves visible to ourselves" (3). John Beverley seems to be making a similar claim when he writes of "the possibility of transculturation *from below*," and asks readers "to worry less about how *we* appropriate Menchú, and to understand and appreciate more how she appropriates *us* for her purposes" (1996 272–73).[5]

Actually, *testimonio*'s specular condition and the positioning it demands from the reader are both closely intertwined, but they do not necessarily occur in obligatory sequence. As I already stated, if *positioning* is an intrinsic component of all acts of reading *testimonio*, and consequently unavoidable, the specular condition lies more in the reader's willful act than in the text itself. In *Rigoberta Menchú and the Story of All Poor Guatemalans*, David Stoll is particularly aware of the close relationship between a reading's output and a reader's identity, and of the impact this relationship has on meaning. Actually, much of Stoll's book is an effort to assert that an interpretation of Rigoberta Menchú's text (and therefore any other testimonial text) is not independent of the reader. He argues that "[h]uman rights is a legal discourse, but what propels its application around the world is solidarity—political identification with victims, dissidents, and opposition movements" (235). I will return to this later, so it is possible to focus on the other aspect I intend to discuss here: the construction of truth in the context of controversy.

In the controversy that was unleashed on December 15, 1998, the argument unravels under the media rules of the global written and oral mass press.[6] Indeed, David Stoll's book was not the catalyst for the flurry of articles in newspapers and magazines, and the appearances on radio news shows. Rather, Larry Rohter's article on the *New York Times*'s front page put the controversy in motion. As an anthropologist, Stoll's investigation of Rigoberta Menchú's *testimonio* and the civil war in Guatemala had already circulated through various channels (conferences, articles, and Stoll's own distribution of his writings to scholars and people connected with Rigoberta Menchú's *testimonio*), and it had already received several rebuttals.[7] The academic community and many of the players central to the writing of *I, Rigoberta Menchú* were aware of Stoll's contentions, and therefore the publication alone of *Rigoberta Menchú and the Story of All Poor Guatemalans* could not have drawn immediate attention, nor have had the impact it has attained.

Stoll's book exhibits obvious methodological problems. It is inconclusive in most of its inquiries—it presents tentative theses that many times cancel each other, uses vaguely defined or completely undefined sources, and it is extremely clear and direct in terms of its political agenda. These characteristics weaken the possibility of its academic success and make difficult a broad and extensive impact. Without Rohter's article, Stoll's book, like his previous contributions, would have achieved only a very limited notoriety.

Rohter's story encompasses its own investigative report and is therefore not offered as a simple book review. Rohter's investigation creates a simulacrum of authentication for Stoll's book, even though the article is based largely on interviews conducted only a few days prior to its publication, and the majority of Rohter's sources are those provided by Stoll himself. The *New York Times* story follows the production rules of mass communication, and as such it embraces and expresses its media charges. Stoll's book is presented as a point of departure—a trigger—that motivates an investigation by the Central American and Caribbean correspondent for the newspaper.

In other words, when the editor in chief decides to send a correspondent to Guatemala to corroborate the "veracity" of Stoll's sources and decides to publish this "verification," a message, a content, is generated. This message stands independently from Stoll's text and separate from the central protagonists, but it is constitutively associated with media dynamics. Within such media dynamics, the front page of a powerful publication is suited far better than Stoll's text to reproduce itself horizontally and uninterruptedly through its global reach, and vertically through the political and institutional power apparatuses.

Consequently, the controversy's inception is locked to the publication of the *Times*'s article—and not the other way around. In its present terms, the controversy does not precede the article, despite the ten long years that Stoll claims he took to develop his inquiry. This fact, however, does not imply that the onset of the controversy is independent of Stoll. As he states in his book, he "can communicate with some of the most influential media in the world" (181), a fact that has played an obvious role here.

What I see as the controversy itself is the fact that an impressive amount of global media has considered it necessary to discuss the "truth" in Menchú's account, interview those who played a role in the writing of *I, Rigoberta Menchú,* and publish the press conferences of the Nobel laureate. Even more than that, commentaries, reactions, and responses have saturated the Web. The controversy is a media output that is shaped by its rules and therefore permeated by its nature. Information in the media is presented in a highly processed and compact form, and it is characterized by immediacy and definite focus. These engineered, instantaneous fragments are generally disconnected from the direct experience they describe—and even from the practical and the ordinary. These highly interpreted units of information must be concise; otherwise, they cannot be processed by the receiver because of the mechanical conditions that define such communication. The units themselves are massively disseminated by owned channels, to which access is given (or denied) by varied commercial transactions, even though they usually present themselves in a vacuum. This process of commercial exchange makes it impossible for any channeled information to be removed from the global economic system of media production, because this is the very system that provides the routes for the creation, dissemination, and multiplication of information. Receiving, processing, and consolidating (including the receiver's methods of identifying information units and the dual operation of storing or discarding information) determine what I will call *residue*. This *residue*, the simulacrum of information, is operative— we make public and private decisions with it; we vote, we dream, we gossip—and we also buy a book.

Stoll's book as an academic text is vaguely established in the field of anthropology (although from my perspective it would be more comfortably placed in the field of political science or investigative journalism). Its central theses may be summarized as follows: Armed struggle is still seen as a viable alternative by some in Latin America, despite repeated failure; it is what Stoll calls "the captivity of *Guevarismo*" (282). Accordingly, it is necessary to criticize such struggle because it has resulted in the radicalization of repression: without the guerrilla, repression would not have taken place in Guatemala (nor in Latin America)—or at least not to the extent that it has. Thus the processes of democratization would have been rapid. U.S. military intervention found justification because of leftist guerrilla activity. Without the guerrilla, the United States would not have intervened. In 1982, Menchú did not represent a mass movement, which had her, an indigenous Maya woman, as one more player in the conflict. The movement depicted by Menchú as one directed toward creating deep and durable modifications in Guatemalan society was not so, in reality, because popular support had long abandoned the struggle—Menchú only expresses a guerrilla mandate whose political agenda gets promoted through the Menchú–Burgos book.

Although the deconstruction of these theses, or of the "textual truth" in Stoll's book, may make for an excellent class assignment, it is not difficult to answer his theses. One need only contrast the historical data on the various processes of the social and political Latin American crises. His thesis, as others critics stated long ago, follows cold war logic and should be understood in that context. The controversy flourishes in a medium far more different than the academic study—the mass media—but it does so in direct relation to Stoll's book. In his Introduction, Stoll asserts how closely embedded mass media, human rights, and academic production are.[8] It is precisely such intimacy, as Stoll says, that couples academic practice, politics, and journalism together, what impels him in the writing of his book (see chapter 17). And it is this same awareness that compels him to operate with the *New York Times* editors when his book is released.

What then constitutes the media message that launches the controversy? What is its content? Clearly, it is not Stoll's theory on Latin American guerrilla movements, nor his thesis on the practice of anthropology in U.S. academe, nor his detailed investigation on Rigoberta Menchú's "autobiography" and the possible inaccuracies portrayed in the book in the making of which Menchú, Elisabeth Burgos, and Cécile Rousseau contributed.[9] In my view, the mass-media message distributed by Rohter and Stoll contains only the contention that Rigoberta Menchú "lies" in the book that carries her name on the cover (in the place of the title or of the author). The mass-media message, thus, is limited to a list of "misrepresentations" that Menchú would have incurred in the telling of her personal life story. Furthermore, this "lie" is not presented simply as Menchú's individual act, but as a gesture representative of many others (including "all poor Guatemalans"). Significantly, in the National Public Radio report that immediately followed the *New York Times* article, Rohter's final comment in the interview goes as follows:

> So, it's distressing to find, you know, these contradictions emerging in her account because the bottom line is that the people who are not sympathetic to the causes of human rights, it gives them ammunition. It allows them to say, "Well if this isn't true, God only knows how many other things are also not true," and the truth of the matter is that as one of Stoll's informants said to him, *the book may not be true about her,* but it is true about Guatemala. And I would agree. But there's no question

that this—these contradictions diminish the effectiveness of the message that human rights groups have been trying to get across for years and years.[10]

The *residue* left by the *New York Times* media operation is that "truth" was compromised in Menchú's telling of her story. In a medium particularly sensitive to this kind of claim about "truth," especially after the investigation of words in the controversy swirling around President Bill Clinton and his associates, a front-page article could have worked only as it did: as a bombshell that would shatter the laboriously acquired consensus about human rights. I can cite here countless illustrations of how effectively and how deeply this impact expanded, but I will relegate only the most poignant to an endnote. In all of them, it is apparent that it was not necessary to have read Stoll's book or Menchú's *testimonio,* not even Rohter's article, or to be at least partially familiar with recent Guatemalan history to start wondering if Menchú "lied" (and with her so many "other people in Guatemala or elsewhere").[11]

If Menchú "lies," the Guatemalans who say that they are the victims of a genocide "lie" too, and so do those who assert that unfortunate repressive politics, entailing economic and social oppression (stimulated many times by the power factors in the United States), has been the source for permanent distress in Central America. If this oversimplification is obviously crass and extremely ideological, it has proven quite attractive and useful for some people in U.S. academe, in Guatemala, and elsewhere. Otherwise, the controversy would not have proliferated the way it did. Its magnitude could probably provide a retort to Gugelberger's question, "What had happened to our 'icon' with a secret?" It could also challenge this author's contention that "[o]bviously the euphoric 'moment' of the *testimonio* has passed" (Introduction 1). The vicious overtones that the debate reached in the first couple of months of the year 2000 constitute a clear proof of how disruptive the presence of *testimonio* is within any canon (be it in Latin American studies or in literature). From a literary standpoint, as Beverley pointedly argues,[12] *testimonio* makes visible the inherited European "literary gesture": reading and analyzing *testimonio* deconstructs the literary tradition as the canon knows it and exposes the social fabric on which its circulation and reproduction relies.

Debunking one of the most famous *testimonios* as "a hoax" could regress the canon to the "official history"—but I cannot see anything less remotely feasible than this. In reality, nothing that the academe may discuss about *testimonio* constitutes the source of its subversive nature. The subversive nature of the genre is generated by the series of political gestures that the *testimoniantes* themselves undertake. In this case, Rigoberta Menchú creates her own mythical construction of herself as it takes her from Quiché to Paris, from Paris to Stockholm, and from Stockholm to her foundation in Guatemala and Mexico.

In examining here the buildup of *residue* through a media operation, I want to address the widespread discomfort that I sense among scholars, teachers, Guatemalans, and people with diverse degrees of familiarity with the war in Guatemala around the December 15 controversy. It is extremely difficult to respond to a highly compact and tangled media message; it leaves us with very little to add or do. We can analyze and discuss its implications, but it is critical to keep in mind the concise media dimensions of the controversy generated by the intended *residue*. Undoubtedly, this *residue* expresses what many people already thought (prior to the media operation and prior to Stoll's book), but is profoundly contradictory to what a "historical truth" can claim. To put it in Stoll's own words: "What will count in the future is what Zygmunt Baumann calls 'remembered history'—what Guatemalans care to remember their history has been, not what a foreign scholar thinks it is" (264).

This is precisely why after the second report on the war in Guatemala was released in February 2000, the controversy in the Guatemalan scene died out of a natural and unavoidable cause. I am referring to the report "Guatemala, memoria del silencio," compiled by the Commission for Historical Clarification (the "truth commission") that originated as part of the peace accords.[13] While visiting Guatemala in March 2000 (at the same time Bill Clinton was in Central America apologizing for the U.S. intervention in the war), I became convinced by media articles and conversations that the forcefulness of the truth commission's report left out any grounds for possible attacks on Menchú's account and made any criticism frivolous.[14]

Historical truth is processed by time, outcomes, and by later interpretations. It is also contingent upon opinion, bias, and political interest, but it is never bound to the instant or to fragments of events, because it is highly charged with accumulation and experience. Historical truth needs certain consensus; it is established, as Stoll states, by "cutting through competing versions of events" (274), and it is never disinterested.

Now, if my argument sounds too removed from the ideal of objectivity that is somehow invoked by Stoll as the origin of his book (particularly in the introduction and in the last chapter), let me offer Richard Rorty's reflection on the polarity of "solidarity or objectivity" and the search for Truth. Rorty presents us with the Greek-originated Western tradition of "the idea of Truth as something to be pursued for its own sake, not because it will be good for oneself, or for one's real or imaginary community." A direct corollary of this aspiration for Truth is the rise of the idea of the intellectual "as someone who is in touch with the nature of things, not by way of the opinions of his community, but in a more immediate way" (21), that is, by the means that "rationality" provides. In Rorty's argument, the ideal of objectivity becomes the dangerous path through which the realist (the one who construes truth as correspondent to reality) creates the universal. The alternative, the truth that stems from solidarity, is "the question of whether our self-description ought to be constructed around a relation ... to a particular collection of human beings" (24). Rorty's criticism illuminates the practice of anthropology that Renato Rosaldo describes in *Culture and Truth* as "imperialist nostalgia."[15] This nostalgia blinds the ethnographer in such a manner that he cannot see himself as an agent, neither innocent nor neutral, in his task of "understanding the situation" he depicts. As Rosaldo puts it, "the observer is neither innocent nor omniscient" (1989, 69).

In one of the most indicative moments of the book, while attempting to address the question of the increasing influence of postcolonial theories in academe, Stoll reprimands—in a highly sarcastic tone—scholars, methods, and theories related to the desire to find more equitable ways of depicting "the Other." In the last paragraph of the section titled "Guatemalan Scapegoat, Gringo Saint," he writes:

> For scholars insecure about their moral right to depict "the Other," *testimonio* and related appeals to the native voice have been godsend. By incorporating native voice into the syllabus and deferring to it on occasion, we validate our authority by claiming to abdicate it. This is not necessarily a bad thing—anthropology and Latin American studies are hard to imagine without it. But in an era of truth commissions, when there is a public demand to establish facts, privileging *one version* of a history of land conflict and homicide will not do. What if, on comparing the most hallowed *testimonio* with others, we find that it is not reliable in certain important ways? Then we would have to acknowledge that there is *no substitute for our capacity* to judge competing versions of

events, *to exercise our authority as scholars.* That would unravel a generation of efforts to revalidate ourselves through idealized reimaginings of the Other. (277; my emphasis)

Precisely the paradox that David Stoll embodies is that through his aspiration for "objectivity," he disassociates himself from a possible solidarity with 93 percent of the victims of violence in Guatemala (figures according to the "truth commission"). Behind a rhetorical gesture in search of objectivity lies the epistemological naïveté that prevents him from seeing his active role in the conflict for land and hegemony in Guatemala. This is the crucial contradiction that permeates all of Stoll's research and therefore its product, *Rigoberta Menchú and the Story of All Poor Guatemalans.* As I see it, Stoll's interaction with *I, Rigoberta Menchú* offers an archetypal dramatization of a reader's vicissitude. For those who have taught *testimonio,* this kind of reader's journey is probably quite familiar. Furthermore, if we agree that there is no other alternative than to position oneself in relation to the text and the world depicted in it, this resistance to testimonial texts should be centrally addressed in a class in which *testimonios* are analyzed. How readers position themselves is not only determined by the text; what they decide to do with the reactions the text has generated is their only privilege.

The connection between the two parts of my argument becomes apparent when one considers the following. The controversy that bursts forth on December 15 operates in the terms of the mass media. The media *residue,* highly political as it is, has been incorporated today in the United States into the historical and textual dissension over Stoll's book. The responses offered by Rigoberta Menchú and the other protagonists involved in the writing of *I, Rigoberta Menchú* have mostly addressed the residue precipitated by the media operation, since their media inscription in furthering the controversy could not be easily erased. Once we clear the table of the pressing and confusing terms with which the media operation completely directed the debate, we can address Stoll's book and his intervention. Stoll's "archetypal dramatization of a reader's vicissitude" takes him on a search for an "objective truth," beyond the necessities of the historical protagonists, beyond their need for solidarity and agency. The deconstruction of Menchú's story on which he embarks becomes an exemplary gesture of the "metaphor of inquiry" criticized by Rorty, in which knowledge becomes associated with truth only if it reflects the viewer's self-image. In this sense, a certain academic practice, or a certain model for social development favored in the eyes of the "inquirer," constitutes the measure, the extent for the right interpretation, and therefore for "truth."

If in the reading of *testimonio,* as stated earlier, positioning is a condition intrinsic to this very act, the specular condition is determined by many factors and could be avoided altogether: it occurs only if the reader willfully examines himself/herself while stimulated by the reading. If an American anthropologist plays with the mass media, it is because he can do it. If, on the other hand, the reading of a *testimonio* prompts his positioning, but does *not* elicit self-reflection while confronting the text, it is simply because he cannot do it. The gesture of transcending the ethnocentric vision is one that is grave and profound, and—as Foucault would argue—brings suffering.

Epilogue

In June 1999, more than a month after I submitted this essay to the editor of this collection, I met Elisabeth Burgos in Paris. There, Burgos showed me the three boxes containing the bits and pieces that went into the writing of *Me llamo Rigoberta Menchú y así me nació la conciencia:* the audiocassettes containing about twenty-four hours of recorded dialogue; the bulky transcription; a series of cards with minute handwriting where Burgos classified the various topics and recorded their location in the transcription; the original manuscript, with thin brown-paper covers for each chapter and handwritten notes on each of the fragile sheaves. I also had a chance to see the first video ever made about Rigoberta, produced by French Channel 3 soon after Burgos's interview, and shown twice in 1983—in May and October. Looking through the manuscript, I was able to corroborate the undeniable literary nature of the text— its emergence and materialization as a written artifact. The literary discursiveness of *Me llamo Rigoberta Menchú y así me nació la conciencia* was not achieved by undermining the oral tradition of which Menchú is heir and also model. Undoubtedly it is Burgos who, by defoliating, ordering, and harmonizing the rhetorical expression of the spoken word, inscribes and incorporates a story and a world vision within the tradition of the book. The *mestizaje* of mediums and languages reaches a point where the double voice becomes one: the voice of Menchú, who speaks out against the disasters of war in Guatemala and demands her people's right to their tradition and their culture. It is in the very text of *Me llamo*

Rigoberta Menchú y así me nació la conciencia that we find the personage that Menchú embodies in Paris in 1982, placed at the junction of
the political and strategic vision of Vicente Menchú; the international
solidarity movement for Guatemala; the Guatemalan guerrilla movement; the authoritarian politics of one of the bloodiest Latin American
dictatorships; the resurgent mobilization of the Maya; the greed of American enterprises that dictated U.S. foreign policy; the politics of exporting
revolution; the lengthy coexistence of the descendents of pre-Columbian
peoples, and the new peoples who stemmed from the European expansion into America; the logic of the cold war. This personage exists within
that moment and it is manifested through the eloquence inherent to
the literary expression. (It is not surprising that the interviews only lasted
several hours, no more than an instant when we consider the length of
the civil war in Guatemala, or the history of colonial politics in the
continent.) Burgos's book generates an image so intense and so powerful
that it has given rise to prolific commentary which reflects on, expli-
cates, or re-creates the emblematic construct that is *Me llamo Rigoberta
Menchú y así me nació la conciencia*. But the complex confluence that
engendered the literary myth also contains a living person, an independent individual, who, thankfully, survived successive waves of repression: Rigoberta Menchú. This individual, already a known activist at
the time of the interview, built her life around the defense of human
rights and the construction of her own role as a representative of the
indigenous community in Guatemala. It was this activist, struggling for
survival and seeking to represent the indigenous community, who was
honored with the Nobel Peace Prize by the Swedish Academy in 1992.
Menchú's activism has been reinscribed as a form of "authorism," where
text, myth, personage, and individual blur together. Thus, Menchú, now
the author of the political myth, is assumed to be the "author" of (authorizes) the textuality that surfaced in those few days in Paris. But that text
also has us, the multiple interpretative communities, as its authors. These
"authors" range from Gallimard, the publishing house whose reading
sanctioned that Burgos's text could be read first by a French-speaking
audience, to the multifaceted North American academe, with all its complexity, that translates and mistranslates, interprets and rewrites the text
to serve no longer the needs of the enmeshed political process in Guatemala, but rather its own involved internal struggles. As any significant
text, *Me llamo Rigoberta Menchú y así me nació la conciencia* today is part

of our patrimony. Constructed out of innumerable hybridities, the book is first of all Guatemalan, Central American, and Latin American, because these are historically the most affected communities in terms of the impact of the text. Next, it is part of the patrimony of anyone who feels that an immense truth, larger than the text in which it has been inscribed, and larger than its protagonists and authors, is constituted every time the book is actualized in a reading. That truth does not need to be spelled out or explicated here. The book's greatness is born both out of its historical transcendence and through its inscription within the continuing debate about the colonial past and the postcolonial present of the Americas, and its inspired language.

Notes

An earlier version of sections of this essay was presented at the 1999 International Conference on Central American Literature (CILCA 99) in Managua, Nicaragua, March 1999.

1. Claudia Ferman, "'Tenía que morir para que me creyeran': la cuestión de la verdad en testimonios sobre las batallas de Centroamérica," International Conference on Central American Literature (CILCA), San José, Costa Rica, February 1997; and "Resisting *testimonio*: From Guatemala to the United States Classroom," Modern Languages Association meeting, December 1998.

2. See, for example, Doris Sommer's "Sin secretos."

3. The following scheme summarizes these concepts: fiction → suspension of disbelief → identification → catharsis, *testimonio* → acts of faith → distance/marginalization → positioning (solidarity/questioning).

4. In commenting on Sklodowska's characterization of the voice of the *testimonio* as a "textual construct," Beverley describes the suspension of fictionality as a characteristic of the genre (1993, 273).

5. This may also be found in John Beverley's article in the collection when he quotes Gayatri Spivak, in the epigraph to his article: "However unfeasible and inefficient it may sound, I see no way to avoid insisting that there has to be a simultaneous other focus: not merely who am I? but who is the other woman? *How am I naming her? How does she name me?*" (1996, 266; my emphasis).

6. It is interesting to point out that the nature of the "news" on the controversy surrounding Rigoberta Menchú, its constitution, prevents the story from getting into the television medium (at least in the United States—and, I would say, probably everywhere else, except in Guatemala, for obvious reasons).

7. See, for example, Marc Zimmerman's *Literature and Resistance in Guatemala: Textual Modes and Cultural Politics from "El Señor Presidente" to Rigoberta Menchú*, vol. 2 (Athens: Ohio University Press, Center for International Studies, 1995), 51–71, or John Beverley (1996, 274–82); or Stoll's own account of the exchange with the same Rigoberta Menchú and John Beverley in 1991, and later with Menchú in 1992 (1999, 226–69) and the confrontation with them and other scholars in the context of the 1991 LASA (Latin American Studies Association) meeting (Stoll 241–42).

8. "In a world swayed by the mass media, in which nations and peoples live or die by their ability to catch international attention, how do the gatekeepers of communication deal with the mixture of truth and falsehood in any movement's portrayal of itself, including those we feel morally obliged to support?" (Stoll 1999, x).

9. Cécile Rousseau is a Canadian psychiatrist whose nom de guerre was Marie Tremblay.

10. Transcript, *All Things Considered,* December 15, 1998; section: News International; my emphasis.

11. First came the advertisement campaign in college newspapers paid for by a think tank based in Los Angeles that describes Menchú as "an intellectual hoax." The president of the Study of Popular Culture (the name of the organization), David Horowitz, said to Denise K. Magner: "Why are we teaching something that is patently false and intellectually dishonest? Unfortunately the answer is, out of loyalty to a *political viewpoint rather than loyalty to the truth*" (my emphasis). Also in a recent issue of the *American Enterprise,* commented upon in the *Chronicle of Higher Education,* it is stated that "public acceptance of lying has increased in recent years." An article by Kenneth Lee, a freelance writer, "points to many professors' forgiveness of the factual errors in Rigoberta Menchú's memoir of Guatemala as evidence of the moral decline in academe." He further states, "This embarrassing episode is only the latest instance of epidemic lying in the ivory tower" (Lee 2000). Furthermore, several articles referred to the controversy in Spain and Mexico in discussing Menchú's "*mentiras piadosas*" (white lies). The last example I want to mention concerns my own naïveté when invited to give a presentation (scheduled before the controversy started) on my interview with Menchú on her book *Crossing Borders* that took place in November 1998, in Maryland. After my presentation, which addressed many aspects of Menchú's leadership, including the relevance of the Stoll controversy in terms of the U.S. academe and the battle over knowledge, I could not ignore some disappointment in my audience. After making inquiries, I came to realize that my talk did not address whether "Menchú had lied or not," which was central to the interest of that class.

12. See John Beverley, *Against Literature,* and also Alberto Moreiras's reflection on the subject in "The Aura of Testimonio."

13. The report may be consulted on the Web at http://hrdata.aaas.org/ceh/report/english (or /spanish).

14. See, for example, Antonio Díaz Cernuda's article "Stoll y la nieta de los mayas" (Stoll and the Mayas' granddaughter), *Prensa Libre,* Guatemala City, Monday, March 15, 1999, 12.

15. "Imperialist nostalgia occurs alongside a peculiar sense of mission, 'the white man's burden,' where civilized nations stand duty-bound to uplift so-called savage ones" (Rosaldo 1989, 70).

Bibliography

Beverley, John. 1993. *Against Literature.* Minneapolis: University of Minnesota Press.
———. 1996. "The Real Thing." In *The Real Thing: Testimonial Discourse and Latin America,* ed. Georg M. Gugelberger. Durham, N.C.: Duke University Press. 266–86.
Gugelberger, Georg M., ed. 1996. *The Real Thing: Testimonial Discourse and Latin America.* Durham, N.C.: Duke University Press.

Lee, Kenneth. 2000. "Untruth in Academe." *American Enterprise* (March 6).

Menchú, Rigoberta. 1998b. *Rigoberta: La nieta de los mayas.* Ed. Dante Liano and Gianni Minà. Madrid: El País/Aguilar.

———. 1998a. *Crossing Borders.* Trans. Ann Wright. London: Verso.

Menchú, Rigoberta, with Elisabeth Burgos-Debray. 1982. *"Moi, Rigoberta Menchu": une vie et une voix, la révolution au Guatemala.* Paris: Gallimard.

———. 1984. *I, Rigoberta Menchú: An Indian Woman in Guatemala.* Trans. Ann Wright. London: Verso.

Moreiras, Alberto. 1996. "The Aura of Testimonio." In *The Real Thing: Testimonial Discourse and Latin America,* ed. Georg M. Gugelberger. Durham, N.C.: Duke University Press. 192–224.

Rorty, Richard. 1991. "Objectivity, Relativism, and Truth." In *Philosophical Papers,* vol. 1. New York: Cambridge University Press.

Rosaldo, Renato. 1989. *Culture and Truth: The Remaking of Social Analysis.* Boston: Beacon Press.

Sklodowska, Elzbieta. 1996. "Spanish American Testimonial Novel: Some Afterthoughts. In *The Real Thing: Testimonial Discourse and Latin America,* ed. Georg M. Gugelberger. Durham, N.C.: Duke University Press. 84–100.

Sommer, Doris. 1992. "Sin secretos." *Revista de crítica literaria latinoamericana* 18.36: 135–53.

Stoll, David. 1999. *Rigoberta Menchú and the Story of All Poor Guatemalans.* Boulder, Colo.: Westview Press.

Zimmerman, Marc. 1995. *Literature and Resistance in Guatemala: Textual Modes and Cultural Politics from "El Señor Presidente" to Rigoberta Menchú.* 2 vols. Athens: Ohio University Press, Center for International Studies.

The Primacy of Larger Truths

Rigoberta Menchú and the Tradition of Native Testimony in Guatemala

W. George Lovell and Christopher H. Lutz

> There can rarely be a definitive version of the past and rarely a
> particular truth, only the larger truths of existence.
> —Merilyn Simonds, *The Lion in the Room Next Door* (1999)

Like many whose work pertains to Guatemala, we find ourselves not
only puzzled by the manner in which David Stoll (1999) approaches
the testimony of Rigoberta Menchú (1984) but also perplexed that Stoll's
dissection of the debatable details of one individual's life serves to divert attention from the undeniable deaths of thousands of others. Although the corrosive effects of the latter are cause for regret, it is the
former disposition that we address here. Stoll appears to believe that,
unless Menchú's version of certain events and circumstances can withstand being subjected to the magnifying glass of social-science inquiry,
any flaws or inconsistencies uncovered in the course of the exercise discredit the testimony in question, cast doubt over its authenticity, and
thus render it suspect. It then becomes possible for the entire narrative
to be dismissed as mere fabrication or perhaps even lies, especially at
the hands of the narrator's adversaries. All this may be far removed from
Stoll's original intentions, whatever they are, but it constitutes an inevitable outcome in a country as politically fraught and divided as Guatemala. Rather surprisingly for an anthropologist whose earlier research
on Ixil country (Stoll 1993) demonstrates a more grounded appreciation
of the past, Stoll seems unconcerned in his analysis with the historical

tradition in which Menchú's testimony is rooted and in which it can readily be contextualized in order to be evaluated more appropriately.

Some of the features that Stoll identifies as problematical in Menchú's testimony, we observe, have antecedents in native texts extant for the sixteenth century, indeed, surface throughout as among their inherent characteristics, the properties of their words. These features include: (1) factual discrepancies or contradictions; (2) questions of authority and representation; (3) the purposeful act of simplifying, embellishing, improvising, and orchestrating what is being said in order to emphasize specific points and to downplay or conceal others, but not to alter the substance of what actually happened; and (4) political protest that is both conscious and overt, fueled by the need to speak out against injustice and repression in an attempt to have one's rights respected. Although a comprehensive survey of the ethnohistorical literature is beyond the scope of our discussion—the work of Robert Carmack (1973), which we highlight prominently, remains the single most insightful commentary available in English—we will illustrate what we have to say with reference to an array of native sources. None of these sources is as well known as Menchú's is today, but they both prefigure and echo her testimony, at times in a striking fashion. First, however, we must establish the salient frames of our comparative perspective.

The Sixteenth Century and the Twentieth

For Maya peoples in Guatemala, the arrival in 1524 of a Spanish military expedition led by Pedro de Alvarado marked the beginning of a process of conquest that has lasted centuries. Several scholars have commented on the enduring nature of conquest in Guatemala, but few have done so with the clarity and succinctness of the late Oliver La Farge (1947, 100). "While these people undoubtedly suffer from drunkenness," he wrote of the Q'anjoba'les of Santa Eulalia, "one would hesitate to remove the bottle from them until the entire pattern of their lives is changed. They are an introverted people, consumed by internal fires which they cannot or dare not express, eternally chafing under the yoke of conquest, and never for a moment forgetting that they are a conquered people."

La Farge viewed conquest not as a distant, historical experience but as a discernible, present condition. Sol Tax (1952) and the anthropologists Carl Kendall, John Hawkins, and Laurel Bossen (1983) concur, interpreting native life as a "heritage of conquest" that connects present-day Mayas with their ancestors of centuries ago. Although, to be sure, the forms of this "heritage of conquest" have varied considerably over the years, conquest as a *way* of life lingers as the central *fact* of life for the five to six million Mayas who today make up roughly half of Guatemala's national population (Lovell and Lutz 1996). To assert otherwise, as Borges once put it, would be "mere statistics," though plenty of these are at hand to counter any credible argument to the contrary.

Just as Menchú's testimony tells of conquest by state terror in the twentieth century, so dozens of native texts record conquest by imperial terror in the sixteenth. For what he calls "Quichean Civilization," Carmack (1973, 24–79) identifies four different categories of native testimony written in the sixteenth century, a total of thirty-nine texts in all. The most important documents, he informs us, "appear to have been based upon prehispanic historical and cultural traditions, which in several cases must have been transcribed in native codices." Carmack concludes that these documents "were written by descendants of the most important ruling lines in prehispanic highland Guatemala, and thus express the 'official' versions of native history."

Although Menchú's testimony has no elite origins beyond "*primero básico*" or grade-seven education, and certainly no "official" seal of approval, its fundamental purpose is the same as many of the Quichean documents that Carmack analyzes—to put memory to work so as to produce a record of the past, furnish an account of the present, and preserve both for the benefit and betterment of future generations. The need to tell one's story comes about in myriad ways and for countless different reasons, but the need becomes more urgent when calamity is the order of the day, when one's very survival is threatened. The Commission for Historical Clarification (1999, 85–86) has established that, during thirty-five years of civil war between 1962 and 1996, some two hundred thousand people (83.33 percent of them Mayas) lost their lives in Guatemala, a disconcerting number of them in horrific massacres carried out by the national armed forces, whom the truth commission holds responsible for 93 percent of recorded human rights violations. Menchú's urge to communicate what was happening to her people arose from, and must be seen in, the murderous context of that conflict. Her testimony is particularly important, for it broke the eerie silence imposed by the fear and violence of those terrible years.

Similarly, the catastrophe that befell Maya populations in the sixteenth century was unleashed by Spanish invasion of their territory, an invasion that resulted almost immediately in the outbreak of hostilities. The devastation and loss of life unleashed by a prolonged war of conquest also triggered an outpouring of testimony, which is again directly linked to the appalling extent of the tragedy in which Guatemalan Indians found themselves. We reckon, for instance, that Maya numbers fell from around two million at contact in 1520 to around 135,000 in 1600 from a combination of conquest-related factors, among them armed confrontation, culture shock, ruthless exploitation, forced migration, and especially the impact of Old World diseases on an immunologically vulnerable native population (Lovell and Lutz 1996). How could the plight of those caught up in such a traumatic spiral of depopulation fail to capture the attention of those charged with recording native history? As with Menchú, Indians in the early colonial period were moved to put into words a record of what life was like under the rule of their oppressors.

Both the sixteenth century and the twentieth thus represent junctures when the disruptive experience of violent conquest spurred native testimony. Let us now consider some of the features connecting Menchú's narrative with the narratives of her K'iche' forebears and those of other relevant actors engaged in constructing vital, if imperfect, memories of what befell them. We will focus our attention more on the historical sources in the hope of providing the reader with a better appreciation of the origins and traditions of native testimony.

Were the K'iche' Kings Hanged or Burned?

Stoll (1999, 63–70) links a good deal of his argument, and attributes much of his being disquieted by Menchú's testimony in the first place, to the depiction in *I, Rigoberta Menchú* of the killing in 1979 of the narrator's sixteen-year-old brother, Petrocinio. Menchú (1984, 176–79) describes it thus:

> The lorry with the tortured came in. They started to take them out one by one. . . . Each of the tortured had different wounds . . . but my mother recognized her son, my little brother, among them. . . . My brother was very badly tortured, he could hardly stand up. . . . He was cut in various places. His head was shaved and slashed. He had no nails. He had no soles to his feet. The earlier wounds were suppurating from infection. . . . I found it impossible to concentrate, seeing that this could be. You could

only think that these were human beings and what pain those bodies had felt to arrive at this unrecognizable state. . . . My mother wept. She almost risked her own life by going to embrace my brother. My other brothers and my father held her back so she wouldn't endanger herself. . . . The captain said, "This isn't the last of their punishments, there's another one yet. . . ." They lined up the tortured and poured petrol on them; and then the soldiers set fire to each one of them.

During fieldwork in which he interviewed a number of people about the episode, Stoll (1999, 69) recounts that "when I brought up Rigoberta's story of prisoners being burned alive in the plaza of Chajul, all I harvested were quizzical looks." Stoll favors another version of events, one gathered while he was investigating the affair and which he corroborates with information contained in an "Open Letter," dated January 31, 1980, distributed by the Democratic Front Against Repression. After the army murdered a number of guerrilla suspects, one man recalls the following scene:

From a military truck they threw down the cadavers, one by one, one by one. I think there were seven. They rang the church bell and summoned the people, to say that [the dead] were guerrillas. The army also said that they were from San Miguel Uspantán. This was done to make the people afraid, to make an example [of the victims]. . . . Yes, they burned a body. But he was already dead; he wasn't alive. (Stoll 1999, 68–69)

Stoll himself acknowledges that, "as best anyone can determine," the group of people killed at Chajul "included her [Menchú's] younger brother" (70).

Just as oral testimony recoverable in the late twentieth century may be plagued by factual discrepancies or contradictions, so too is the ethnohistorical record of the early sixteenth. Two of our most valued sources for understanding Maya history and culture, the *Popol Vuh* and the *Memorial de Sololá*, allow us to reflect on one case in point. These "major documents" in the eyes of Carmack, as with Stoll versus Menchú on the killing of Petrocinio, differ on the means by which Pedro de Alvarado executed two K'iche' rulers. One English edition of the *Popol Vuh* (Recinos 1950, 230) runs: "Oxib-Queh [Three Deer] and Beleheb-Tzi [Nine Dog], the twelfth generation of kings. These were those who reigned when Donadiú came, and who were hanged by the Spaniards."

In Nahuatl, the language of the Aztecs, Donadiú or Tonatiuh means "the Sun" and is the name that several early sources give for Alvarado, on account of his fair complexion and blond hair. Another English edition of *The Book of the Dawn of Life* (Tedlock 1985) reads: "Three Deer and Nine Dog, in the twelfth generation of lords. And they were ruling when Tonatiuh arrived. They were hanged by the Castilian people."

The *Memorial de Solalá*, also known as the *Annals of the Cakchiquels*, records the K'iche' kings, identified as Ahpop and Ahpop Qamahay, as having been tortured and burned at the stake, not hanged. Adrián Recinos and Delia Goetz (1953, 119–20) render the incident as follows:

On the day 1 Ganel [February 20, 1524] the Quichés were destroyed by the Spaniards. Their chief, he who was called Tunatiuh Avilantaro, conquered all the people. Their faces were not known before that time.
    Having arrived at Xelahub [Quetzaltenango], they defeated the Quichés; all the Quichés who had gone out to meet the Spaniards were exterminated.
    Then [the Spaniards] went forth to the city of Gumarcaah [Utatlán], where they were received by the kings, the Ahpop and the Ahpop Qamahay, and the Quichés paid them tribute. Soon the kings were tortured by Tunatiuh.
    On the day 4 Qat [March 7, 1524] the kings Ahpop and Ahpop Qamahay were burned by Tunatiuh. The heart of Tunatiuh was without compassion for the people during the war.

Writing to his commander in chief in Mexico, Hernán Cortés, a month later from Gumarcaah, Alvarado himself provides us with an account of the incident that matches the *Memorial de Solalá* version of the killing of the kings, not that of the *Popol Vuh*. Sedley J. Mackie (1924, 62–63) translates the conquistador as stating:

And seeing that by fire and sword I might bring these people to the service of His Majesty, I determined to burn the chiefs, who, at the time that I wanted to burn them, told me, as it will appear in their confessions, that they were the ones who had ordered the war against me and were the ones also who made it. They told me about the way they were to do so, to burn me in the city, and that with this thought in their minds they had brought me there, and that they had ordered their vassals not to come and give obedience to our Lord and Emperor, nor help us, nor do anything else that was right. And as I knew them to have such a bad disposition towards the service of His Majesty, and to insure the good and peace of this land, I burnt them, and sent to burn the town and to destroy it, for it is a very strong and dangerous place, that more resembles a robbers' stronghold than a city.

The question we would put to Stoll is this: Does it matter whether the Guatemalan army shot Menchú's brother or torched him alive, any more than whether Alvarado had the K'iche' kings hanged or burned? Does it matter that one source of information says one thing and another something slightly different? Is not the most pertinent piece of information the incontestable fact that murder took place for political reasons in an atmosphere of terror that all parties not only agree upon but can also describe with as much convergence as divergence of opinion?

Stoll (1999, 70) concedes that "in and of itself, the contrast between Rigoberta's account and everyone else's is not very significant," but he goes on to assert that "the important point is that her story, here and at other critical junctures, is not the eyewitness account that it purports to be." Stoll's sense of what "the important point is" raises our next query. Does Menchú actually claim that her testimony is exclusively an eyewitness account, any more than did scores of native sources in the sixteenth century?

Speaking for All Poor Guatemalans

Questions of authority and representation are difficult ones to resolve when dealing with most texts, but more so with ones that have oral origins, as Menchú's certainly does, or in all likelihood are offshoots of an oral tradition, as are many sixteenth-century native documents. Let us consider Menchú's claim to authority and representativeness first.

Stoll lifts the title of his book from the opening lines of Menchú's testimony (1984, 1), in which the protagonist states:

> My name is Rigoberta Menchú. I am twenty-three years old. This is my testimony. I didn't learn it from a book and I didn't learn it alone. I'd like to stress that it's not only *my* life, it's also the testimony of my people. It's hard for me to remember everything that's happened to me in my life since there have been many very bad times but, yes, moments of joy as well. The important thing is that what has happened to me has happened to many other people too: My story is the story of all poor Guatemalans. My personal experience is the reality of a whole people.

Rather than establish the worth of her testimony purely on the basis of eyewitness credentials, we contend that Menchú's words make it clear that the narrative strategy she is about to adopt leans as much on collective memory as individual recall. "It's not only *my* life," she takes pains to stress, "it's also the testimony of my people." Menchú reiterates this essential point not once—"What has happened to me has happened to many other people too"—but twice: "My personal experience is the reality of a whole people." The repetition of an idea, expressed for emphasis and for effect in slightly different ways, is a standard rhetorical tactic, in this case deployed unequivocally to establish not only personal but also communal validity. The communal validity of Menchú's words, having been made quite apparent at the outset of her testimony, in our eyes makes redundant, or at least minimizes, the relevance of Stoll's elaborate exercise in fact checking, which he conducts as if Menchú's account was *only* cast as that of one eyewitness.

Although the historical record allows us to recover the names of certain individuals as being the ones who actually penned native testimonies in the sixteenth century, it is usually the case that what is documented as having occurred is worded so as to have not individual but group applicability. Consider the following poignant extract from the *Memorial de Sololá*, which may be a description of how smallpox reached and ravaged Guatemala three or four years before the arrival of Alvarado:

> It happened that during the twenty-fifth year the plague began, oh, my sons! First they became ill of a cough. They suffered from nosebleeds and illness of the bladder. It was truly terrible, the number of dead there were in that period. The prince *Vakaki Ahmak* died then. Little by little heavy shadows and black night enveloped our fathers and grandfathers and us also, oh, my sons! when the plague raged.
>
> It was in truth terrible, the number of dead among the people. The people could not in any way control the sickness.
>
> Great was the stench of the dead. After our fathers and grandfathers succumbed, half of the people fled to the fields. The dogs and the vultures devoured the bodies. The mortality was terrible. Your grandfathers died, and with them died the son of the king and his brothers and kinsmen. So it was that we became orphans, oh, my sons! So we became when we were young. All of us were thus. We were born to die! (Recinos and Goetz 1953, 115–16)

Use of a collective voice to capture a collective lot is a feature of several other native texts besides the *Memorial de Sololá*, among them a genre Carmack identifies as *títulos*. These "titles" were often presented, long after they were written, as "evidence" in land disputes, frequently between Indian communities. Carmack (1973, 19) observes that *títulos* were written "primarily for legal and political purposes." The original reason for penning *títulos* was to defend the interests of elite Maya lineages. In a curious twist of fate, however, their subsequent use as land titles benefited not just the nobility but the common folk as well, especially those who worked the land and who depended on it to meet their tributary obligations.

Unlike *títulos* in which members of an elite make reference to pre-Hispanic ancestors in order to establish their status and authority, the composers of the Nahuatl *memorias* had lost a sense of association with, or awareness of, their pre-Conquest origins. This unusual situation came about, in part, because some members of the communities in question, which were located on the margins or in the vicinity of Santiago de Guatemala, were immigrants or the descendants of immigrants who had fought alongside Alvarado as Mexican auxiliaries. Most residents of these particular *barrios* and *pueblos,* however, were former slaves or the descendants of slaves held by Alvarado or by his companions in conquest between the mid-1520s and emancipation around 1550.

A good example of elite invocation of the past is the *Título Tamub* from the Totonicapán area, identified as such by Carmack (1973, 31–32) but referred to by Recinos (1957, 25ff.) as the "Historia Quiché de Don Juan de Torres." This document alludes to "migrations by ancestors from the East" and describes lineage genealogy in some detail. On the other hand, only a few communities for which we have *memorias* could recall the different towns, regions, and language groups from which their pre-Conquest ancestors originated. The authors of the *memorias* make no grandiose claims, as their elite counterparts often do, but instead speak to us from the heart in simple but poetic language. They do not hesitate, as elected members of town councils or *cabildos,* to restrict themselves to their own grievances but instead seek to draw attention to the suffering of elderly widows, orphaned children, and the physically impaired. The *memorias* thus represent, as in our time do the testimonies of Menchú and her Popti' colleague Victor Montejo (1987), a cry from the humble depths of society. It is not without hazard, we concede, but it is possible for texts to be put together that speak, if not for *all* poor Guatemalans, then for a significant number of them, in a valid collective voice.

Accommodating Textual Distortions

Stoll (1999, x–xi) goes to painstaking lengths in his scrutiny of Menchú's testimony to highlight what he correctly identifies, among a plethora of other narrative conventions, as the "condensing," "concealing," "revising," "glossing over," or "filtering out" of information. Why, as a diligent researcher who has spent time not only interviewing in the field but also poring over archival documents, he should be surprised by such tendencies we find rather odd. Even a cursory examination of the historical record indicates (1) a notable incidence of the practice and (2) the need to accommodate such distortions as an integral part of the research process, especially if we wish to know more about native points of view and thus gain a better appreciation of how what happened in history might look through their eyes.

In order to engage a more indigenous perspective, let us now examine some historiographical issues in terms of changes that may have had an impact on how the ancestors of Mayas such as Menchú viewed and articulated their sense of the past. Why might those who wrote native history more than four hundred years ago not necessarily have followed the methodologies used by colonial-period, non-Indian chroniclers, let alone modern social scientists?

Carmack points out the existence in K'iche' society, up to the time of the Spanish Conquest, of a scholarly community known as *aj tz'ibab*. These men of letters were priest-historians trained to read, interpret, and write sacred texts and calendars. After the arrival of the Spaniards, the *aj tz'ibab* did not maintain their prestigious social position for long. Having witnessed what they held to be pagan excesses among the Aztecs and other Mexican peoples, Spanish clergymen set out to destroy all aspects of Maya religious practice. Their acts of destruction included (1) tearing down temples and altars, as noted by Carmack (1973, 301) and Tzaquitzal Zapata (1993, 25) in the *Título C'oyoi'* or *Coyoy;* (2) destroying sacred texts, as noted by Carmack (1973, 17), who cites as his source Las Casas (1958, 2:348); and (3) hunting down and persecuting all those whom the invaders considered practitioners of a demonized religion, among whom were the *aj tz'ibab.* Carmack (1973, 17) puts it succinctly thus: "Shortly after the conquest," he writes, the *aj tz'ibab* "ceased to function in the way they had before the conquest."

Once the practice of training "historians" was curtailed—it was a Kaqchikel custom also, we should note—the loss must have had a serious impact on the accuracy and care with which Maya authors later wrote *títulos, memorias,* and *relaciones.* The disappearance of professionals such as the *aj tz'ibab* would surely have affected how Maya oral tradition was passed down through the generations.

Mercedes de la Garza (1975, 110–11), however, notes that "[even] if the codices were destroyed and the priests persecuted and murdered, Maya historical memory could not be destroyed, [and] precisely because of it, we have information of their ancient history, their myths, and their customs." According to de la Garza, "historic memory" did *not* die because (1) learned native elders passed their knowledge on to Spanish friars, who recorded what had been told to them in their chronicles; and (2) some Indians learned to write in their own languages using the Latin alphabet, producing new texts based on pre-Hispanic codices and oral traditions. Although, to be sure, these cultural processes were at work far more intensely in Mexico, their importance in Guatemala cannot be disputed. But although "historical memory" may have lived on, the training that came with the continuity of an unbroken tradition, as well as the discipline and precision of *aj tz'ibab* composition, was seriously eroded.

A striking exception, however, is the author of the *Memorial de Sololá*, Francisco Hernández Arana (ca. 1505–ca. 82), grandson of a Kaqchikel ruler of the Xajil lineage, who was an eyewitness to the outbreak of sickness quoted earlier as well as other events leading up to, and following, the Spanish Conquest. Hernández Arana began to record the events he had witnessed, as long ago as sixty years earlier, in the 1570s, paying particular attention to dates and details. His text holds up to critical scrutiny far better than most other surviving documents. Before we furnish some examples of the latter, a comment about who these new post-Conquest authors were seems appropriate.

Like Hernández Arana, most post-Conquest Maya authors were lineage or clan leaders who received instruction from Franciscan or Dominican friars in the rudiments of European forms of writing. This new generation of scribes, with few exceptions, only began to be taught how to read and write in native languages in the 1540s. This means that there was often a lapse of two decades between the destruction of the *aj tz'ibab* and the appearance of a new historiographic order. Much would have been lost in the hiatus.

The loss, of course, was compounded by the fact that Indians now had to function in a radically different political setting. The *aj tz'ibab* and other such priest-historians belonged to elite groups who governed independent political realms. Newly formed native leaders cum authors, on the other hand, were placed in charge of perhaps only a town and its surrounding territory, and were always beholden to Spanish civil and religious authorities. Although vestiges of pre-Hispanic social organization survived, any sense of exercising absolute control over land and resources soon evaporated. Thus the challenge for native authors frequently involved making a case for the importance of their particular lineage or social group by any means possible, in order to convince Spanish authorities that their demands for recognition were sound and just. Carmack (1973, 19–20) notes:

> Most documents refer to either local rights of administration or to rights of tribute. Administration rights, usually, were based on mythologegendary associations between the land and the local groups, or on mere occupancy, in which case land boundaries and markers were given. Tribute rights were based on narration of the conquest of the territory and subsequent instances of tribute payment by the subjected peoples.

He adds:

> Besides land claims, some documents contain claims to special cacique privileges given by the Crown to *señores naturales* (members of the aboriginal ruling stratum, though not priests). Most claims were made in the decade of 1550–1560, possibly in response to the Crown's attempt to limit the tribute rights and other privileges of Indian caciques.... Evidently, under increasing pressure for acceptable verification of ties with prehispanic nobility, the Spanish courts began to demand of the caciques special native documents on their genealogy and history. (19–20)

One such special K'iche' document Recinos (1957, 74–91) refers to as the "Títulos de la casa Ixquín-Nehaib, señora del territorio de Otzoyá," which Carmack, whose designation for this same document we follow, calls "Nijaib I." It belongs to a set of four titles that Carmack reckons "contain claims to prehispanic territorial holdings by the Nijaib branch of the Quiche" (32). *Nijaib I* records elaborate information on lineage matters and on strategic aspects of K'iche' conquest, but some of its contents are difficult to accept at face value.

Without specifying a date, the document claims that, during the reign of Moctezuma, word was sent to "our ancestors" that they pay tribute to the Aztec ruler. This they did, or so asserts the document: "They sent many quetzal feathers, gold, emeralds, pearls, diamonds, cacao, *pataxte* [white cacao] as well as cloths, everything that here they gave to the leaders, the same things they sent to Moctezuma in Tlaxcala, which is where the said Moctezuma was" (Recinos 1957, 84). Recinos rightly queried the veracity of this claim, observing that no other document known to him registers that the K'iche' ever paid tribute to Moctezuma. Carmack, however, identified at least one other such case years after Recinos was investigating the topic. If, indeed, tribute was paid to Moctezuma, why wouldn't this notable fact be mentioned in other more important K'iche' sources? Also, why wouldn't mention of K'iche' tributary status be included in Mexican codices that recorded the tribute furnished by distant peoples? Would the K'iche' have had easy access to all the items listed, especially diamonds and emeralds? And what was Moctezuma up to in Tlaxcala, a city well known to be hostile to the Aztecs, rather than seeing to affairs in his own capital, Tenochtitlán?

Nijaib I also claims, contrary to a host of other sources, that "for many years the K'iche' were not involved in acts of conquests, staying instead in their town and paying tribute to Moctezuma, until the time of the new conquest by the Spaniards and by Don Fernando Cortés and the [one] they call *Tunadiú*." The document goes on to state that, in 1512, Moctezuma sent a messenger, Uitzitzil, to the K'iche', advising them that the Spanish Conquest was about to begin and that they should take all necessary measures in order to defend themselves. Other peoples were advised to follow suit. According to this account (Recinos 1957, 84–85), the lords of Utatlán "raised their banners" and began preparations for war with the invaders. Time here is telescoped and events distorted to have us believe that the K'iche' were warned of the Spanish Conquest more than a decade before Alvarado invaded Guatemala and some seven years before Hernán Cortés even reached Mexico.

In making claims regarding, first, payment of tribute and, second, being in contact with Moctezuma about events that had not yet occurred, the purpose is clearly to associate the ancestors of the writer(s) with the glory that once was Moctezuma and the Aztec empire. Similar claims of close ties between the K'iche' and the Aztecs, including a tributary relationship, surface in the "Buenabaj Pictorials" from Momostenango. An inscription in this document, according to Carmack (1973, 63), makes the "startling statement" that "Moctezuma had married two of his daughters to the Quiché rulers." Carmack interprets this distortion as illustrating a desire to "establish the legitimacy of cacique privileges held by the rulers of Momostenango *(Chwa Tzak)* by showing their affiliation with the ruling line of Utatlán" (Carmack 1973, 63). A map, Carmack tells us, "shows Momostenango to be one link in a chain extending west from Utatlán." The depiction of a Spanish coat of arms, he contends, demonstrates "the acceptance of the Utatlán rulers by the Crown, while the linkage with the house of Moctezuma shows an acceptance of their prehispanic nobility and rulership by the Aztecs." However, if Moctezuma arranged for two of his daughters to marry K'iche' rulers, why don't other *títulos* and other documents mention what would have been highly significant links with the Aztecs?

Nijaib I, furthermore, states that four Franciscan friars accompanied Pedro de Alvarado in the conquest. These friars, it is alleged, baptized a number of caciques in the Quetzaltenango area. *Nijaib I* also states that thirteen lineage heads, all recently baptized as Christians, and forty K'iche' soldiers accompanied Alvarado as guides in his campaign of conquest. Rather than seek legitimacy and acceptance through Moctezuma, here it is maintained that the ancestors embraced Christianity quickly and then played a key role in helping Alvarado attain his military goals. Franciscans, despite what the *título* asserts, did *not* enter Guatemala with Alvarado. It also seems improbable that other K'iche' nobles would have participated voluntarily in the Spanish conquest of Utatlán, which followed soon after the battles near Quetzaltenango. The *Título del Ajpop Huitzitzil Tzunún* (Gall 1963), however, which was written around 1567 by lords of Utatlán, Quezaltenango, and "probably other towns," depicts the K'iche' leader Huitzitzil Tzunún, according to Carmack (1973, 41–42), as a "Christian leader among his people" who aided the Spaniards in the conquest of Utatlán as an effort to "procure special privileges for him and his descendants."

Why did members of the K'iche' nobility make these claims? Why did they undermine their credibility by advancing information that runs the gamut from doubtful to absurd? Was it because of a lack of sophistication on their part, or was it because they saw themselves and their society in a state of severe crisis and decline and thus acted out of a sense of desperation?

Another matter that has generated debate and is the subject of controversy is that of Tecún Umán, grandson of the great King Quikab and the "captain general" reputed to have led K'iche' forces against Alvarado at El Pinar (Pachah) near Quezaltenango (Xelaju'). Tecún Umán, according to some K'iche' sources, engaged in man-to-man combat with Alvarado and died as a result of it. Legend has it that Tecún Umán transformed himself into a quetzal bird and propelled himself toward the mounted Alvarado, decapitating the conquistador's horse with his weapon. According to *Nijaib I*, Tecún Umán was startled to see that Alvarado did not die after he had beheaded his horse. Almost instantly, Alvarado himself lanced and killed the K'iche' leader.

Legend aside, although Alvarado does mention that a prominent K'iche' warrior died in this first battle and that, the following day, a number of important K'iche' leaders were taken prisoner or died in a subsequent engagement, no specific reference is made of Tecún Umán (Mackie 1924, 58–60). The K'iche' hero also escaped the notice of Alvarado's contemporary Bernal Díaz del Castillo in his account of the conquest of Guatemala (Díaz del Castillo 1974, 410–15). Only much later, toward the end of the seventeenth century, did the chronicler Francisco Antonio de Fuentes y Guzmán (1969–72) and, after him, other historians begin to write about Tecún Umán. In our day, Tecún Umán has been appropriated and embraced by the Guatemalan army (Anonymous 1963) as a national hero. Menchú herself makes reference to the K'iche' figure, as do countless others.

Recently, however, historians Jorge Luján Muñoz and Horacio Cabezas Carcache (1993, 52–53) have cast doubt on whether Tecún Umán ever existed, let alone died in mortal combat with Alvarado. Although we cannot begin to do justice to the story of Tecún Umán, it serves to illustrate the complexity of such issues: what seems a matter of fact to many, including the Guatemalan army, Robert Carmack, and Rigoberta Menchú, appears at best hazy and contradictory to ourselves and strikes two historians of Guatemala as baseless legend. At times the research we do calls for us simply to accept ambiguity, accommodate distortions, and move on. The fact that we have good reasons to query certain statements in sixteenth-century Maya documents, or in the testimony of Menchú, hardly means that they are fraudulent and next to worthless in terms of the information they contain.

Our Sorrow, Our Suffering

Stoll is in no doubt about the raison d'être of Menchú's testimony: "Rigoberta's purpose in telling her story the way that she did," he writes, "enabled her to focus international condemnation on an institution that deserved it, the Guatemalan army" (1999, viii–xi).

Menchú's account is many things, but above all else it is an act of political protest aimed at capturing the attention of an international audience that she believes, rightly or wrongly, can ameliorate the dire situation of her people. In its clamor to be heard, Menchú's testimony has a fascinating if little-known counterpart in sixteenth-century Guatemala, when Indian communities in the environs of the colonial capital of Santiago, today Antigua, wrote a series of *memorias* (Dakin and Lutz 1996) to King Philip II of Spain, "memoirs" or "memorials" that describe in moving detail "our sorrow, our suffering."

In a strict linguistic sense these testimonies are not Maya, because they are written mostly in Nahuatl, the lingua franca of New Spain and, to a lesser extent, of early colonial Guatemala. In other ways, however, they are very much Maya testimonies, for they express the deeply felt sentiments of a score of native communities, the overwhelming majority of whose inhabitants were Maya (Lutz 1994). Only one of the original twenty-one *memorias*, as well as a letter of introduction from a past president of the Audiencia or Royal Court of Guatemala, Francisco Brizeño, were written in the language of the conquerors. Due, most likely, to failure on the part of Spanish officialdom to respond to the grievances being aired, the same *pueblos* and *barrios* furnished the Crown with another set of *memorias*, this time composed in Spanish (AGI, Guatemala 54). The first set of *memorias* dates to 1572, the second to 1576.

Like Menchú, the authors and signatories of the *memorias*, almost without exception, were of humble origin; in fact, most of their ancestors had been enslaved a half-century earlier, in the course of military conquest. If their forefathers at one time had been members of the nobility, it was, by the 1570s, beyond anybody's ability to prove it. Thus, while those who signed the *memorias* were male authorities serving as *alcaldes* (mayors), *regidores* (aldermen), or *escribanos* (scribes) of municipal councils, like Menchú they spoke not just for themselves but on behalf of entire communities. Having been emancipated for more than twenty years, these communities wrote to the king to protest the excesses they suffered at the hands of several parties, including low-level and high-ranking royal officials, Spanish settlers, and even African slaves who saw fit to serve their Spanish masters by themselves abusing Indians.

The *memorias*, in many respects, are more inclusive and democratic than the elite-generated texts we have discussed so far. Maya *títulos* often had a political motivation, but they do not speak out against social injustice in the direct manner that the *memorias* do. Whereas the native voices of Menchú, and those articulated by Victor Montejo and Q'anil Akab (1992), may have been heard, the *memorias* sent to the Crown in 1572 and 1576 languished in silence for four centuries in the Archivo General de Indias in Seville. Despite having been forgotten for so long, the voices of protest that surface in the *memorias* continue to be relevant, resonating even today for Mayas who maintain that aspects of contemporary life in Guatemala, especially the way they are treated by government officials, Ladino landowners, and city housewives, remind them constantly of their status as "second-class" citizens.

Unlike today, however, when we describe certain behavior and attitudes in terms of discrimination and racism, the authors of the *memorias* did not possess such a terminology. Instead, in their plaintive, poetic style, they recount the slanders and insults they had to endure at the hands of Spaniards, detailing mistreatment at all levels of society, from the behavior of the Audiencia's top judges or *oidores* to the slights of a lowly jailer or *carcelero*. Narrative repetition in the wording of the *memorias* is seldom boring. On the contrary, it makes it easier for the reader, as with Menchú, to pay attention and become absorbed by a compelling story.

The *memorias* are filled with harrowing details of the hardships of daily life. By the early 1570s, Indians who lived close to Spanish settlements in Guatemala knew Spaniards personally—they lived on their lands, they labored in their fields, and they worked as servants or artisans in their houses. Most paid burdensome tribute to the Crown and complained bitterly of Spanish census takers. Many had to provide labor under the terms of a draft known as *servicio ordinario,* which saw them not only work but also supply commodities such as fodder for livestock for a pittance. Because of the heavy demand placed on the best lands surrounding the capital city, native communities there complained of a scarcity of land to grow essential foodstuffs, especially corn. Other woes included the seizure and sale of orphaned children and the mistreatment leveled at Indian *alcaldes* and *regidores* who were responsible for the flow of labor and tribute and who were punished when the system inevitably faltered. Another thread that runs through the *memorias* is the high incidence of physical and verbal abuse, of institutionalized violence. We will now touch briefly on these subjects, selecting appropriate quotations to illustrate the key points.

Paying Tribute

> Everyone pays tribute, even blind persons who cannot see.
> —*Memoria* 8 (Dakin and Lutz 1996, 37)

In their petitions to the Crown, the Indians who lived near or on the outskirts of Santiago complained most bitterly about the tribute they had to pay. They were especially aggrieved by irregularities in how new tributary lists were compiled, for they were subject to systematic overassessment. The heavy-handed manner in which Spaniards went about tribute collection also pained them. One judge in particular, Licenciado Valdés de Cárcamo, who was personally responsible for carrying out the tributary counts of nearly all of the *pueblos* and *barrios* that composed the *memorias,* was singled out for his obnoxious behavior. In Santa Ana, adjacent to the capital city, local officials wrote to their parish priest in the hope that he would draw Valdés's indiscretions to the attention of the king:

> You must already know how Licenciado Valdés made us suffer when he carried out his tribute count. He lived among us, here in Santa Ana, for nine days. Each day he ate four chickens. The *nahuatlato* [interpreter] Bobadilla paid *one real* for every four chickens. He who did not deliver a chicken went to jail. The men were frightened. They gave him their chickens. You know this already, our Father Friar Sebastián. There are twenty loads of fodder that they take to [his] house every day, and four loads of firewood to cook [his] food. Nothing has been paid. They collect forty eggs from the houses each day. They don't even pay at the houses where they go [to collect]. . . . Inspections were carried out. [Valdés] registered in the tribute census all the men, their children, the poor, and the orphans, who only eat and drink with the help of the rest. . . . By order of the *Corregidor* Gabriel Mejía, the tribute of those who died also [had to be] paid. The *alcalde,* the *regidor,* and the *alguaciles* (constables)— . . . everyone pays tribute, even blind persons who cannot see. (Dakin and Lutz 1996, 36–37)

In the Barrio of Santo Domingo, inhabited by Mexicans as well as Kachiqueles, the *cabildo* officials wrote: "Some who are very old and poor or who are one-handed and crippled or who are blind and maimed, we don't dare demand [tribute] of them, and for this reason they apprehend us and throw us in jail until it is collected" (Dakin and Lutz 1996, 73). The allegations appear not to have been exaggerated, for they are recounted time after time with remarkable consistency, community after community, not just in Santa Ana and the Barrio of Santo Domingo.

Providing Services

> They give these services to the Spaniards, [who] are our masters.
> —AGI, Guatemala 54: "Los indios que eran
> esclavos . . . [1576]," folio 25

The fulfillment of *servicio ordinario* ("ordinary service") entailed for Indians the provision of labor, often on a daily basis, for Spanish households in Santiago in addition to working on Spanish estates in the countryside. Routine city chores included cleaning, cooking, baking bread, carrying water, supplying firewood, and ensuring that a plentiful supply of fodder was on hand to feed Spanish horses. Rural obligations were equally diverse, involving all sorts of agricultural activities, including the tending of livestock. *Servicio ordinario* in time gave way to *repartimiento*, a system of low-paid forced or corvée labor. Whether they were residents of an urban *barrio* or a rural *pueblo*, Indians would count on being called to perform tasks that were frequent, onerous, and poorly rewarded, if paid for at all. To make matters worse, on top of heavy demands for their labor, the Spanish officials extorted illegal fines and payments from their native charges. In the Milpa de Dueñas, local leaders clearly felt overwhelmed by the labor duties imposed on them:

> Here is the labor obligation of the men who work in Dueñas. Each week twenty men harvest maize. When they finish harvesting maize, they then cut sugar cane close to Dueñas. There [live] here those who go to carry fodder [to the Spaniards in the city] and one worker who is sold [rented]. Six bring fodder by order of Valdés. Others work on the streets. They make them sweep. Now the people suffer with that. Now they weep a lot out of sadness. (Dakin and Lutz 1996, 65)

For Guatemala, historical testimony of this nature is hard to come by. It may strike the reader as little more than an odd piece of information removed from a longer or larger context. This is why it is important to note that, in 1572, the leaders of San Antonio Aguas Calientes likewise protested that "each week six men deliver six loads of fodder for one *tomín*," a meager sum worth only one-quarter of a *tostón*. A century later, in 1672, the *alcalde* and *regidores* of San Antonio petitioned the authorities that, as was well known, their community was obliged to provide fodder to the city all year long. As the people of San Antonio had neither fodder nor sufficient land to spare, they were obliged to go elsewhere to buy the fodder, which they did at great cost, in order to meet their tribute requirements. An indifferent response would not have been any less than was expected: instead of delivering the fodder, it was decreed that an equivalent amount in cash would suffice (Dakin and Lutz 1996, 49 and 113 n. 13). The conditions that the authors of the *memorias* complained about, which often vanish from the historical record, in this case did not disappear from the daily grind for some time.

Selling Orphans

> Valdés asked for the orphans he was going to sell, for whom we were held to ransom at the sum of five reales each.
> —*Memoria 7* (Dakin and Lutz 1996, 31)

One of the most nefarious practices of early colonial officialdom, in which Spanish residents were also involved, was the seizure and subsequent sale of Indian orphans, both boys and girls, to willing accomplices and, on occasion, to native families in the children's home community who wanted them back. As in the 1980s, when tens of thousands of Maya offspring were left orphaned by army counterinsurgency campaigns, untold numbers of children lost one or both parents in the wake of the Spanish Conquest. The orphan issue dates back in the historical record to the 1550s and 1560s (Dakin and Lutz 1996, xxxiv–xxxvi). Even after the period of intense fighting had ended, Indians continued to die or to flee from epidemics that struck, with heavy loss of life, throughout the colonial period (Lovell and Lutz 1996). Native men in particular often saw flight, to escape tribute and labor obligations, as their best option, leaving their wives and children behind to fend for themselves. Population displacement as well as population decline thus meant that Spaniards always had to be on the lookout for innovative ways to overcome shortages of labor. Trafficking in orphans was one such strategy.

As early as July 1, 1570, a newly appointed inspector of all the native towns ten leagues around Santiago was instructed to record the number of orphans and place them in useful employment. His instructions went so far as to decree that if he were to find that some two-parent families "had many children," some of them should be put to work. Although the policy was vigorously enforced by the infamous Valdés de Cárcamo in the early 1570s, it appears to have been used predominantly as an extortion racket, a means of exacting bribes from communities that did not wish to have their children siphoned off and so paid up in order to hold on to them.

Numerous *memorias,* both urban and rural, bemoan the seizure of orphans. Officials of the Barrio of Santo Domingo lament:

> They have done many things to us here. They have taken step-children and orphans, sons and daughters from us, in order to give them to the Spaniards. And when they return the boys and girls to us, we pay seven *reales* to the scribe Juan de Chávez and one *tostón* for an official retention order and another *tostón* for the constable who goes to retrieve the child. (Dakin and Lutz 1996, 73, 75)

These "charges" put the total cost of ransoming one child at nearly two pesos. Santo Domingo's officials claimed that, in one transaction, they had to pay two hundred *tostones* to recover abducted children, meaning some fifty of them were "brought back" from captivity in this manner. Far from being a unique case, the experience of Santo Domingo befell other neighboring communities, and the noxious practice continued until at least the end of the sixteenth century.

Usurping Land

> Now we don't have lands where we can harvest hay to sell.
> —*Memoria* 2 (Dakin and Lutz 1996, 7)

Spaniards expropriating land from indigenous populations is nothing especially unusual in the history of Latin America. What is notable about the area around Santiago de Guatemala, however, is that native inhabitants began to complain of a shortage of land relatively early on, even when their numbers were in steep decline (Lutz 1994, 63–78; Lovell and Lutz 1996). In Guatemala, Spanish appropriation of land in the vicinity of Santiago began in 1527, resulting in the steady erosion of Indian holdings, and in the appearance of scores of private estates held by Spanish conquerors and colonists. On these estates were settled recently acquired Indian slaves. The communities that came into being in this way still characterize Santiago's distinctive cultural landscape. Aside from these rural settlements, the Spaniards founded two cities: in 1527, Santiago in Almolonga, destroyed by mudslides in 1541 and subsequently relocated a short distance to the north as Santiago de Guatemala. Such a flurry of activity within a few decades of conquest, followed by the emancipation of some three to five thousand Indian slaves at mid-century, led to the founding of indigenous *barrios* around the edges of the capital. Indian communities required land from which to derive a livelihood. They had to compete for land, however, with Spanish properties that occupied the best valley locations in order to grow wheat and graze livestock. By the 1570s, as Santiago expanded, Indians in both rural and urban areas began to feel the pressure, exerted also, especially in city districts, by poor Spaniards, free blacks and mulattoes, and mestizos who had appeared on the scene.

Land scarcity was not viewed by the authors of the *memorias* as an isolated problem. On the contrary, they relate it directly to the myriad economic demands of Spanish rule, which in their case included paying a land rent known as the *terrazgo*. In 1572, the inhabitants of the Barrio of La Merced told the king: "We who are here in Santa María de la Merced suffer greatly because we live on land for which we [each] have to pay two *tostones* a year" (Dakin and Lutz 1996, 9). Rent in this instance was paid to the Mercedarian Convent.

The inhabitants of the Milpa de Ceballos made their *terrazgo* payments to the landowner Pedro de Ceballos in kind as well as in cash: "Our tribute to Pedro de Ceballos is twelve loads of maize, twelve chickens, and twelve *tostones* each year" (Dakin and Lutz 1996, 61). Even though Pedro de Alvarado and Francisco Marroquín, Guatemala's first bishop, were by now long deceased, and even though Indian slavery had formally ended twenty years or so earlier, the Kaqchikel and K'iche' inhabitants of Jocotenango, situated at the northern edge of the Spanish capital, wrote to the king as if they were still slaves who lived on the properties of their onetime masters. They proclaimed:

> No longer are there royal lands where we could live.... We now ask that King Philip of Castille help us. That he grant us a provision here for the lands of Don Pedro de Alvarado and Bishop Francisco Marroquín. That he may help us in our need. That he help the sons of the Emperor, King of Spain. (Dakin and Lutz 1996, 81)

Four years later, the leaders of the Barrio of Santo Domingo spoke even more forcibly about their lack of land:

> We, the poor Indians of this city, have no land to call our own, it having been taken away from us for the benefit of the Spaniards. We have to pay

terrazgo to them, to work [the land] for them, or to lease it for pasture or to grow wheat. They want to take from us the little land and house lots [we have left]. Because we live close to the city, they harass and bother us. (Dakin and Lutz 1996, xxxviii)

Like Menchú, the leaders of the Barrio of Santo Domingo had no difficulty and saw nothing problematical in contradicting themselves in order to get a crucial point across. The people of the *barrio* are acknowledged still to have some land remaining, yet their representatives depict the gravity of the situation as one in which "we have no land to call our own." A statement surely does not have to be literally true in order for it to have validity and meaning.

Abusing Indian Representatives

Always, our sole award was to be imprisoned.
—*Memoria* 12 (Dakin and Lutz 1996, 49)

In Guatemala, as elsewhere in Spanish America, one of the most persecuted social groups was local Indian officials whose job it was, in a variety of ways, to function as intermediaries between the colonial bureaucracy and members of the community they were either elected or delegated to represent. Whether on the doorstep of the Spanish capital or far away in some remote and isolated province, it was these often luckless individuals who were held responsible for collecting tribute and administering the operation of labor drafts.

When tribute was not fully paid or when native workers were not provided in the requisite numbers at the assigned time, even when orphans were not handed over before a declared deadline, Spanish officials soon confronted Indian representatives, bullying and intimidating them to take action. No doubt colonial authorities were themselves under pressure to deliver the goods, as was the case with Valdés de Cárcamo, charged with the impossible task of furnishing the Crown with Indian tribute at a time of precipitous native depopulation. Valdés's strategy, as we have noted, was to register anyone and everyone as an eligible tributary, including many who previously had been exempted from the obligation. Enlisting widows, the blind, and the physically handicapped was one thing; another matter entirely was to collect from them, which is what Indian leaders were expected to do. When they failed, punishment was swift and demeaning. *Alcaldes* made up the shortfall by enforcing fines or exacting bribes. Spanish retribution, furthermore, was accompanied by a barrage of abuse and derogatory remarks. The *cabildo* members of the Milpa de Juan Pérez Dardón were among those community representatives unfortunate to incur the wrath of Valdés and his nasty henchmen:

> They punished us when Valdés de Cárcamo, his scribe, Juan de Chávez, and his interpreter, Juan de Bobadilla, arrived. They came on a Saturday and on the Sunday they threw us in jail. None of the men attended Mass. On the Monday he had us pulled on to the street by horses, which scared us. They gave us two hundred lashes in the street. Twice the punishment was carried out, that is two times, here in our town. They gave twenty lashes to each of us and then they shaved off our hair. This was done in the month of August. (Dakin and Lutz 1996, 23)

Town after town, *barrio* after *barrio*, the stories go on and on. The indignity of it all is nowhere more poignantly expressed than by the words of the *cabildo* members of Santa María de Jesús. At the end of an eight-day stay, the Indian leaders tell us, Valdés, Chávez, and Bobadilla brought their tribute assessment to a close by saying: "You are sodomites. You are pigs. You are bestial men." It all proved too much for the *alcalde* and *regidores* to bear. "That is what they said. Here we became very sick because of their words."

Conclusion

> A woman who knows how to tell a good story effectively, one that sounds true, is aware that she can skillfully conceal many another fault she might have.
>
> —B. Traven, *Trozas* (1936)

The Maya nobility who were the authors of sixteenth-century *títulos* appealed for Crown recognition of their status and privileges, marshaling and embellishing "facts," as they saw them, in an attempt to restore or, at the very least, try to preserve what remained of a way of life that was fast disappearing. Likewise, the common folk of more popular or unknown origins who authored the Nahuatl *memorias* called out for action to counter the abuses they endured at the hands of royal officials as well as Spanish settlers and landowners: "Help us, you, *our* King, Don Felipe," was the cry from the Indian *pueblos* and *barrios* of Santiago de Guatemala. Their cry actually reached Spain in 1572, but it fell on deaf ears, prompting the same communities to call out again in 1576. Perhaps the tributary reforms implemented in Guatemala in the late 1570s and early 1580s by President García de Valverde constituted a form of state response to native protest, but if so it was another sorry instance of too little, too late.

Similar to these sixteenth-century appeals for justice, Rigoberta Menchú also cried out against even greater horrors perpetrated against her people by twentieth-century equivalents of Pedro de Alvarado and Valdés de Cárcamo. Alas, unlike her sixteenth-century counterparts from in and around Santiago de Guatemala, Menchú had no delusions that an appeal to the president of the republic would do any good. She made her pitch, instead, to the international community in the form of moving speeches and a powerful testimony given the permanence of print by her collaboration with Elisabeth Burgos-Debray. However problematical the latter may appear to David Stoll, we contend that it is the primacy of larger truths that should concern us, in the sixteenth century as much as today, in order to get at the essence of what has happened in Guatemala since the Spanish Conquest on.

We close with one final reflection: What is the point of it all? Does not Stoll, in effect, exhibit exactly the same selectivity in constructing his text as Menchú does in constructing hers? As best we can discern, Stoll could easily have arranged his findings to support what Menchú has to say as much as criticize her for how she goes about saying it. Stoll, well aware of the work of the Catholic church's project for the Recovery of Historical Memory (REMHI 1998) and the United Nations' Commission for Historical Clarification (1999), could equally have fleshed out the truthfulness of one person's testimony with the disclosures of lots of others, including some of his own informants. Why he chose to do things the way that he did remains a mystery not only to us but also to many of his fellow scholars of Guatemala.

Bibliography

AGI, Guatemala 54. 1576. "Los indios que eran esclavos . . . [1576]." Archivo General de Indias, Legajo Guatemala 54. Seville.

Anonymous. 1963. *La muerte de Tecún Umán: Estudio crítico de la conquista del altiplano occidental de la República*. Guatemala: Editorial del Ejército.

Carmack, Robert M. 1973. *Quichean Civilization: The Ethnohistoric, Ethnographic and Archaeological Sources*. Berkeley, Los Angeles, and London: University of California Press.

Commission for Historical Clarification. 1999. *Guatemala: Memory of Silence*. Guatemala City: Litoprint.

Dakin, Karen, and Christopher H. Lutz, trans. and eds. 1996. *Nuestro pesar, nuestra aflicción/tunetuliniliz, tucucuca: Memorias en lengua náhuatl enviadas a Felipe II por indígenas del valle de Guatemala hacia 1572.* Mexico City: Universidad Nacional Autónoma de México.

de la Garza, Mercedes. 1975. *La conciencia histórica de los antiguos mayas.* Centro Estudios Maya, Cuaderno 11. Mexico City: Universidad Nacional Autónoma de México.

Díaz del Castillo, Bernal. 1974. *Historia verdadera de la Conquista de la Nueva España.* 10th ed. Introduction and notes by Joaquín Ramírez Cabañas. Mexico City: Editorial Porrúa.

Fuentes y Guzmán, Francisco Antonio de. 1969–72. *Obras históricas de D. Francisco Antonio de Fuentes y Guzmán.* Ed. Carmelo Sáenz de Santamaría. 3 vols. Biblioteca de Autores Españoles, nos. 230, 251, and 259. Madrid: Ediciones Atlas.

Gall, Francis. 1963. *Título del Ajpop Huitzizil Tzunún: Probanza de Méritos de los León y Cardona. Guatemala City: Ministerio de Educación Pública.*

Kendall, Carl, John Hawkins, and Laurel Bossen, eds. 1983. *Heritage of Conquest: Thirty Years Later.* Albuquerque: University of New Mexico Press.

La Farge, Oliver. 1947. *Santa Eulalia: The Religion of a Cuchumatán Indian Town.* Chicago: University of Chicago Press.

Las Casas, Bartolomé de. 1958. *Apologética histórica de las Indias.* 2 vols. Biblioteca de Autores Españoles, nos. 105, 106. (Vol. 2, no. 106 cited in current study.) Madrid: Ediciones Atlas.

Lovell, W. George, and Christopher H. Lutz. 1995. *Demography and Empire: A Guide to the Population History of Spanish Central America, 1500–1821.* Dellplain Latin American Studies, no. 33. Boulder, Colo.: Westview Press.

Lovell, W. George, and Christopher H. Lutz. 1996. "'A Dark Obverse': Maya Survival in Guatemala, 1520–1994." *Geographical Review* 86.3: 398–407.

Luján Muñoz, Jorge, and Horacio Cabezas Carcache. 1993. "La Conquista." In *Dominación Española: Desde la Conquista hasta 1700,* vol. ed. Ernesto Chinchilla Aguilar, general ed. Jorge Luján Muñoz. *Historia General de Guatemala,* vol. 2, 47–74. Guatemala City: Asociación de Amigos del País, Fundación para la Cultura y el Desarrollo.

Lutz, Christopher H. 1994. *Santiago de Guatemala, 1541–1773: City, Caste, and the Colonial Experience.* Norman: University of Oklahoma Press.

Mackie, Sedley J., ed. and trans. 1924. *An Account of the Conquest of Guatemala in 1524 by Pedro de Alvarado.* New York: The Cortés Society.

Memorial de Sololá. See Recinos and Goetz, *The Annals of the Cakchiquels.*

Menchú, Rigoberta. 1984. *I, Rigoberta Menchú: An Indian Woman in Guatemala.* Ed. and introd. Elisabeth Burgos-Debray. Trans. Ann Wright. London: Verso.

Montejo, Victor. 1987. *Testimony: Death of a Guatemalan Village.* Translated by Victor Perera. Willimantic, Conn.: Curbstone Press.

Montejo, Victor, and Q'anil Akab. 1992. *Brevísima relación testimonial de la continua destrucción del Mayab' (Guatemala).* Providence, R.I.: Guatemala Scholars Network.

Recinos, Adrián, ed. and trans. 1957. *Crónicas indígenas de Guatemala.* Guatemala City: Editorial Universitaria.

———, trans. 1950. *Popol Vuh: The Sacred Book of the Ancient Quiché Maya.* English version by Delia Goetz and Sylvanus G. Morley. Norman: University of Oklahoma Press.

Recinos, Adrián, and Delia Goetz, trans. 1953. *The Annals of the Cakchiquels.* Norman: University of Oklahoma Press.

REMHI (Recuperación de Memoria Histórica). 1998. *Guatemala: Nunca Más.* 4 vols. Guatemala City: Oficina de Derechos Humanos del Arzobispado.

Simonds, Merilyn. 1999. *The Lion in the Room Next Door.* Toronto: McClelland and Stewart.

Stoll, David. 1993. *Between Two Armies in the Ixil Towns of Guatemala.* New York: Columbia University Press.

————. 1999. *Rigoberta Menchú and the Story of All Poor Guatemalans.* Boulder, Colo.: Westview Press.

Tax, Sol, ed. 1952. *Heritage of Conquest: The Ethnohistory of Middle America.* New York: Macmillan.

Tedlock, Dennis, trans. 1985. *Popol Vuh: The Mayan Book of the Dawn of Life.* New York: Simon and Schuster.

Traven, B. *Trozas.* 1998. Translated from the German [1936] by Hugh Young. Chicago: Ivan R. Dee.

Tzaquitzal Zapata, Alfonso Efraín, trans. 1993. *Título de los señores Coyoy.* Edición bilingüe K'iche'-Español transcripción k'iche' de Robert M. Carmack. Guatemala: Comisión Interuniversitaria del Quinto Centenario del Descubrimiento de América (CIGDA).

Telling Truths

*Taking David Stoll and the Rigoberta Menchú
Exposé Seriously*

Kay B. Warren

On December 15, 1998, journalist Larry Rohter broke a disturbing scandal on the first page of the *New York Times*. By all appearances, indigenous rights activist and Nobel Peace Prize winner Rigoberta Menchú had significantly misrepresented her life in the world-famous autobiographic account *I, Rigoberta Menchú: An Indian Woman in Guatemala* (1984). Through independent interviews in Menchú's home village, Chimel, just outside San Miguel Uspantán in the western highlands of Guatemala, Rohter had apparently verified key aspects of anthropologist David Stoll's new book, *Rigoberta Menchú and the Story of All Poor Guatemalans* (1999). Rural Guatemalans who knew the family and even some of Menchú's relatives disputed her story of political activism. If these charges were accurate, the book that had kindled the international scrutiny of Guatemala's abusive military and its wartime torture and killing of tens of thousands of civilians during the late 1970s and 1980s was full of inaccuracies, half-truths, and events that did not happen as portrayed. Not only had Rigoberta Menchú misconstrued the world around her but she had dramatically altered her own past.

In a narrow sense, what seems to be at stake is the integrity of a public intellectual and human rights leader. From a wider angle, however, the stakes are higher and strikingly diverse. Professors in universities throughout the United States and Europe have used her book in classes; some have cited it in their research. Many now wonder if they can still legitimately teach the book to undergraduates. The virtue of the book has always been its accessibility and the way its first-person account connects so well with students on important issues distant from their life experiences. Activist Guatemalans and their international sympathizers worry about the political fallout from this well-publicized attempt to discredit the rebels and the popular opposition to state violence during the counterinsurgency wars of 1960–86. At stake is not only whether the insurgent left was fighting a just war with broad civilian support, but also whether the rebellion, supported by an international solidarity movement centered in the United States and Europe, did more harm than good.

One has the feeling that the Stoll versus Menchú controversy will join the pool of legendary debates in anthropology: Lewis versus Redfield, Freeman versus Mead, Sahlins versus Obeyesekere. But this is what is so interesting. The other debates have involved anthropological peers challenging each other in academic venues over the quality of field research, clashing analytical framings, and the significance of distinctive findings. By contrast, Stoll, a Latin Americanist and professor of anthropology at Middlebury College, is publicly disputing the credibility of a Mayan leader and nonacademic observer. At first glance, something very new appears to be happening in the discipline of cultural anthropology.

In this essay, I argue that anthropology's transformation in the last decades of the twentieth century from a field that reveled in the distinctiveness of local communities to one that studies translocal processes and politics means that anthropologists will increasingly engage public intellectuals and other peers from the countries we study.[1] Thus, rather than dismissing Stoll as an ideologically motivated outlaw, as some have, it makes more sense to understand him as someone who reveals telling dilemmas that have propelled the discipline into the new millennium. This shift in anthropology's scope makes it all the more essential to ask why his work generates such heated criticism.

The Power of a Personal Testimony, Displaced

Stoll is aware that Rigoberta Menchú dictated her wartime autobiography as a *testimonio*, as testimonial literature. This genre gained fame in Latin America as a strategy to air subaltern voices in the court of world opinion. *Testimonios* have always had a political edge. They are designed to describe state violence, corrosive poverty, and inhuman working conditions in a way that makes a compelling case for dramatic change. The *testimonio* genre attempts to make abstractions—violence, poverty, and degrading living conditions—real by personalizing their effects and recounting heroic stories of individual resistance to entrenched inequities in the face of overwhelming odds.

Rigoberta as a young child takes readers on a journey to experience life on coastal plantations through her eyes. We see her family loaded into the back of an airless truck and follow the story of children who toil alongside adults in the fields. This little girl yearned to work harder, to do her part and fill the heavy bags of harvested cotton and coffee. Day laborers were forced to work long hours to fill the mandated quota or face additional work the next day. In exchange, adults received $1.20 per day and children 20 cents. As Rigoberta observed: "Watching [my mother] made me feel useless and weak because I couldn't do anything to help her except look after my brother. That's when my consciousness was born. It's true. . . . I wanted to work, more than anything, to help her, both economically and physically" (Menchú 1984, 34). These personal stories evoke the tensions between the striking work ethic of Mayan families, whose members struggle to make the best of their difficult situation, and a system that cruelly steals their accomplishments and family members away from them. Rigoberta's two-year-old brother lay dying of malnutrition—years earlier her older brother had succumbed to pesticide poisoning—and their mother could not find help or medicine to try to save him. Their isolation was frightening: the search for work had dispersed the rest of the family to other farms, neither Rigoberta nor her mother could effectively communicate to other workers across Mayan languages or in Spanish, and the overseers were unconcerned. At the child's death they are thrown off the plantation for being disruptive—without their two weeks' pay.

As an adult, Rigoberta reflects on the larger dynamic her family could not escape:

> Those fifteen days working in the finca was one of my earliest experiences and I remember it with enormous hatred. That hatred has stayed with me until today. . . . It's one long process of robbing them of their pay. They're charged for absolutely everything, even for the loading of the lorry. Then, in the fincas, the overseers steal from the workers from the very first day. The cantina steals from them too. It continues until the last day. (Ibid., 42)[2]

The intimate family history rivets readers early in the book. It prepares the audience for continuing stories of exploitation and humiliation and for subsequent moments when Rigoberta's consciousness would be triggered. The autobiography captures her continued radicalization through the suffering of her family: the army's kidnap, torture, and murder of her brother, a political organizer; the death of her activist father in the burning of the Spanish embassy; and the gang rape and torture killing of her mother—all in 1979 and 1980.

David Stoll's challenge to the Menchú account draws readers up short with a jarring revelation that marks the beginning of a stream of allegations that dispute her status as an eyewitness to the events she describes: "Although Rigoberta has often said that she grew up bilingual and illiterate, this is not how she is remembered in Uspantán. What distinguished her was that Catholic nuns took her away to boarding school" (Stoll 1999, 159). Stoll believes that Rigoberta Menchú did not directly experience the rigors of plantation work until she was twenty and worked as a leftist organizer on the coast. He finds that much of Menchú's childhood was spent in a series of Catholic schools beginning at the age of six or seven when she was taken to a school in Chichicastenango in southern Quiché for a year or two.[3] It is important to add that this was not an uncommon pattern for those in her generation from modest backgrounds whom local priests and nuns identified as especially promising. Facing an inadequate school system and struggling against the odds of a 75 percent illiteracy rate for Mayan women (AVANCSO 1991) called for great personal sacrifice.

But the question remains: How do we make sense of Rigoberta Menchú's *testimonio* and David Stoll's exposé in light of such radical discrepancies?

Realist Representation and the Latin American *Testimonio*

Testimonio writers share a commitment to realism with anthropologists, who use similar conventions when they introduce life stories and thick description vignettes into their ethnographies. Realist modes of representation create the illusion of an unmediated window on the world to allow the vicarious experience of social realities outside the reader's own life experience. *Testimonios* gain their narrative power through the metaphor of witnessing. They offer eyewitness experiences of injustice and violence in cinematographic detail, and thereby create the effect of witnesses presenting evidence to the court of public opinion.

In the 1980s, Latin American *testimonios* were written in the language of cold war politics. Although autobiographical in their self-presentation, *testimonios* are for the most part compiled by literate professionals to raise international awareness about state violence, pressure foreign governments for political leverage, and generate funding for their organizations. As in the Menchú account—where Elisabeth Burgos-Debray, a European-based Venezuelan anthropologist who actively supported revolutionary movements, was the intermediary—these writers record and transcribe interviews, and edit accounts to produce an "autobiography" that the protagonist would not otherwise have written.[4]

It is highly unlikely that Menchú would have produced an autobiographical account like this one on her own. In fact, autobiography, in a literary sense, is not indigenous to Mayan culture, though gifted storytellers are prized in Mayan communities. Instead, their favored genres include mythistories, surreal narratives, formal oratory, divining rituals, festival street theater, and abstract social critique. In the 1990s, Mayan intellectuals have experimented with other forms, including fiction, newspaper commentaries, and *testimonios*. Mayan expressive forms, old and new, appear less self-consumed than the Western fascination with biography and autobiography.

Latin America was the major source of works by indigenous Marxists in the 1970s and 1980s, arguing for the sui generis character of class-based political organizing. Rigoberta filled the "indigenous slot" for this genre in striking ways.[5] Interspersed and sometimes crowding out her accounts of growing political militancy are idealized ethnographic descriptions of Mayan culture. For Western readers she re-creates the cohesive Mayan community: the enactment of ceremonies at birth, marriage, and death and at key moments in the agricultural cycle; the respectful greeting of elders that has long been the essential metaphor for Mayan civility; and Mayan religiosity and the belief in personal animal doubles (called *nahuales*).

Being ethnically different—a monolingual Mayan in a world of hateful Spanish-speaking Ladinos—is central to her self-presentation. In much of the book, Rigoberta narrates the dehumanizing racism of Guatemala's Ladinos rather than focusing uniquely on class conflict and exploitation. After joining the organized opposition, she channels her political consciousness in fresh directions. The insight that despite cultural difference and widespread racism she has important Ladino allies in the struggle—workers, intellectuals, and militants—marks her personal transformation into a committed leftist activist (Menchú 1984, 119).

Like other forms of realist representation, *testimonios* are marked by their history of production and consumption. In the United States, *I, Rigoberta Menchú* has been a best-seller on college campuses, where it has been consumed by distinctive audiences since it appeared.[6] The testimony has also been read widely in Europe and other parts of Latin America. The book, however, did not circulate publicly in Guatemala until the 1990s because it was simply too dangerous to own a copy of anything so seditious.

The Exposer and Exposed

Stoll's critique of the Rigoberta Menchú *testimonio* bridges very different historical periods. His denunciations and the strong backlash generated by his position stem in part from this fact. Successive waves of internal warfare battered the country from 1960 to 1996. Menchú's narrative focuses on the apogee of the violence in 1980–82 when an estimated 26,000 to 35,000 people were killed in army massacres of whole villages in the western highlands.[7] In the wake of continuing violence, the Spanish edition of the book appeared in 1983 and the English edition a year later.

Stoll's exposé, however, found its 1999 North American and Guatemalan audiences at a very different political moment a decade after the fall of the Berlin Wall. Not only have cold war polarities been dismantled internationally, but academic views of identity politics now emphasize the multiplicity of identities and interests individuals assert in their lives. In Latin American countries with indigenous populations, ethnic resurgence has frequently displaced the older discourse of class conflict (Kearney 1996). After more than a decade of political limbo in Guatemala during which guerrilla and counterinsurgency demilitarization proved an illusive goal, the country finally emerged from the war period. The full implementation of the 1996 peace accords may turn out to be a daunting task, given the stunning failure of indigenous rights and other institutional reforms to garner national support in the May 1999 referendum.[8] Forging an inclusive democracy will be an ongoing project. Nevertheless, there are two important measures of the tremendous change the political system has undergone since the early 1990s. Former guerrillas are now part of the political party system, clashing and maneuvering for power with other leaders in an array of newly constituted parties on the left. The momentum for widening indigenous representation in national affairs survived the 1999 election of the new president, Alfonso Portillo, from the conservative Guatemalan Republican Front (FRG). Parties across the spectrum are recruiting their own politicized Mayan representatives. These axes of democratic inclusion would have been unthinkable in the mid-1980s.

Stoll's critique of Menchú involves the empiricist battle of facts versus politics. In effect, he refuses to read Menchú's autobiography as an instance of testimonial literature in which, by design, there is room for maneuver between collective and individual veracities. Rather, Stoll elects to judge the work within the paradigm of factual science, and concludes that he has uncovered an instance of fraud, the equivalent of fabricating experimental data. To put the book to the test, he questions and attempts to "corroborate" or "invalidate" each event and claim. He looks for eyewitnesses to events, puzzles over "evasions" in his interviews, cultivates "sources," pursues factual "inconsistencies," generates "evidence." He becomes a transnational detective: "Absent an official inquiry, I showed newspaper photos of the [burning of the Spanish embassy] to two arson investigators in California" (Stoll, 82).

In the process, Stoll conjures what he judges to be a very different image of rural politics, one in which Mayan conflicts can be just as important as Ladino/Mayan tensions, communal feelings coexist with feuding, and patterns of politicization are shifting and complex. Anthropologists have been interested in precisely these issues (Brintnall 1979; Annis 1987; Carmack 1995; AVANCSO 1991). Over the course of the civil war, violence became internalized in many communities as neighbors and kin reported about the behavior of their local enemies to the army or the guerrillas (Carmack 1988; Montejo 1987; Montejo and Q'anil Akab' 1992; Warren 1993; Carlsen 1997). As military tactics changed, army sweeps and clandestine death squads redirected and intensified local violence (Schirmer 1998). These findings are consistent with community-based ethnography in the western highlands. Here Stoll's exposé owes an underacknowledged debt to a history of scholarly engagement with rural realities in Guatemala.

In poor agrarian communities, land conflicts among Mayan families and sibling rivalries within extended families are not uncommon. Longstanding disputes between adjacent communities and, where there are large plantations, between large landholders and smallholders are endemic in a country where a tiny economic elite holds 75 percent of the agricultural land. Communal and shamanistic rituals focus on forging a sense of community and common purpose in the midst of a world driven by *envidia* (corrosive envy) where one person's gain (of education, wealth, ample harvests, large families, and good health) is often perceived as another's personal loss. Factionalism can follow these lines and, in recent decades, has often been spelled out in religious terms, with Catholics, evangelicals, and traditionalists taking different sides politically.

In the 1960s, highland communities were influenced by the spread of Catholic Action community groups, evangelical congregations, agrarian cooperatives, and the United States Peace Corps.[9] Local leaders, such as Menchú's father, routinely had contact with United States development organizations. It does not make sense to discredit their radicalism because of these early ties, as Stoll does. Some young Mayan leaders broke with traditionalism through the new groups; others found that the continuing land crisis overwhelmed the incremental advances they achieved through access to credit and fertilizer via the cooperative movement and opted for more radical political change. In some cases, Catholic Action groups were radicalized with the introduction of theology of liberation politics by foreign priests (Falla 1978). Still other youths looked to Mayan cultural resurgence instead of revolutionary politics. There is no universal story for Guatemalan communities because of the variations in access to agricultural land, regional economies, the impact of plantations, ethnic demographics, and distinctive political histories (Smith 1990; Wilson 1995). Few escaped the war and chronic economic uncertainty during the 1970s and 1980s. Most Mayans saw their personal subordination to local Ladino entitlements as a major issue in their lives, but not as the only challenge.

My larger point here is that there are a variety of ways of engaging *testimonios* and that seeing this instance as flawed academic history or autoethnography rather than as multiply authored transnational wartime propaganda from the onset has important repercussions. Stoll needs to be understood as one of a host of possible readings of *I, Rigoberta Menchú* whose differences spring from the ways the truth value of the book is conceived.

Ethnographic Writing as Exposé

With an empiricist approach, Stoll appears less aware that his work is framed by its own genre—the exposé—and, as a result, is also marked by a set of unspoken narrative conventions. The exposé has a singular goal of revealing truths that have been hidden from public view. It has the excitement of a pursuit, a detective adventure of discovering something not yet understood. The exposé focuses in a particularly interesting way on the exposer as well as on the exposed. The goal of this inquiry is to generate facts that will discredit accepted accounts and interpretations. Facts outside the frame of the immediate quest are ignored. We associate exposés with a dramatic leveling of those with power and prestige. Thus, exposé by its nature is a political genre.

I would suggest that one way of understanding the Stoll–Menchú controversy is to see it as a clash of genres or paradigms for political expression. Interestingly enough, exposé and *testimonio* share important characteristics. Both achieve their immediacy and authority as first-person accounts based on direct experience. Both involve a narrow, relentless framing to achieve a deeper truth. In this case, both take readers on journeys of political self-discovery and personal transformation. Because of their similarities, ethnographic exposé and testimonial literature become potent antagonists.

Stoll sees the mission of interrogating the wartime insurgency as more important than his choice of ethnographic genre. Yet, as anthropology has moved to multisited and transnational research, the question for the field has been how to best convey our findings.[10] If one takes Stoll's work seriously as social science rather than dismissing it as journalism, as some critics have, then it is also important to assess this book as an experimental ethnography. As one would do for other ethnographies, the issue is how the medium and findings interact and shape each other.

Stoll's book shares with other contemporary experiments the willingness to portray the process of doing field research as integral to the final product. We see Stoll gather information through a chain of interviews, follow his curiosity through personal adventure to the discovery process, and accompany him through an emerging counteranalysis of Menchú's community and personal history. This is a much more interactive representation than the classical testimonial that suppresses the compilers' interview questions. The narrative also serves to make the case for Stoll's care in amassing the evidence for his case, that his conclusions were based on an inductive method, not on ideologically preconceived lines of reasoning: "In the early 1980s, [compiler Elisabeth Burgos] was still a supporter of the revolutionary movement, along with myself and many others appalled by the brutality of the Guatemalan army. Since then my

thinking has changed because of my conversations with peasants, including many who once supported the guerrillas" (Stoll 1999, 184). For a significant number of current readers, however, Stoll's claim of personal
transformation is astonishing, given the selective framing of the project, his findings, and the tone of his earlier publications.

In another self-reflexive move, Stoll uses the account to discuss his
own situation and to position himself as someone who has been marginalized by postmodern trends in the discipline (231–47). His is the
heroic marginalization of the whistle-blower, in this case struggling
against the political correctness of the postmodern and left-leaning academic establishment. Here the exposé turns into a David and Goliath
story of Stoll versus the academic establishment. As Stoll asserts:

> Under the influence of postmodernism (which has undermined confi-
> dence in a single set of facts) and identity politics (which demands
> acceptance of claims to victimhood), scholars are increasingly hesitant
> to challenge certain kinds of rhetoric. They do not want to be accused
> of "blaming the victim"—an all-purpose, preemptive indictment, like
> "racism," which has been very effective in suppressing unwelcome
> information and replacing it with defensive theorizing. In the case of
> Guatemala, I was to avoid focusing on how peasants contribute to their
> poverty by having large families, or how guerrillas triggered political
> killing in some locales, or how the left is out of touch with the people
> it wants to represent. (244)

With this move, Stoll dismissively stereotypes recent research, neglects
scholarship outside this grammar of polarities, and slights the dilemmas faced by ex-rebels and formerly marginalized Mayan cultural activists who are operating for the first time in the world of national electoral politics. His sweeping judgments become additional catalysts for
strong reactions to the publication. Those of us who have written on
the war are, in fact, politically diverse.[11] Perhaps Stoll's tendency to stereotype the groups he criticizes is amplified by the choice of the exposé
genre, which individualizes the relation of the exposer to the exposed.

Stoll envisions himself as the truth teller who weighs different interview accounts to find the truth and who decides when "problems in
[Menchú's] account should be brought to wider attention" or "not to
call a press conference" as his research progresses. The rugged individualism of the journalistic exposé and its fascination with wider publics
contrast with other forms of academic ethnography—in which ana-

lysts seek to situate their work in wider scholarly networks and lines of research.

Stoll's dominant focus is on *the facts* so as to question the veracity of the testimonial account. What more could there be? Not much if one accepts this framing. But this is where Stoll chooses a distinctive path from ethnographers who are as interested in *the cultural and social contexts* of their informants' lives and portrayals as in the particular facts they provide. For most anthropological writing, exploring the context for the production of knowledge—the ways ongoing social relations influence the production of ideas and judgments in everyday life and in scholarship—leads investigators down multiple rather than unitary paths. One way to phrase this difference is that Stoll follows the facts as they relate to Menchú's life in the 1970s and early 1980s, whereas other ethnographers pursue the facts to highlight contested interpretations in the past and their political stakes in the present. The interplay of past and present in history and memory is not of particular interest to the exposé. That the past has striking relevance for the present, however, is clear from the controversy.

What does it mean that over the course of several months Menchú appears to have conceded important issues, such as her educational background?[12] On the one hand, it demonstrates that Stoll is a rigorous investigator in his own terms. Furthermore, he has shown that economic tensions *among* Mayan families in communities such as Chimel can be as trying as tensions between Ladinos and Mayans. This is a point that popular left researchers, such as Matilde González at AVANCSO, have been working on as well.

Stoll appears eager to undermine one set of polarities—the ethnic distinctiveness of Ladino and Mayan in Guatemala—at the same time as he asserts an ethnic-like division in the American academy: scientists versus leftists. This latter polarity echoes the polemics of the U.S. culture wars, which have involved conservative denunciations of liberal social movements and university professors. It denies social scientists the heterogeneous personal and professional identities that we have in practice. Often, this rhetoric strategically blurs and essentializes the labels "liberal," "Marxist," and "communist" and appears to confuse teaching political works with uncritical political advocacy. As Jacob Weisberg recently argued (1999), the survival long beyond the cold war of this polarized language on both sides of the U.S. conservative–leftist divide hides more than it reveals about contemporary politics. Cast in this mold, Stoll's revelations cannot, for many readers, extinguish the power of testimonial autobiography in which one person symbolically takes on the burden of the wider veracity of social suffering during a counterinsurgency war.

Coming in from the Cold: The Politics of Transitions

Stoll has interrogated the counterinsurgency war across two books. To summarize the argument of *Between Two Armies* (1993), he sees guerrilla offensives as being destructive, as having cynically provoked military atrocities against civilians in the Ixil region of the western highlands. One can read the Rigoberta Menchú critique as an interesting attempt to humanize his earlier analysis—to challenge an icon who stands as the symbol of a just insurgency. Stoll questions accounts that root the insurgency and its civilian supporters such as the Committee for Peasant Unity (CUC) in local communities. Instead he argues that Mayan peasants joined the guerrillas under duress or became disenchanted with the insurgent left for personal or ideological reasons. Finally, he is one of several ethnographers who have described various sorts of social positioning and active neutrality that Mayans employed to survive the army and guerrilla sweeps that resulted from the army's scorched-earth policy (Carmack 1988; Warren 1993; Schirmer 1998).

When the Menchú scandal first broke, I was more concerned about how the work would be used in the present. The peace accords, signed by the Guatemalan army, the URNG guerrilla alliance, and the government, advocated important reforms for the reconstruction of the country (ASIES 1996). The rebels voluntarily disarmed and transformed themselves in December 1998 into a political party, the Guatemalan National Revolutionary Unity (URNG). They initially shared the left of the political spectrum with the Democratic Front for a New Guatemala (FDNG), whose leadership was drawn from wartime popular organizations. By the time of the November 1999 elections, former guerrillas participated in a coalition of leftist parties, the New Nation Alliance (ANN), which won 11.6 percent of the national vote and eight congressional seats. This was just one facet of a wider set of institutional reforms designed to democratize civil society and deal with legacies of the war.

As the peace accords mandated, the army has been downsized and military bases throughout the countryside closed. Refugees from Mexico have been allowed to return to their home regions, though many have found their houses and fields occupied and have resettled elsewhere, often in difficult circumstances (MINUGUA 1998).

The Commission for Historical Clarification (CEH) was given the task of documenting the atrocities during the war on both sides. At issue is how the country will remember the war, its scope, and its legacies.[13] Because amnesty was given to both the military and the guerrillas as part of the peace process, the goal of these proceedings was not to name and prosecute offenders but rather to take measure of the horror and to establish a rough sense of who the perpetrators and victims were.

When the Stoll book was released, I worried about its potential impact on discussions about the need to incorporate representatives of Guatemala's indigenous majority into all public institutions in leadership positions. That indigenous issues became an integral aspect of the peace accords was a surprise to many, given the track record of the insurgents and the army, both of whom thoroughly subordinated ethnic concerns to their own political agendas. Inevitably, the exposé of an indigenous leader would be used by the right in its attempts to undercut the momentum for reforms, discredit congressional adversaries, and sideline indigenous issues in the peace process (Jonas 2000). Given the tremendous amount of organizing that has gone on—and the creation during the peace process of umbrella groups such as the Coordination of the Mayan People of Guatemala (COPMAGUA), which represented indigenous peoples from a variety of viewpoints during the peace process in the Assembly of Civil Society—there is no dearth of leadership on the grassroots left. However, many Mayan activists have found other organizations more congenial, especially those specializing in language revitalization and cultural rights as promulgated by the Mayan Movement, a nonaligned civil and cultural rights movement that gained a national profile in the late 1980s. Postwar politics is not dependent on Menchú, who, in any event, has lived much of her adult life out of the country as an international rights activist.

The publicity surrounding the February 1999 release of the truth commission's summary findings and the impending release of the full nine-volume report displaced the initial furor in Guatemala over the Stoll book. Most telling is the astounding volume of documented violence, the disproportionate government authorship of violence, and the genocidal dimension of the conflict. As documented by the Commission for

Historical Clarification, the army committed 93 percent of the violence, guerrillas 3 percent, and the rest is unattributed. An estimated 83 percent of the fully identified victims were Mayan versus the 17 percent who were Ladinos (CEH 1999). Thus, the blame for wartime atrocities has been unequivocally placed at the feet of the army. Yet, the commission also concluded that "the fundamental reasons for the Guatemalan armed confrontation cannot be reduced to the simplistic logic of two armed factions" (New York Times, February 26, 1999). Rather, the report identified a wide range of structural and political factors—national and international—that influenced the genesis of the war.

Details of the report triggered President Clinton's March 11, 1999, apology to the people of Guatemala during his Central American trip for the United States involvement in the war, including the stateside training of Guatemalan officers in counterinsurgency techniques at the School of the Americas. Former URNG guerrillas offered an apology for wartime excesses two days afterward. The army remained silent.[14]

In conversations with a variety of Mayan leaders and their allies in and around the May 30–June 3, 1999, Second Pop Wuj Conference in Quetzaltenango, I was struck by the profound significance for the Mayan community of the recent revelations of direct U.S. support for the Guatemalan counterinsurgency state, which, in effect, legitimized the genocidal repression of rural communities in the name of national security. In the context of this exposé of the U.S. involvement in Guatemala's war, my half-hour presentation of the Stoll analysis for a panel on political issues generated more than an hour of heated discussion. Although people explicitly stated that they did not want "to demonize" Stoll, many saw his work as an extension of this longer history of foreign intervention in Guatemalan affairs. Members of TIMACH (Tijolb'al Mayab' Adrián Inés Chávez), the Liga Maya Guatemala, and the Comunidad de Universitarios Mayas; professionals such as Otilia Lux de Cotí and Victor Montejo; graduate students pursuing doctorates at the University of Texas at Austin, including Ven de la Cruz and Irma Velásquez Nimatuj; activist teachers at rural elementary schools; and North American Mayanists at the conference—all articulated strong opinions then and afterwards. The book evoked varying mixtures of nationalism and anticolonialism among its politicized Guatemalan readers. Some Mayan observers responded by noting similarities between Stoll's self-portrayal as a detective and the surveillance they endured during the counter-insurgency period.

In response to my comment in passing that Stoll was rigorous in his own terms, doctoral student Irma Velásquez Nimatuj retorted, "Rigorous for whom?" This comment unleashed a torrent of pointed questions and comments from a wide cross section of the audience. Young intellectuals are helping to create a new politics of cultural rights and land issues.[15] At the conference, they argued that the real problem was not, as Stoll portrayed it, Mayans fighting each other in the courts for agricultural land, but rather the underlying reality that most of the country's land is in the hands of a small elite, thus consigning rural communities to endemic poverty.

Doctoral student Ven de la Cruz went on to complain that Stoll's emphasis on Mayan neutrality, during armed clashes between the army and guerrillas, strips rural communities of their agency during the war and disregards those Mayans who were involved in the insurgency. Critics questioned his singling out of one particular national figure to critique and worried that he had handed ammunition to Ladino conservatives at an important moment in the democratic transition. After the meetings, one participant also privately shared the thought that Stoll's critique might, nevertheless, serve as a positive corrective to the left's overshadowing of other efforts promote cultural reforms to remake the state and national culture.

Activists see the truth commission and Stoll as locked into a wider debate about the causes and consequences of the war. Increasingly, public intellectuals, such as Victor Montejo, argue that the Clinton administration's declassification of documents in the National Security Archives, which detail United States involvement and the resulting human rights abuses, is not enough. Rather, a commission should now be established to examine the issue of war reparations to those communities that were most deeply affected. Stoll's book, which was not accessible to wider Guatemalan audiences because its translation had not found a Latin American publisher, was being rewoven by Mayan activists into narratives of transnational intervention and responsibility.

Finally, where do I stand on the issue of exposé as an ethnographic genre for anthropology? This analysis has argued that David Stoll has not escaped the dilemmas of being political any more than Rigoberta Menchú had in her wartime quest for justice. Anthropologists will continue to be interested in alternative representations of conflict—though, more often, I anticipate, to show the fuller variety of parties in debate. This approach is not the result of some sort of foundational relativism that treats all explanations as equally valid. Rather, it is a commitment to the study of complex realities that in their diversity and dynamism call for multifaceted understandings. For instance, Stoll could have framed his study in a more encompassing way by taking General Héctor Gramajo, the author of the country's pacification strategies for civilian communities, and developing an analysis (to parallel the Menchú exposé) of the general's wartime activities and commentaries, the genres he used, and the transnational circulation of this policy language in military circles. Jennifer Schirmer's work (1998) shows that such projects are feasible.

At issue, given the centrality of meaning to anthropological research, are the limits of any one line of analysis. Debates over the significance of events, their representation, and the media for their public airing will continue to be central to the field. The third vantage point, an anthropological one that attempts to capture the fuller controversy—and, in this case, that traces what has been lost with an intense focus on only two of many protagonists—requires its own scrutiny as yet another position rather than a transcendent rationality.

For North American readers, however, the Stoll–Menchú controversy may only obscure the important retooling of politics that is occurring in Guatemala.[16] A Mayan agenda in public affairs has emerged since the early 1980s through a multistranded history of organizations and movements. Although these organizations have found leverage from Menchú's UN work on transnational indigenous issues, many do not share her history of revolutionary activism. One of the survivors of civil-war repression is the politically independent Mayan Movement with its goal of forging a pan-community identity, revitalizing Mayan languages and culture, and transforming Guatemala into a "multiethnic, culturally plural, and multilingual nation."[17]

The Mayan Movement has created hundreds of cultural organizations, national networks, book publishers, and Mayan schools. A wide variety of interest groups and public intellectuals now meet regionally and nationally to forge new alliances and issue consensus statements on issues of common concern. The Movement critiques Ladino assimilationism and promotes political and cultural rights that defy older polarities. Younger students and leaders who might in the past have sought out transethnic activist groups now appear to be aligning themselves with the Mayan Movement and widening its agenda. Whereas the Stoll–Menchú controversy remains anchored in the deep waters of the cold war, the Mayan Movement appears more immediately concerned with the internal dynamics of the range of organizations that it currently encounters—state institutions, religious groups, political parties, international donors, NGOs, and foreign universities—whatever their political inclinations.

The transition from cold war polarities to more inclusive political orders has generated much unfinished business for Latin America and the United States. Perhaps that is why, in 1999, the Stoll–Menchú clash riveted attention on the interface between politics and public culture across nations. As this essay has argued, there is much to learn about the past and the present in the process. The trick, of course, is not to conflate the two, and to realize that recent events have produced more than one exposé.

Notes

Discussions with Diane Nelson, Jennifer Schirmer, Doris Sommer, David Stoll, Arturo Arias, Victor Montejo, Alberto Esquit Choy, Claret Vargas, Lee Warren, and Nancy Houfek and exchanges with the participants, including Irma Velásquez Nimatuj, Ven de la Cruz, Otilia Lux de Cojtí, John Watanabe, Gary Gossen, and Abigail Adams, at the Segundo Congreso Internacional sobre el Pop Wuj, May 30–June 3, 1999, in Xela, Guatemala, and the Tercer Congreso de Estudios Mayas, August 31–September 4, 1999, in Guatemala City stimulated the development of this essay. The analysis was first developed for my inaugural lecture at Harvard on March 22, 1999. The responsibility for the final line of analysis remains mine.

1. The trend will grow as social critics throughout the world deploy discourses of cultural distinctiveness and as foreign and national anthropologists engage public intellectuals in the societies they study. My own debates with Mario Roberto Morales (Warren 1998) reflect this tendency.

2. Note the change in pronouns in this passage, the built-in ambiguity between Rigoberta as a narrator of her own experience and an observer of the experiences of others.

3. According to Stoll, she finished first and second grades at the age of twelve to fourteen, supported by the Belgian Order of the Holy Family, continued third through sixth grades in the capital, and pursued a final year in Huehuetenango (Stoll 1999, 160–61). Young students faced long separations from their families, fragmented schooling because of their poverty, and demanding combinations of work and study.

4. In 1982, Elisabeth Burgos-Debray—who had no direct experience with Guatemala—interviewed a twenty-three-year-old Rigoberta Menchú for twenty-four hours

over one week to produce a typescript of some five hundred pages. Historian Arturo Taracena sat in on the sessions. After Menchú left, the interviews were edited down to a book-length manuscript and shown to URNG guerrilla reprentatives in Mexico to be cleared for publication. Burgos described her role in the following terms: "I allowed her to speak and then became her instrument, her double by allowing her to make the transition from the spoken to the written word. . . . I had to insert linking passages if the manuscript were to read like a monologue, like one continuous narrative. I then divided it into chapters organized around the themes I had already identified. I followed my original chronological outline, even though our conversations had not done so, so as to make the text more accessible to the reader" (Menchú 1984, xx).

5. See Trouillot (1991) and Field (1996).

6. There is much more to be said about the genre, its circulation, and commodification. See Gugelberger (1996), Carey-Webb and Benz (1996), and Erdemir (1999). To show that sisterhood is international, *I, Rigoberta Menchú* has been assigned in women's studies courses to challenge students' ethnocentrism and to illustrate women's political agency in a strikingly different cultural setting. In comparative social science and Latin American studies courses, it has been used to humanize the region's political and economic struggles and to represent opposition social movements and revolutionary organizing in violent states. In the revision of core curriculums, it has been included as a good-faith effort to expand the literary canon beyond high status Western classics (Mary Louise Pratt, in this volume).

7. For discussions of these estimates and the patterns of wartime violence, see Schirmer (1998), the Guatemalan Commission for Historical Clarification (CEH) (1999), and Ball, Kobrak, and Spirer (1998).

8. For the peace process, see Arnson (1999), ASIES (1996), and Warren (1998). In hindsight, it is clear that the referendum was destined for defeat because disparate reforms were packaged together and voters had only a yes or no vote for each of four heterogeneous subsets of issues (Warren 2000).

9. For the history of Catholic Action and distinctive forms of politicization in different regions of the country, see Warren (1989), Falla (1978), and Wilson (1995).

10. From Clifford and Marcus (1986) and Clifford (1988) to Fox (1991) and Appadurai (1996), the trend in cultural anthropology has been to widen the alternatives for ethnographic expression.

11. I, for one, am a political moderate and social progressive who has written on the ambiguities of wartime violence and on the complex relation of pan-Mayanism with the grassroots left.

12. See, for example, the *New York Times,* January 21 and February 12, 1999.

13. See Warren (1999) for a discussion of the blurring of civilian and military authority through the creation of civil patrols during the war.

14. Given the nature of the civil war—where violence was often designed to hide the identities of the perpetrators—it would not be surprising to see continuing evasions of responsibility (see Warren 1998, 1999). Wilson (1997) and Stoll (1997) have shown how tricky it is to argue unilaterally in terms of human rights abuses.

15. See, for example, Velásquez (1999) and de la Cruz (1999).

16. When Stoll's work has been appropriated in the United States, the polemics have less to do with Guatemala's complex transition to democracy than with U.S. domestic politics. The story of state violence is depoliticized and repoliticized to

suit a very different political agenda. One culture war's hub for the appropriation of the Stoll book has been David Horowitz's Los Angeles-based Center for the Study of Popular Culture, which began its college newspaper ad campaign with the following headlines: "Rigoberta Menchú. Nobel Laureate and Marxist Terrorist as an Intellectual Hoax. This Fraud Was Originally Perpetuated and Is Still Defended by Your Professors and by the Nobel Prize Committee" (*Harvard Crimson*, March 3, 1999). Horowitz seeks to reignite the culture wars by condemning "the tenured radicals who dominate the American academic community" (frontpagemag.com, February 26, 1999). At stake in this seemingly esoteric debate about literary canons are questions about the role of higher education and alternative images of national culture (see Pratt, in this volume). Is the national identity to be rooted in the country's historical connection with Britain or, given the antecedent indigenous population and the diasporas that have continually reconfigured the country, is the United States fundamentally a multicultural, multiethnic, and multilingual nation? Thus, one theme reverberates across national borders, the global preoccupation with the problem of monocultural and monoethnic national identities and the reality of ethnically and linguistically distinctive groups that now demand representation in systems that have conventionally marginalized them (Warren 1999; Nelson 1999).

17. See Cojtí Cuxil (1995, 1996, 1997), Bastos and Camus (1995), Fischer and Brown (1996), and Warren (1998).

Bibliography

Annis, Sheldon. 1987. *God and Production in a Guatemalan Town.* Austin: University of Texas Press.

Appadurai, Arjun. 1996. *Modernity at Large: Cultural Dimensions of Globalization.* Minneapolis: University of Minnesota Press.

Arnson, Cynthia, ed. 1999. *Comparative Peace Processes in Latin America.* Palo Alto, Calif.: Stanford University Press.

ASIES. 1996. *Acuerdo de paz firme y duradera: Acuerdo sobre cronograma para la implementación, cuplimiento y verificación de los acuerdos de paz.* Guatemala City: Asociación de Investigación y Estudios Sociales.

AVANCSO. 1991. "'Vonós a la capital': Estudio sobre la emigración en Guatemala." *Cuadernos de Investigación* no. 7. Guatemala City: Asociación para el Avance de las Ciencias Sociales en Guatemala.

Ball, Patrick, Paul Kobrak, and Herbert F. Spirer. 1998. *State Violence in Guatemala, 1960–1996: A Quantitative Reflection.* American Academy for the Advancement of Science and CIIDH. <thrdata.aaas.org/ciidh>

Bastos, Santiago, and Manuela Camus. 1995. *Abriendo caminos; las organizaciones mayas desde el Nobel hasta el Acuerdo de Derechos Indígenas.* Guatemala City: FLACSO.

Brintnall, Douglas E. 1979. *Revolt against the Dead: The Modernization of a Mayan Community in the Highlands of Guatemala.* New York: Gordon and Breach.

Carlsen, Robert S. 1997. *The War for the Heart and Soul of a Highland Maya Town.* Austin: University of Texas Press.

Carmack, Robert. 1995. *Rebels of Highland Guatemala: the Quiché-Mayas of Momostenango.* Norman: University of Oklahoma Press.

————, ed. 1988. *Harvest of Violence: The Maya Indians and the Guatemalan Crisis.* Norman: University of Oklahoma Press.

Carey-Webb, Allen, and Stephen Benz, eds. 1996. *Teaching and Testimony: Rigoberta Menchú and the North American Classroom.* Albany: State University of New York Press.

CEH (Commission for Historical Clarification). 1999. *Guatemala: Memory of Silence Tz'inil Na'tab'al.* <hrdata.aaas.org/ceh/report>

Clifford, James. 1988. *The Predicament of Culture: Twentieth-Century Ethnography, Literature and Art.* Cambridge: Harvard University Press.

Clifford, James, and George E. Marcus, eds. 1986. *Writing Culture: The Poetics and Politics of Ethnography.* Berkeley: University of California Press.

Cojtí Cuxil, Demetrio. 1995. *Ub'aniik Ri Una'ooj Uchomab'aal Ri Maya' Tinamit; Configuración del pensamiento político del pueblo maya.* Part 2. Guatemala City: Seminario Permanente de Estudios Mayas and Editorial Cholsamaj.

————. 1996. "The Politics of Mayan Revindication." In *Maya Cultural Activism in Guatemala,* ed. Edward Fischer and R. McKenna Brown. Austin: University of Texas Press. 19–50.

————. 1997. *Ri Maya' Moloj pa Iximulew; El movimiento maya (en Guatemala).* Guatemala: Editorial Cholsamaj.

de la Cruz, Ven. 1999. "The Politics of Truth, Memory, and Historical Representation in Guatemala: A Critical Look at David Stoll's *Rigoberta Menchú and the Story of All Poor Guatemalans.*" Unpublished essay, University of Texas at Austin.

Erdemir, Aykan. 1999. "Kurdish Testimonial Narratives: Commodification, Reterritorialization, and Containment in the Middle East." Unpublished paper.

Falla, Ricardo. 1978. *Quiché rebelde: Estudio de un movimiento de conversión religiosa, rebelde a las creencias tradicionales, en San Antonio Ilotenango, Quiché (1948–1970).* Guatemala City: Editorial Universitaria.

Field, Les. 1996. "Mired Positionings: Moving beyond Metropolitan Authority and Indigenous Authenticity." *Identities* 3.102: 137–54.

Fischer, Edward, and R. McKenna Brown, eds. 1996. *Maya Cultural Activism in Guatemala.* Austin: University of Texas Press.

Fox, Richard G., ed. 1991. *Recapturing Anthropology: Working in the Present.* Santa Fe: School of American Research Press.

Gugelberger, Georg M., ed. 1996. *The Real Thing: Testimonial Discourse and Latin America.* Durham, N.C.: Duke University Press.

Jonas, Susanne. 2000. *Of Centaurs and Doves: Guatemala's Peace Process.* Boulder, Colo.: Westview Press.

Kearney, Michael. 1996. *Reconceptualizing the Peasantry: Anthropology in Global Perspective.* Boulder, Colo.: Westview Press.

Menchú, Rigoberta, with Elisabeth Burgos-Debray. 1984. Trans. Ann Wright. *I, Rigoberta Menchú: An Indian Woman in Guatemala.* London: Verso.

MINUGUA (United Nations Verification Commission in Guatemala). 1998. "The Situation in Central America: Procedures for the Establishment of a Firm and Lasting Peace and Progress in Fashioning a Region of Peace, Freedom, Democracy and Development." A/52/757. New York: United Nations.

Montejo, Victor. 1987. *Testimony: Death of a Guatemalan Village.* Willimantic, Conn.: Curbstone Press.

Montejo, Victor, and Q'anil Akab'. 1992. *Brevísima relación testimonial de la continua destrucción del Mayab' (Guatemala)*. Providence, R.I.: Guatemala Scholars Network.

Nelson, Diane. 1999. *The Finger in the Wound: Ethnicity, Nation, and Gender in the Body Politic of Quincentennial Guatemala*. Berkeley: University of California Press.

Schirmer, Jennifer. 1998. *The Guatemalan Military Project: A Violence Called Democracy*. Philadelphia: University of Pennsylvania Press.

Smith, Carol, ed. 1990. *Guatemalan Indians and the State: 1540–1988*. Austin: University of Texas Press.

Stoll, David. 1993. *Between Two Armies in the Ixil Towns of Guatemala*. New York: Columbia University Press.

———. 1997. "To Whom Should We Listen? Human Rights Activism in Two Guatemalan Land Disputes." In *Human Rights, Culture and Context: Anthropological Perspectives*, ed. Richard Wilson. London: Pluto Press. 187–215.

———. 1999. *Rigoberta Menchú and the Story of All Poor Guatemalans*. Boulder, Colo.: Westview Press.

Trouillot, Michele-Rolph. 1991 "Anthropology and the Savage Slot: The Poetics and Politics of Otherness." In *Recapturing Anthropology: Working in the Present*, ed. Richard Fox. Santa Fe: School of American Research. 17–44.

Velásquez Nimatuj, Irma. 1999. "¿Quién nos ha Representado?" Unpublished essay, University of Texas at Austin.

Warren, Kay B. 1989. *The Symbolism of Subordination: Indian Identity in a Guatemalan Town*. Austin: University of Texas Press.

———. 1993. "Interpreting la Violencia in Guatemala: Shapes of Kaqchikel Silence and Resistance in the 1970s and 1980s." In *The Violence Within: Cultural and Political Opposition in Divided Nations*, ed. Kay B. Warren. Boulder, Colo.: Westview Press. 25–56.

———. 1998. *Indigenous Movements and Their Critics: Pan-Maya Activism in Guatemala*. Princeton, N.J.: Princeton University Press.

———. 1999. "Death Squads and Wider Complicities: Dilemmas for the Anthropology of Violence." In *Death Squad: The Anthropology of State Terror*, ed. Jeffrey Sluka. Philadelphia: University of Pennsylvania Press. 226–47.

———. 2000. "Lessons from the 'Failure' of the 1999 Referendum on Indigenous Rights in Guatemala." APSA meetings, August 31, 2000.

Weisberg, Jacob. 1999. "Cold War without End." *New York Times Magazine*, November 29, 1999, 116–58.

Wilson, Richard. 1995. *Mayan Resurgence in Guatemala: Q'echi' Experiences*. Norman: University of Oklahoma Press.

———. ed. 1997. *Human Rights, Culture and Context: Anthropological Perspectives*. London: Pluto Press.

What Happens When the Subaltern Speaks

Rigoberta Menchú, Multiculturalism, and the Presumption of Equal Worth

John Beverley

In one of the most powerful sections of *I, Rigoberta Menchú*, Menchú narrates the torture and execution of her brother Petrocinio by elements of the Guatemalan army in the plaza of a small highland town called Chajul, which is the site of an annual pilgrimage by worshipers of the local saint. Here is part of her account:

> After he'd finished talking the officer ordered the squad to take away those who'd been 'punished', naked and swollen as they were. They dragged them along, they could no longer walk. Dragged them to this place, where they lined them up all together within sight of everyone. The officer called to the worst of the criminals—the *Kaibiles*, who wear different clothes from other soldiers. They're the ones with the most training, the most power. Well, he called the *Kaibiles* and they poured petrol over each of the tortured. The captain said, 'This isn't the last of their punishments, there's another one yet. This is what we've done with all the subversives we catch, because they have to die by violence. And if this doesn't teach you a lesson, this is what'll happen to you too. The problem is that the Indians let themselves be led by the communists. Since no-one's told the Indians anything, they go along with the communists.' He was trying to convince the people but at the same time he was insulting them by what he said. Anyway, they [the soldiers] lined up the tortured and poured petrol on them; and then the soldiers set fire to each one of them. Many of them begged for mercy. Some of them screamed, many of them leapt but uttered no sound—of course, that was because their breathing was cut off. But—and to me this was incredible—many of the people had weapons with them, the ones who'd been on their way to work had machetes, others had nothing in their

hands, but when they saw the army setting fire to the victims, everyone wanted to strike back, to risk their lives doing it, despite all the soldiers' arms. . . . Faced with its own cowardice, the army itself realized that the whole people were prepared to fight. You could see that even the children were enraged, but they didn't know how to express their rage. . . . [T]he officer quickly gave the order for the squad to withdraw. They all fell back holding their weapons up and shouting slogans as if it were a celebration. They were happy! They roared with laughter and cried "Long live the Fatherland! Long live Guatemala! Long live our President! Long live the army!"[1]

Much of the force of this passage derives from the fact that it pretends to be the account of a witness, that is, testimony in both the legal and evangelical sense. Menchú was there; she and her family traveled all night over mountain paths to be in Chajul; like the writers of the Gospels, she saw with her own eyes the terrible wounds on her brother's body, saw him being burned alive, felt that surge of rage of the crowd against the *Kaibiles*.

"What if much of Rigoberta's story is not true?" David Stoll asks in his book about *I, Rigoberta Menchú*.[2] On the basis of interviews in the area where the massacre was supposed to have occurred, Stoll concludes (63–70) that the killing of Menchú's brother did not happen in exactly this way, that Menchú was not a direct witness to the event, as her account suggests, and that therefore this account, along with other details of her *testimonio*, amounts to, in his words, a "mythic inflation" (232).

It would be more accurate to say that what Stoll has been able to show is that *some* rather than "much" of Menchú's story is not true. It is important to distinguish this claim from the claim subsequently made by some right-wing commentators that *I, Rigoberta Menchú* is fraudulent. Stoll is not saying that Menchú is making it all up. He does not contest the fact of the murder of Menchú's brother by the army. And he stipulates in his preface that "[t]here is no doubt about the most important points [in her story]: that a dictatorship massacred thousands of indigenous peasants, that the victims included half of Rigoberta's immediate family, that she fled to Mexico to save her life, and that she joined a revolutionary movement to liberate her country" (viii). But he does argue that the inaccuracies, omissions, or misrepresentations he claims to find in her narrative make her less than a reliable representative of the interests and beliefs of the people she claims to be speaking for.

If (in my own account of the form) "*testimonio* [is] a narrative...
told in the first person by a narrator who is also the real protagonist or
witness of the events he or she recounts,"[3] then (referring in part specifically to this definition) Stoll argues that "[j]udging by such definitions, *I,
Rigoberta Menchú* does not belong in the genre of which it is the most
famous example, because it is not the eyewitness account it purports to
be" (Stoll 242).

In response to Stoll's charges, Menchú has publicly conceded that she
grafted elements of other people's experiences and stories onto her own
account. In particular, she has admitted that she was not herself present at the massacre of her brother and his companions in Chajul, and
that her account of the event came instead from her mother, who (she
claims) was in fact there. She says that these interpolations were a way
of making her story a collective account, rather than an autobiography.[4] I personally don't find this explanation (or the related idea that
Mayan forms of storytelling merge the individual experience in the collective) entirely convincing. I think it would have been better for Menchú
to have indicated when she was speaking from or about someone else's
experience. But, of course, that would have diminished the force of direct witness that the account carries. And Menchú, who tells us in her
testimonio that she was trained to be a catechist of the word (*catequista
de la palabra*)—that is, someone charged with explaining biblical stories
to people of her community in a way they could understand in terms
of their own language and experience—is far from being a naive narrator. She cannot fail to be aware at some level of the resonance between her description of the death of her brother at the hands of the
Kaibiles and the biblical story of the crucifixion. Would the truth the
crucifixion has for Christians be altered if it could be shown, for example, that Luke was not actually present at the event, or that the accounts
in Matthew, Mark, and John differ in some crucial details from his—
assuming, of course, that Luke is one person, and not, as seems more
likely, a palimpsest of different authors and revisions?

The argument between Menchú and Stoll is not so much about what
really happened as it is about who has the authority to narrate. What
seems to bother Stoll above all is that Menchú *has* an agenda. He wants
her to be a "native informant," who will lend herself to *his* purposes (of
information gathering and evaluation); but she is instead something like

what Gramsci meant by an "organic intellectual," concerned with producing a text of "local history" (to borrow Florencia Mallon's term)—
that is, with elaborating hegemony.

The basic idea of Gayatri Spivak's famous, but notoriously difficult,
essay "Can the Subaltern Speak?" might be reformulated in this way: If
the subaltern could speak—that is, speak in a way that really *mattered*
to us, that we would feel compelled to listen to, then it would not be
subaltern. Spivak is saying, in other words, that one of the things being
subaltern means is not mattering, not being worth listening to. By contrast, Stoll's argument with Rigoberta Menchú is precisely with the way
in which her book "matters." It concerns how the canonization of *I,
Rigoberta Menchú* was used by teachers like myself or solidarity and human rights activists to mobilize international support for the Guatemalan
armed struggle in the 1980s, long after (in Stoll's view) that movement
had lost whatever support it may have initially enjoyed among the Mayan
peasants that Menchú claims to speak for. The inaccuracies and omissions in Menchú's account lend themselves, Stoll feels, "to justify violence" (274). That issue—"how outsiders were using Rigoberta's story
to justify continuing a war at the expense of peasants who did not support it" (241)—is the main problem for Stoll, rather than the inaccuracies
or omissions themselves. By making Menchú's story seem "the story of
all poor Guatemalans," *I, Rigoberta Menchú* misrepresented a more complex and ideologically contradictory situation among the indigenous
peasants.

In one sense, of course, there is a coincidence between Spivak's concern with the production in metropolitan academic and theoretical
discourse of a "domesticated Other" in "Can the Subaltern Speak?" and
Stoll's concern with the conversion of Menchú into an icon of academic political correctness in order to sustain a vanguardist political
strategy in Guatemala he thinks was profoundly flawed. In a way that
seems to echo Spivak, Stoll notes that

> books like *I, Rigoberta Menchú* will be exalted because they tell
> academics what they want to hear. . . . What makes *I, Rigoberta Menchú*
> so attractive in universities is what makes it misleading about the
> struggle for survival in Guatemala. We think we are getting closer to
> understanding Guatemalan peasants when actually we are being borne
> away by the mystifications wrapped up in an iconic figure. (227)

But Stoll's argument is also explicitly *with* Spivak, as a representative of the very kind of "postmodern scholarship" that would privilege a text like *I, Rigoberta Menchú.*[5]

I will come back to this point. For the moment, it may be enough to note that where Spivak is concerned with the way in which elite representation effaces the effective presence of the subaltern, Stoll's case against Menchú is precisely that: a way of, so to speak, *resubalternizing* a narrative that aspired to (and achieved) hegemony.

Although Stoll talks a lot about "facts" and "verification," it turns out that he also has an ideological agenda. He believes that the attempt of the left to wage an armed struggle against the military dictatorship in Guatemala put the majority of the highland indian population "between two fires," driven to support the guerrillas mainly by the ferocity of the army's counterinsurgency measures rather than by a belief in the justice or strategic necessity of armed struggle. By contrast, the narrative logic of *I, Rigoberta Menchú* suggests that the Guatemalan armed struggle grew *necessarily* out of the conditions of repression the indigenous communities faced in their attempts to hold the line against land seizures and exploitation by the army, paramilitary death squads, and rich landowners anxious to appropriate their lands and exploit their labor. For Stoll to sustain his hypothesis, he has to impeach the force of Menchú's testimony.[6]

But is the problem for Stoll the verifiability of Menchú's story or the wisdom of armed struggle as such? Stoll's position is *political,* in a way that is not susceptible to "factual proof," just as, say, being a Democrat or a Republican is a political-ideological rather than a rational-empirical choice. If it could be shown that all the details in Menchú's account were in fact verifiable, would it follow for Stoll that the armed struggle was justified? Obviously not. But, by the same token, the gaps, inaccuracies, "mythic inflation," and so on he finds in Menchú's account do not necessarily add up to an indictment of the armed struggle. It may well be that armed struggle was a mistake: Stoll observes that Menchú has sought in recent years to place some distance between herself and the umbrella organization of the revolutionary left, the URNG.[7] But that judgment does not in itself follow from his attempted impeachment of Menchú's narrative authority. In other words, the question of verifiability and representativity is subordinate to the question of Stoll's ideological disagreement with the strategy of armed struggle, which he claims *I, Rigoberta Menchú* is inextricably connected to.

In particular, it is a long way from saying, as Stoll does, that not *all* highland peasants supported the armed struggle, which is at best a truism, to claiming that the guerrilla movement lacked, or lost, any significant popular roots among them, that it was imposed on them against their will and interests. Stoll gives us no more "hard" evidence to support this contention than Menchú does to argue the contrary, and other close observers of the conflict, Carol A. Smith (in this volume), have argued that the guerrillas were in fact relatively successful in recruiting the highland indigenous peasants to their cause, indeed, that the integration of the previously predominantly ladino guerrilla groups with significant elements of this population constituted a powerful challenge to the military dictatorship, that it was precisely that possibility the army was seeking to destroy in the genocidal counterinsurgency war Menchú describes in her narrative. Who are we to believe? As in the impeachment trial of President Clinton, it comes down to a matter of "he said, she said," which in the last instance will be decided on *political* as well as epistemological grounds.

Moreover, one could certainly read *I, Rigoberta Menchú* as an indictment of the near-genocidal violence of the Guatemalan army and ruling class, without necessarily agreeing with the strategy of armed struggle (or with the particular way in which that strategy was carried out). I would argue that this is the way *I, Rigoberta Menchú* has been read, in fact, most often outside Guatemala: not so much as a celebration of guerrilla struggle (like, for example, Che Guevara's *Reminiscences of the Cuban Revolutionary War,* Omar Cabezas's *Fire from the Mountain,* or Mario Payeras's *Days of the Jungle*), but rather as a way of mobilizing international opinion in favor of an end to the violence (and also, as I elaborate on later, as a defense of indigenous cultural autonomy and identity politics, rather than left-wing revolutionary vanguardism). Referring to the tasks of the truth commissions established as part of the peace process in Guatemala, Stoll notes that "[i]f identifying crimes and breaking through regimes of denial has become a public imperative in peacemaking, if there is a public demand for establishing 'historical memory,' then *I, Rigoberta Menchú* cannot be enshrined as true in a way it is not" (273). Fair enough. But if the Guatemalan army had simply destroyed the guerrillas and imposed its will by force on the population, then there would have been no truth commissions in the first place. Yet Stoll faults Menchú's story, among other things, for helping guerrilla leaders "finally obtain the December 1996 peace agreement" (278). Does he think it would have been better *not* to have done this?

In the process of constructing her narrative and articulating herself as a political icon around its circulation, Menchú is becoming not-subaltern, in the sense that she is functioning as a subject of history. But the conditions of her becoming not-subaltern—her narrative choices, silences, "mythic inflation," "reinvention," and so on—entail necessarily that there are versions of "what really happened" that she does not or cannot represent without relativizing the authority of her own account. In any social situation—indeed, even within a given class or group identity—it is always possible to find a variety of points of narratives, points of view, that reflect contradictory agendas and interests. "Obviously," Stoll quite properly observes,

> Rigoberta is a legitimate Mayan voice. So are all the young Mayas who want to move to Los Angeles or Houston. So is the man with a large family who owns three worn-out acres and wants me to buy him a chain saw so he can cut down the last forest more quickly. Any of these people can be picked to make misleading generalizations about Mayas. (247)

The presence of "other" indigenous voices in Stoll's account makes Guatemalan indigenous communities—indeed, even Menchú's own immediate family—seem irremediably riven by internal rivalries, contradictions, different ways of telling.[8] But, in a way, this is to deny the possibility of political struggle as such, because a hegemonic project by definition points to a possibility of collective will and action that depends precisely on transforming the conditions of cultural and political disenfranchisement, alienation, and desperation that underlie these contradictions. The appeal to heterogeneity—"any of these people"—leaves intact the authority of the "outside" observer (that is, Stoll) who is alone in the position of being able to both hear and sort through the various testimonies. It also leaves intact the *existing* structures of political military domination and cultural authority. The existence of "contradictions among the people"—for example, the interminable internecine fights over land and natural resource rights within and between peasant communities that Stoll puts so much emphasis on—does not deny the possibility of contradiction between the "people" as such (say, a worker-peasant-professional alliance of ladinos and indian poor peasants) and an ethnicity, class, and state felt as deeply antagonistic and repressive. Yet Stoll seems uncomfortable with notions of class and ethnic conflict as such, as if to appeal to such notions were in itself to encourage the sort of politics he dislikes.

But, of course, Stoll's argument is not only about Guatemala. It is also with the discourses of multiculturalism and postmodernism in the North American academy, which he feels consciously or unconsciously colluded to perpetuate the armed struggle in Guatemala by promoting *I, Rigoberta Menchú* and making Menchú into an international icon. Thus, for example: "[i]t was in the name of multiculturalism that *I, Rigoberta Menchú* entered the university reading lists" (243). Or, "[u]nder the influence of postmodernism (which has undermined confidence in a single set of facts) and identity politics (which demands acceptance of claims to victimhood), scholars are increasingly hesitant to challenge certain kinds of rhetoric" (244). Or, "the identity needs of Rigoberta's academic constituency play into the weakness of rules of evidence in postmodern scholarship" (247). Or, "with postmodern critiques of representation and authority, many scholars are tempted to abandon the task of verification, especially when they construe the narrator as a victim worthy of their support" (274).

What starts off as a critique of the truth claims of Rigoberta Menchú's *testimonio* and the strategy of the Guatemalan guerrilla movement metamorphoses into an attack on what the neoconservative writer Roger Kimball memorably called "tenured radicals" in European and North American universities. The connection between postmodernism and multiculturalism that bothers Stoll is predicated on the fact that multiculturalism carries with it what Canadian philosopher Charles Taylor calls a "presumption of equal worth."[9] The presumption of equal worth implies a demand for epistemological relativism that coincides with the postmodernist critique of the Enlightenment paradigm. If there is no one universal standard for truth, then claims about truth are contextual: they have to do with how people construct different understandings of the world and historical memory from the same set of facts in situations of gender, ethnic, and class inequality, exploitation, and repression. As noted, the truth claims for a testimonial narrative like *I, Rigoberta Menchú* depend on conferring on the form a certain special kind of epistemological authority. But for Stoll this amounts to an idealization of the subaltern to favor the prejudices of a metropolitan academic audience, in the interest of a solidarity politics that (in his view) is doing more harm than good. Against the authority of testimonial "voice," Stoll wants to affirm the authority of the fact-gathering procedures of anthropology and journalism, in which testimonial accounts such as Menchú's will be treated simply as raw material that must be processed by more objective techniques of assessment.

In a recent discussion, Homi Bhabha argues that, for Taylor, the presumption of equal worth "does not participate in the universal language of cultural value . . . for it focuses exclusively on recognition of the excluded." In other words, the presumption is not dictated by an ethical principle that exists prior to the claim of cultural recognition itself. Rather, it depends on what Taylor calls a "processual judgment" that involves working through cultural difference to arrive at a new "fusion of horizon" (Taylor's term). But, Bhabha counters, such

> working through cultural difference in order to be transformed by the other is not as straightforwardly open to the other as it sounds. For the possibility of the "fusion of horizon" of standards—the *new* standard of judgement—is not all that new; it is founded on the notion of the dialogic subject of culture that we had *precisely at the beginning* of the whole argument. . . . that makes the fusing of horizons a largely consensual and homogenizing norm of cultural value or worth, based on the notion that cultural difference is fundamentally synchronous.[10]

What is clear in Bhabha's point about the nonsynchronicity of difference is that it is not an abstract legal, ethical, or epistemological principle that drives the "presumption of equal worth": it is rather the *specific* character of the various relations of subordination, exploitation, and marginalization produced by capitalist modernity itself, involving as they do at all moments racism, Eurocentrism, colonialism and its aftermath, the destruction or displacement of native populations and territorialities, demographic catastrophe and waves of mass immigration, combined and uneven development, boom and bust cycles, the imposition or perpetuation of patriarchal forms of authority and women's inequality, and so on.

If Bhabha is right, the thrust of Taylor's argument is to recode multiculturalism within the possibilities offered by the existing institutional-ideological superstructure of globalized capital and liberal democracy, including the academy. But for Bhabha there is clearly something more corrosive in the principle of multiculturalism. Would it be possible to derive from multiculturalism a more radical consequence politically? The question has to do in turn with the relation of multiculturalism to, under conditions of globalization, the cultural identity of the nation.

I, Rigoberta Menchú is, among other things, an argument for understanding Guatemala itself as a deeply multicultural and multilingual nation, in which indians like herself—who make up more than half of the population—deserve greater cultural and legal autonomy. Mario Roberto Morales's recent book, *La articulación de las diferencias*, centers in particular on the "interethnic debate" that has accompanied the 1996 signing of the peace accords in Guatemala and their subsequent implementation.[11] Morales shares with David Stoll a preoccupation with the way in which *I, Rigoberta Menchú* has been canonized by multiculturalism and postcolonial and subaltern studies theory in the U.S. academy; but, unlike Stoll, he is more concerned with the effects of this *inside* Guatemala, which, he feels, are to legitimize the emergent discourse of a separatist Mayan identity politics.

For Morales, what is at stake in the interethnic debate in Guatemala is the future of the country and the Central American region as a whole in the conjuncture formed by the defeat or stalemate of the project of the revolutionary left and the effects of globalization that the region is experiencing in the wake of that defeat and will continue to have to confront in the coming millennium. His way of posing the problem stems from a double personal crisis: the crisis of the revolutionary left with which he had identified as a writer; the crisis of the traditional concept of the Latin American writer as a sort of literary Moses—a *conductor de pueblos*—who was uniquely charged with representing the *national.* [12]

The idea of a synergistic relation between literature and the processes of national development in a country like Guatemala found its most powerful expression in the 1960s and 1970s in Ángel Rama's concept of "narrative transculturation": *transculturación narrativa.*[13] Transculturation functioned for Rama (as for the Cuban ethnographer Fernando Ortiz, from whom Rama borrows the concept) as a *teleology* of the national, not without moments of violent confrontation, cultural genocide and loss, desperation, adaptation, and tenacious resistance, but *necessary* in the final analysis for the formation of an inclusive national-popular culture. In relation to what came to be known as the "indian question," in particular, Rama believed that the only viable option for the indigenous peoples of the Americas was racial-cultural *mestizaje,* a *mestizaje* that his concept of transculturation both represented as an empirical social given and postulated as a normative model for intercultural relations.

Rama's idea of transculturation coincided with the heyday of dependency theory in Latin America. Transculturation would be, so to speak, the "cultural" correlative of the process of economic "delinking" and autonomous development the dependency economists were advocating. Both transculturation and dependency theory stressed the "underdeveloped" character of Latin American states—their inability to represent culturally and politically and to utilize productively all of the human and natural elements of the continent. But to articulate the indigenous, the regional, the anachronistic, the subaltern, the marginal as a problem of their *integration* by the nation-state—that is, in relation to the "incomplete project of modernity" (I am alluding, of course, to Habermas's well-known slogan)—does not open up a conceptual space to represent these as entities in their own right, with their own demands, values, cultural practices, and historical narratives (which may or may not coincide with the narrative of the formation and evolution of the state). In particular, Rama's insistence on transculturation prevented him from being able to anticipate the emergence in the 1980s of the so-called new social movements in Latin America—one of whose main characteristics was that, unlike the formal political left in both its communist and reformist forms, they not only did not base themselves on a narrative of transculturation but also felt compelled many times to resist or negate the force of such a narrative.

A similar failure, in my opinion, afflicts Morales's analysis of Guatemalan cultural politics today. The principal achievement of *La articulación de las diferencias* is to free Central American cultural criticism from the limits of a purely literary or "high-culture" concept of cultural agency. In its pages, we can see the cultural life of Guatemala as a heterotopic or "mixed" space in which the agendas of international NGOs and human rights organization, the novels of Miguel Ángel Asturias and *testimonios* based on the authority of oral culture such as *I, Rigoberta Menchú,* the Tex-Mex songs of Selena broadcast from stations in the United States and twenty-two (or more) distinct indigenous groups—each with its own language and cultural forms and practices—co-exist. But something also survives in Morales's argument of Rama's idea of transculturation, albeit now expressed in a postmodernist idiom of "cultural studies" and "hybridity" (*La articulación de las diferencias* could be read as a Guatemalan version of Néstor García Canclini's *Hybrid Cultures*).

Although he concedes that Mayan identity politics are born out of conditions of extreme poverty and oppression, Morales feels that at best the discourse of cultural identity proposes a negotiation between indigenous cultural (and economic) elites with the Guatemalan state and globalization, and their insertion in both. In this sense, he feels (like Stoll about *I, Rigoberta Menchú*) that this discourse (1) does not represent—in the sense of speaking *about*: that is, mimetically—the life-world of Guatemalan indigenous peoples in their multiple accommodations and negotiations with both the surrounding ladino world and globalized or transnational cultural flows and products; and (2) does not represent—in the sense of speaking *for*: that is, politically—the possibility of what he calls an "interethnic alliance" capable of displacing the hegemony in Guatemala of groups espousing a neoliberal model of development and the continuing power of elements connected to the old military-oligarchic state.

Against the sharp indigenous/ladino binary in the discourse of Mayan identity politics, Morales defends in his book a process of what he calls "*mestizaje cultural.*" Morales wants to mean by "*mestizaje cultural*" not so much the sublation of cultural difference in favor of the emergence of a "common" or "shared" national identity, as in the idea of *mestizaje* in earlier Latin American cultural thinking (in, e.g., Vasconcelos or Martí), but rather a complex and permanent, never completely achieved, process of expression, negotiation, and hybridization of these differences. He recognizes the persistence of the multiethnic and multilinguistic character of the population of a country such as Guatemala, the justice of many of the demands of indigenous groups, even the desirability and practical possibility of semiautonomous indigenous regions within the "national" space of Guatemala.

But if, for Morales, both indigenous cultures and ladino culture participate in a common process of *mestizaje,* hybridization, and "negotiation," then the question is, What (or where) is their difference? Because there is, finally, a *difference* between indians and ladinos that the fact of racial-cultural *mestizaje* does not cancel, just as there are differences—antagonistic and nonantagonistic, of "identity," values, access to capital, power, or privilege—between blacks and whites in the United States, or between men and women in all class societies. Morales's concern in attacking Mayan identity politics is nominally with the reconstruction of the project of the left in Guatemala after the defeat of the armed struggle. But a new form of the left that could become hegemonic cannot be founded on a notion of "hybridization" of differences. Rather, it is precisely (racial, ethnic, gender, class, etc.) "differences" that would potentialize a revised politics of the left as a *transformative* force. In other words, it is *from* multicultural difference that the possibility of reconstituting (or perhaps of constituting really for the first time) a genuinely popular bloc appears. (Morales sometimes indulges in an essentialism of his own, identifying multiculturalism with "Anglo" moralism and *mestizaje* with the Latin American as such.)

What is important in identity politics is not so much the claim of cultural difference per se, which (as Morales properly notes) all too often can play into the hands of elites, and sustain or even widen existing power and economic differentials, within subaltern or minority groups. But the "presumption of equal worth" that underlies these claims lends them a kind of communality in their very incommensurability. If multiculturalism is essentially a demand for equality of opportunity—in accord with the category of the subject and the principle of individual rights—then not only is it compatible with neoliberal hegemony but, in a sense, it actively requires the market and liberal democracy and legal categories to constitute itself as such. In turn, the logic of the state and corporate planning is to organize hybrid or heterogeneous populations into fixed identity categories: poor, black, gay, indigenous, latino, woman, person with AIDS, Catholic, and so on. (Part of the problem with identity politics is, of course, that one person can be all or some of these things at once.)

But if the demand is not so much for formal equality—the "level playing field"—as for *actual* epistemological, cultural, economic, and civic-political equality and self-realization, such that cultural difference (say, the fact of being a non-Spanish speaker in Guatemala) does not imply a limitation on citizenship, then the logic of multiculturalism will necessarily have to question the existing forms of cultural and political hegemony. To paraphrase a well-known argument of Chantal Mouffe and Ernesto Laclau: multiculturalism conforms to liberal pluralism because the identities in play in multiculturalism find in themselves the principle of their validity and rationality, rather than in a transcendental social principle or goal. On the other hand, to the extent that the auto-constitution of multicultural identities is tied to forms of subalternity, the identity claims participate in a common "egalitarian imaginary"—as Mouffe and Laclau call it—that is potentially subversive of the existing order of things. What fuels identity politics, in other words, is hatred and negation of social inequality and discrimination *as such.* Even the trope of simple inversion—the first shall be last and the last first, "we have been naught, we shall be all"—that is the driving force of subaltern agency has at its core a displaced form of egalitarian imaginary (for if the relation of master and slave can be reversed, then these are simply "roles" and not ontological destinies).

This makes it possible to produce from identity politics not only the essentialism and separatism Morales is concerned about (in their most negative form, as ethnic cleansing), but also what Mouffe and Laclau call a "popular subject position"—that is, a position that divides the political-cultural space of the nation into two antagonistic blocs: the bloc of the "people" and the bloc of the elite or ruling class. The idea inherent in this argument is that one can derive a new form of popular-democratic hegemony from the principle of multiculturalism. In other words, the "egalitarian imaginary" is a *necessary* rather than a contingent aspect of popular-democratic identity. The "people" is "essentially" multicultural (in the sense that Spivak intends in her concept of "strategic essentialism").

This is something quite different from generalizing the principle of heterogeneity to the whole social space, such that economic, racial, class, and gender inequalities and differences are seen as coincident with "civil society" as such. This would be, as I argued earlier apropos of Stoll's critique of Menchú's representativity, a way of neutralizing the political force of multicultural (as well as class and gender) difference. Rather, muticultural heterogeneity is *internal* to the identity of the people, which in turn has to be articulated against that which it is not, what Laclau and Mouffe call its "constitutive outside." The reason I have given so much critical attention to Morales's defense of *mestizaje* is that the "constitutive outside" of the "people" would have to be in some sense the logic of acculturation or transculturation of capitalist modernity itself.

To put this another way, the unity and mutual reciprocity of the—necessarily heterogeneous—elements of the "people" depends (as the idea of the Rainbow Coalition meant to symbolize) on a recognition of the inevitability and desirability of "contradictions among the people," without the need to resolve cultural difference and incommensurability into a transcendent or unitary cultural or political teleology. A potentially hegemonic articulation of multiculturalism would not seek to transcend differences and affectivities. In this sense, in order to form the interethnic ladino-indigenous-mestizo alliance of the sort Morales would like to see in Guatemala, a struggle against ladino hegemony and for the affirmation of the value of indigenous culture and identity may be necessary *in the first place,* because the "negotiation" of difference can only come as a response to a *demand.*[14]

If hybridity, *mestizaje,* transculturation, and the like are understood by Morales primarily as the field of this "negotiation" or—to use Bhabha's concept—of the "translation" of difference, then the dispute is merely terminological: hybrid or binary, transcultured or heterogeneous, shared or incommensurable—it is more or less the same. But one also suspects in Morales's activation of these concepts against the force of Mayan identity politics the persistence of a form of class (bourgeois or petty-bourgeois) and ethnic (ladino-*letrado*) *anxiety* about being displaced at the center of the national culture by a multiform popular subject (akin to what Jean-François Lyotard means by "the pagan"), an anxiety that works itself out in the desire to contain the protagonism of that subject within limits that are familiar and acceptable *for us.*

It would be yet another version of the "native informant" to grant a narrator such as Rigoberta Menchú only the possibility of being a witness, but not the power to create his or her own narrative authority and negotiate its conditions of truth and representativity. This would amount to saying that the subaltern can, of course, speak, but only through *us,* through our institutionally sanctioned authority and pretended objectivity as journalists or social scientists, which gives us the power to decide what counts as relevant and true in the narrator's "raw material." What *I, Rigoberta Menchú* forces us to confront is not someone who is being represented for us *as subaltern,* but rather an active agent of a transformative cultural and political project that aspires to become hegemonic in its own right: someone, in other words, who assumes the right to tell the story in the way she feels will be most effective in molding both national and international public opinion in support of the ideas and values she favors, which include a new kind of autonomy and authority for indigenous peoples.[15]

Stoll and Morales point in somewhat different directions politically, although both share a critique of the project of the Latin American revolutionary left as such and its relation with solidarity politics and multiculturalism in the United States. To the extent that they make that critique through a neutralization and containment of Menchú's own claim to authority, both of their books seem to me contemporary instances of what Ranajit Guha calls (apropos of the official histories and accounts of peasant rebellions in nineteenth-century India) "the prose of counter–insurgency": that is, texts that capture the fact of subaltern agency and insurgency essentially through the cultural assumptions and values of the elites that agency is directed against.[16]

Notes

1. Rigoberta Menchú, with Elisabeth Burgos-Debray, *I, Rigoberta Menchú: An Indian Woman in Guatemala*, trans. Ann Wright (London: Verso, 1984), 178–79.

2. David Stoll, *Rigoberta Menchú and the Story of All Poor Guatemalans* (Boulder, Colo.: Westview Press, 1999), viii.

3. John Beverley, *Against Literature* (Minneapolis: University of Minnesota Press, 1993), 70.

4. Rigoberta Menchú, interview by Juan Jesús Arnárez, "Those Who Attack Me Humiliate the Victims," El País, January 24, 1999 (in this volume).

5. For example, in the following passage: "At this point, the identity needs of Rigoberta's academic constituency play into the weakness of rules of evidence in postmodern scholarship. Following the thinking of literary theorists such as Edward Said and Gayatri Spivak, anthropologists have become very interested in problems of narrative, voice, and representation, especially the problem of how we misrepresent voices other than our own. In reaction, some anthropologists argue that the resulting fascination with texts threatens the claim of anthropology to be a science, by replacing hypothesis, evidence, and generalization with stylish forms of introspection" (Stoll 247).

6. Moreover, as he makes clear at the end of his book, Stoll intends not only a *retrospective* critique of armed struggle in Guatemala; he also means his book as a caution against enthusiasm for contemporary armed struggle movements such as the Zapatistas in Mexico (see, e.g., pp. 279–80). Indeed, for Stoll rural guerrilla strategies *as such* "are an urban romance, a myth propounded by middle-class radicals who dream of finding true solidarity in the countryside"; such strategies have "repeatedly been fatal for the left itself, by dismaying lower-class constituents and guaranteeing a crushing response from the state" (282). The "mythic inflation" or simplification of indigenous life and rural realities that *I, Rigoberta Menchú* supposedly performs colludes with this urban romance.

7. My own view is that under conditions of military and paramilitary rule in which even the most cautious ladino trade unionists and social democratic or Christian Democratic elected officials were likely to be "disappeared," and in the context

of the Sandinista victory in 1979, it is not surprising that armed resistance came to seem to many people in Guatemala as a desperate but plausible strategy.

8. To give credit where credit is due, the point about "other" narratives of Guatemalan indigenous life that contradict or relativize aspects of Menchú's *testimonio* was first made by Marc Zimmerman, in his essay "El otro de Rigoberta," in *La voz del otro. Testimonio, subalternidad, y verdad narrativa*, ed. John Beverley and Hugo Achugar (Pittsburgh and Lima: Latinoamerica Editores, 1993), 229–43.

9. Charles Taylor, *Multiculturalism: Examining the Politics of Recognition*, ed. Amy Gutman (Princeton, N.J.: Princeton University Press, 1994).

10. Homi Bhabha, "Editor's Introduction," *Front Lines/Border Posts*, a special issue of *Critical Inquiry* 23.3 (1997): 458–60.

11. Mario Roberto Morales, *La articulación de las diferencias: El debate inter-étnico en Guatemala* (Guatemala City: FLACSO, 1999). See also his essay in this volume.

12. Like many Central American intellectuals of his generation, Morales condenses in his own person and career the intersection of these two forms of practice. In the 1970s and 1980s, he was a cadre in one of the organizations that protagonized the armed struggle in Guatemala, an experience he describes in his tragicomic memoir *Los que se fueron por la libre* (1998). At the same time, he was becoming known as an emerging voice in Guatemalan literature in a series of novels that touched on the political crisis his generation of middle-class youth experienced: *Los demonios salvajes* (1977), *El esplendor de la pirámide* (1986), *Señores abajo los arboles* (1994), and *El ángel de la retaguardia* (1997). His first book of literary criticism, *La ideología y la lírica de la lucha armada* (1992), was one of the most rigorous efforts to theorize the relationship between revolutionary militancy and the new forms of Latin American literature coming out of vanguardism and the boom.

13. Ángel Rama, *Transculturación narrativa en América Latina* (Mexico: Siglo XXI, 1982).

14. Wendy Brown has analyzed acutely the political impasse that identity politics may lead to (I am indebted to Gareth Williams for bringing this passage to my attention): "In its emergence as a protest against marginalization or subordination, politicized identity... becomes attached to its own exclusion both because it is premised on this exclusion for its existence as identity and because the identity as the site of exclusion, as exclusion, augments or 'alters the direction of the suffering' entailed in subordination or marginalization by finding a site of blame for it. But in so doing, it installs pain over its unredeemed history in the very foundation of its political claim, in its demand for recognition as identity. In locating a site of blame for its powerlessness over its past—a past of injury, a past as a hurt will—and locating a 'reason' for the 'unendurable pain' of social powerlessness in the present, it converts this reasoning into an ethnicizing politics, a politics of recrimination that seeks to avenge the hurt even while it reaffirms it, discursively codifies it. Politicized identity thus enunciates itself, makes claims for itself, only by entrenching, restating, dramatizing, and inscribing its pain in politics; it can hold out no future— for itself or others—that triumphs over this pain. The loss of historical direction, and with it the loss of futurity characteristic of the late modern age, is thus homologically refigured in the structure of desire of the dominant political expression of the age: identity politics" (Wendy Brown, *State of Inquiry: Power and Freedom in Late Modernity* [Princeton, N.J.: Princeton University Press, 1995], 73–74). The point is

well taken, and coincides with Morales's skepticism about Mayan identity politics in Guatemala. But, like Morales, Brown presupposes that identity politics cannot aspire to become hegemonic without losing its raison d'être, that subaltern negativity can only affirm impotence, resentment, and suffering. One thing is identity politics without the transformative possibility of hegemony—that is, within the "rules of the game" of the dominant class and political-legal institutions (Brown notes in this respect that identity politics paradoxically runs the risk of becoming "a protest that . . . reinstalls the humanist ideal [of the inclusive/universal community] so far as it premises itself on an exclusion from it" [65]); another—what Chantal Mouffe and Ernesto Laclau are trying to point to in their notion of the "egalitarian imaginary" as the articulating principle of a new kind of popular-democratic alliance politics—is identity politics with that possibility, since, by definition, even the prospect of attaining hegemony would necessarily transform the identities that enter into play in a process of hegemonic articulation to start with. But if the subaltern has to become like *that which is already hegemonic* in order to become itself hegemonic, then what will have been gained? Obviously, *something* of its initial "identity" as subaltern, marginal, "excluded" would have to be present in any new discursive structure or *combinatoire* of hegemony. It cannot enter into politics simply by renouncing or "deconstructing" its identity claims without also affirming a fictive universalism or "humanism." Mouffe and Laclau note that "[t]he original forms of democratic thought were linked to a positive and unified conception of human nature," whereas identity politics confronts us with "the emergence of a *plurality of subjects,* whose form of constitution and diversity it is only possible to think if we relinquish the category of the 'subject' as a unified and unifying essence" (Chantal Mouffe and Ernesto Laclau, 180–81). But is not "democratic thought" itself a class- and ethnically specific form of thought (the thought of the European bourgeoisie in its struggle against feudal power), and is not *all* politics in this sense identity politics?

15. As a graduate student in my department noted recently apropos of the Stoll–Menchú debate, the question is not Can the subaltern speak? but Can the subaltern speak in a way that manipulates or dupes us to serve her interests?

16. Ranajit Guha, "The Prose of Counter-Insurgency," in *Selected Subaltern Studies,* ed. Ranajit Guha and Gayatri Spivak (New York: Oxford University Press, 1988). I am indebted to José Rabasa for this observation.

Las Casas's Lies and Other Language Games

Doris Sommer

Truth or Lies

David Stoll is probably right about some objections he raises to Rigoberta Menchú's 1983 *testimonio*. It may well be partial, in both senses of that word: both limited to the information she remembers or chooses to share, and biased toward her father and to the comrades she inherited from him. And sympathetic readers may therefore feel justifiably disappointed, even offended, if, in fact, they have been somewhat deceived. This is hardly reason to dismiss Rigoberta, as if she were an intimate friend, invested with our personal trust that could be betrayed with almost any breech of confidence. Even a critical note about Stoll's presumption, and his sometimes tedious or sloppy scholarship, does not shake Tim Golden's demand to know Rigoberta the person. About her new book, he complains, "What seems not to have changed is the difficulty readers will have in seeing the woman behind the symbol" (*New York Times Book Review,* April 18, 1999).

But other readers sense that the sympathy she elicits is shy of intimacy; it is defensive and strategic. To acknowledge this is no reason to stop reading her, as if the only legitimate reason to continue were to know a person, or to know the full truth. If it were, how would we continue to read the discontinuous versions of Frederick Douglass's autobiography? Notoriously, the three versions show contradictions, from the first where, for example, his mother is a brief memory to the last where she is the intellectual spirit and trainer of the future statesman. Does he disqualify himself as an informant? Perhaps he performs a kind of creative control over his "life," as theorists of autobiography might argue, unless, of course, a slave narrative or a *testimonio* creates fundamentally different expectations than does a standard autobiography. If the expectation is transparency, confession, lack of guile or control, then our reading habits need reflection, because the very autonomy or agency that the genre promises is short-circuited by an asymmetrical reception. Writers exercise control; and demanding readers wrest that control by requiring submission. Language games are many, far exceeding the telling of facts or finding falsehoods. These certainly do not exhaust the possibilities, as both J. L. Austin and Ludwig Wittgenstein used to tell more rigid philosophers who created trouble for themselves. The therapy for philosophy's penchant for problem making was simply to appreciate the many functions language performs.

Do we dismiss the testimonies of genocidal holocaust in World War II because of controvertible details, when the incontrovertible fact of genocide is in the balance? Some revisionist historians do just that, Jean-François Lyotard worried in *The Differend*.[1] The neologism refers to a conflict "that cannot be equitably resolved for lack of a rule applicable to both arguments." Referring to the Holocaust, Lyotard asks how a survivor can testify to what should have killed him. "The burden of proof always falls on the plaintiff. Reality is always the plaintiff's responsibility. For the defense, it is sufficient to refute the argumentation—as recognized by Aristotle (*Rhetoric* 1402b 24–25). The defense is nihilistic" (Lyotard, 10). This is the double bind that leads Lyotard into a sidetrack: the *differend*, "the case where the plaintiff is divested of the means to argue and becomes for that reason a victim . . . the 'regulation' of the conflict that opposes them is done in the idiom of one of the parties while the wrong suffered by the other is not signified in that idiom" (Lyotard. 12).

Now, Rigoberta has not been silent; and it would be hasty to call her a victim in a litigation initiated by Stoll. She is by no means passive or ignored in public arenas, as Douglass was not. And she may indeed have "perjured" herself in her (literary, strategic) testimony, but a measure of creative writing and reading is, as I said, unobjectionable in most first-person narratives, including the politically motivated and deployed slave narratives that survive their inconsistencies. What exactly is Stoll demanding of Rigoberta's story, and is the demand fair? Another way to pose the question is to consider which "phrase regimen" defines her

testimony. Is it the same that defines Stoll's critique? In the case of coincidence, no damage is done, to follow Lyotard, since both parties submit
to the same criteria of communication: "There are a number of phrase
regimens: reasoning, knowing, describing, recounting, questioning, showing, ordering, etc. [one could add denouncing, consciousness raising,
apologia]. Phrases from heterogeneous regimens cannot be translated
from one into the other." In general, he observes, "there is no universal
rule of judgment between heterogeneous genres." And certainly the two
are playing games in different regimens: Rigoberta is "showing" genocide and staking her claim to agency, whereas Stoll is "questioning" her
right to that agency. The games "can be linked one onto the other in
accordance with an end fixed by a genre of discourse," says Lyotard, and
with a certain goal in mind: "to know, to teach, to be just, to seduce, to
justify, to evaluate" (xii). This last and least friendly option is the one
that links Stoll's investigation to Rigoberta's denunciation.

I will therefore not dispute Stoll's information about her father's pre-
political competitions over land that brought him into conflict with in-
laws (*Anthropology Newsletter,* April 1998). Nor will I debate Stoll's summary of the historical and continuing conflicts over land between Quiché
and Ixil people in northern Guatemala (*Active Voices,* May 14, 1998).
Whether or not the information is accurate is beside the point I would
like to raise here, which is about the incompatible phrase regimen he
deploys, and the loose language games he is playing. Stoll's alleged care
to learn and to tell the truth falters on conceptual carelessness, when
information gathering links onto Rigoberta's narrative through evaluation. The movement produces a slip, as his language of description and
investigation skids into playing games with policy considerations. From
evaluating Rigoberta's story, he moves into evaluating the policies that
take for granted the antagonisms between government-backed large landholders and peasants. We would be wise to wonder why he wants to shift
public attention from the genocidal war waged by the Guatemalan government against its indigenous population to a particular internecine
struggle between native groups. What is his purpose in foregrounding
current peasant conflicts while the country is urgently debating how to
develop public institutions that acknowledge indigenous rights? Why
are the competitions between peasants made so weighty in Stoll's story?
He does not fully exonerate the greedy *latifundistas,* who have made
arable land scarce, have ignited and fanned much of the internecine

competition, and whose collaboration with the government is obvious both in Rigoberta's account and in the reports from international commissions. But Stoll certainly mitigates the landowners' responsibility for violence, with his focus on the tensions between the plantations' loyal employees and frustrated occasional workers. The effects of his fact-finding, I am saying, are hardly neutral, especially as they are linked to critiques of international funding for peasant initiatives. That is one reason to worry about Stoll's procedure.

Apologia and Dismissal

Does he pursue the truth? Or does he purvey opinions? In other words, what is the relationship in his work between getting knowledge and giving advice (to foundations, policy makers, educators)? Stoll is probably right to quibble over Rigoberta's facts, given the tension between her particular political agendas and her universal, almost saintly, Nobel laureate stature, and given also the nature of his own work as fact-finder and analyst. Other scrupulous fact-finders have also quibbled with passionate and interested accounts of atrocities in Latin America. Objections begin with the well-known criticisms of the histories written by Bartolomé de Las Casas. His faultfinders, and even many of his admirers, have accused him of being no historian at all, but a fabricator of tales spun out of the data he used in (mis)leading ways. "He has been called noble Apostle to the Indians, piously fanatic . . . ; but few men in his time or later have considered him to be a true historian," Lewis Hanke wrote in an apologetic prologue to the *Historia de las Indias*. Las Casas's defenders complain that the objections are narrow, that they mistake exaggerations in statistics for significant distortions of meaning. Whatever the accurate numbers of dead Indians and victorious Spaniards, the ineluctable fact of history is that a short generation after the "discovery," Hispaniola's indigenous population was practically exterminated, and the rest of the Caribbean peoples were essentially wiped out soon afterwards. Hanke's apologia concedes that Las Casas may indeed have been writing legend, but it adds that legends tend to be as true in substance as they are false in detail.

Poetic Truth and Technical Lies

Stoll might have apologized for Rigoberta in a similar spirit, conceding the "legendary" effect of her book and defending its usefulness in bring-

ing embattled indigenous people to the world's attention. This hypo-
thetical apologia would not be at all far-fetched if Stoll had addressed
himself, reflexively, in his own quip about the spirit of truth: "If *poetic
truth* is good enough for you," the part of her story that matches versions of Guatemala's genocidal campaign told by Rigoberta's neighbors,
and that resonates with the general indigenous population, "*is all too
true*" (*Anthropology Newsletter*, April 1998, 11; my emphasis). But Stoll
does not link up history to apologia; instead, he links it to analysis,
through evaluation.

Wittgenstein would have noticed that these various genres of writing
are distinct "language games." They have a "family resemblance," insofar
as particular features (e.g., the appeal to responsibility, a consideration
of alternative versions) repeat from one game to another.[2] Defense and
prosecution are evidently linked by a shared logic of proofs, otherwise
nothing could be settled through these language games. And each is
equally possible—in the tautological sort of way Wittgenstein practiced
philosophy after abandoning logical speculation—because they both
exist. So do many other games. But Stoll's polarization of the discussion
concerning Rigoberta allows only these two judgmental games, and
within this narrow playing field, he rushes toward rejection, even though
her "poetic truth" might have been a cause for validation. Then the game
slips beyond that field and plays with policy considerations.

To his credit, Stoll's game acknowledges that judgments should derive from a historical record that can and should be as complete as possible, even when completion includes countervailing narratives. These
are not, however, the "phrases in collision" that Lyotard describes as
ethically irreconcilable differences, in his conflictive development of
Wittgenstein's games. Lyotard understood the conflict between a hegemonic system of judgment and a subaltern code of values to be worthy
of respect, not simply a nuisance to be overridden in favor of "the law."
Stoll, on the other hand, proceeds as if all parties concerned were, or
should be, transparent before the same system of logic and law. His blind
justice would equalize the Guatemalan government, the guerrilla, landowners, peons, peasants, Quiché, Ixil, foreign foundations, American
anthropologists. Once the players are leveled to occupy the same field,
Stoll can shift focus from the state-sponsored abuses that outraged and
energized others (writers as well as volunteers, philanthropists, and international peacekeepers), to the murkier aggressiveness among peas-

ants who compete over the area's insufficient land. The difficulty with this procedure should be patent: its raze-and-burn effect on the constitutive asymmetries of culture and economics in Guatemala does damage to the players, recoils from their particularities, even before the nefarious game of judging begins. To repeat, Stoll's ideally disinterested, almost innocent, game of fact-finding gets mired in the tangled terrain of persistent social and cultural difference. Information gathering, in Stoll's hand, links onto the game of analysis; and, as I said, it comes very close to policy recommendations.

Investigation and Recommendation

The slippage is not philosophically necessary, as Wittgenstein would have sensed in his appreciation for the variability of games, and as Lyotard spelled out in a discussion of phrase regimens that sometimes link onto one another and sometimes do not. Stoll might have remained inside the game of multiple perspectives and of historical contradictions. He might have honored Rigoberta's account of the conflicts—understanding that her version is itself a game of strategy, a "speech act" inside the war, and not merely an account of the war—at the same time that he recorded other partial and strategic versions. But Stoll does not stay in the complexity-of-history game. He insists and persists—for more than a decade now—in debunking Rigoberta's version. John Beverley has already pointed out that Stoll had first exaggerated the liberties that Rigoberta allegedly took as a narrator, even though Stoll privileges other informants whose facts are just as mired in narrative and possibly partial as is her *testimonio*. Why debunk her? Is it because countervailing accounts of history can implode into a *Roshomon* kind of relativism that does not leave much ground to stand on? Then the worried reader may wonder, Why does Stoll need to take a stand? This is where history slips into the game of policy. The move is not logically necessary, we know. Is it, then, a political, or an ethical, requirement? This is not a rhetorical question.

Secrets

Rigoberta forces this very real but underexamined question on her readers, by wedging an empty space into the debate, a chasm between the outsider's information and his possible interference. Keeping secrets is her most significant language game, I believe. Rigoberta Menchú's secrets astonished me when I read her testimonial in the early 1980s. Her secrets stopped me then, and instruct me now, whatever the validity of the information or the authenticity of the informant. Why should she make so much of keeping secrets instead of just keeping quiet? I wondered. And why do these cultural secrets matter, if they have no apparent military or strategic value in this denunciation of Indian removal politics in Guatemala? Here is an exposé that refuses to share information. The dissonance raised a question about Rigoberta: Was she an authentic witness to abuse, a vehicle for truth beyond her control and vulnerable to a compromised and enfuriated government? Or was she being coy on the witness stand, exercising control over apparently irrelevant information, perhaps to produce her own strategic version of truth? The difference is significant, even if the alternatives stay tangled.

A reference to Nietzsche could suggest the fine line between telling and troping, informing and performing. And lessons from Enrique Dussel, Paul Ricoeur, and the shades of church-affiliated victims of Guatemalan death squads might remind us that bearing witness has been a sacred responsibility throughout Christianity, which is why witnesses are martyrs etymologically and historically. Rigoberta glosses those lessons in her performance of responsible survival. Her techniques include maintaining the secrets that keep readers from knowing her too well. One conclusion to draw is that productive alliances respect cultural distances among members. Like the rhetorical figure of metonymy, alliance is a relationship of contiguity, not of metaphoric overlap. To shorten the distance between writer and readers would invite identifications that makes one of those positions redundant. Rigoberta is too smart to prepare her own reduction, in the logic of metaphoric evaporations. Embattled Indians generally know that reductions are dangerous. It is the word for conquered communities.

We should notice that the audible protests of silence are responses to anthropologist Elisabeth Burgos-Debray's line of questioning. If she were not asking possibly impertinent questions, the Quiché informant would have no reason to resist. From the introduction to *Me llamo Rigoberta Menchú* (1983), we know that the testimonial is being mediated at several levels by Burgos, who records, edits, and arranges the information, so that knowledge in this text announces its partiality. The book never presumes immediacy between the narrating "I" and the readerly "you." Nor does Rigoberta offer intimacy when she claims authorship for the interviews that remain cataloged under the interrogator's name.[3] Yet many readers have preferred the illusion of immediacy, perhaps from certain (autobiographical, or old-line anthropological?) habits of reading that project a real and knowable person onto the persona we are hearing, despite being told that the recorded voice is synthesized and processed, and despite the repeated reminders that our access is limited. Could the ardent interest, and our best intentions toward the informant, amount to construing the text as a kind of artless "confession," like the ones exacted by surveillance techniques of nineteenth-century colonizers? Maybe empathy for an informant is a good feeling that covers over a controlling disposition, what Derrida calls "an inquisitorial insistence, an order, a petition. . . . To demand the narrative of the other, to extort it from him like a secretless secret."[4] The possibility should make us pause. Natives who remained incalculable, because they refused to tell secrets, obviously frustrated colonial state control.[5]

I have already argued that the projections of presence and truth are less than generous here.[6] Empathy is hardly an ethical feeling, despite the enthusiasm for identifying with Others among some political activists, including some first-world feminists. In effect, the projections of intimacy and requirement of transparency allow us to shorten the stretch between writer and reader, disregarding the text's rhetorical (decidedly fictional) performance of keeping us at a politically safe distance. To close in on Rigoberta would threaten her authority and leadership.[7]

The very fact that I am able to call self-critical attention to our culture-bound appetites is a sign that I have been reading Rigoberta. When I began, her forthright refusals to satisfy my interest woke me to the possibility that the interest was being cultivated in order to produce the sting of rebuff. Concerns about the text's authenticity seemed beside the point, as I began to appreciate the evident manipulations. Perhaps the informant was being more active and strategic than our essentialist notions of authenticity have allowed. The possibility triggered memories of other books that had refused intimacy, and their distancing tropes came into focus as corollaries to Rigoberta's lesson.

Interpret Away

Masterful reading, even as a motive and short of a presumption, is what some particularist narrators try to baffle. Secrets can cordon off curious and controlling readers from the vulnerable objects of their attention.

Secrecy is a safeguard to freedom, Emmanuel Levinas argues against Hegel, who ridiculed it; it is the inviolable core of human subjectivity that makes interaction a matter of choice rather than rational necessity. "Only starting from this secrecy is the pluralism of society possible."[8] Notice that Rigoberta's refusals remain on the page after the editing is done. The refusals say, in effect, this document is a screen, in the double sense that Henri Lefebvre uses the term: something that shows and that also covers up.[9] From the beginning, the narrator tells us very clearly that she is not going to tell: "Indians have been very careful not to disclose any details of their communities."[10] They are largely "public" secrets, known to the Quichés and kept from us in a gesture of self-preservation. By some editorial or joint decision, the very last words of the testimonial are, "I'm still keeping secret what I think no-one should know. Not even anthropologists or intellectuals, no matter how many books they have, can find out all our secrets" (1984, 247; 1983, 377).

Readers have noticed the inevitable interference of the ethnographer in these transcriptions. And they have been critical or disappointed at the loss of immediacy, perhaps with a resentment born of ardor that chafes at insulating frames around heartwarming stories. Most offensive to many readers is Burgos-Debray's unreflexive Introduction, where she presumes to share intimacy and solidarity with Rigoberta as they share meals of black beans in Paris. Almost unremarked, however, but far more remarkable for being unanticipated, are the repeated and deliberate signs of asymmetry throughout Rigoberta's testimony. Either the informant, the scribe, or both were determined to keep the admonitions in the published text. Uncooperative gestures may be typical of ethnographic interrogations, but they seldom survive in scientific reports.[11] Here, however, scientific curiosity turns out to be impertinent, to judge from the refusals to respond. If Rigoberta had not refused audibly and repeatedly, we might mistake her resistance for passivity. This contrast between the possibility of speech and an impossibility imposed by others is what Jean-François Lyotard adapts from Aristotle in order to distinguish between a plaintiff (who can attest to a crime against her) and a victim (who is silenced by her fear or is dismissed as irrelevant).[12] Are we being warned, by Rigoberta's active refusal, that our curiosity may be an impulse to warm cold bodies with the fuel of violated lives? In the backhanded logic of metaleptic effects, our curiosity may be the result of Rigoberta's resistance. Before she demurs, how desirous are we? I wonder if she staged even more questions than she was asked, just to perform more refusals. This seductive possibility does not occur to Lyotard's legal logic.[13] Without refusing our putative interest often enough for us to notice, she could hardly have exercised the uncooperative control that turns a potentially humiliating scene of interrogation into an opportunity for self-authorization.

Nevertheless, the almost four hundred pages of testimony are full of information—about herself, her community, traditional practices, the armed struggle, strategic decisions. Therefore, a reader may wonder why her final statement insists, for a last and conclusive time, that we "cannot know" her secrets. Why is so much attention being called to our insufficiency as readers? Does it mean that the knowledge is impossible or that it is forbidden? Is she saying that we are *incapable* of knowing, or that we *ought* not to know?

Rigoberta continues to publicly perform this kind of silence, like a leitmotif. At the Political Forum of Harvard University, in April 1994, she opened her address with some literally incomprehensible words. It was an incantatory flow pronounced between smiling lips under friendly eyes, words that a student asked her to translate during the question period. "No," was her polite response, "I cannot translate them." They were a formal and formulaic greeting in Quiché, she said, and they would lose their poetic quality in a different rendering. This speech act was not hostile, but it was a reminder of difference that located meaning elsewhere, beyond translation, in the very foreignness of words.

As in the case of Nietzsche's meditation on the nature of rhetoric in general, the choice between ethics and epistemology is undecidable. Because even if her own explicit rationale is nonempirical, ethical (claiming that we should not know the secrets because of the particular power attached to the stories we tell about ourselves), she suggests the other reason. It is the degree of our foreignness, our cultural difference, that would make her secrets incomprehensible to the outsider. We could never know them as she does, because we would inevitably force her secrets into our framework. "Theologians have come and observed us," for example, "and have drawn a false impression of the Indian world" (1984, 9, translation modified; 1983, 42).

Guatemalan Indians have a long history of being read that way in European languages. From the sixteenth century to the present, the Maya have been "surviving Conquest," as a recent demographic analysis puts it. If some readers perceive a certain ahistorical inflection in Rigoberta's sense that the Spanish Conquest is an event of the recent past, W. George Lovell might corroborate her sense of continuity in this new period of cultural genocide:

> Viewed in historical perspective, it is disconcerting to think how much the twentieth century resembles the sixteenth, for the parallels between cycles of conquest hundreds of years apart are striking. Model villages are designed to serve similar purposes as colonial *congregaciones*— to function as the institutional means by which one culture seeks to reshape the ways and conventions of another, to operate as authoritarian mechanisms of resettlement, indoctrination, and control.[14]

The less comprehension in/by Spanish, the better; it is the language that the enemy uses to conquer differences. For an Indian, to learn Spanish can amount to passing over to the other side, to the Ladinos, which simply means "Latin" or Spanish speakers. "My father used to call them 'ladinized Indians,'... because they act like *ladinos,* bad *ladinos*" (1984, 24; 1983, 66). This kind of caution has managed to preserve Mayan cultural continuities, and the political solidarity it can activate, beyond the social scientific paradigms that have tried to account for it.[15]

Paul Ricoeur might have guessed at her designs, given the mediation of language in testimony. The incorrigibly compromising medium of fallible human languages derails God's truth; it translates between a truth to die for and a life that goes on. Charged with a communicative duty imposed by absolute truth, language cannot avoid humanizing, debasing the message by interpreting it. There is no help for it. Even sacred testimony passes through the contingency of interpretation. So, Ricoeur concludes, the only possible philosophy of testimony is hermeneutics, interpretation.[16] Testimony is hermeneutical in a double sense. It gives a content to be interpreted, and it calls for an interpretation; it narrates facts, and it confesses a faith during the juridical moments that link history to eternity.[17]

Rigoberta apparently appreciates testimony's double duty: the message of liberation pulls in one (ideal) direction, and the (earthly) medium of political persuasion pulls in another. To collapse the two is foolish, maybe disastrous. She will not mistake (ideal) demands for justice with sentimental interest from (earthly) interrogators. Offers of solidarity probably confuse doing good with feeling good. The double challenge for this Christian leader, as new and as beleaguered as Christ's first witnesses, is to serve truth in ways that make a difference in the world. Testimony to that truth and coyness about how to convey it turn out to be voices in counterpoint. If we cannot hear the complexity, perhaps our inability is simply that, as Nietzsche reminded us, rather than a sign that contradictions cannot exist.

Whose Game?

Even more significant than the information she offers (whether or not it is all accurate, or complete, or even biased) is her performance of self-authorization in a situation that threatens to replace her indigenous authority with foreign advice. She keeps reminding readers that we are too foreign to presume to analyze her world, certainly too ill-informed to solve its problems. More provocative than her facts, facts that can be quibbled with or contradicted, much more startling than the competing political postures (learned from Catholic missionaries, Marxist revolutionaries, peasant mothers, displaced men), postures that can be struck, adjusted, unstuck, is Rigoberta's game of distancing readers to a point from which they cannot possibly offer advice. "I keep secrets," is her insistent leitmotif; "my people know them, but you will not." This surely infuriates some traditional anthropologists. Perhaps they are deaf to the message of propriety, or they feel goaded to know more than she will tell. A possible, but simple, reading of her *testimonio* is, of course, that it condemns Guatemala's government and defends the guerrilla in ways that flatten a complex reality.

This is Stoll's criticism. But any careful reader will note that her book does not proselytize to potential comrades; it does not try to win souls for combat or to welcome outsiders into the struggle. Readers are cautioned against their own zealousness for information and for involvement. "I have secrets" means that you will never know enough to analyze our war or to make policies for peace. A careless reading of this caution would mistake it for a hands-off intransigence against alliances with foreigners, an endorsement for the kind of cultural relativism that justifies political indifference and paralysis. Evidently, Rigoberta's *testimonio* is an appeal for international support (otherwise, why write it?), and it is a lesson in the distinction between giving support and giving orders. Readers may feel moved to lobby against military aid to a cruel regime, perhaps to send medical supplies or food, and to reflect on the long history of slippages between wanting to know Indians and thinking you know enough to make policy for them.

Notes

1. Jean-François Lyotard, *The Differend: Phrases in Dispute,* trans. Georges Van Den Abbeele (Minneapolis: University of Minnesota Press, 1992; orig. Minuit, 1983).

2. Ludwig Wittgenstein, *Philosophical Investigations,* trans. G. E. M. Anscombe (New York: Macmillan, 1953, 1968), 67.

3. Alice Britton and Kenya Dworkin, "Rigoberta Menchú: 'Los indígenas nos quedamos como bichos aislados, immunes, desde hace 500 años. No. Nosotros hemos sido protagonistas de la historia,'" *Nuevo Texto Crítico* 6 (1993): 214+ Rigoberta Menchú, *Crossing Borders,* trans. Ann Wright (London: Verso 1998). "The moral rights of author and the translator have been asserted." (This note by the publisher appears along with the ordinary publication data.)

4. Jacques Derrida, "Living On: Border Lines," in *Deconstruction and Criticism,* ed. Jacques Derrida, Paul de Man, J. Hillis Miller, Harold Bloom, and Geoffrey Hartman (London: Routledge and Kegan Paul, 1979), 87.

5. Homi Bhabha, *The Location of Culture* (New York: Routledge, 1994), 99.

6. Doris Sommer, "Rigoberta's Secrets," *Latin American Perspectives* 18 (1991): 32–50.

7. David Stoll, among many others, questions her claims to leadership by referring to indigenous informants who do not authorize Rigoberta. See John Beverley's reference in "The Real Thing," in *The Real Thing: Testimonial Discourse and Latin America,* ed. Georg M. Gugelberger (Durham, N.C.: Duke University Press, 1996), n. 15. Her legitimacy is not at issue for me. Rather, it is her rhetorical defense of decision making among Indians. This implies making alliances with others, so that readers will be obliged to make judgments in order to participate. But this is different from replacing local leadership by presuming our political sophistication. The difference is Rigoberta's rhetorical lesson.

8. Emmanuel Levinas, *Ethics and Infinity: Conversations with Philippe Nemo,* trans. Richard A. Cohen (Pittsburgh: Duquesne University Press, 1985), 75–81; 78–79.

9. Henri Lefebvre, "Toward a Leftist Cultural Politics Remarks Occasioned by the Centenary of Marx's Death," in *Marxism and the Interpretation of Culture,* ed. Cary Nelson and Lawrence Grossberg, trans. David Reifman (Urbana: University of Illinois Press, 1988), 75–88; quote from 78.

10. Rigoberta Menchú, with Elisabeth Burgos-Debray, *I, Rigoberta Menchú: An Indian Woman in Guatemala,* trans. Ann Wright (London: Verso, 1984), 9; see also *Me llamo Rigoberta Menchú,* ed. Elisabeth Burgos-Debray (Havana: Casa de las Américas, 1983), 42. Page references are to the translation, followed by references to the original.

11. See, for example, Vincent Crapanzano, "Life Histories," *American Anthropologist* 86.4 (1984): 953–60.

12. Lyotard, *The Differend,* 14: "Not to speak is part of the ability to speak, since ability is a possibility and a possibility implies something and its opposite . . . To be able not to speak is not the same as not to be able to speak. The latter is a deprivation, the former a negation (Aristotle, *De Interpretatione* 21 b 12–17; *Metaphysics* IV 1022 b 22ff.)"

13. Lyotard, *The Differend*, 26. Silence can indicate my incompetence to hear, the lack of any event or relevant information to recount, the unworthiness of the witness, or a combination of these.

14. W. George Lovell, "Surviving Conquest: The Maya of Guatemala in Historical Perspective," *Latin American Research Review* 23.2 (1988), 47; see also Beatriz Manz, *Refugees of a Hidden War: The Aftermath of Counterinsurgency in Guatemala*, SUNY Series in Anthropological Studies of Contemporary Issues (Albany: State University of New York Press, 1988).

15. See June Nash's important contribution, "The Reassertion of Indigenous Identity: Mayan Responses to State Intervention in Chiapas," *Latin American Research Review* 30.3 (1995): 7–41; 9: "The rebellion attests to the extraordinary durability of distinctive cultures in Middle America. Anthropologists have attributed this persistence variously.... Protagonists on both sides of this older [essentialist versus constructionist] debate have shown that the persistence of distinct beliefs and practices among indigenous populations of the Americas arises from internal resources and from pressures exerted by the dominant group. Current debates are taking into account the combined force of antagonistic but interpenetrating relationships between *indígenas* and *ladinos* as they generate and sustain ethnic diversity.... By looking inward at 'narrative strategies for resisting terror' (Kay B. Warren, ed., *The Violence Within: Cultural and Political Opposition in Divided Nations* [Boulder, (Colo.:) Westview (Press,) 1993]), evoking dialogue between ancient and present traditions, and assessing the economic opportunities that condition their survival, researchers are constructing a theory that recognizes both the structural imperatives of the colonial and postcolonial systems encapsulating indigenous peoples and their own search for a base from which to defend themselves and generate collective action."

16. Paul Ricoeur, "The Hermeneutics of Testimony," in Essays in Biblical Interpretation, ed. Lewis S. Mudge (Philadelphia: Fortress Press, 1980), 119–54.

17. Ibid., 142.

The Poetics of Remembering, the Politics of Forgetting
Rereading I, Rigoberta Menchú

Elzbieta Sklodowska

> Whether it happened so or not I do not know; but if you think
> about it you can see that it is true.
>
> —*Black Elk Speaks*

This essay was written during a time when the controversy about Rigoberta Menchú's testimony was impelled by ad hominem attacks and fraught with sensationalism. It is my hope to contribute to this ongoing exchange without partaking of its contentious rhetoric. Faced with the evidence for obvious misremembering of some of the most compelling interpretations of *testimonio* among those involved in the current debate, I begin my essay by framing Latin American testimonial writing both historically and methodologically. This, in turn, opens up the space for my own rereading of *I, Rigoberta Menchú* by focusing on the role of memory in the mediation of telling, writing, reading, and critical interpretation.

In an era that has redirected its critical energy from investigating "the truth" toward the study "of inventing, making, creating or . . . constructing" (Scarry 214), the recent debate surrounding the "truthfulness" of Rigoberta Menchú's testimony seems oddly out of place. After all, recent studies from across a broad range of disciplines in the humanities and social sciences focus on the "constructed" or "invented" nature of such notions as ethnicity, sexuality, nationality, and gender. If all these concepts fit the category of "created objects," our postmodern wisdom tells us that Rigoberta Menchú's testimonial account, too, should be approached with "a self-conscious acknowledgement of [its] artifactual nature" (Scarry 215).

This seems a fitting moment to recall that two disciplines that bear "family resemblance" to testimonial narrative—history and anthropology—have been involved in an intense process of self-questioning for more than two decades. In the early 1970s, Clifford Geertz and Hayden White admitted, respectively, that the anthropologist's and historian's activities consist in producing texts. Consequently, they suggested that rhetorical analysis should take precedence over scientific truth claims, and White went almost as far as denying the "outside the text" altogether when he declared that "truth remains captive of the linguistic mode" (xi).

In *Rigoberta Menchú and the Story of All Poor Guatemalans*, David Stoll tackles some of these problems by stating that along with other sociocultural anthropologists he has been "much affected by literary theory and postmodern skepticism about the very possibility of knowledge. Like other scholars influenced by these trends, we increasingly doubt our authority to make definitive statements about subordinate groups" (12). As a believer in the project of "deferring to the perspective of the people we study and broadcasting their usually unheard voices," Stoll proposes to "complement" one indigenous voice (that of Rigoberta Menchú) "with others that were not being heard" (ibid.). Given the symbolic status achieved by Menchú, Stoll is well aware of the possible consequences of his approach: "To some scholars . . . challenging the reliability of *I, Rigoberta Menchú* is little short of outrageous. It casts doubt on the entire project of bestowing authority on the voices of the oppressed—and on the authority that they themselves derive from it" (ibid.). In the course of recent debate, Stoll's critique of the scholarship pertaining to Latin American testimonial literature has been somewhat eclipsed by his questioning of Menchú's testimony. I believe, however, that Stoll's indictment of multiculturalist scholars deserves attention as an integral part of his overall argument.

Speaking from the position of a critic who has worked with Spanish-American *testimonio* for almost two decades, I consider Stoll's assessment of testimonial literary criticism rather superficial. It is certainly true that in some of the most influential early studies on Spanish-American testimonial literature the focus on authenticity took precedence over discursive analysis. For George Yúdice, for example, *testimonio* "may be defined as an authentic narrative" that summons truth in order to denounce exploitation and to set right official history (17). This action-oriented approach assumes that the testimonial word that emerges out of oppression—the word of the victim—is irrefutable, and as such has unquestioned power to redress sociopolitical grievances. In short, despite the considerable differences in tone and focus, numerous studies of *testimonio* underscore its premise to recover the unspeakable experience of collective suffering that would otherwise go untold. The following definition of *testimonio* proposed by Mary Chamberlain and Paul Thompson highlights this primacy of radical ideology within the genre: "[it is] a secular spiritual testimony, telling a life, as a left-wing moral, with the overt intention of raising consciousness" (6).

Nonetheless, in a more recent reading of *I, Rigoberta Menchú*, Brett Levinson broaches the issue of critics' reluctance to de-idealize or de-mythify Menchú's testimony by arguing—not unlike Stoll—that the avoidance of close readings rests on a rigid understanding of political commitment:

> Indeed, the critics who have authored the most powerful interpretations of *I, Rigoberta Menchú* have also deployed the text as a key political device: as a means to rethink the question of colonial/post-colonial oppression, the role of literature in writing in the new Latin American social movements, and the politics of Latin American studies. To offer a fundamentally new reading of *I, Rigoberta Menchú*, therefore, is also potentially to upset the delicate balance between hermeneutics and politics. (33)

In light of Levinson's comment one could easily imagine that the lack of a "fundamentally new reading" of Menchú's testimony created a sort of vacuum that has now been filled by Stoll's book, the accompanying endorsement from the front-page article in the *New York Times,* and the ensuing "scandal."

I would argue, however, that prior to Stoll's book there was hardly a critical vacuum around *testimonio.* Despite all the ideologically motivated resistance to "demythify" *testimonio,* since the late 1980s numerous literary critics (see Gugelberger, *The Real Thing*) have effectively challenged the presupposition that revealing *testimonio*'s rhetorical modus operandi would "condemn" it as a political tool. Stoll's statement that "Beverley and his colleagues have been promoting testimonio in a way that does not allow questioning its reliability" (242) shows how easily one can be led astray when reaching across a plurality of disciplines not in search of a genuine dialogue, but in order to select suitable ingredients for a cut-and-paste approach.

For a literary scholar such as myself, the immediate lesson derived from the current whirlwind of messages and pronouncements surrounding Menchú's account is that the interpretation of *testimonio* is still relative both to ideological purpose and to disciplinary focus. By virtue of its hybridity, *testimonio* has invited approaches from literary criticism, anthropology, oral history, philosophy, and political science, and in many ways it continues to be an open text that can be read according to different paradigms. Consequently, specialists from various fields have acquired a taste for exploring *testimonio*, but they also feel it is their right to impose their own discipline's criteria as a touchstone of *testimonio*'s aesthetic beauty, ideological worth, or objective validity. Of course, unlike the anthropologist Stoll, whose modus operandi is circumscribed by factual evidence, literary critics feel free to read across disciplines (especially in the era of cultural studies), searching for "the truth of possibility" rather than "the truth of material events" (Portelli 38).

Nobody denies that there is powerful appeal in the stories of Menchú, Esteban Montejo, or Domitila Barrios de Chungara.[1] However, as researchers in different areas continue to have some autonomous disciplinary stake in the topic, their view of *testimonio* is still tainted with suspicion in a quite tribal sense: whereas in certain quarters *testimonio*'s factual dimension may be deemed not rigorous enough to be included in the domain of social sciences, some literary critics are not quite sure whether *testimonio* has a sufficient measure of "literariness" to be worthy of their scrutiny. For all the flourishing of scholarship in this area, a joint exploration of the genre that would bring together current thinking in both literary criticism and social sciences has never taken place. Although a genuinely cross-disciplinary dialogue has taken place at recent Latin American Studies Association (LASA) meetings, it has been limited to a fairly narrow circle of fellow academics. Perhaps the most promising approach to *testimonio* would result from a method similar to the one adopted by anthropologist Elizabeth Tonkin, whose *Narrating Our Pasts* aims at "a reintegration of literary perception and social scientific research on the basis that 'facts and opinions do not exist as freestanding objects, but are reproduced through grammar and larger conventions of discourse'" (in Chamberlain and Thompson 10).

Stoll undoubtedly makes an effort to reach beyond his own discipline and uncover new evidence, but he ultimately runs up against the self-imposed thesis about the multiculturalist conspiracy to canonize Menchú. Stoll takes us behind the scenes of his book's construction and highlights his efforts to establish contacts with literary critics (John Beverley and Marc Zimmerman) renowned for their work on *testimonio*, only to prove over and over again that those "sophisticated literary scholars" have no patience "with contradictory evidence" when it comes to demythifying "native voices" that serve their own political interests (242). It would have been commendable, of course, if—keeping with the premise of his own book of "complementing" one set of voices with others (12)—Stoll had looked at a broader range of *testimonio* critics (Lucille Kerr, Rosemary Geisdorfer Feal, Alberto Moreiras, to name a few).

I have to admit that I have found Stoll's critique of my own field rather vitriolic, but not entirely unfounded. His comments have made me look back at my writings and see the ways in which I had used *testimonio* as a pretext, as a testing ground—in my case not for political ideas but for the latest trends in literary theory. Contemporary theories certainly challenge us to read at a breakneck pace through the swiftly changing lenses of flashy concepts and catchy theories and, with hindsight, I would second Hernán Vidal's concern that the sheer quantity of work being published in the field known as Latinamericanism, as well as the speed at which it appears in the critical marketplace, end up obfuscating the ostensible object of inquiry—the text. The race to keep abreast of arcane terminology and short-lived fashions has become part and parcel of graduate seminars, publishing venues, and academic symposia. It scarcely needs repeating after Vidal that all of us working in American academia are expected to be constant innovators, as opposed to puzzle solvers. For Stoll, the flourishing of postmodern multiculturalism has had a particularly negative impact on the quality of scholarship, regardless of discipline: "At a time when rumor, myth, representation and the construction of what we consider 'real' pose fascinating issues, it has become all too easy to deprecate the task of separating truth from falsehood, deferring instead to the authority of fashionable forms of victimhood" (274).

I first wrote about Menchú's book in the early 1990s. I have taught it at several universities, to graduates and undergraduates, in Spanish, Polish, and English. Given the fact that *testimonio* represents the interface between several disciplines, I have often ventured outside the traditional scope of literary criticism and I have become particularly interested in the heterological operations that enable the "translation" of the primary story through a number of conventions derived from the disciplines of law, anthropology and psychoanalysis (Gugelberger 91). Since I have always seen testimonial texts as a peculiar mixture of experience, creation, manipulation, and invention, more akin, perhaps, to a novel, than to a scientific document, I have never relinquished my interest in the "literary." On the outset of my work I armed myself with an awareness of the text's artifactual nature, including the inevitable embroidering of the facts for dramatic, political, or aesthetic effect. Throughout this process I must have developed antibodies that make me immune to the kind of revelations we have heard recently about Menchú's book. So, where Stoll spots lies and fabrications, I see allegories and metaphors. In short, I see a text.

Of course, over the years my thinking about testimonial literature has become more stratified, as it has evolved and undergone revisions, perhaps even grown in sophistication. To be sure, I have been guilty of some false starts, overstated conclusions, twisted arguments, and excesses of interpretation and more often than not I have been led astray by my methodology du jour. Clearly, some of my statements have not passed the test of time and to have to reread them (or see them quoted) is not an uplifting experience.

And now the Menchú/Stoll controversy has forced me and many others—ordinary readers, journalists, politicians, and specialists from various disciplines—into painstaking rereadings, likely to be followed by an outpouring of corrective and revisionary dissertations, essays, and conference papers. Hopefully, this process—as painful as it may be—will go beyond the effort to devalue or defend Menchú's testimony. Perhaps it will make us, the critics, set aside our postmodern toolbox and realize that Rigoberta Menchú will never conform to the model we try to construct for her. In a larger context, the attack on her may trigger a revival of interest in *testimonio,* which, in turn, should help refocus public opinion on experiences of collective suffering that once resonated with great force—through the voices of Tlatelolco, Esteban Montejo, Domitila Barrios de Chungara, Menchú, and others—but have since lost their power to mobilize both outrage and solidarity.

As paradoxical as it may sound, *testimonio*—as a form of narrative predicated on memory—is particularly vulnerable to oblivion. The relevance of the dynamics between memory, oblivion, and representation is articulated by Jean-François Lyotard in terms of erasure lurking behind every scripted sign: "Whenever one represents, one inscribes in memory, and this might seem a good defense against forgetting. It is, I believe, just the opposite. Only that which has been inscribed can, in the current sense of the term, be forgotten, because it could be effaced" (26). This observation is revealing in that—writing as he is in the post-Holocaust context—Lyotard poses memory as a mechanism whereby human suffering can be made ordinary, dismissed, "taken care of," exorcised (ibid.). In short, Lyotard's ethical philosophy hinges on the premise that with the poetics of remembrance also comes the politics of forgetting.

Curiously enough, Paul de Man—whose links with Lyotard are ideologically remote, to say the least—develops a similar thought in his essay on autobiography. As Brad Epps explains, "For de Man, the memory of the face is, like everything else, subject to oblivion, to defacement (*at least when the image of the face is verbally produced*)" (161; emphasis added). Richard Terdiman, in turn, links "the politics of forgetting" to the realm of hegemonic discourse perceived as "a highly ideologized form of recollection that brackets fully as much as it restores" (20). Finally, working in a related area, Raphael Samuel argues that, regardless of its political affiliation, memory "is historically conditioned, changing colour and shape according to the emergencies of the moment. . . . It is stamped with the ruling passions of its time" (8). Only now, in the light of the most recent outpouring of information regarding the construction of *I, Rigoberta Menchú*, can we begin to understand the extent to which "the emergencies of the moment" might have shaped the original account.

In addition to the chameleonic nature of memory—as articulated here by Lyotard, de Man, Terdiman, and Samuel—the testimonial contract hinges on the precarious position of the witness. For critics operating within the parameters of postmodernism there is no longer a "biographical self capable of reflection, or a biographical reality upon which to reflect" (Chamberlain and Thompson 3), and Gianni Vattimo is quick to warn us that the disintegration of the bourgeois/Christian notion of the subject—defined in terms of the hegemony of consciousness—has severed the link between the individual and truth on which the testimonial contract is built. Vattimo is convinced that "the notion of testimony goes 'out of date' as a result of the inversion of the traditional hierarchy of the elements of the individual psyche. This inversion has meant an increasingly dominant role for the unconscious" (47).

All this theorizing notwithstanding, even the most cynical critics lost in the fun house of postmodernism would stop short of arguing that *testimonio* is just "fiction for print, tape, and live voice." It is quite evident that *I, Rigoberta Menchú* allocates testimonial authority to one narrator, and the book bears the authenticating seal of a real witness through the use (in the English title) of the pronoun "I," the name, and the inclusion of Menchú's picture. On the other hand, the subtitle—*An Indian Woman in Guatemala*—meets a social demand for exemplarity. If we agree with Chamberlain and Thompson that "what people narrate in their autobiographical stories is selected and shaped by the repertoire of genre available to them" (14), at first sight *I, Rigoberta Menchú* appears to give primacy to the individual as established by Western (auto)biographical tradition.

However, in view of the political and cross-cultural complications involved in the making of *I, Rigoberta Menchú,* it would be impossible to attribute the choice of any of the generic and rhetorical strategies to the witness/narrator alone. As we all know, Rigoberta—the already constructed self of the original interview—was further "reconstructed" by various advisers and editors, although the actual twists and turns of this multilayered process are still in dispute. Moreover, there is a significant difference between the original title—with bildungsroman connotations of "y así me nació la conciencia"—and its English equivalent. Students of autobiographical writing who have a keen interest in the motivations for life-telling in terms of different "quests" could certainly read the Spanish title as indicative of a quest for empowerment and self-identity (Gullestad 26). If we go beyond the packaging of the book for different audiences and consider the text itself, it becomes clear that storytelling, remembering, and denouncing are primarily a collective enterprise, and that any foregrounding of Rigoberta's agency is done on behalf of her community. What the text allows us to see is that the ethos of individualism so dear to Western tradition is not as prevalent as the title (Spanish and English) might have implied.

We have to bear in mind, of course, that many of Rigoberta's followers and detractors locked in the recent controversy are not interested in the postmodern questioning of the subject. Furthermore, a nonacademic reader is unaware of the pitfalls of cross-cultural dialogues. Instead, most readers will probably agree with Paul Ricoeur's opinion that persuading is always a highly subjective process, and that an aura of authenticity is ultimately created by "the dispositions of the audience and *the character of the orator*" (127; my emphasis). In this light it comes as no surprise that Stoll's book managed to undermine the credibility of the witness by focusing on a number of allegedly willful fabrications. What is less understandable is the widespread desire to topple Rigoberta from her pedestal, to stigmatize her, and to make the entire testimonial edifice crumble.

In the remaining pages of this essay I would like to go back to *I, Rigoberta Menchú* without performing any kind of exorcism. I do not intend to forget about Menchú besieged by detractors, but it is not my goal to make this text into a plea for her defense. As much as I would wish to see Menchú emerge out of this controversy unscathed, I know that an essay like this one will not make much difference. As a reader, however, I would like to understand why and how *I, Rigoberta Menchú* has kept me under its spell through countless rereadings and misreadings, including the most recent controversy.

As a student of literature, I was taught to approach texts in slow motion, to reread them over and over again through a corrective lens of images retained by memory, accrued knowledge, new critical findings, uncovered evidence, and accumulated life experience. In fact, memory plays such a fundamental role in the mediation of all telling, writing, reading, and interpreting that the theme of remembrance and forgetting emerged almost of its own accord when I was first invited to write on Menchú for this volume. Returning to a well-known text—especially in the context of newly "uncovered" evidence—invites "perverse readings," as Epps has shown in a more "literary" context. One should be prepared to face the challenge because such revisiting tends to "counter the memory of a canonized and classified text" and open up space for reviving/refiguring/relocating remembered meanings (Epps 147).

Memory as an archive of experience is undoubtedly a complex puzzle. Despite the long tradition of probing into its workings—from Aristotle (*De Memoria et Reminiscentia*) and Plato to Freud and de Man—and despite the recent surge of interest in "autobiographical memory," no one can claim a full understanding of the mechanisms that make us re-member, reminisce, or forget. By the same token, any examination of paths through which memory finds its way into writing seems particu-larly suited for interdisciplinary undertakings, especially when we deal with communities whose traditions have little to do with Plato, Freud, or de Man. A host of other concerns come to mind when tackling the topic. As a discipline concerned with remembering per se, psychology offers invaluable insights into the inscription of memory in testimonial texts. According to Craig R. Barclay, most autobiographical memories are true but inaccurate: "What is remembered in particular probably does not reflect the way some event really happened.... The sense of fa-miliarity created by an event is associated with a judgment that the event is true to what most likely occurred and consistent with what should have happened" (97). Psychologists tend to agree that life stories are of-ten deeply ambiguous texts, based on schematization of real events for the sake of fitting them into a coherent story. Furthermore, life stories are marked by frequent transition from episodic to semantic memory, which allows for several experiences to merge into one.

Speaking from the standpoint of a historian, Raphael Samuel has ar-gued that memory is "an active, shaping force" and the "conscious act of recollection" is an intellectual labor "very much akin to that of the historian: a matter of quotation, imitation, borrowing and assimilation" (x). However, one can hardly forget about the fact that we live at a time when, as Andreas Huyssen has aptly suggested, "the notion of memory has migrated into the realm of silicon chips, computers and cyborg fic-tions" (249). With its heavy reliance on information retrieval and mem-ory upgrades, our era is not conducive to the slow-paced reflection in-spired by Mnemosyne, the goddess of wisdom and the mother of the muses. Moreover, a critic working from the postcolonial perspective should not ignore what Terdiman has identified as the "massive disrup-tion of traditional forms of memory" associated with the processes of modernization (14).

It is perhaps for all the reasons just mentioned that the scripting of memory in the testimonial genre is still largely unexplored, even though the mnemonic process has such a pervasive role to play in its construc-tion. Ultimately, it is the perception of memory as a subjective, instinc-tual, and emotional force (Samuel ix) that does not agree with the critical construction of *testimonio* premised on a bond of trust, truth, and authenticity.

What we first glean from the pages of *I, Rigoberta Menchú* is that memory figures in the book both as a structuring device and as a cultural force. The value of memory is inscribed in Rigoberta's culture, and in her testimony she draws as much from the collective repository of memory, history, and myth as from her "real-life" experience. The often-quoted opening of the book—which sets the tone for the rest of the narrative—underscores the collective dimension of the account: "This is my testimony. I didn't learn it from a book and I didn't learn it alone. I'd like to stress that it's not only *my* life, it's also the testimony of my people" (1). The theme of remembrance and cultural continuity is reinforced throughout the text: "Everything that is done today, is done in memory of those who have passed on" (17). Tellingly, these first lines also offer a disclosure about the difficulty in remembering: "It's hard for me to remember everything that's happened to me in my life since there have been many very bad times but, yes, moments of joy as well. The important thing is that what has happened to me has happened to many other people too" (1).

I recall these opening lines not only to refresh our memory of the text, but also to give due attention to the fact—now widely confirmed by feminist research—that "women's spoken autobiographical acts reveal features of their own" (Paul Thompson 141). Among the factors that could assist us in demarcating the realm of autobiographical experience, the gender-specific construction of life stories should be considered along the lines suggested by Paul Thompson: whereas men "consider the life they have lived as their own," women, by contrast "talk of their lives typically in terms of relationships, including parts of other life-stories as their own" (157). Whether we choose to follow Thompson's lead or not, the fact is that this kind of "appropriation" of stories other than her own appears throughout Rigoberta's narrative and is particularly obvious in her rendering of family lore. Fragments of family history are recounted by Rigoberta out of what she had learned from her parents. Occasionally, her account is interspersed with words pointing to the source of the story ("my father told me," "my mother said," 4), and she seems to be thinking out loud when recalling her mother's words: "My mother already had five children, I think. Yes, I had five brothers and sisters and

I'm the sixth. My mother said that she was working down on a *finca* until a month before I was born" (5). At times Rigoberta quotes her mother when evoking events she was unable to understand as a child because of her inability to speak Spanish: "When the owner began to speak, he spoke in Spanish. My mother understood a little Spanish and afterwards she told us he was talking about the elections" (25). More often than not, however, a recollection of a story told by her mother appears to merge with Rigoberta's memory of the actual event:

> From when I was very tiny, my mother used to take me down to the *finca*, wrapped in a shawl on her back. She told me that when I was about two, I had to be carried screaming onto the lorry because I didn't want to go. I didn't even know what it was, but I knew I hated it because I hate things that smell horrible. (21)

Whereas her mother's stories are told from within mother–daughter relationship, her father's accounts appear to be set in a broader public context of historical events. Once again, however, Rigoberta's current interpretation of the past becomes part of her account: "In the defeat of 1954, he said they captured men from our region, and from other regions. They took our men off to the barracks. My father was one of those caught. He has very black memories of those days" (26).

The degree to which stories actually lived and told by others become intertwined is best illustrated by the following juxtaposition of two examples. In the first one, when referring to the events that took place at the *finca* after she and her mother had been forced to leave, Rigoberta is very careful in providing the source of information: "We were told by one of our neighbours who stayed on there" (24). However, in the story of the soldier ambushed by her community and ultimately released, Rigoberta does not consider it pertinent to clarify how she learned about his fate: "We didn't kill the soldier. The army itself took care of that when he got back to camp. They said he must be an informer. . . . So they killed him" (139).

Among psychologists, one of the most agreed-upon characteristics of memory is that a certain degree of "suggestibility" and "problems of source attribution" are quite common, especially when recalling childhood experiences. As for Rigoberta, she admits that most of what she remembers is after she was five (5). Without getting into the theoretical explanation of "false memory" creation, I would like to refer to Ira Hyman and Erica Kleinknecht's argument that in family settings, "listening to the stories may eventually lead the children to imagine the experiences as if they actually did happen and accept the stories as personal memories" (182). Both researchers see the positive side of this process by arguing that "Generally in families and other social settings, the malleability of memory is a good thing. One goal of remembering is the strengthening of social bonds" (ibid.).

The strange hybrid we have come to call *testimonio* thus offers an amalgam of shreds of memory and cohesive narrative. It involves a series of erasures, emendations, and amalgamations quite similar to those that Freud sets out in his account of "screen memories," where the unconscious mind performs the operations of displacing, projecting, splitting, and telescoping. From a literary standpoint, this is an intriguing blend; from the perspective of more "scientific" disciplines it is, at best, an uneasy combination.

To complicate the picture still further, some of Rigoberta's memories stand out as more vivid even though they may seem of little relevance within a larger discursive frame, such as the recollection of "going along in the lorry and wanting to set it on fire so that we would be allowed to rest" (24). Not surprisingly, a frightening childhood experience—however, not threatening enough to be "screened" by other memories (Conway 73)—is presented with dramatic immediacy and detail. Even though Rigoberta does not remember her exact age ("I think I was about twelve"), her recollection of the first encounter with a local landowner is very vivid: "I remember the first time I saw a *finca* landowner, I was frightened of him because he was very fat. I'd never seen a *ladino* like that. He was very fat, well dressed, and had a watch" (25). The image of this man returns later to haunt the girl in her dreams: "The landowner left, but afterwards...I dreamed about him over and over again....it must have been the fear, the impression made on me by that man's face. I remember telling mother: 'I dreamed about that old *ladino* who came here'" (26).

This is not the place to explore how some of these memories may have been summoned in response to the theme of oppression and resistance underlying Rigoberta's personal myth of "emerging consciousness." Suffice it to say that memories of powerful emotions, such as hatred or anger, are not easily forgotten: "It's something I've never forgotten, because of the anger I felt at the way we live" (29), she says at one point, to elaborate later: "Those fifteen days working in the *finca* was one of my earliest experiences and I remember it with enormous hatred. That hatred has stayed with me until today" (41).

Rigoberta's strong confidence in the accuracy of emotional recollective memories is reinforced by clear images of concrete physical settings. It is of course a cliché that images of places can often evoke the past in vivid detail, whereas temporal references are subject to dismissal, distortion, or displacement. According to Peter Morris, the suggestion that memory could be helped by "selecting places and forming mental images of the things to be remembered in those places" dates back to the story of Simonides, a Greek poet who was able to identify the bodies of his relatives mangled in a collapsed building "because he could remember who had been sitting in each place" (Morris 2). Such spatial mnemonics—as Frances A. Yates demonstrates in her well-known study—lie at the very foundation of Western rhetorical tradition. Whether the art of remembrance as practiced by Menchú owes much to Western rhetorical tradition is difficult to assess, especially in the light of recently released information about the multilayered editing process to which her account was subjected. Readers of the book will recall, however, the primacy of "place" in most of her childhood memories. This sort of "mental mapping in which space rather than time" provides "significant markers" (Samuel viii) is particularly obvious in Rigoberta's account of getting lost in the mountains at the age of seven (28). Similarly, her first trip to the capital is scripted through mostly visual memories of previously unknown sights: "It was the first time I'd ever sat on a seat in a truck—*and* one with windows" (3).

The exploration of the ways in which *I, Rigoberta Menchú* seeks to transfer the mechanisms of memory into the realm of writing could follow any number of paths I cannot take here. Those include issues usually tackled by psychologists, such as the temporal organization of remembering, the difference between storing private and public events, the process known as amalgamation of facts, and the interplay between childhood memories and the "personal myths" forged on the threshold of self-discovery. I would like, however, to return briefly to the initial concern that framed my essay—the interlacing between disciplinary methodologies, memory, and rereading—to see whether the mechanics of remembering and forgetting has any significance at all in the context of Stoll's book and the ensuing polemics.

Stoll's *Rigoberta Menchú and the Story of All Poor Guatemalans* does not deal with strictly private events that cannot be either verified or refuted, hence the facts that come under Stoll's scrutiny are limited to a public realm. Among the most dramatic events recalled by Menchú and not corroborated by Stoll's witnesses are the specific circumstances of the torture and death of her brother Petrocinio. Although I do not intend to go as far as drawing analogies between Guatemalan massacres and other acts of genocide from recent history, I am reminded here of Dori Laub's argument in his study of Holocaust testimonials that acts of genocide preclude the existence of a witness from "inside the event" (Laub 66). Hence, the ethical dilemma of the survivor—so persuasively studied by Lyotard in *The Differend*—is either to embody his/her truth of the event s/he did not witness or to remain silent.

Although I understand that Stoll's attempt to maintain the boundary between "fact" and "fiction" is dictated by the internal logic of his methodology, I want to stress once again that *the text* of *I, Rigoberta Menchú* cannot be made "hostage" to the rules or demands of any single discipline. Just for the record, and for the sake of fostering cross-disciplinary understanding, I want to mention an article written in 1990, in which Rosemary Geisdorfer Feal summoned the text of *I, Rigoberta Menchú* as her only witness and showed that the book could not be read as factually accurate. Writing as she was to like-minded readers of *Modern Language Studies,* Feal simply assumed that no autobiographical account is scrupulously concerned with facts. The premise that a story—any story—is ultimately reconstructive and, therefore, susceptible to distortion, underlies Feal's reading of Rigoberta's recollection of her mother's torture and death. In a related register, Doris Sommer has brilliantly argued that Rigoberta's testimony is built around stories withheld and never to be shared. For Menchú, then, the remembrance of the past inevitably entails some loss, and the ongoing tension between forgetting and denial, the censorship of memory and trauma, the act of witnessing and the act of telling are at the core of her account.

In my reading of *I, Rigoberta Menchú* I agree with Feal's stance that poetic truth is not precluded by historical inaccuracies. Curiously enough, Stoll admits that he would rather remain under the poetic and human spell of Rigoberta's story: "Her narrative strategy is easy to defend because her most important claims, about the Guatemalan army's killings, are true" (273). However, on reflection, Stoll goes back to his original premise that "factuality" remains "a legitimate issue for any narrative claiming to be an eyewitness account, especially one that has been taken as seriously as Rigoberta's" (273). It is, of course, rather curious that Stoll ends up blaming Menchú for the fact that her book became part of the canon: "Rigoberta's story may have given voice to the dead in the early 1980s, but by the late 1980s it had become so sacrosanct that it was drowning the voice of other Guatemalans" (278).

What specific readers make of specific texts at different times and places is, obviously, a complex matter. What is relevant for me personally— and that goes beyond the factual verification of *I, Rigoberta Menchú*— is the palpable human truth of her retelling of experiences for which we have no words. To reinforce the point about the enduring power of Menchú's testimony from a disciplinary perspective other than my own and to avoid an increasingly unproductive debate about the borderlines between fact and fiction, I suggest we learn from fellow researchers in the field of oral history who have long recognized both the artificiality and the artifactuality of life stories without diminishing the value of human experience (see Portelli).

Ultimately, the most obvious lesson derived from this rereading is that any study of autobiographical memory is ultimately self-reflexive. One of the unmistakable benefits of this swing of the pendulum could be a heightened sense of methodological responsibility and a close encounter with one's own critical practice. Moreover, given the cross-disciplinary interest in memory, choosing it as a topic of inquiry is bound to expose our modus operandi to the corrective influence of insights from other disciplines. The downside is that this kind of inquiry may lead us back into the overgrown garden of theory, where among the forking paths of political agendas and methodological fads someone's truth can easily turn into fiction for print, tape, and live voice.

Notes

I gratefully acknowledge the support from the Washington University Graduate School of Arts and Sciences Faculty Research Grant that enabled me to write this essay.

1. Esteban Montejo's *Biografía de un cimarrón* and Domitila Barrios de Chungara's *Si me permiten hablar* are among the best-known Latin American *testimonios*. Both were edited by professional writers (Miguel Barnet and Moema Viezzer, respectively).

Bibliography

Banta, Martha. 1999. "If I Forget Thee, Jerusalem." Editor's Column. *PMLA* 114.2 (March): 175–83.

Barclay, Craig R. 1986. "Schematization of Autobiographical Memory." In *Autobiographical Memory: Theoretical and Applied Perspectives*, ed. David Rabin. Cambridge and London: Cambridge University Press. 82–99.

Barrios de Chungara, Domitila. 1980. *Si me permiten hablar: testimonio de una mujer de las minas de Bolivia.* 5th ed. Ed. Moema Viezzer. Mexico City: Siglo XXI.

Berkner, Lucy, and John Briere. 1999. "Trauma, Memory and Clinical Practice." In *Trauma and Memory*, ed. Linda M. Williams and Victoria L. Banyard. Thousand Oaks, Calif.: Sage Publications. 3–18.

Birkerts, Sven. 1998. "Some Thoughts on Rereading." In *Second Thoughts: Focus on Rereading*, ed. David Galef. Detroit: Wayne State University Press. 340–44.

Brown, Laura S. 1995. "Not Outside the Range: One Feminist Perspective on Psychic Trauma." In *Trauma: Explorations in Memory*, ed. Cathy Caruth. Baltimore: Johns Hopkins University Press. 100–112.

Canby, Peter. 1999. "The Truth about Rigoberta Menchú." *New York Review of Books* (April 8): 28–33.

Caruth, Cathy, ed. 1995. *Trauma: Explorations in Memory.* Baltimore: Johns Hopkins University Press.

Chamberlain, Mary, and Paul Thompson, eds. 1998. *Narrative and Genre.* London and New York: Routledge.

Conway, Martin A. 1986. "Autobiographical Knowledge and Autobiographical Memories." In *Autobiographical Memory: Theoretical and Applied Perspectives*, ed. David Rubin. Cambridge and London: Cambridge University Press.

de Man, Paul. 1979. "Autobiography as De-facement." *MLN* 94: 919–30.

Donato, Eugenio. 1974. "Topographies of Memory." *SubStance* 4.1: 40–44.

Epps, Brad. 1993. "Realizing the Self: Autobiography, Genealogy, and Death in *Sonata de Otoño.*" *Journal of Interdisciplinary Literary Studies* 5.1: 147–79.

Feal, Rosemary Geisdorfer. 1990. "Spanish American Ethnobiography and the Slave Narrative Tradition: *Biografía de un cimarrón* and *Me llamo Rigoberta Menchú.*" *Modern Language Studies* 20.1: 100–111.

Gugelberger, Georg M., ed. *The Real Thing: Testimonial Discourse and Latin America.* Durham, N.C.: Duke University Press, 1996.

Gullestad, Marianne, ed. 1996. *Imagined Childhoods: Self and Society in Autobiographical Accounts.* Oslo, Stockholm, Copenhagen: Scandinavian University Press.

Handley, George B. 1995. "'It's an Unbelievable Story': Testimony and Truth in the Work of Rosario Ferré and Rigoberta Menchú." In *Violence, Silence and Anger: Women's Writing and Transgression.* Charlottesville: University Press of Virginia. 61–79.

Huyssen, Andreas. 1993. "Monument and Memory in a Postmodern Age." *Yale Journal of Criticism* 6.2 (fall): 249–63.

Hyman, Ira E., and Erica E. Kleinknecht. 1999. "False Childhood Memories: Research, Theory and Application." In *Trauma and Memory*, ed. Linda M. Williams and Victoria L. Banyard. Thousand Oaks, Calif.: Sage Publications. 175–88.

Krieger, Murray. 1992. "Literary Invention, Critical Fashion, and the Impulse to Theoretical Change: 'Or Whether Revolution Be the Same.'" In *Studies in Histor-*

ical Change, ed. Ralph Cohen. Charlottesville: University Press of Virginia. 179–206.

Laub, Dori. 1995. "Truth and Testimony: The Process and the Struggle." In *Trauma: Explorations in Memory,* ed. Cathy Caruth. Baltimore: Johns Hopkins University Press. 13–60.

Lazreg, Marnia. 1988. "Feminism and Difference: The Perils of Writing as a Woman on Women in Algeria." *Feminist Studies* 14.1 (spring): 81–107.

Levinson, Brett. 1996. "Neopatriarchy and After: *I, Rigoberta Menchú* as Allegory of Death." *Journal of Latin American Cultural Studies* 5.1: 33–50.

Lyotard, Jean-François. 1988. *The Differend: Phrases in Dispute.* Trans. Georges Van Den Abbeele. Minneapolis: University of Minnesota Press.

Menchú, Rigoberta. 1998. *Crossing Borders.* Trans. Ann Wright. London: Verso.

———. 1998. *Rigoberta: La nieta de los mayas.* Ed. Dante Liano and Gianni Minà. Madrid: El País/Aguilar.

Menchú, Rigoberta, with Elisabeth Burgos-Debray. 1984. *I, Rigoberta Menchú: An Indian Woman in Guatemala.* Trans. Ann Wright. London: Verso.

Montejo, Esteban. 1966. *Biografía de un cimarrón.* Ed. Miguel Barnet. Havana: Instituto de Etnografía y Folklore.

Morris, Peter E. 1994. "Theories of Memory: An Historical Perspective." In *Theoretical Aspects of Memory,* ed. Peter E. Morris and Michael Grunberg. 2d ed. London: Routledge. 1–28.

Morris, Peter E., and Michael Grunberg. 1994. *Theoretical Aspects of Memory.* 2d ed. London: Routledge.

Nora, Pierre. 1989. "Between Memory and History: *Les Lieux de mémoire.*" *Representations* 26 (spring): 7–25.

Portelli, Alessandro. 1998. "Oral History as Genre." In *Narrative and Genre,* ed. Mary Chamberlain and Paul Thompson. London and New York: Routledge. 23–43.

Pratt, Mary Louise. 1996. "*Me llamo Rigoberta Menchú:* Autoethnography and the Recoding of Citizenship." In *Teaching and Testimony: Rigoberta Menchú and the North American Classroom,* ed. Allen Carey-Webb and Stephen Benz. Albany: State University of New York Press.

Ricoeur, Paul. 1980. "The Hermeneutics of Testimony." In *Essays on Biblical Interpretation,* ed. Lewis S. Mudge. Philadelphia: Fortress Press. 119–54.

Rosen, Harold. 1998. *Speaking from Memory: A Guide to Autobiographical Acts and Practices.* London: Trentham Books.

Rubin, David. 1986. "Beginnings of a Theory of Autobiographical Remembering." In *Autobiographical Memory: Theoretical and Applied Perspectives,* ed. David Rubin. Cambridge and London: Cambridge University Press. 47–68.

———, ed. 1986. *Autobiographical Memory: Theoretical and Applied Perspectives.* Cambridge and London: Cambridge University Press.

———. 1996. *Remembering Our Past: Studies in Autobiographical Memory.* Cambridge and London: Cambridge University Press.

Samuel, Raphael. 1996. *Theatres of Memory: Past and Present in Contemporary Culture.* London: Verso.

Scarry, Elaine. 1996. "The Made-Up and the Made-Real." In *Field Work: Sites in Literary and Cultural Studies,* ed. Marjorie B. Garber, Paul B. Franklin, and Rebecca L. Walkowitz. New York: Routledge. 214–24.

Sommer, Doris. 1999. "No Secrets for Rigoberta." In *Proceed with Caution When Engaged by Minority Writing in the Americas.* Cambridge: Harvard University Press. 115–37.

Stoll, David. 1999. *Rigoberta Menchú and the Story of All Poor Guatemalans.* Boulder, Colo.: Westview Press.

Terdiman, Richard. 1985. "Deconstructing Memory: On Representing the Past and Theorizing Culture in France since the Revolution." *Diacritics* (winter): 13–36.

Thompson, Charles P., ed. 1998. *Autobiographical Memory: Theoretical and Applied Perspectives.* Mahwah, N.J.: Lawrence Erlbaum Associates.

Thompson, Paul R. 1988. *Voices of the Past: Oral History.* 2d ed. Oxford and New York: Oxford University Press.

Vattimo, Gianni. 1993 "The Decline of the Subject and the Problem of Testimony." In *The Adventure of Difference. Philosophy after Nietzsche and Heidegger.* Baltimore: Johns Hopkins University Press. 40–60.

Vidal, Hernán. 1991. "The Notion of Otherness within the Framework of National Cultures." *Gestos* 11 (April): 27–44.

Warnock, Mary. 1987. *Memory.* London: Faber and Faber.

White, Hayden. 1973. *Metahistory: The Historical Imagination in Nineteenth-Century Europe.* Baltimore: Johns Hopkins University Press.

Yates, Frances A. 1966. *The Art of Memory.* Chicago: University of Chicago Press.

Yúdice, George. 1991. "*Testimonio* and Postmodernism." In *Voices of the Voiceless in Testimonial Literature,* ed. Georg M. Gugelberger and Michael Kearney. Special issue of *Latin American Perspectives* 18.3: 15–31.

Whose Truth? Iconicity and Accuracy in the World of Testimonial Literature

Daphne Patai

A Saint's Life

In an essay on teaching *I, Rigoberta Menchú,* a North American university professor explains her dismay at her students' criticism of the book by telling us that for her, Rigoberta's text is "sacred" and "untouchable" (Jones 1996, 153).[1] Arturo Arias, in the same volume, tells us that Rigoberta has, for good or ill, become a "living icon" in Guatemala, and that her receipt of the Nobel Peace Prize in 1992 "singlehandedly changed the configuration of Guatemalan politics" (Arias 1996, 29, 40). Here, I suspect, is the heart of the problem. In the hostile responses that have greeted David Stoll's (1999) critique of Rigoberta's story, there is revealed a depth of commitment on many readers' parts to Rigoberta and to her book that is closely akin to hagiography and the absorption of it by the faithful.

The comparison is suggestive. The adventures of medieval saints are for the most part fanciful, and in any case cannot ordinarily be verified by scholarly research. But to the pious reader, the historicity of these incidents is unimportant because both the lives and reading about them are acts of faith. In their brave deeds, above all in their passions, saints and martyrs demonstrated the truth of their religion, so it hardly matters to the devout reader whether a particular story is historically accurate or not. The saint's life, told reverently, is an exemplary narrative. It is taken to embody a higher kind of truth to which its hero is the witness.

Our secular world, too, has its rites of unquestioning reverence. Is there not something indecent about quibbling over evidence when the subject is suffering an oppression? The case of Tawana Brawley some years ago—the African-American teenager who claimed to have been assaulted and raped by six white men—is instructive. When the girl's story was shown to lack any foundations, attorney William Kunstler asserted that "[i]t makes no difference anymore whether the attack on Tawana really happened. It doesn't disguise the fact that a lot of young black women are treated the way she said she was treated" (qtd. in Siegel 1998, 72).

A continent away and more than a decade later, the same apologia has been offered by different people, inside Guatemala and out, who have sought to discredit David Stoll and minimize what they have perceived as the political damage done by his carefully documented challenge to Rigoberta's famous *testimonio*. In the face of Stoll's evidence showing that Rigoberta's brother did not die as she said he did, and that, furthermore, contrary to her horrifying account, she had not been a witness to his death, the Guatemalan Dante Liano (1999, 99) asks rhetorically: "At any rate, is a death by bullets better than one by burning?" And to Rigoberta's false claim that she learned Spanish only a few years before her meeting with Burgos in 1982, Dante Liano merely rejoins: "Is partial illiteracy better than total ignorance?" (ibid.). Rigoberta is being subjected to a "smear campaign," he charges, the real object of which is to exonerate Guatemala's ruling oligarchy. His conclusion is uncompromising: "To say that Rigoberta Menchú has lied is taken to mean that no social injustice has taken place in Guatemala" (101).

In the United States, too, many academics have leaped to Rigoberta's defense. One of them, Marjorie Agosin, chair of the Spanish Department at Wellesley College, told a reporter for the *Chronicle of Higher Education* that criticisms of Rigoberta serve only to attack multiculturalism. As to trust in Rigoberta, Agosin side-stepped the issue: "Whether her book is true or not, I don't care. We should teach our students about the brutality of the Guatemalan military and the U.S. financing of it" (Wilson 1999, A14). Besides, says Agosin, "Even if she didn't watch her little brother being murdered, the military did murder people in Guatemala" (ibid., A16).

Speaking for myself, I am deeply skeptical about the motives underlying such a defense (the tactical aspects of which Stoll addresses in his book). I am certain that, were the object of this controversy not a figure revered by leftists but one out of favor with them, the reaction to half-truths, misrepresentations, and outright falsehoods would be very different. What this tells me is that "truth"—with or without scare quotes—is, in this case (as in so many others), being made subservient to politics. And that is a dangerous, if hardly original, stance for intellectuals to take. For what is the value of a human rights activism that is driven by an a priori loyalty to certain political causes, and not to others, rather than being rooted in a commitment to the defense of human rights wherever they are abused? Of what merit is it for academics to praise some *testimonios* as heroic literature, when other testimonies, those that offend their own politics—the many, for example, that have been written by dissidents persecuted in Castro's Cuba—are ignored? This double standard, the existence of which is easily exposed by a survey of the literature, is enough to demonstrate the political corruption at the heart of the prolific academic industry on *testimonios*.

Whose Testimony?

When, one might therefore ask, is a *testimonio* not a *testimonio*? Answer: when it attacks a sacred idol of the left.

A review of some of the most often-quoted definitions of *testimonio* makes the ideological triage at work here abundantly clear. In a well-known essay, "The Margin at the Center: On *Testimonio* (Testimonial Narrative)," John Beverley defines *testimonio* as "a new form of narrative literature in which we can at the same time witness and be a part of the emerging culture of an international proletarian/popular-democratic subject in its period of ascendancy" (1992, 106). It is a form of writing, he says, that engages readers in the struggles of particular communities and involves them in significant human rights and solidarity movements. *Testimonio*, according to Beverley, arises from "an urgency to communicate, a problem of repression, poverty, subalternity, imprisonment, struggle for survival" (94).

Interestingly, when writing this essay in the late 1980s, Beverley had not excluded *testimonios* such as Armando Valladares's *Against All Hope*, chronicling his twenty-two years in Castro's prisons (Beverley 1992, 103). The theme common to all *testimonios*, including those, such as Valladares's, that Beverley labeled as coming from the "political Right," was "the need for a general social change in which the stability of the reader's world must be brought into question" (ibid.). Beverley had stressed the "urgency" of *testimonio*, its concern with "sincerity" rather than literariness, and the fact that "it is not, to begin with, fiction." And, like other commentators on *testimonio* as a genre, Beverley emphasized that in *testimonio* the narrator always represents or speaks for a community or a group (94–95). He had also made the extremely astute observation (in light of what Stoll would later disclose) that the episodes in which Rigoberta describes "in excruciating detail" the torture and murder of her brother and mother differed markedly in tone from the rest of her account, expressing a "hallucinatory" intensity that Beverley labeled "magic realism" (101).

By the mid-1990s, however, Beverley had grown more restrictive in deciding what to count as a proper *testimonio*. In his 1996 essay "The Real Thing," he calls *testimonio* "the voice of the body in pain, of the disappeared," and then adds: "of the losers in the rush to marketize" (1996, 281).[2] More significant, Beverley now takes an entirely new approach to the question of authenticity in Rigoberta's story. Having in the meantime become aware of Stoll's work, he begins to treat Rigoberta as a sophisticated author. She is no longer limited to being a mere witness to events, as anthropologists would like to have it. Instead, Beverley—no doubt aided by his self-critical conviction that "literature and the university are among the institutional practices that *create* and sustain subalternity" (1996, 271)—now sees testimonial narrators as possessing, as he puts it, the "power to create their own narrative authority and negotiate its conditions of truth and representativity" (276). Perhaps hoping to clinch his argument, he adds that Stoll can only replace Rigoberta's narratives with other narratives he has gathered (277), as if the problem of truth and accuracy could be dismissed as nothing more than an infinite regress. *Testimonio*, in Beverley's new understanding, "is both an art and a strategy of subaltern memory" (ibid.).

To speak here of "strategy" is, in effect, to redeem Rigoberta from the consequences of her misrepresentations by suggesting that these falsehoods were tactical choices with no bearing on the deeper questions of truth and trust. Postmodernist obfuscations notwithstanding, however, it is a fact that commentator after commentator has praised the reliability of Rigoberta's plainspoken narrative, treating as axiomatic the truth of what she recounts. It is this supposed authenticity that has made the book a staple in the classroom, where scores of teachers have, by their own reports, taught it as real history and *not* as a version of "truth" to be read like poetry and the novel, from which students are to draw no precise historical conclusions. Only when challenged on their interpretive shifts do such professors retreat to oracular equivocations about the indeterminacy of truth and the ambiguities of narrative.

Before Stoll, why did none of the many celebrants of Latin American *testimonio* think to question basic elements of Rigoberta's narrative? Clearly it is because they wanted the story to be true in all its painful details, believing that the more graphic the suffering depicted, the more impressive—and useful—the story and its protagonist. A rather different attitude is adopted toward testimonial accounts that do not support these readers' own political commitments. In other words, there is presumption of truth telling in the testimonies of "subalterns," and suspicion of unreliability for everyone else. Given this permissive reception of her story, Rigoberta's narrative elicited little distance, few doubts. Instead, in academic circles, she became an epistemologically privileged spokesperson, whose status as an exemplary Other was powerfully reinforced by her North American readers.

What Stoll undertook to do, and what many cannot forgive him for, was to intervene in Rigoberta's story. As he tells it, he did not set out to destroy her. But scholarly rigor made it impossible for him to avoid asking basic questions once he became aware of the many discrepancies in her story. These are the sorts of questions we should always ask of accounts claiming to be a true reflection of events on the basis of which we are asked to engage in political action: Did they really happen? Is the teller trustworthy? Is there corroborating evidence? Philosophical speculations about the nature of truth or the reliability of our senses are irrelevant to this level of investigation, which concerns the degree of agreement between what is told and what actually occurred. Certainly such questions must be asked if political programs and actions are contemplated.

It is true that oral histories of the "life-history" type—which is what Rigoberta's original story is (notwithstanding the distinctions sometimes drawn between oral-history and *testimonio*)—tend to be taken at face value. Indeed, this is one of the criticisms directed at oral history methodology: too often it does not attempt to ascertain the truth or falsity of what is told. The usual answer to the question of facticity and accuracy in oral history is: there are no lies in oral history. This assertion, however, has a very specific and limited meaning. It refers to the proposition that in "constructing a self," the speaker reveals her intentions, her projection of the self she wants to present to the world, regardless of its conformity to the objective facts of her life. And in that sense, her self-portrait is indeed "true"—truly reflective, that is, of the self she is offering up to the world. Rigoberta, for her part, presents a self that is a victim. She is one of the oppressed. But above all she is a proud fighter for her indigenous identity. The distortions in her story serve to advance the creation and acceptance of this double image. Its persuasiveness outside her own country has, in turn, been much enhanced by a notion pervasively present in the scholarly and academic world of North America, that of "the authority of experience." This oft-repeated and versatile shibboleth has it that when one of the oppressed—especially a third-world woman or a woman of color—tells her story, she herself is the authority on that experience and what she says should remain beyond challenge. The truthfulness of any specific allegation can thus always be validated by an implicit appeal to the broader experience of the group. Raising questions, let alone testing the allegation for its specific accuracy, becomes that much more problematic.

Constructing a Self

"Inaccuracies are common in oral history interviews," Wílliam Cutler III has written; "but if the researcher can identify them, especially those resulting from dishonesty or reticence, he can profit handsomely, for sometimes they provide an important avenue of insight into a respondent's state of mind" (1984, 84). It is in this sense that one can say that there are no lies in oral history—which is not to claim that all statements are accurate, but to say only that all statements are meaningful and reflect pertinently on the speaker. In a far more sophisticated treatment of the same issue, Agnes Hankiss, in her essay "Ontologies of the Self: On the Mythological Rearranging of One's Life-History," discusses the way in which, in the narration of a life history, certain episodes are endowed with a symbolic significance that in effect turns them into myths. She explains that this is a never-ending process, for the adult constantly selects new models or strategies of life, by which the old is transmuted into material useful for the new—the new self and the new situation. Everyone attempts, "in one way or another, to build up his or her own ontology" (1981, 204). Hankiss discusses four strategies for doing this; of these Rigoberta clearly chose the one in which the scenario of a bad image of childhood is shown to lead to a good image of the present self (ibid.). From the point of view of an effective narrative, Rigoberta's embellishment of her experiences, to make them harsher and crueler than they really were, causes her adult heroism to stand out all the more strongly.

As I wrote in *Brazilian Women Speak: Contemporary Life Stories* (1988a, 18), the very act of telling one's life story involves the imposition of structure on experience. In the midst of this structure, a subject emerges that tends to be represented as constant over time. Concerning "the truth" of the accounts we (as intermediaries) record, I wrote, reflecting on my own experience interviewing sixty women in Brazil:

> While I cannot address this issue with any certainty, I am satisfied that the women who talked to me were telling me a truth, which reveals what was important *for them.* This does not, of course, exclude the possibility of intentional misrepresentation, self-censorship, or unintentional replication of a given society's myths and cherished beliefs about the world, itself, or the roles that distinctive individuals or groups play.

Perhaps not coincidentally, Rigoberta chose to defend her book on similar grounds. It was "my truth," she said, that she had told to Burgos (Preston 1999). This was, however, Rigoberta's second line of defense, following the collapse of the first, which was simply to blame Burgos for any inaccuracies in the account. But what is most telling in the current perspective is that Rigoberta at some point began to use the language of intellectuals schooled in postmodernist evasions. She seems to know the rhetoric of truth as contingent. This is part of her careful crafting of an identity likely to be pleasing to her academic supporters.

These supporters have staunchly affirmed Rigoberta's early assumption of another posture, one they would never willingly grant to most speakers in our own culture: that of spokesperson for "her people." On the very first page of *I, Rigoberta Menchú*, Rigoberta confidently announced that her tale is that of all her people (Menchú 1). It is also on this very first page that Rigoberta tells us she received no schooling—a false assertion, as Stoll has established.

The predictable rejoinder that such falsehoods result from Burgos's emphasis in editing the book, or from Burgos's mistaken conflation of a number of different stories told her by Rigoberta, has already been neutralized by Stoll's discovery that Rigoberta set forth the basic outlines of her public persona before she ever met with Burgos. Stoll located a narrative, dating from 1981, in which Rigoberta lays out the pivotal tale of her father's brave resistance to the "landlords," and the torture and death of her brother Petrocinio and of her mother. Equally important, Stoll found that the representational stance Rigoberta took in her interviews with Burgos had also been anticipated in that earlier narrative: "My sorrow and my struggle are also the sorrow and struggle of an entire oppressed people who struggle for their liberation" (Stoll 183). There is every reason, Stoll concludes, to believe that *I, Rigoberta Menchú* is indeed Rigoberta's own account of her life (183), not a tale distorted by Burgos.

It is interesting to note how Rigoberta's initial attempt to blame Burgos feeds into the lengthy debates in certain North American intellectual circles about who controls the story. There have been some notable conflicts over this issue between ethnographers and storytellers. A famous case is that of Adélaïde Blasquez, who published a book called *Gaston Lucas, serrurier, chronique de l'anti-héros* (1976). The French scholar Philippe Lejeune called this book a masterpiece of ethnographic truth telling—until he learned that Blasquez had erased each interview with Lucas after transcribing it. When Blasquez's publisher invited Lejeune to interview Blasquez for a video, Lejeune suggested that Gaston Lucas, who was still alive, should be included. Blasquez refused, insisting that the living Gaston Lucas had nothing of value to say. Rather, she asserted, he truly existed only as a character that she, through her art, had created (Eakin xvii–xix).

Closer to Rigoberta's situation is a conflict between ethnographer and narrator discussed by Sondra Hale in an essay describing her problematic relationship with a Sudanese communist named Fatma Ahmed Ibrahim, Sudan's most visible woman politician and, for more than thirty years, a leading activist. In the course of their interview, Hale's Western feminist expectations of sisterly exchange and mutual recognition turned to disillusionment as Fatma presented her with a carefully contrived account in which she revealed only what she considered strategic to her political objectives, for which she clearly expected Hale to be her mouthpiece.

Hale is unusually forthright in describing how this meeting upset her. She felt relegated to the category of "mere listener" (131). Her own long residence in the Sudan, and her status as a "sister feminist" from the

West, seemed to count for nothing: "My 'dream of a common language,'" she confesses, "had been dashed by the interview, but perhaps that was because, although I had remembered a form of 'feminism,' I had forgotten some anthropology, politics, and history" (134). She is certainly correct in this suspicion. And Rigoberta's case makes it even more clear how strongly North American responses to this "subaltern" narrative have been shaped by politics and iconicity, rather than by the search for accuracy and truthfulness. The fervor of these responses can be gauged from the extremely hostile reaction Stoll's work has generated, because Stoll, though warmly sympathetic to both Rigoberta and her cause, is above all committed to scholarly standards not subjected to political oversight.

Lying

Sissela Bok has argued that lies (even so-called white lies) have consequences, and that lies tend to spread by repetition (1978). It is not surprising, then, that Rigoberta's lies are regularly repeated in the literature about her. In a children's book about Rigoberta, for example, published in 1996 (Brill), we find all her exaggerations and distortions recycled: her older brother is tortured and burned to death before her eyes; her younger brother succumbs to starvation; she is deprived of education and spends her childhood laboring on plantations; and, of course, the foundational tale—key to the mythic view of community of which so many U.S. academics are enamored—her father's conflict with Ladinos over land in Chimel, these Ladinos being described as "rich landowners," always the enemy in this children's book.

What exactly is the nature of Rigoberta's "misrepresentations" (as some have discreetly called them)? Unlike "white lies," which typically attempt to spare someone else's feelings, or otherwise innocuous fibs (though even those are not necessarily without negative effects, as Bok argues), Rigoberta's distortions were evidently done predominantly with a political purpose. But this represents an altogether different order of dishonesty, for—as Bok points out—such dishonesty has the unavoidable consequence of destroying trust. Thus, lies that are told originally in order to increase the power of their teller (or of the teller's cause) paradoxically, when exposed, have the effect of decreasing that power, and replacing it with mistrust (Bok 27).

The specifics of some of Rigoberta's lies also carry some unexpected implications. By inflating her own agonies, especially in falsely describing herself as a witness to the burning to death of her brother, Rigoberta suggests, implicitly, that her actual sufferings were insufficient to make the kind of powerful impression she wants to leave with her readers. Given her eagerness to win support for the guerrilla cause, it is perhaps understandable that she should have made this decision. But it also shows that she was consciously constructing a story that would be useful for her immediate purpose—which was a political one. Until Stoll wrote his book, few readers had bothered to notice the agenda she was promoting in her conversations with Burgos—or, rather, many academic readers seem to have automatically assented to that agenda and hence avoided subjecting it to critical scrutiny. Post-Stoll, of course, the rhetoric about Rigoberta has changed. Even John Beverley now suggests that we should "worry less about how *we* appropriate Menchú, and . . . understand and appreciate more how she appropriates us for her purposes" (1996, 272–73).

Perhaps nothing in Rigoberta's account is quite as revealing of the artful construction of her life story as her representation of herself as an unschooled person with only broken Spanish recently learned. This lie (she had in fact been a well-regarded pupil in a nuns' school) is of a somewhat different order than her misrepresentation regarding Petrocinio's death or the equally politically motivated cover-up of the land struggle between her father and his in-laws. Here Rigoberta attempts to manipulate the reader's take on her whole person, and clearly she knew what counts as positive in the "outside world" of her readership. Most people lie by inflating their accomplishments. But Rigoberta does the reverse, as if she were wise to the strange competition going on in the contemporary world over what groups are to be accorded most-oppressed status. As Stoll comments, Rigoberta's denial of knowledge of Spanish and literacy should be seen as "a preemptive defense of her authenticity." Why? "It is not true," writes Stoll, "that solidarity activists require their Indians to be barefoot and illiterate. But it is not hard to find people on the Left and on the fringes of anthropology who disparage Indians wearing a tie as inauthentic" (1999, 195).

Here, too—as noted earlier—the main damage done by Rigoberta's misrepresentations is to the cause of human rights. It cannot help human rights activists to be reminded that their witnesses are apt to deceive them. And it can only diminish the public's humane responses to repression and privation to discover that a leading icon of the international struggle to improve the human lot has built her reputation at least in part on falsehoods.

Teaching Rigoberta

I once made the point, based on sad personal experience, that in the field of women's studies "empowerment" means the equal disempowerment of each by all. The major exception to this is women of color and third-world women, who have come to occupy a special status within feminism. When we are being urged to believe in the privileged consciousness of nonwhite narrators, it becomes risky at times for scholars to defend objectivity and common sense. Nowhere is this risk more apparent today than in the classroom.

An entire volume has been devoted to the teaching of Rigoberta's book: *Teaching and Testimony: Rigoberta Menchú and the North American Classroom,* edited by Allen Carey-Webb and Stephen Benz. Its twenty-eight chapters, in addition to showing how widely used a text *I, Rigoberta Menchú* has become in colleges and universities, make abundantly clear how readily many professors and students seem to accept Rigoberta's account as a true one, and how frequently it is precisely the harrowing episode of her brother's torture and death that particularly impressed students.

Rigoberta's book was a required text in a first-year general education core course at Mount Vernon College, a small liberal arts college for women in Washington, D.C. A teacher comments: "[O]nly after they read Rigoberta's moving accounts of the torture and death of her sixteen-year-old brother burned alive in front of his family and of the kidnapping, torture, rape, and murder of her mother... did many students grasp fully the meaning of the term *human rights violations* that had figured centrally in the history outlined for them" (Carey-Webb and Benz 1996, 265).

Other authors report similar experiences. Catherine Ann Collins and Patricia Varas, who used Rigoberta's book in an obligatory freshman "World Views" course taught at Willamette University, in Salem, Oregon, quote a colleague who complained that "students wanted to believe

[Rigoberta] literally, rather than metaphorically" and was dismayed that when students realized something was not literally true, "it tended to discredit her" (144). The teachers here criticize their students for insisting on the "facts" and blame this on the influence of Western narratives that—so the essay informs us—condition students to be "in search of an authoritarian, first-person hero/heroine who controls the narrative and talks directly to the reader. If that hero/heroine isn't present, they can feel betrayed" (ibid.). That sort of voice is, of course, very much in evidence in Rigoberta's account, and it appears to be the professors who cannot hear it. They insist that Rigoberta is "voiceless"—following Gayatri Spivak's much-touted contention that the "subaltern cannot speak" (Spivak 1988; see also Patai 1988b)—and disparage their students' view of her as an extraordinary person, winner of the Nobel Peace Prize. Their students' problem, Collins and Varas say, is that their reading of *I, Rigoberta Menchú* "has not developed the necessary relationship to testimony as a discourse that (1) moves the reader toward change; (2) gives voice to the voiceless, especially women; and (3) questions 'not only Western versions of what is true, but even Western notions of truth'" (quoting from Gugelberger and Kearney 1991, 9). Unlike their students, Collins and Varas regret what they take to be the typical Western emphasis on individual effort and use the occasion for a trendy blast at their own culture: "The collective voice of the testimony, again, is undermined by Western notions of truth and objectivity" (144).

Yet another essayist, Robin Jones, who taught the book in a course on women writers at the University of Colorado at Boulder, was initially taken aback at her students' skepticism about Menchú's narrative. It is Jones whom I quoted at the beginning of this essay as stating that: "The work to me had taken on sacred dimensions and had become untouchable" (153). She tells of a student who, by focusing on environmental issues in Rigoberta's book, was "avoiding" the issues of ethnicity and gender (155). Jones, too, makes much of the episode of Rigoberta's brother's death and of her own difficulty in teaching "such a personal and painful work" (which she likens to teaching about the Nazi Holocaust [158]). Her students'

> main reaction to the violence was that Menchú was being "too graphic." If she wanted to arouse sympathy she should have "softened" the images. In other words, she should have retold the story in a gentler fashion so

> the reader could stay within the story. Students did not feel horrified as much as manipulated, as if this was indeed a slasher movie, not a real account of the death of a family member. (159)

Needless to say, Jones was "disappointed" (ibid.) at this reaction.

Jones also provides a clear example of the multicultural mode now current in North American pedagogy: "I suggest that when students describe a work as 'too depressing,' this statement be interrogated to find out which element of the story they find most depressing. I suspect that what is really at stake is the student's reaction to being decentered as a subject and feeling disempowered by the strength of an unfamiliar life experience" (160). "I am still troubled," she concludes, "by the students' resentment towards Menchú and her work, reflecting a backlash against multiculturalism and an unexamined response to the politics of 'political correctness'" (161). She promises to give her students more historical preparation in the future.

In another essay Mary Louise Pratt tells us that, in teaching Rigoberta's book, she instructs her Stanford students as follows: "Take notes about where you find yourself resisting its force, where it forces you into rejection or denial" (57). She teaches the book, Pratt explains, not in order to get her American students to change Guatemala, but "to do something about North America" (71).

For her part, in an essay in the same volume Meri-Jane Rochelson addresses the importance of finding an "authentic voice in making one's history known" (248). Rochelson, like most commentators, highly approves of Rigoberta's "repeated insistence that she was speaking for her group rather than for herself," and accepts this "as part of the revolutionary status of her *testimonio*." We have seen this proposition asserted by critics such as John Beverley, who deem it characteristic of *testimonio*, thereby elevating it to a status superior to that of the individual memoir, dismissible as a bourgeois-individualist exercise.

Doris Sommer, whose work on Rigoberta is, like Beverley's, frequently cited, speaks in an essay titled "Not Just a Personal Story: Women's *Testimonios* and the Plural Self" (1988, 110) of the "helpless solitude" that she thinks plagues Western women, in contrast to the "collective self" evidenced by *testimonios* such as Rigoberta's. Along with many of her colleagues, Sommer, too, feels compelled to parade her postcolonialist anti-Western attitude, as when she laments that even the collective subject bears witness to "Western penetration" when it is expressed through the individual *testimonio* (111).

It is intriguing to contemplate these critics' patronizing view that non-"hegemonic" people somehow cannot possess (or at least do not have the poor taste to display) an individual sense of self. And it is even more fascinating to speculate on why such high-profile academics express so much disdain for the intellectual values that have bestowed so many honors and rewards on them. The work of these writers is filled with unexamined *obiter dicta*—for example, Sommer's statement that "historical change cannot *[sic]* be mandated from the top down" (114)—and modish declarations, such as the oft-reiterated doctrine that "community" and "communal values" are necessarily more desirable than "individuality" (123).

This latter assertion, in particular, is an astonishing belief to be professed by someone living today, when so many horrors have been committed worldwide in the name of some community or other in the service of its vaunted ideals. Consider a kind of *testimonio* that is rarely heard in the classrooms where Rigoberta is celebrated: Ana Rodríguez's *Diary of a Survivor: Nineteen Years in a Cuban Women's Prison.* Like many Cuban dissidents of her generation, Rodríguez was first anti-Batista, then anti-Castro, and at about the age of twenty was imprisoned. Describing Cuba's Reeducation Program (renamed the Progressive Plan in the late 1960s), she sheds quite a different light on "community" and the obligations it imposes on the individual:

> [T]o me it looked like the same old Orwellian stuff. You signed a confession of your sins against the Revolution, implicating others to prove your sincerity; with other prisoners, you went to 'self-criticism' sessions . . . and you performed slave labor to show your gratitude for the whole process. [There was also] . . . mandatory participation in the idiotic Spoken Choruses. These consisted of groups of prisoners chanting in unison musty passages from Castro's speeches and letters. Perfect Communist art: It required neither talent nor imagination. (1995, 228–29).

One wonders what personal experiences with "community" American academics have had that lead so many of them to laud communal over individual values.

Conclusion

The saga of Rigoberta's story is a morality tale for our time. Whom can we trust? Whom do we celebrate? Must we mythologize figures in order to respect them? Is truth a Western ploy? What are the obligations of intellectuals—especially those fortunate enough to live in countries where they are free to pursue their vocations?

It seems to me that, at the present moment, demystifying Rigoberta is an important part of answering these questions. Opposition to human rights violations should not depend on misrepresentation—whether it is about land conflicts, one's family history, one's own education, or who did what to whom and who was there to see it. Truth and integrity matter, and we should not rush to give willing credence to stories just because they fit our preconceived ideas, all the while insisting on sound evidence for those that do not.

As far as Rigoberta's own role is concerned, a simple and probable explanation exists for the choices she made in presenting herself to the world, and it is an explanation that makes short work of the endless rhetoric about *testimonio* and collective voices, which, no doubt, tells us more about first-world intellectuals' needs and longings than about third-world testimonials. Rigoberta had, as Stoll's work makes convincingly and sympathetically clear, mixed motives. She wanted to promote her cause *and* she wanted to project a certain image of herself. Both objectives were served, in her view, by distorting her life story, and even lying about it when that seemed expedient. When confronted with evidence of her falsehoods, she sought to blame others. Why should this surprise us? It should not—unless we have fallen in thrall to notions about the superior virtues of the oppressed, or have come to imagine, or hope, that by idealizing the "subaltern," some of the charm will rub off on us.

As for scholars, clearly it is their duty to put scholarship first in their work and "advocacy" second. There is life outside the university, and plenty of time for acting on one's political commitments without turning either one's scholarly writing or one's teaching into propaganda. Is there anyone left on the left, I have wondered in recent years, who is prepared to defend the autonomy of intellectual work, and hence disinclined to reduce all questions to political bottom lines? Is no one on the academic left concerned about the perils of conflating political and intellectual goals (Patai 1994, 70)? Must everything we do be absorbed into politics, and be justified by the pretense that we (we academics) become "activists" every time we write another essay about the "oppressed"? Have we made the study of "subalterns" into a holy relic by association with which we hope to gain absolution from our sinful state as "oppressors"?

David Stoll addresses this delusion in his book, and illustrates it with a telling quotation from Bertrand Russell (1950):

> The stage in which superior virtue is attributed to the oppressed is transient and unstable. It begins only when the oppressors come to have a bad conscience, and this only happens when their power is no longer secure.... Sooner or later the oppressed class will argue that its superior virtue is a reason in favor of its having power, and the oppressors will find their own weapons turned against them. When at last power has been equalized, it becomes apparent to everybody that all the talk about superior virtue was nonsense, and that it was quite unnecessary as a basis for the claim to equality. (Qtd. in Stoll 1999, 194)

Only one thing is missing from this passage. Russell could not have imagined that in our time the self-proclaimed "oppressors" would themselves insist on the superior virtue of the oppressed, and that bizarre internecine disputes would ensue over who should be granted the distinction of this honorable status. Much less did he foresee that academic reputations would be made and unmade in the course of waging this unseemly quarrel.

Notes

1. John Beverley (1996, 267–68) has written at some length about the practice of referring to Rigoberta by her first name, making the predictable comments about the familiar usage. I nonetheless follow it. It is common practice in Latin America to refer to famous figures by their given names—"Oswald" for Oswald de Andrade; "Getúlio" for Getúlio Vargas; "Fidel" for Fidel Castro; "Clarice" for Clarice Lispector, and so on.

2. Interestingly, despite entitling his essay "The Real Thing," Beverley makes no reference to Henry James's short story of the same name, which brilliantly depicts the problems confronted by a painter when a "gentleman and a lady," fallen on hard times, wish to sit for him as models. The story recounts the painter's increasing discovery that the "real thing" cannot successfully represent the real thing, which the painter's usual déclassé models can do to perfection. As James's artist-narrator puts it (1996), he had "an innate preference for the represented subject over the real one: the defect of the real one was so apt to be a lack of representation. I liked things

that appeared; then one was sure. Whether they *were* or not was a subordinate and almost always a profitless question."

Bibliography

Arias, Arturo. 1996. "From Peasant to National Symbol." In *Teaching and Testimony: Rigoberta Menchú and the North American Classroom*, ed. Allen Carey-Webb and Stephen Benz. Albany: State University of New York Press.

Beverley, John. 1992. "The Margin at the Center: On *Testimonio* (Testimonial Narrative)." In *De/Colonizing the Subject: The Politics of Gender in Women's Autobiography*, ed. Sidonie Smith and Julie Watson. Minneaplis: University of Minnesota Press. 91–114. Beverley's essay first appeared in *Modern Fiction Studies* 35.1 (spring 1989).

———. 1996. "The Real Thing." In *The Real Thing: Testimonial Discourse and Latin America*, ed. Georg M. Gugelberger. Durham, N.C.: Duke University Press. 266–86.

Blasquez, Adélaïde, 1976. *Gaston Lucas, serrurier, chronique de l'anti-héros*. Paris: Plon.

Bok, Sissela. 1978. *Lying: Moral Choice in Public and Private Life*. New York: Vintage Books.

Brill, Marlene Targ. 1996. *Journey for Peace: The Story of Rigoberta Menchú*. Illustrated by Ruben De Anda. New York: Dutton, Lodestar Books.

Carey-Webb, Allen, and Stephen Benz, eds. 1996. *Teaching and Testimony: Rigoberta Menchú and the North American Classroom*. Albany: State University of New York Press.

Collins, Catherine Ann, and Patricia Varas. 1996. "The Freshman Experience at Willamette University: Teaching and Learning with Rigoberta Menchú." In *Teaching and Testimony: Rigoberta Menchú and the North American Classroom*, ed. Allen Carey-Webb and Stephen Benz. Albany: State University of New York Press. 133–47.

Cutler, William, III. 1984. "Accuracy in Oral History Interviewing." In *Oral History: An Interdisciplinary Anthology*, ed. David K. Dunaway and Willa K. Baum. Nashville: American Association for State and Local History. 79–86.

Eakin, Paul John. 1989. Foreword to Philippe Lejeune, *On Autobiography*, ed. Paul John Eakin. Trans. Katherine Leary, Minneapolis: University of Minnesota Press.

Guerra, Jonnie G., and Sharon Ahern Fechter. In *Teaching and Testimony: Rigoberta Menchú and the North American Classroom*, ed. Allen Carey-Webb and Stephen Benz. Albany: State University of New York Press. 261–70.

Gugelberger, Georg, and Michael Kearney. 1991. "Voices for the Voiceless: Testimonial Literature in Latin America." *Latin American Perspectives* 18.3: 3–14.

Hale, Sondra. 1991. "Feminist Method, Process, and Self-Criticism: Interviewing Sudanese Women." In *Women's Words: The Feminist Practice of Oral History*, ed. Sherna Berger Gluck and Daphne Patai. New York: Routledge. 121–36.

Hankiss, Agnes. 1981. "Ontologies of the Self: On the Mythological Rearranging of One's Life-History." In *Biography and Society: The Life History Approach in the Social Sciences*, ed. Daniel Bertaux. Beverly Hills, Calif.: Sage Publications. 203–9.

James, Henry. 1996. "The Real Thing." In *Complete Stories, 1892–1898*. New York: Library of America.

Jones, Robin, 1996. "Having to Read a Book about Oppression: Encountering Rigoberta Menchú's Testimony in Boulder, Colorado." In *Teaching and Testimony: Rigoberta Menchú and the North American Classroom,* ed. Allen Carey-Webb and Stephen Benz. Albany: State University of New York Press. 149–62.

Liano, Dante. 1999. "I, Rigoberta Menchú? The Controversy Surrounding the Mayan Activist." Trans. Will H. Corral. *Hopscotch* 1.3: 96–101.

Menchú, Rigoberta, with Elisabeth Burgos-Debray. 1984. *I. Rigoberta Menchú: An Indian Woman in Guatemala.* Trans. Ann Wright. London: Verso.

Patai, Daphne. 1988a. *Brazilian Women Speak: Contemporary Life Stories.* New Brunswick, N.J.: Rutgers University Press.

———. 1988b. "Who's Calling Whom 'Subaltern'?" *Women and Language* 11.2:23–26.

———. 1994. "When Method Becomes Power." In *Power and Method: Political Activism and Educational Research,* ed. Andrew Gitlin. New York: Routledge. 61–73.

Pratt, Mary Louise. 1996. "*Me llamo Rigoberta Menchú:* Autoethnography and the Recoding of Citizenship." In *Teaching and Testimony: Rigoberta Menchú and the North American Classroom,* ed. Allen Carey-Webb and Stephen Benz. Albany: State University of New York Press. 57–72.

Preston, Julia. 1999. "Guatemala Laureate Defends 'My Truth.'" *New York Times,* January 21, A8.

Rochelson, Meri-Jane. 1996. "'This Is My Testimony': Rigoberta Menchú in a Class on Oral History." In *Teaching and Testimony: Rigoberta Menchú and the North American Classroom,* ed. Allen Carey-Webb and Stephen Benz. Albany: State University of New York Press. 247–57.

Rodríguez, Ana, and Glenn Garvin. 1995. *Diary of a Survivor: Nineteen Years in a Cuban Women's Prison.* New York: St. Martin's Press.

Russell, Bertrand. 1950. "The Superior Virtue of the Oppressed." In *Unpopular Essays.* New York: Simon and Schuster.

Siegel, Fred. 1998. "Taking It to the Streets." *Reason* (June): 72–73.

Sommer, Doris. 1988. "Not Just a Personal Story: Women's *Testimonies* and the Plural Self." In *Life/Lines: Theorizing Women's Autobiography,* ed. Bella Brodzki and Celeste Schenck. Ithaca, N.Y.: Cornell University Press. 107–30.

Spivak, Gayatri Chakravorty. 1988. "Can the Subaltern Speak?" In *Marxism and the Interpretation of Culture,* ed. Cary Nelson and Lawrence Grossberg. Urbana: University of Illinois Press. 271–313.

Stoll, David. 1999. *Rigoberta Menchú and the Story of All Poor Guatemalans.* Boulder, Colo.: Westview Press.

Wilson, Robin. 1999. "Anthropologist Challenges Veracity of Multicultural Icon." *Chronicle of Higher Education,* January 15, A14–16.

Menchú Tales and Maya Social Landscapes
The Silencing of Words and Worlds

Duncan Earle

The Alice-in-Wonderland quality of the "debate" about Rigoberta
Menchú's account finds me moved to comment on an issue over which
I have long been publicly silent, but about which I feel informed enough
to, as it were, join the fray. I say this because I spent the majority of my
time in the period just before the "Violence" of 1980–84 in Guatemala,
living with and working with K'iche's in the southern part of Quiché
province, and my work brought me into close, continuous, personal contact with all the social players of the region, in eleven *municipios,* and
103 communities within them.[1] At the same time, I find myself in an
uncomfortable place writing this essay, and I tell myself I must do it,
because the issue is so important. I say that with the disclaimer that the
issues that began this "debate" as I read about it in the news are, for me,
not all that important: I do not think that changing one's personal story
line to incorporate others' lives is a great sin—and it does wonders for
the dramatization of the narrative line, one that did, after all, help
Menchú's book become a major cultural, literary, and political event.
This is important. The way in which the book was able to expose the
scope, brutality, and scale of the killings and abuse in the context of Maya
culture and sociobiography and within the context of a colonial-style,
hyperracist country, was a superb, brilliant way to move toward making
sure it does not happen again, a way to make the world become more
committed to seeing to it that genocide against indigenous peoples stops.
In that vein it must be said at the outset that the Nobel Peace Prize was

for precisely this gift: to make genocide come to life so that the community of nations, concerned as it has been for other genocidal, militarized, large-scale violence, could reveal its hypocrisy. In exposing this crime, it represents a blow against genocide, the antithesis of peace in the extreme.

At long last to have the world confront the inequity, the injustice, the blood on all of us for having let the massive killings of 1979–84 happen. Menchú documents with verve the latest legacy of large-scale indigenous murder that began five centuries ago. The power of attention drawn to Menchú by the prize also drew attention to the genocidal crimes she decried. I had given fifty-four public lectures during the first two years of the megamassacres and could not get people even to listen, let alone believe it was happening. But Rigoberta Menchú did. In the politics of silence of the time, the anthropological voice was not authorized, but a Maya voice, for once, was. That the prize should come in 1992 gives away the point of the award, a recognition of this silenced violence in both structural and visceral forms that continues to enslave the indigenous. By comparison to this stunning achievement, the fibbing that has grabbed headlines has seemed to me trivial at best, suspect at worst.

This is what I always told David Stoll, too. I said exposing Menchú's contradictions would do harm and abet the perpetrators and their ideological allies while making a smaller, more specific series of points lost on most people. That, not to mention the heaps of derision he would receive for doing it. I agreed that some of the things said in his book were misleading, but the personal biographical facts were far more trouble than they were worth. What bothered me was what I saw as issues best taken up within the context of those sympathetic to Rigoberta Menchú's main point about violence against the Maya, and those concerned with the social well-being of indigenous Guatemalans. My complaints are at a more subtle level of social analysis than questions of who saw who get burned where and when. It is unfortunate in this daytime talk-show culture that such personal issues become the focus of media—and thus public—attention. That was not Stoll's intention, but then as now I saw it as inevitable, and I do lay those realities at his feet. From an intellectual standpoint, I could not justify imposing censorship. But from the standpoint of the struggle for indigenous justice, and despite all the compelling arguments, the refutation of anything Menchú said risks a popular refutation of everything she said, and that is not good. So I held my tongue.

Experience and Outrage

But now that this flap has ushered in the issue of textual verities, perhaps it is a fair moment to raise my own heretofore unpublished concerns. I do not think that, by themselves, they will give much succor to the perpetrators or their apologists or their investors. I am reluctant, in any case. Having lost many close personal friends in the bloodbath (more than one hundred people I knew well), for my major applied fieldwork experiences were during the period of 1975–79 in the province of Quiché, I cannot abide the thought of saying anything that would make people question whether things were as bad as Menchú said they were. Based on what I was told and saw, they were worse, if that can be imagined.

In fact, it is from my outrage at the killings, and my concern about justice, that I gave some study to the violence in the part of Quiché I knew well—the south. I had just finished working for a community development and aid program a few years earlier. It was funded by Save the Children and we worked in nine *municipios* around Santa Cruz, as far east as Sacualpa, as far west as San Antonio Ilotenango (where Ricardo Falla worked; Falla 1979), to the north San Pedro Jocopilas, and to the south Chichicastenengo and Patzite', mostly focused on reconstruction and housing, forestry and community organization (Earle 1977). I knew many of the people who had become Western-educated *catequistas* (catechists) because some of their members got most of the jobs we offered to housing promotors and other aid program positions. The reconstruction efforts after the 1976 earthquake favored them because of their high levels of literacy, Spanish-language use, and general acculturation. I also knew the local Ladinos, because I dealt with them in terms of local town powers and politics, and through many social contacts associated with eateries and stores, as well as at work. And I knew the traditional or *costumbre* K'iche', because I lived with a family of them. They were the least like my own culture, and required the most time for me to understand. This experience, plus many summer revisits and inquiries both before and after the Violence (1980–84), make up what informs my essay.

I too have had a Stollian moment, though thankfully less public. I once gave a talk to a gathered group of churchy solidarity folks on Guatemala, and in the discussion afterward I was asked about Rigoberta's book, specifically in terms of the religious representation of Maya traditions.

Here I thought I was on safe ground. Anyone familiar with the divining system and the calendar knew that there were twenty days (not ten). In short, there were a lot of inaccuracies about K'iche' traditional beliefs because, I explained, clearly Rigoberta was a catechist (*catequista*) and, like so many others of her background, did not know much about the subject. I had known other *catequista* Mayas with the same kind of partial and jumbled, even romanticized, notions of a tradition to which they had little direct exposure. I was often asked by catechist coworkers what the "chimanes" (a term also used in the book) or "zajorines" (both Ladino Spanish terms for *aj q'ij,* "calendar diviner," literally, "day-keeper") were all about, and how K'iche' calendar divination worked, as it was a subject they knew I had studied. These more urbane friends were not apologetic about their lack of understanding of their ancestral religious traditions, because they viewed such practices as backward and suspect from a theological point of view. To those of us who lived in the highlands, the religious split and the theological contrasts and frequent animosities among Mayas along lines of religious affiliation were just part of the normal social landscape. Both perspectives to me seemed comprehensible alternatives in their own social and economic contexts, with virtues and drawbacks (this all before the evangelical Protestants had gained much of a voice to muddy the dichotomy with further divisions).

The vehemence of the response from the man who organized my talk took me aback. In front of the whole group he insisted that the book was "authentic" down to the last jot and I must have gotten it wrong, since I was the white foreigner. She was the Maya, she was the authority. I began to realize that I was only welcome so long as I reconfirmed their perspective, as I did with my lecture presentation on the massive killings by the military and the refugee crisis. The point I tried to make about the killings being even more unjustified in places where there was next to no guerrilla presence (such as Chiché, Sacualpa, Chinique, and many other southern Quiché townships) did not reach them, because they were still seeing a war, not a form of genocide of the marginal simply based on their race and remote or strategic location (I called it "preventative counterinsurgency"). I got nowhere with my field-learned perspective. This was a war. The book was viewed as gospel. I felt my voice, and the perspectives of the many voiceless Mayas I had spent so many years with, being aggressively silenced by this man who had never been there. I had violated the literal-minded readings of some seeming scripture. What could I say, I thought, to this orthodoxy? I bowed out as soon as possible, resigned to the fact that things were too complicated to get into with this crowd, and reminding myself as always that the important thing was to focus on the killing fields.

The Silenced Divide

For people familiar with Quiché department, highland Guatemala, and the social processes at work in the decade before the mass killings, the Menchú book is a challenging text by what it says and does not say. Perhaps the most significant issue the book plays down by making frequent references to indigenous unity is the fierce internal social division in most highland indigenous townships, that between the followers of the reform lay group called *catequistas* (also known as Catholic Action, or Acción católica) and the followers of the traditional Maya religion. The divide was established in most parts of Quiché starting in the 1960s or early 1970s (see Falla 1979; Brintnall 1979; Smith 1977; Carmack 1988; Earle 1983; Le Bot 1995). By the time of the 1976 earthquake, it was the defining social division within most indigenous towns, often overshadowing even indigenous relations with the Ladinos, and there were frequent and heated conflicts. In Chichicastenango, the fighting had locally famous roots in the Acción católica attack on a well-known shrine called Pascual Abaj, in which the central stone figure was broken in half and thrown into the canyon, condemned as an "idol." It was later retrieved, and now serves as a tourist attraction, also serving as an important shrine for its followers. While I was working in the town, a conflict erupted when a new priest tried to encroach on the space the *costumbre* people use to put down their votive candles, to have more pews. These conflicts were a constant in my field notes, from 1975 until my last pre-holocaust entries in the summer of 1981.

Every township of the nine I worked in, and many more that I visited, in the 1970s endured this division, and conflicts were often lived out regarding who controlled sacred space in the town church and the rural shrines. In San Pedro, the priest rebuilt the church so the *costumbre* offerings would blow out in the wind. In Chiché, the priest assisted the catechists to build a separate church so they would not have to share space with the "pagans," as Father Amibalec referred to them. Many other authors mention this division throughout the highlands (Falla, Warren,

Brintnall). The hostilities made community work difficult, especially with the more aggressive and this-worldly *catequistas* monopolizing most community aid and organization efforts. The "Old Ways" people resented this, and felt marginalized by the aid efforts, and in many cases that I myself witnessed, they were (Earle 1977). At the same time, in their defense, the catechists were becoming involved in collective efforts to better themselves economically, through education, cooperatives of many sorts, and labor organizing, as well as by working in international development agencies—alongside people like me. No one was the bad guy. But there was not the needed effort by the clerics managing Catholic Action to involve the other, more marginalized sector. The progressive intervention was also very divisive.

Before the coming of the new priests and Acción católica, the system of religion and community government in the western highlands had been tied together by the fiesta system, the worship of saints being the basis of the development of indigenous authority (Earle 1990; Smith 1977). This is the "civil-religious hierarchy," well documented in Guatemala and Mexico by anthropologists of earlier eras (Tax 1937; Wolf 1967; Reina 1966; Bunzel 1967). It was fashionable of those who sought to critique this earlier ethnography to interpret the calendar of religious festivities in Maya villages as an imposition of the colonial system to make natives go into debt so they would work on their farms and plantations to pay it off (Smith 1977). Although it is true that many people went into debt because of religious costs and worked it off on the coastal plantations, and some still do, this interpretation of exploitation ignored the benefit that the heavy costs paid for. The benefit was the reiteration of the totemic hegemony of the saint spirits over the village, such that those who were their caretakers and judges earned their political maturity by serving the saints. Those elders who had served well, and who had served on the civil town corporation as well, became the *principales,* elders whom all people of the town deferred to in resolving conflicts, of which there were many. The gerontocracy was a way of keeping the outside out, and people from becoming divided from within the township, as well as spreading food around the town in the saints' name. Put another way, Maya religious practices associated with saint veneration developed in the colonial period were actively anticolonial in intent and effect (see Earle 1990 for an elaboration of this for Chiapas; Farris 1984 for colonial Yucatán). Unable to form strong ties beyond municipalities, this was the one area where solidarity against cultural conquest could be exercised (Earle 1990).

Such a role of what James Dow (1977) has called "informal authority formally acquired" (seeing the same structure of resistance in an Otomí community) came to function as an ultimate authority only because everyone was enrolled in the same system of beliefs, and continued to respect the saints and the brotherhoods who care for them. Religious leadership was the basis of political authority, regardless of who became mayor or what the priests wanted. This was the situation still in most Maya communities in Guatemala when, as a response to the perceived threats of communist secularism of the 1944–54 revolution, the Catholic church launched Catholic Action. It served as a part of the follow-up of the 1954 Armas counterrevolution, another political outrage planned and bolstered by the CIA and other powerful buddies of the Dulles brothers and the United Fruit Company.[2] Construing indigenous practices as backward, paganlike, and caught up in ignorant interpretations of Catholicism, the movement sought to rationalize and modernize the church and bring the Mayas into the larger world through education, greater access to Western goods and services, and, of course, repudiation of the past religion and its practitioners. This missionary zeal of the movement remained with Catholic Action as it became more "liberal," following the progressive changes in the Latin American church, and moved from soul saving to social analysis, cooperatives, medical clinics, the introduction of fertilizers and pesticides to increase agricultural production, and community organizations addressing social issues. This work was carried out at the hamlet (*aldea,* canton) level, circumventing the township centers where the traditionalist authorities were located.

According to Ricardo Falla (1979) and testimonies I have taken, the catechists were able to recruit well among younger people because many wanted to escape arranged marriages, ceremonial posts, and the authority of parents and the religious elders in general. When young men wished to escape the burdens of religious offices, now there was the Acción católica alternative to provide an out from having to financially support community feasting. The group also offered access to things often enjoyed by Ladinos of the region, such as literacy, goods, and control of transportation, as well as introduction through the priests to more profitable ways of managing agriculture, craft production, and marketing, and even the organizing of neighborhoods for self-improvement. The young men were also able to take advantage of Western pharmaceuticals, which, along with the rejection of shamanic faith healing, displaced spiritual healers. The system of unified support for the saints was broken, and in many highland towns the *cofradías* died out or shrank dramatically in size and support (Carlsen and Prechtel 1991; Annis 1987).[3] And the communities became divided, sometimes violently. There was no longer a legitimate authority as there had been for centuries, that everyone accepted within the community of Mayas in a township. Many communities devolved into factionalism, making them more vulnerable to outsiders and their interests (Earle 1992). At the same time, the group most involved with the priests, most prosperous, most Spanish-speaking, and most acculturated, became the group from which would come supporters of the CUC and the guerrilla.

The central problem from the *costumbrista* standpoint was the intolerance of the old practices by the *catequistas* and the priests who backed them up. The *costumbristas* often felt under attack for practicing their religion, and in heavily *catequista* areas such as around Santa Cruz the practice became almost entirely hidden from view. The family I lived with had to sneak around in Santa Cruz del Quiché when trying to do an offering ritual. In their formation as *catequistas,* followers learned from the reformist priests that such things as diviners who used the ancient Maya calendar were allies of the devil, or worse, simply deluded by their ignorant ancestors. It was utterly unnecessary antagonism. "You believe in logs," was a slogan that developed in the cradle of Catholic Action's influence, referring to Maya saint worship. In the 1960s and more so in the 1970s, as Catholic Action grew, in general the greatest factional splits in indigenous towns without significant numbers of Ladinos such as Chiché, San Pedro, San Antonio, and Lemoa, were, according to the *catequistas,* followers of the old traditions. These divisions were sometimes bitter.

In general, most anthropologists of the 1970s portrayed the catechists in a positive light, ignoring the negative impacts of facilitating capitalist penetration, fertilizer dependency, pesticide poisoning, and creating a climate of conflict over religion. Nor was there much complaint by scholars about the paternalism of the priests (which the catechists themselves complained of all the time), their imposition of Western cultural beliefs and practices in ignorance of what they were displacing (including, in some cases, effecting the loss of the K'iche' language), and their launching into community development projects without the background sufficient to prepare them for such efforts, many of which failed. Even their aggressive posture against the poorest and weakest segment of the Mayas, so characteristic of the Sacred Heart padres headquartered in Santa Cruz del Quiché (some of whom I knew personally), has hardly been commented on. The admiration many of us share for the late Father Sam Rother, who was machine-gunned to death in 1981 in Santiago Atitlán (where he was parish priest), was that he stood out in his efforts to bring the factions together, an effort symbolically demonstrated in the religiously integrated *retablo* still in the town church that he had commissioned. His ecumenical approach and efforts to reunite the religious factions no doubt contributed to the military decision to murder him. His ecumenism was, unfortunately, an exception. In most parts of the highlands, the 1960s and 1970s were a landscape of religious strife aided and abetted by Catholic priests and their acculturating followers, and later this initial change gave an opening for Protestant sects (Smith 1977). The activist Catholic orthodoxy did little to lessen the Ladino racism either, for that social sector felt threatened by the new Mayas and their aggressive economic activities in areas of Ladino monopoly (Earle 1983).

Unity, Mystification, and Appropriation

Reading the Menchú book, it is confusing to me because, while the author is a *catequista* or Catholic Action affiliate, as was her father, she often talks about issues that border on *costumbre* practices on one hand, and paints a social scene of communalist unity among the Maya on the other. It gives the impression of appropriation and mystification: appropriation because much of what is claimed as traditional either falls into the domain of *costumbre* (at that time the theological enemy) or appears to be new; mystification because, on the one hand, indigenous culture is said to be one of secrets, even as many religious practices are discussed, and yet the discussions of many of the traditions are highly anomalous, and in some cases just plain incorrect. An obvious case is the discussion of the Maya calendar in use in Menchú's region (mentioned earlier). There are many, many others.

One could say Menchú is misrepresenting these cultural practices intentionally, a form of disguise, her "secrets." This is possible. Given the details she does describe, it does not make that much sense to me. Her patchy discourse on traditional Maya culture reminds me of another Maya raised in Catholic Action whom I know very well, a cooperative leader from La Estancia whose brothers knew Rigoberta's father. One of the man's brothers, a *catequista* leader, was actually crucified by the military in mockery of the brothers' Catholicism (Carmack 1988). To me, Menchú's book reads as if it were written by someone who knows of the religious practices and beliefs from a distance. I knew dozens of second-generation *catequistas* in the 1970s. The problem arises when this distanced view comes to be seen as gospel. Although Menchú's text has a tendency toward the essentialist "we the indigenous" and "the story of all," to me the title of the book defines it, ultimately, as a perspective of one person, at one point in time, and one position in the social landscape. Other perspectives languished and still languish in silence, and too many readers have simplified the Maya social landscape by thinking this particular position, numerically a minority of one, is representative of everyone when it comes to indigenous people and culture. This is not Menchú's doing, but that of her constituencies. The question is to what degree this was the intent of the author, and what was the result of the partiality of one perspective—a troubling question raised by Stoll's inquiry. But I am less concerned with whether the omission was conscious (the cult of personality raises its Oprah head) and more with the many ways that it creates an unbalanced picture of indigenous Guatemala for those not already aware of the complexities.

Martyrs are no good to a movement if they are revealed to not be true believers, but killing innocent bystanders increases the heinousness of the crime, because it removes the army's only remaining justification for having done it. Even if the military cast itself as having come to believe the guerrillas' claims of mass support in areas where there was only some, its behavior even in supposed ignorance is inexcusable. Here lies the root of my complaint about Menchú's book. In many people's reading of it, the impression is given that there was more guerrilla support, national political consciousness, and involvement than is in fact the case. This is also a shortcoming of Manz's (1988) book, whose discussion was confined to areas where there was a guerrilla presence (see Earle book-review essay, 1992). I do not wish to debate who supported whom and why in the Ixil case, as I do not know it close up. But what of cases like the rural south of Quiché, most of which appears to have had little or no guerrilla presence and yet had equally bad massacres. A careful reading of the recent reports on the rural violence of the time demonstrates the absence of a close correlation between Maya deaths and guerrilla-held space.

This purported pan-Maya unity hides a profound division that no one had wanted to talk about. But now we must. It is not just the issue of giving the EGP more revolutionary credit than it deserves, or its possible influence over the military's response. Such imagined unity promotes an illusion that in turn could be used to justify the response, because arguing the military was killing in villages made up largely of committed guerrillas and their cadres makes it easier for the Guatemalan and international courts to let it get away with it, through the amnesty for "political" murders. Few of the massacres I knew of well in Quiché (excepting northeast Chichicastenango) qualified as political killings, except in the most twisted and ridiculous of definitions, such as the sick idea of preventative counterinsurgency, a kind of "don't even think of considering joining the rebels" form of terror and savagery. This would not pass in courts of law. The myth of an authentic war has helped the military, even as it may have helped the failed rebel movement, as Stoll claims. But again, it does not help the Mayas if it weakens their collective case regarding crimes against humanity. The great secret Menchú's book ends up preserving is that the military slaughtered thousands in areas without any credible evidence of significant involvement or support for the guerrillas or their political cause—this quite apart from the complex and not always textbook reasons behind why some people did join up, in the areas where they did so (Le Bot 1995; Manz 1988).

The Dialectic of Conquest: Other Maya Voices Speak

One silenced voice I would like to enliven here comes from a Maya man whose real name I never knew. Rigoberto was all he offered. I met him while working on various craft and aid projects for widows in Guatemala in 1984. He was involved in crafts, using tourist sales of them to help his and other Maya communities with social programs of recovery. It was all hidden, based on cells divided by language groups, so no one could be tortured into revealing the other groups or their activities. He would only talk to me in a place he knew in zone 9, sitting next to a loud marimba in a place with lots of space between tables. He said he had gone to the university, but felt rejected by the students for being an "Indian." He studied politics but found the spectrum of left and right to be arid:

> For me they are sides of a legislature in France, from Europe. This is not our dialectic. I see the townships of Mayas to be within the dialectic of Conquest. This dialectic is about invaders and invaded, the crimes of theft, rape, and racism for five centuries that no one will address, even though it is everywhere present, even though we continue to live those crimes. Until the invaders face their criminal history and make amends to arrive at equity, or wipe us out so we don't keep reminding them of their failure to face up, the dialectic will continue. We will have to keep fighting the Conquest. No other social or power dialectic is as deep in the life of Guatemala.

He went on to say:

> The left organizations want our involvement but not our agenda. They think of us as racist to want to emphasize our cultural differences. But that just preserves their prejudice, and makes them blind to it as well. They do not understand the dialectic of Conquest. They seem to think our culture is an obstacle to progress and political change; some even say it is not ours, not authentic, a colonial creation. They find many ways to not take our views or culture into account. In this they are similar to the rightists, who would like to have us for quaint folklore and as a tourist attraction, but hate to have us be people on a par with them, hate to hear our voices. We who want to continue to be Maya have no allies in places with money. We are all like I am here with you, our words covered by louder noises with catchier tunes, easier to listen to as well.

I cannot help but think of the well-meaning priests of the counterrevolution period forward as unwitting agents of the Conquest, preaching their social vision so poorly fit to the larger social, cultural, ecological, and political environment in which they experimented. Just like their secular counterparts, these "agents of change" had unintended consequences that to this day no one seems to want to face. One of them was promoting a divide-and-convert strategy, one that split townships deeply, and later facilitated the government terror that always exploits divisions. Surely it is an error less egregious than the crimes of the military—but still, it is an error we should not silence or keep hidden behind a mythic unity.

The Time of the *Itzel Winak,* or All Politics Is Local

In 1984 I gave a Chajul elder or *principal* a ride from the town center to his "Development Pole," an upbeat term for a squalid resettlement camp for Ixiles of the region displaced by the military. The loud roar in the private car animated him to talk about the tragedy of the lost people and the events leading up to the military massacres:

> When the guerrillas first came, we thought they were *capaz* [literally "capable," in control]. We liked what they said about getting land back from the Ladinos, but some of us did not like it about killing the *finca* owners. Where would we get work if they were all killed? Where would we find our pay for a little maize? Well, we saw then, when the army came, that the first ones were not *capaz*. So here we are. No, we do not like the military, but they are like our mother and our father.

It struck me that this was not the kind of political consciousness that Rigoberta had attained, and I wondered how typical he was of the old guard, and of the catechists and other reform groups as well.

It made me return to places where I was known and trusted in the southern Quiché department, to ask people to characterize their impressions of the guerrillas and their supporters. I began with the family where I had lived, beyond Chiché to the east. The army had confronted the family early on about "the subversion" (la subversión), and the family had answered that they knew nothing but their machetes and their hoes; they feigned ignorance as a cynical response of the intrusion. They would reiterate that such new groups were people who knew things, "que tienen escritorios" (literally, "who have offices"—meaning educated, usually Ladino). They played into the stereotype of their own imagined ignorance and were left alone. But, according to family members, some of the *catequistas* made the mistake of saying that they "knew things" when the army grabbed them, so some were taken back to the base. The subsequent torture compelled them to speak badly about others, also *catequistas* but from a rival group:

> So the *pintos* [the common name for the military, based on the multiple colors on the uniform] went up there and got them, and before they were taken away they "sang" about the guilt of the relatives of the first *catequista*. And so it went, week by week for months, until they were all finished off. The whole *aldea*, nothing but the dogs. It was left abandoned, until widows from Chiché moved in a year later.

Another anthropologist who has worked in the same area wrote me:

> As for disconnection between guerrilla support and killings, I think Chinique is a clear case in point. It seems that at the beginning "se lo llevaron a" many *aldea* catechists, who may or may not have gone to

some "meetings" with CUC or with the EGP. But from what I gathered, the guerrillas only came into the pueblo once early on, were unsuccessful, and then the Ladino-led PACS [Civil Self-Defense Patrols] took full reign in terrorizing the place into siding with the army. Many people (whose families nonetheless had been devastated) told me they never even saw guerrillas at all, and had quite mixed feelings and knowledge about who they were and what they represented; the guerrillas were essentially an image of evil created by the army. I was told by a Ladino in Paraxquin that the PACS would stage guerrilla fights in the *aldeas*, planting "folletos" [leaflets], etc., so that they could then come in with an excuse to terrorize. The violence in Chinique had everything to do with local power and economics (PACS got rich on people's *leña* [firewood] and land), and with vengeances, and not with ideology. Two hamlets (La Puerta and Ximbaxuc) were completely razed. (Patricia Foxen)

The neighboring town of Chiché was devastated; friends said half the town was killed, in military and later patrol assaults, but mostly military. Here tensions were also very high between the two factions, and nearly half the town was *accionista,* many of whom went to the coast or traded. The claims of no guerrilla presence there are harder to substantiate because of the level of killings and the possibility of terror-based historical revisionism. My *accionista* friends who survived maintained that they were not involved in anything but their *capilla* prayer meetings (in rural chapels), the reconstruction committees, and other community improvement organizations. The attacks were completely unprovoked and unjustified, I was told. No one I could find knew anyone from Chiché involved with CUC, although they knew of people in labor movements in Santa Cruz. People could have been covering up, or rewriting their level of interest in opposition movements after the terror, although I knew some of these people very well from before the Violence. On the part of the *costumbristas,* the period was characterized as the time of the "bad men," when the whole order of society went to pieces, when people hid in their houses or went to the coast, sometimes for years.

People I knew very well in one *aldea* in a township close by shared that they had speculated on who the *guerreros* ("warriors" literally, a corruption of *guerrilleros*) really were—they had only come through the region twice, and no one knew them:

Once they made a scene in the marketplace and shot a Ladino nobody liked, and another time they shot Don Roberto, the poor Ladino right next door. Lots of people owed him money, and he had a nice truck. His wife got shot too, but she lived. Some say they are not humans but soldiers sent by the World ["Earth Lord," one of the most important traditional spiritual entities], because sometimes they have nice boots and light faces, and sometimes they have bare feet and look like us *indígenas*. Some say they must know how to change from one appearance to the other, which shows why they are not human. Some say they come to punish us for having abandoned the old ways, the ancestors, and becoming arrogant. Others say they are from the volcano Tacaná, where thousands of them live, and a priest has the keys to let them out, which he does two or three at a time, and they only speak "lengua," our native speech, these *guerreros*.

This construction of the guerrillas was not as class or ethnic allies, but as mysterious and dangerous strangers (see Carmack, in Carmack 1988).

"What is certain is that soon after they came by there began the time of the '*itzel winak*,' the bad men, when nothing was as before and even the dog was closed inside the houses by eight o'clock, so afraid were we all." The term *itzel winak* showed up in many parts of the region, and around Lake Atitlán as well, as a way to talk about the peak violence period, and it suggests an understanding of the events quite different from the perspective of those in solidarity with the EGP or the CUC. The evil men included guerrillas, military, civil patrol leaders, ex-*comisionados*, and violence opportunists who profited by the arrival of de facto martial law, using it to settle long-standing local scores. "*Itzel winak* liked to bring death for whatever excuse." The excuses were often totally unrelated to the so-called war that was supposed to be going on. Local conflicts became "nationalized" and the national "war" was used to further the local conflicts. Mutual, negative appropriation of mutually unintelligible labels helped to get a lot of people killed beyond the territory of war.

Outside of interviews with urban catechists in Santa Cruz del Quiché *municipio* and close by, this kind of characterization was the norm. My Santa Cruz friends who had involvement with aid organizations had mostly fled, except for the Ladinos. Their relatives claim they were threatened and left. Some became refugees, some joined the rebels, some hid on the coast or the capital city. I know of three close friends who all felt they had to leave after the 1980 violence in La Estancia, a hamlet outside Santa Cruz. Even with the extensive presence of CUC sympathizers in the region since about 1978, residents of La Estancia denied "that the Indians had arms or that they were tied to the guerrillas in any way" (see Carmack, in Carmack 1988, 53–54). With a second major massacre in the hamlet, forty community members left to join the guerrillas to the north, one EGP member from La Estancia claimed (ibid., 52–53). I provided money for one of the families living in Santa Cruz to go to Mexico. None of these catechists knew of anyone who was involved directly with the guerrillas, but because they were not present in that part of Quiché then, they explained, one would have had to leave to join up.

All of these are subjective reports, I realize, and I can only speak with any authority at all in the parts of Quiché I knew from before and that I revisited. But I know that most of the south of Quiché, apart from some of the Chichicastenango mountains and a part of Tululche, almost never had a sustained guerrilla presence (in this the solidarity literature of the time squares with reports from my contacts in the nine municipalities), and one cannot correlate the vast majority of military killings with that factor. Presence in the Acción católica, however, made one almost automatically a suspect, as did living in a suspect hamlet, especially in this region, as people said again and again (Carmack 1988). When the Sacred Heart order left, following the shooting death of the priest in Joyabaj and other death threats and murder attempts, it was clear that its followers would be targeted. It did not help them then that the priests had encouraged them to take actions that antagonized the Ladinos and the *costumbristas* over the preceding two decades. Now that the communities had been divided for a generation or more, the military would take full advantage of it to get some people to rat on others. The unleashed racism of the local Ladinos, in towns where they still maintained a notable presence, also accounts for many deaths and acts of terror.

The military was good at breaking people who "thought they knew something." One of my closest catechist coworkers was taken to the military base on an accusation by G-2 (military intelligence) in 1982. Two of his brothers had already been murdered by soldiers. He was a head of a community betterment committee and a member of a weaving co-op. At the base he was beaten to within an inch of his life. Fortunately, the protests of his community got him out before every bone in his body was broken. He had been able to focus on his own case when his torturers tried to get him to talk about others, repeating, "What is my crime? This is a democracy. What is my crime? Show me my crime, then

I shall agree to my death." His bravery and focus meant no other deaths in his community. Many detentions did result in death, he explained. Some people would simply give the name of someone they did not like, so as to try to be let go. With all the *divisionismo* and conflict of the last twenty years, there were plenty of people not to like, completely aside from any consideration of guerrillas or the national political conflict. The military tactics encouraged such a local settling of scores. The military thought it was rooting out the "subversion" that was supposed to be all around but that no one actually saw.

As is becoming increasingly clear in some killings in Chiapas, Mexico, local conflicts repeatedly become exploited for larger ends. Case after case of "mutual negative appropriation" is misread by the outside world. We need more careful and focused research on the social processes that in the 1960s and 1970s led to the conflicts that were negatively appropriated for a war that, from reports I have gathered from the zone I am familiar with, does not seem to have been a war.

Who Speaks for Whom?

Many who are outraged by the impugning of the Menchú tale should reflect on what legitimacy the anthropologist has in bringing forth indigenous voices we do not want to hear if they conflict with other ones we do want to hear. The power of Menchú's book as an epic tale (re Gary Gossen's article) for identification by a variety of groups for a variety of reasons should not blind us to the multivocality of social life on the ground where this all happened. It is more than a setting, a trope to tell a transcendently true tale. Black hats and white hats thinking regarding conflicts between groups who both owe their origins and ideas to a location and culture outside the indigenous region should be suspect on the face of it. Much as we would have liked to see in Guatemala the level of cultural sensitivity and organizational integration that we appear to see from the Zapatista leaders, who have taken the trouble to learn the culture and language of the Chiapas Mayas before armed action, this sensitivity was harder to find in most of the armed left (or the foreign priests) in Guatemala. A number of Mayas whom I interviewed after they left the guerrillas complained about the continued cultural prejudice and racism among the rebel troops. There is no space for the details of their testimony here, but it raises the question: Who speaks for those who have no constituency, nationally or abroad, who cannot speak for themselves but who do not agree with Eurocentric political projects or alien religions? Who will dare to report or speak the voice of those who repudiate rationalist "progressive" Catholicism as a cultural assault, and those who have a vision inspired by Maya political concepts more than those of Che? This perspective now has growing support in the Maya cultural identity movement. But for most who have sought to understand indigenous Guatemala, it is still heresy. Should our fear of gifting our political enemies make us silent to that which has silenced the least empowered sector of Maya society, especially when that other truth may serve to punish genocide?

Conclusion

I return to my main points. First, it must be recognized that Menchú and Burgos-Debray were able to accomplish a huge feat by making the book, drawing world attention to a crime of huge and wrenching proportions done to a people already living in a state of abject injustice and grinding poverty. The value of the book as a vouchsafement against a repeat performance of the times of the *itzel winak* transcends all else, for now many influential people around the world know the scale of the crimes, and many of them only because of Rigoberta Menchú's words. Any hint of undermining that truth by questioning Rigoberta Menchú's portraits of herself, her family, and/or her local social landscape misses the point. The killings were very real, as the mass grave exhumations and church and UN truth commission reports suggest, and the vast majority were carried out by a vicious military. My own calculations for the deaths of the early 1980s still exceed the "official" count by more than 20 percent. Like Cambodia, East Timor, Uganda, and similar third-world killing fields, the silenced outrage had to be exposed, and no one has done more for that than the only indigenous American Nobel laureate to date.

Second, Rigoberta Menchú's position needs to be situated where she was located when she dictated it. Stoll attempts to do this in terms of the CUC and EGP influences on the *catequistas* at the time she went to Paris. I would situate it in the context of priest-based religious organization that determines a position historically in relation to the depreciated *costumbristas* on one side and the depreciating Ladinos on the other, one that silences the first and vilifies the second. Such a reduction of the social landscape serves external interests at the expense of approximations of the truth in all its complexity at a local level. But such simplification serves to make coherent and unified statements that are hopeful and empowering, without contradictions or inner conflicts. Especially bad personal circumstances, and equally stark social and political ones, for foreign consumption, increase people's attention and retention. Menchú's book has served a heroic purpose, but at a cost I think we now ought to consider.

Third, what is hidden and silenced in the book about solidarity and unity of the Maya are the ways they do not get along, the internal conflicts, and how they were used and even manipulated at times by the major actors, and how national issues were used to (mis)address local conflicts. To put too much emphasis on solidarity with the guerrillas ignores the fact that the guerrillas bear some responsibility in the tragedy, that their tactical, strategic, and ideological errors were expensive—and not always paid in lives of those who backed them or even knew who they were or what they dreamed of. To place too much emphasis on religious and social unity obscures not only the factionalism but who was responsible for it. Shall we say it is the fault of the *costumbristas,* those who have tried the hardest to fulfill the ideals of the ancestors spoken of so respectfully in Menchú's book, and those whose tradition has successfully rejected the cultural invasions and intrusions from outside for so many centuries? This would not be accepted by anyone. Evidence of social schisms would be blamed on the other faction, the church and its followers, a constituency close to the author in a number of ways. I fear that this helps explain why the schisms were played down so dramatically. If the value of this period of reflection on this tragedy is confronting the truth, the *hechos* along with the *derechos,* then this part of indigenous Guatemala's social history must be demystified, just as the cold war justifications that Reagan gave for underwriting the genocide had to be demystified. It is a time for *all* outsiders to confess their errors and offer an apology for their role in the latest bloody episode of the Conquest. This is hard for people to do. It is a position that has no powerful nonindigenous constituency.

All of this would be of less pressing importance were it not for the current political and legal realities surrounding the peace process. The standard left position that Rigoberta Menchú's book helps to authorize ironically serves to justify the killing from the standpoint of law and the military logic of counterinsurgency. I have heard publicly and read military testimony advancing this argument, and using the position of the guerrillas claiming mass Maya uprising to validate their claims of having won a nasty war. But what if it were true that in many places where the military killed people there were no rebels, just local conflicts that the military cynically preyed upon? Genocide and crimes against humanity are more substantiated by cases of massacres of people not involved in the fight. The killing of truly innocent bystanders simply because of their race and the presumption of possible future involvement—this is a crime for which there is no amnesty. For this reason, I think it is worth considering other voices situated in other locations within the Guatemalan Maya social landscape. I hope the future brings us more of them.

Notes

1. I worked in Santa Cruz del Quiché for the summer of 1974, Chinautla and Quiché from January to August of 1975, and then in the southern Quiché region (Quiché, Chinique, Chiché, Chichicastenango, Saculalpa, San Antonio, San Pedro Jocopilas, San Bartolomé, San Andrés Sajcabajá, Joyabaj, Patzité) in 1976 through the summer of 1977, and was in that region each summer through 1981. I returned briefly in 1984 and then each summer again through 1992, and less frequently since. Because I was working during my 1976–77 period for a reconstruction NGO funded by Sweden, I was exposed to all sectors of the society, and worked closely with Mayas of all stripes and orientations, as well as Ladinos, rural and town-based.

2. In June 1954, Colonel Carlos Castillo Armas, aided by a CIA coup and with support from both the Somoza and Trujillo dictatorships, entered Guatemala City and overthrew the democratic government of President Jacobo Arbenz.

3. *Cofradías* is a religious brotherhood established around a Catholic image, to promote the socialization of personal goods between wealthy and poor families in the same community.

Bibliography

Annis, Sheldon. 1987. *God and Production in a Guatemalan Town*. Austin: University of Texas Press.

Brintnall, Douglas. 1979. *Revolt against the Dead: The Modernization of a Maya Community in the Highlands of Guatemala*. New York: Gordon and Breach.

Bunzel, Ruth. 1967. *Chichicastenango: A Guatemalan Villlage*. Seattle: University of Washington Press.

Carlsen, Robert S., and Martin Prechtel. 1991. "The Flowering of the Dead: An Interpretation of Highland Maya Culture." *MAN* 26:23–42.

Carmack, Robert, ed. 1988. *Harvest of Violence*. Norman: University of Oklahoma Press.

Dow, James. 1977. "Religion in the Organization of a Mexican Peasant Economy." In *Peasant Livelihood,* ed. Rhoda Halperin and James Dow. New York: St. Martin's.

Earle, Duncan. 1977. "Roofs of Tin in El Quiché: Cultural Logic and the Southern Quiché Reconstruction Program." In National Symposium on the 1976 Guatemalan Earthquake, proceedings. Guatemala City: National Reconstruction Committee.

———. 1983. "Changes in Ethnic Population Proportions in the Quiché Basin: A Case of Reconquest." In *Historical Demography of Highland Guatemala,* ed. Robert Carmack, Early, and Lutz. Albany: Institute for Mesoamerican Studies, publication no. 6, State University of New York Press.

———. 1990. "Appropriating the Enemy: Maya Religious Organization and Community Survival." In *The Politics of Popular Religion in Mexico and Central America,* ed. L. Stephen and James Dow. Washington, D.C.: American Anthropology Association. 115–42.

———. 1991. "Measuring the Maya Disconnection: Violence and Development in Guatemala." *American Ethnologist* 18.4:793–98.

———. 1992. "Authority, Social Conflict and the Rise of Protestants: Religious Conversion in a Maya Village." *Social Compass* 39.3: 379–90.

———. 1995. "The Unquiet Dead of Guatemala." *American Anthropologist* 99.4 (winter).

Falla, Ricardo. 1979. *Quiché Rebelde.* Colección Realidad Nuestra. Vol. 7. Editorial Guatemala City: Universitaria de Guatemala.

Farris, Nancy. 1984. *Maya Society under Colonial Rule: The Collective Enterprise of Survival.* Princeton, N.J.: Princeton University Press.

Le Bot, Yvon. 1995. *La guerra en tierras mayas: Comunidad, violencia y modernidad en Guatemala (1970–1992).* Mexico City: Fondo de Cultura Económica.

Manz, Beatriz. 1988. *Refugees of a Hidden War: The Aftermath of Counterinsurgency in Guatemala.* Albany: State University of New York Press.

Reina, Ruben. 1966. *The Law of the Saints.* New York: Bobbs-Merrill.

Smith, Waldemar. 1977. *The Fiesta System and Economic Change.* New York: Columbia University Press.

Stoll, David. 1993. *Between Two Armies in the Ixil Towns of Guatemala.* New York: Columbia University Press.

———. 1999. *Rigoberta Menchú and the Story of All Poor Guatemalans.* Boulder, Colo.: Westview Press.

Tax, Sol. 1937. "The Municipios of the Midwestern Highlands of Guatemala." *American Anthropologist* 39.3: 423–44.

Warren, Kay. 1978. *The Symbolism of Subordination: Indian Identity in a Guatemalan Town.* Austin: University of Texas Press.

Wolf, Eric. 1957. "Closed Corporate Peasant Communities in Mesoamerica and Central Java." *Southwest Journal of Anthropology* 13: 1–18.

Teaching, Testimony, and Truth

Rigoberta Menchú's Credibility in the
North American Classroom

Allen Carey-Webb

> Autobiography like *I, Rigoberta Menchú* calls on first-world readers
> to take responsibility, not for the third world but for the locatedness
> and therefore the limitations of our own perspective. Acknowledging
> those limitations might contribute to the survival of us all.
> —Janet Varner Gunn (278)[1]

> The situation is so dire, ignorance and disinterest so widespread that
> the hours we devote to the inquiry take on an unusual importance.
> —Daniel Goldrich (289)

I first met David Stoll and heard his now well-publicized accusation that
Rigoberta Menchú exaggerated her testimony when we happened to be
together on the same panel at the 1990 conference of the Western Humanities Association in Berkeley, California. The panel was titled "The
Politics of Establishing Revisionary Literary Canons" and three presen-
ters each had twenty minutes to read prepared papers with little ostensible relation to each other. My paper was about postcolonial literature
in Kenya, Mexico, and Guatemala and Rigoberta Menchú's testimonial
was one of three texts to which I referred. The second paper was by
Yiingjin Zhang and addressed Chinese texts. David Stoll's paper was
focused on testimony he had gathered on a brief visit to Chajal, Guatemala, the year before. He had spoken with a man in the village who told
him that there had been no public burning of victims by the Guatemalan army in his town, and Stoll had thus concluded that Rigoberta
Menchú's brother Petrocinio could not have died as Menchú had de-

scribed. At the time of the panel Stoll, Yiingjin Zhang, and I were all graduate students, Zhang and I in comparative literature and Stoll in anthropology. Rigoberta Menchú had not yet received the Nobel Prize and was, outside Latin American studies, relatively unknown.

In the fifteen-minute discussion period after the papers I responded to Stoll by suggesting that his emphasis on the detail of the burning of Menchú's brother seemed out of proportion, especially given the magnitude of the violence in Guatemala. Stoll did not dispute that the war in Guatemala had been a near genocide and that Menchú's parents had been killed, yet he had what seemed to me a flippant attitude toward Menchú, asserting that she was now out of touch with Guatemala and living the high life in "la-la land," a phrase he repeated several times. I asked him what he meant by "la-la land" (I never found out) and I tried to explain that I thought it would be difficult for native Guatemalans to trust a North American anthropologist, especially one just visiting their town. I added that before he publicly accused Menchú of fabricating parts of her story he might want at least to speak with her and hear her response. I told him I thought he should think carefully about the charges he was making because there were groups that would like to use such charges, such as the Guatemalan military and the U.S. State Department, to discredit not only Menchú, but also the efforts of groups in Guatemala and in the United States that were trying to advance the peace process. (George Bush was president and actively supporting Guatemala's military regime.)

After the panel and discussion, I invited Stoll and two anthropologists whom I had met at an earlier session to continue the conversation over lunch. As we strolled across the sunny Berkeley campus, we kept talking and Stoll told us about his fieldwork in other parts of Guatemala and the sympathies he had developed for the evangelical Christian movement in that country. Over soup and sandwiches we discussed how he might bring his concerns about Menchú's story to other audiences; I suggested he send a copy of his remarks to John Beverley, one of the best-known scholars of *testimonio*.

A reporter for the *Chronicle of Higher Education* had been attending the session when Stoll and I presented. Apparently this reporter did not regard any of our papers as newsworthy; nothing appeared in the *Chronicle* with reference to them. On the other hand, two years later, when Menchú received the Nobel Prize this reporter remembered my name and called to ask if I was still working with Menchú's story. I mentioned I had thought of creating a book about the experiences of teachers using her testimony; the remark was published in a brief paragraph in a sidebar to the article about the prize, and a professor I did not know, Stephen Benz, phoned offering to help me with the book. His call actually started our project, and together eventually we edited a twenty-eight-chapter book, *Teaching and Testimony: Rigoberta Menchú in the North American Classroom*, a collection of stories by teachers about the difficult, complex, and ultimately rich learning that can take place when North American students study Menchú's story.

Let me apologize for beginning what you might have expected to be a general examination of "teaching, testimony, and truth" with this personal reflection about a minor conference panel many years ago. Yet this panel has some relevance to the issues and events that put the question of Rigoberta Menchú's credibility before us. One can, for instance, read a quite different version of this panel in David Stoll's book *Rigoberta Menchú and the Story of All Poor Guatemalans* (239). In Stoll's version, I serve as the representative of "left liberal scholars" at a conference of "experienced academics" who have never been to Guatemala but need Rigoberta Menchú for "moral validation." Our interchange becomes the only real "confrontation" at the whole conference, a conference that is, according to Stoll, "at a high level of abstraction." Stoll's paper becomes the one exception to this abstraction as he makes his point about the burning of Menchú's brother. In Stoll's version, I am his "adversary" taking at "face value Rigoberta's portrait of Indians living in harmony." Stoll describes me as less concerned by what he says about Menchú and more troubled by his comment that "many of us wished to privilege a voice that met our own needs at the cost of understanding the situation." This comment somehow becomes "unavoidably personal" and I engage in "ideologically policing" with my "reaction" that Stoll was "falling into the army's propaganda line."

Stoll does not use my name. Interestingly, in his book replete with vague references to "leftist scholars" that do not want to hear what he has to say and somehow threaten to prevent him from speaking, it is my anonymous self that serves as one of the few specific examples he offers. I guess we could say that in the version of events Stoll wishes to narrate he has turned me into an icon, an icon of the politically correct leftist scholar his book seeks to combat.

From this experience I can see that it is not particularly pleasurable to be turned into an icon without being consulted and I can also see that having once become an icon, trying to extricate oneself from the narrative becomes problematic, even suspect. Yet readers of Stoll's book will, no doubt, be in a position to sense some irony here. Just as with the Guatemalans whose stories he contrasts to Rigoberta Menchú's testimonial, Stoll and I have two different versions of the same events. We have these different versions even though we were both present and actors, and, unlike witnesses to the events in Guatemala, neither of us, I presume, was severely traumatized. It is clear that Stoll writes his book with a mission to find "the truth" rather than explore subtle interpretations, what he calls "abstractions," yet he ends up focusing on details that become marvelously abstract in themselves (was Petrocinio Menchú burned before or was he burned after he was detained, tortured, shot, and his body put on public display?). He contradicts one version of events, Rigoberta Menchú's, with other versions. From his vantage point supposedly above the fray, he wants to show that Menchú distorted the truth to make herself into an icon of the Guatemalan and international left. At the same time, his own narrative is subjective and polemical. He distorts, exaggerates, and interprets events. He creates his own icons and countericons. And, in a way I admit I find offensive, he in effect denies the suffering of impoverished and tortured victims of the Guatemalan and American military juggernaut in the service of furthering his own argument against the academic left.[2]

What we have, then, is juxtaposed experiences, opposing testimonies, and discordant stereotypes, imagery, and interpretation. We are, in other words, precisely in the place in which and from which any pedagogy that seeks to explore the truth of Rigoberta Menchú's testimony and its credibility in the North American classroom must begin.

By this I do not mean that David Stoll's book *Rigoberta Menchú and the Story of All Poor Guatemalans* sets the terms for future teaching of Rigoberta Menchú's testimonial. Indeed, I will argue quite the contrary. I mean instead that teaching Rigoberta Menchú's testimony to North American students is, at its most essential level, about bringing together distinct pasts and potentially and actively conflictive worldviews with some hope of opening up new perspectives, addressing and even breaking down barriers between people, and trying to find ways to communicate. In this context, Menchú's testimony bears a powerful and transforming truth. It is not a truth that cannot be questioned, but a truth that creates, opens up, and initiates questions. At the most profound level, the issue is not so much Menchú's credibility as a witness to the Guatemalan holocaust (not even Stoll doubts this), but instead her credibility within the contemporary and relatively comfortable North American classroom as a voice speaking to our students about poverty and violence, and the courage to survive and struggle against them.

The North American Classroom Context for Menchú's Truth

Most American high school and college students know very little about Guatemala, not to mention Central America, Latin America, or even, to use that omnibus term, the "third world." Global poverty, inequality, and the developing economies, American foreign policy in Latin America, land distribution, repressive military regimes, and revolutionary movements–these topics rarely surface in the American curriculum. Despite charges of "politically correct" reading lists in literature courses, the most current and extensive research indicates that no works by American minority authors are yet to be among the most taught texts in this country and that no writers from the third world appear in the list of the fifty most commonly used texts in American high schools.[3] By and large, history and social-science courses continue to be taught with a Eurocentric focus and literature curricula continue to be dominated by Shakespeare, Dickens, Twain, and Steinbeck. If and when American students address Native American cultures, it is usually as an issue of the past and/or one within current U.S. borders. Jessica Miller, teaching advanced Spanish in a Michigan high school, reports that many of her "students were surprised to learn that Spanish is not the only language spoken in Latin America and that hundreds of indigenous groups communicating in over one thousand seven hundred different languages also inhabit this region."[4] Miller's experience is not unique.

Massive public ignorance and misunderstanding of Central America can be said, I suppose, to free the hands of American policy makers. I do not remember an outcry when, in a speech in the 1980s, Ronald Reagan justified his assistance to the Nicaraguan contras by warning that the Sandinista threat was a mere "day's drive from Texas." It does not take much knowledge of Guatemalan and Mexican geography (and roads) to know how absurd this remark was, yet similar rhetoric has supported many an American intervention, including in Guatemala in 1954. Considering the position of the United States as the one world superpower and the readiness of American governments to meddle in the internal politics of other nations, it is not strange that many people find American ignorance about the world disturbing, even frightening.

The paucity of academic study of Central America, Native Americans, or the third world is certainly not made up for by the appearance of these topics in the mass media. Although American students may have heard of "global sweatshops," in large measure the origin and production of consumer goods in the third world, the conditions of workers, and the utilization and the exploitation of resources in these countries remain subjects that are rarely addressed. Seemingly peripheral to propagating modern Western lifestyles and consumption patterns, indigenous third-world peoples are so profoundly stereotyped that what does appear in the media is often worse than no information at all. Consider, for instance, Juan Valdez, the mythical hero of Colombian coffee commercials who sometimes appears in tidy white clothes with a friendly burro or, as I have seen in at least one commercial, water-skiing in what looks like the Gulf of Mexico.

In the absence of systematic knowledge, fragments become stereotypes and take on greater significance. Before teaching chapters from Rigoberta Menchú's testimony to high school sophomores in the small town of Coloma in southwestern Michigan, Andrea Smith tries to find out what her students know of America's neighbors to the south:

> We began by asking students what they already knew about or what stereotypes they already had of Guatemalans, Mexicans, and/or Central America in general. As we put words like "drugs," "lazy," "dirty," "alcoholics," "poor," "lots of kids," "hot peppers," "overpopulated," "farmers" on the board, we asked students to tell us if their answer was a "fact" or a "stereotype." Students began to realize that the stereotypes were all they knew. I suggested we could revisit this list during and after our reading.

To understand the context that Menchú's testimonial enters in the American classroom, we need to recognize that this class's brainstormed list is a re-presentation of images repeated from the mass media, images to which all Americans, even those more knowledgeable about Central America, are relentlessly exposed. This class's list of terms is self-explanatory; poverty is the result of laziness, dirtiness, alcohol addiction, and having "lots of kids." Suggesting cultural difference, "hot peppers," the list also captures fear and a sense of threat. Americans are endangered not only by "drugs" but also by the overpopulated, unwashed masses across the border. The Mexicans and Central Americans of this list of terms are a static caricature and a profound "Other," people from a world to which North American students sense little connection.

Given the limitations and the erroneousness of the information American students have about Guatemala, Central America, and the third world, it is not surprising that many react by not penetrating very deeply into Menchú's testimonial as they begin to read it. American students often find it unpleasant, "depressing," and above all "boring"—that powerful word of rejection in the student vocabulary that, to the attentive teacher, means not only repetition of stereotype but also "I don't understand." The result can be emotional distance and intellectual passivity:

> My students began by distrusting the text and the teller, disliking the information, being bored, depressed, and in general having a negative reaction and attitude toward the work. (Women's study course in Boulder, Colorado) (149)

> [I, Rigoberta Menchú] is too much for the majority of students where I teach. Too much blood and gore, too much rhetoric and politics, too much indigenous culture. (Latin American culture students in Chester, Pennsylvania) (175)

> Reading Rigoberta Menchú's testimony to the oppression of the Indians in Guatemala posed a challenge . . . and, no doubt for this very reason, some students deemed it "too morbid" and "depressing." (Mount Vernon College in Washington, D.C.) (265)

> Out of forty-six students in two sections of third semester Spanish at the University of Wisconsin-Madison, about half said that they were bored by the excerpt [of Me llamo Rigoberta Menchú] that appears in Paisajes: Literatura. The other half were about equally divided between those that "did not care" and those that were genuinely "interested." (209)

> One of my students, a woman in her late twenties, remarked in class one day that reading I, Rigoberta Menchú was, because of the alienness of Menchú's experiences, like "reading science fiction." (Comparative literature student in Harrisburg, Pennsylvania) (227)

Reading Rigoberta Menchú's testimonial presents American students with an experience of "cultural shock" to which a frequent response is rejection and retreat: How can this be true? Why do these people live this way? Why have I never heard about it before? Addressing this shock and distancing is frequently a concern of teachers. As Stephen Benz explains, "Teachers must be prepared to understand that without some background, some context for approaching Menchú's narrative, many students, resorting to their preconceived notions of 'primitive Indians,' will simply dismiss the text or greatly misunderstand it" (19). A first step for most American readers of Rigoberta Menchú's testimonial is simply a recognition of their own experience of shock, and from this, an increased awareness of themselves in relation to others living in poverty and under a violent regime:

> What saddens me even more about this story is the lack of feeling I have. The thought, of course, sickens me that that kind of injustice still goes on in these "modern" days, but my life has been so sheltered to this kind of violence and life-style. I can't imagine living like that; not knowing if I'll have food the next day, a house the next day, or even be alive the next day. Americans don't realize what we have. We're all so naive. I'm glad, though, that I have the choice to be naive—not thrust into such a life. Stories like this one make me a grateful girl. (Alternative high school student in Michigan)[5]

> Before this class, many students I have talked to never knew this sort of condition existed for the indigenous person of Latin America. The stories of beatings and killings were something that was supposed to have happened in the past and not in the present day society. It is still happening now, however, and many students have become aware of these situations . . . this understanding that is gained about the world around us is an important part of development for students. (Willamette University freshman in Oregon) (147)

Although these reflections might not constitute a complete or sophisticated analysis, an important ethical dimension is engaged in by students when they relate their own situation to Menchú. Dan Goldrich has been teaching courses on Central America for many years and used a variety of forms of testimony from the region, including many in-person presentations. He sees the ethical dimension as something that arises as part of the teaching of testimony:

> Here's a real human being, this is someone's real experience. This dynamic is heightened if the testimony is presented in a social setting focused on it, where connections are made between presenter and audience, where values and principles shared between them are noted. This makes it harder to turn off. In such a setting, a shocking personal crisis can be created. We've heard it. Do we let it in or try to shut it out, restoring our safer, more comfortable world? . . .

Then, an awful question arises, "What do I do, what can I do, what should I do?" This is a crisis of personal responsibility. Testimony can generate this dynamic. It tends to generate, I believe, a sense of guilt. I'm aware that guilt has a bad name with many people contemporarily, but I think guilt arises in a process beginning with the perception of a gap between the ideal and the real, right and wrong, and through testimony such as Menchú's, the question appears, "What should I do?" The psychohistorian Robert J. Lifton terms this the anxiety of responsibility. (288)

Critical Thinking, Ethics, and Credibility

Joining critical understanding to personal and ethical responses has always been seen as crucial by teachers of Menchú's testimony. Although no two classes call for the same focus or approach, teachers want students to think carefully about Guatemalan society, American involvement in Latin American politics, and the nature and purpose of representations themselves, including the testimonial form.

> I think that an emotional response to Menchú's description of torture is both natural and important: it is precisely this emotion that helps my students stop seeing Rigoberta Menchú as an "exotic, romantic, mythical Indian." But in order for them to also start seeing Menchú as an intelligent, articulate spokeswoman whose cause includes promoting international solidarity with oppressed Guatemalans, they need to go one step further. This additional step requires a serious attempt at objective (relatively objective) textual analysis in response to the question, How do Burgos and Menchú achieve solidarity with their readers? (Teresa Longo, teaching at William and Mary College in Virginia) (306)

> I encourage a critical faculty in my composition students by asking them to read with a sense of the writer's historical, social, and political context; to respond to texts with a sense of their own historical, social, and political context; to construct a rhetorical situation that contains both themselves and the text; and, most of all, to become aware of the tensions and contradictions within the text, within themselves, and within their responses to the text. (Clyde Moneyhun, with freshman college students in Arizona) (237)

> In showing that the unfamiliarity of Menchú's *testimonio* in fact unsettles what it means to find a text "useful" for students I find I must elaborate on the idea that the testimonio is not so much unmediated, "transparent" truth as it is a product of strategies of narrating and the cultural assumptions embedded in those strategies; as such, testimonio

shares many characteristics with fiction. (Tace Hedrick, teaching women's studies in Pennsylvania) (228)

Think, I would tell students the week it was assigned, about what gives this book its force. How does it mobilize your mind and your imagination? How does it force you to think and know things you would not otherwise think or know? Take notes about where you find yourself resisting its force, where it forces you into rejection or denial. *Force* seemed to me a term that might generate a viable poetics of the testimonio, one not at odds with its political compromise and activist imperative. (Mary Louise Pratt, teaching Stanford College freshmen) (57)

Teachers I know who work with Rigoberta Menchú's testimony are eager to have their students increase their knowledge about Guatemala and investigate further the situation in that country. They try to incorporate a variety of materials in their classes, willingly share reading lists, encourage student research to verify the conditions Menchú reports on, and push their students to seek out a variety of sources of information. Latin American scholars usually share Steve Mathews's view and approach:

Contrary to many U.S. representations of it, Latin American culture is *not* a monolithic entity; therefore our readings will lead us across multiple and shifting borders of ethnicity, gender, nationality, and politics. (163)

Teachers working with Menchú's testimonial who are not Latin American specialists are frequently inspired to learn more. Judith Peterson, teaching in a Jesuit high school in Nebraska, reports that despite the absence of Central American literature from standard textbooks, she has researched and developed a diverse unit on the subject (105–11). Unable to answer student questions generated by Menchú's testimony, June Kuzmeskus turned the study of the testimonial into a class research project. Passionate interest in the unit led her to create an entire research course on Guatemala for her eleventh-grade students (128–29).

As I have suggested, Menchú's testimony presents experiences quite foreign to many North American students and they find the level of poverty and violence Menchú reports in Guatemala to be difficult, if not impossible, to believe. Comparing Menchú's testimony with other sources of information becomes vital and part of the process of critical thinking, one that many teachers engage in. Given the questioning of Menchú's veracity in the *New York Times* ("Tarnished Laureate," December 15, 1998, also in this volume), it is appropriate that I share the approach of a young teacher in Michigan who engages his ninth-grade students in a comparative examination of the credibility of Menchú's testimonial and *New York Times* reporting in 1980, during the height of the violence and repression in Guatemala.

> Since this book *[I, Rigoberta Menchú]* is not officially in the curriculum or on the approved reading list at our school, I couldn't purchase or assign the whole text but was only able to use certain selected chapters. I chose those that would not only be informative about the background of this peasant woman, but would also tell a gripping episode of her life. One of the chapters was chapter 25, Menchú's account of the death of her father in the Spanish Embassy in Guatemala. The chapter is Menchú's retelling of the occurrence after gathering facts, stories, and interviews from friends who had firsthand knowledge. Along with this chapter I had students read an article printed in the *New York Times* on February 1, 1980, covering the same event at the embassy. Their assignment was to read both the chapters and the newspaper article for the next day and be ready for a class discussion on whatever discrepancies they found between the two accounts.... When they arrived ... we began a discussion on what they thought of the chapter, and they immediately became involved with the textual details. They pinpointed cruelties that the indigenous people were facing. Many students were disgruntled by the fact that the Guatemalan government was not listening to the peasants or understanding the difficulties they faced....
>
> During the comparison, we identified several differences in the two accounts of the embassy takeover. Many wondered about vagueness in the newspaper article about the history of the Guatemalan peasants. They also questioned who the "officials" were that the journalist used as sources. Another detail they searched for was how could a "gasoline bomb" have been "accidentally dropped" as the newspaper reported. The word "mistreatment" was floating around the room. These ninth-grade students were incredibly perceptive about what was going on in the testimonial and the newspaper article. Facts that once meant little were stirring feelings and emotions. The students seemed to be increasingly sensitized to the atrocities we were examining in Guatemala by making the comparison between the testimony and the newspaper article.
>
> After reading both portions of *I, Rigoberta Menchú* and a *New York Times* article their final task was to write about which source they found more credible and why. Do you believe this uneducated peasant woman? I asked them. Or, do you believe what a major American publication reported and published? The fact that the vast majority of students found this [Latin American woman's] testimony more credible than the *New York Times* became a starting point for further investigation.[6]

This teacher's ninth-grade students wrote comments such as the following:

> The *New York Times* article gives the reader a "public" point of view while *I, Rigoberta Menchú* gives the reader a perspective from the Indian peasants. It also presents more feeling and a more clear background situation than that of the *New York Times* article. The article also favors the officials more than the peasants. It covers up some of the truth (peasants' perspective). The article also blames the peasants for starting the fire.

> In the *New York Times* article they mention five of the peasants had weapons, but in the article by Rigoberta Menchú she said that none of the peasants had any arms. Also peasants, according to Rigoberta Menchú, were not holding hostages in the embassy. The *New York Times* article is basically on the side of the officials. I believe Rigoberta's story is true because it fits together better. How could peasants take hostages if they only have rocks as weapons?

The Classroom Significance of David Stoll's *Rigoberta Menchú*

Given the public controversy, it is important for teachers to carefully examine the charges that David Stoll has made in *Rigoberta Menchú and the Story of All Poor Guatemalans*. An attentive reading of Stoll's book makes it clear that initial press reports on his research were sensationalistic. While the *New York Times* (December 15, 1998) claimed that Rigoberta Menchú "fabricated," "seriously exaggerated," and told "one lie after another," Stoll's research, on the contrary, serves to affirm the truth of Menchú's account in all of its major points, certainly those points that are most relevant to the vast majority of American teachers and students who have worked with Menchú's testimonial.

After years of research focused on identifying errors, exaggerations, shortcomings, and bias in Menchú's 1982 oral testimonial, Stoll himself begins the preface of his book by asserting that there is "no doubt about the most important points" Menchú makes.[7] Moreover, despite press reports about requests to the Nobel Prize Committee to rescind the Peace Prize, Stoll states that he believes awarding the Nobel Prize to Rigoberta Menchú was a "good idea" and that "she has been the first to acknowledge that she received it, not for her own accomplishments but because she stands for a wider group of people who deserve international support" (ix).

Specifically, Stoll corroborates the following information in Menchú's testimony:

1. Rigoberta Menchú's father was burned alive when the army attacked the Spanish embassy he was occupying to protest human rights abuses, an occurrence that is widely known in Guatemala. Stoll believes Menchú's account of the events at the embassy is more balanced than most others (80).

2. Rigoberta Menchú's mother was detained, raped, tortured, killed, and her body was mutilated by the Guatemalan army. Rigoberta Menchú's gruesome description of what happened to her mother is corroborated by independent sources (127).

3. Rigoberta Menchú's sixteen-year-old brother Petrocinio was seized, tortured, and shot by the army and his mutilated body was left in the street of the town of Chajul. Rigoberta Menchú reports that her brother was burned alive; Stoll argues he may have been burned after he was killed, but that it "was not rare" for the army to humiliate, torture, and burn people alive in front of their families (70).

4. Rigoberta Menchú's village, Chimel, was attacked by the army, and the villagers used self-defense strategies to protect themselves, much as Menchú describes (129).

5. Rigoberta Menchú's two younger sisters did join the guerrillas after the murder of their mother (130).

6. Ladinos in the highlands near Menchú's village were, at least during the war, closely associated with the army and attacks on indigenous people and Menchú's family (136).

7. Guatemalans regard Menchú's testimonial as a "truthful portrayal of their country" (246).

David Stoll also adds information that Rigoberta does not include in her testimony:

1. The military coup in Guatemala in 1954 was "organized" by the United States, through the CIA, to overthrow a popularly elected democratic government. This military coup can be held directly responsible for a loss of political development and the country's economic collapse, military violence, and the revolutionary movement. Had the coup not taken place, Stoll believes, Guatemala

"could have evolved in the direction of Costa Rica, which leads Latin America in per capita income and political stability" (46).

2. Rigoberta Menchú's village was completely destroyed by the Guatemalan army not long after her testimony was recorded.

3. Rigoberta Menchú's brother Víctor was shot and killed by the army after peacefully turning himself in (135).

4. Rigoberta Menchú's sister-in-law was killed and her nieces, age three and five, were starved to death while in army custody (134–36).

5. Rigoberta Menchú's closest friend at school, Bernadina Us Hernández, was killed by the army, as were Bernadina's father, her brother (in front of the family), and six other male family members (46).

6. Stoll documents many other violent murders of innocent indigenous people in the region Menchú comes from, frequently using words such as *slaughter, massacre,* and *holocaust.*

7. Menchú and her book contributed to the international pressure that led, eventually, to negotiation between the guerrillas and the government and a reduction in the power of the army—in Stoll's words, "quite an achievement" (278).

8. In the 1990s Rigoberta Menchú became a powerful leader for reconciliation between a wide cross section of constituencies in Guatemala and was considered a possible candidate for presidency of the country.

There are several factual and interpretive points that Stoll disputes with Menchú and to which Menchú has responded:

1. Testimonies from other Guatemalans indicate that Rigoberta Menchú's brother was not burned alive (after being tortured and before being killed) and that Menchú herself was not present when his body was dumped in the street outside Chajul. Menchú responds that her testimony repeats the firsthand account her mother gave her and that, until she is presented with the evidence of her brother's body itself, she will continue to believe her mother. Independent human rights records do record the public burning of indigenous people by the army in Chajul at roughly the same period.[8]

2. Based on conversations with neighbors and archives in the national land office, Stoll argues that Rigoberta Menchú's father was

not involved in a land dispute with Ladinos but with relatives of Rigoberta Menchú's mother, the Tums. Rigoberta Menchú responds that her family believed that Ladinos had secretly bought the land from some of the Quiché and were using their Quiché names in the dispute as a front for land they owned. Although Stoll elaborates disputes between indigenous Guatemalans over land, he does not mention that the vast majority of land in Guatemala is in the hands of a tiny minority of Ladino elite and that only 10 percent of rural families have enough land to live on (62).

3. Stoll argues that Rigoberta Menchú was a student in a boarding school for three years, an experience she does not mention in her 1982 oral testimony. Menchú responds that she did not speak about the school in 1982 to protect it from reprisals by the army. (Stoll mentions that the school was surrounded at various times by the army, that students were interrogated, and that Menchú's best friend at the school was killed by the army–thus making Menchú's silence credible.) Menchú also explains that she was on a charity scholarship at the school that only allowed her three hours of classes per day, and the rest of her time was spent cleaning the school as a servant.

4. Stoll claims that Rigoberta Menchú's brother Nicolás could not have died from malnutrition as she claims in her testimonial because he met her brother Nicolás alive and well in Guatemala. Rigoberta explains that her father was married twice and named two different sons "Nicolás," a common tradition among indigenous Guatemalans. She maintains that it was the older Nicolás who did, indeed, die of malnutrition.

5. Stoll can find no evidence of the death of "Petrona Chona" on the coffee plantation he believes that Rigoberta Menchú might have worked on (Rigoberta Menchú reports Petrona Chona's killing by the landowner's son when she refuses his amorous advances). Stoll does find evidence of the death of a "Pascuala Xoná Chomo" whose husband was accused of killing her based on rumors of a relationship with the landowner's son.

6. Stoll can find no specific evidence supporting Rigoberta Menchú's claim of having worked on coffee or sugar plantations or as a maid in the capital. Aside from wondering how Menchú could have fit these activities in with everything else she was doing, Stoll offers

no evidence to refute Menchú's account. He corroborates that many indigenous Guatemalans do work in these plantations and that Menchú's description of working conditions is accurate. Menchú describes these conditions as abject, exploitative, abusive, and violent.

7. Stoll blames the revolutionary guerrillas for the violence of the army. He sites several instances where the Guatemalan army was helpful to native Guatemalans, yet he does not dispute human rights reports that blame the army for the murder of a hundred thousand innocent indigenous Guatemalans.

8. Stoll believes that Rigoberta Menchú's testimonial portrays indigenous Guatemalans as more sympathetic to the guerrilla movement than they actually were. He bases his belief on interviews nearly ten years after the events Menchú describes. This is a point of contention that scholars more qualified than I respond to in other essays in this book. Yet, it seems obvious to me that after ten years of unbelievably harsh repression of indigenous people by the Guatemalan army—a period during which any mention of sympathy or support for guerrillas led to almost certain death not just of individuals, but also of entire families and villages—it is not surprising that Stoll does not interview many indigenous Guatemalans who tell him of their support for armed rebellion.

Teaching the Conflicts

In comparison with the overall picture of violence in Guatemala, David Stoll's concern over obviously minor factual points may seem unbalanced, even misplaced, yet, in his view these discrepencies are important precisely because they led readers, he assumes, to believe that indigenous Guatemalans enthusiastically joined guerrillas in a revolutionary response to their oppression. After working extensively with students and teachers studying Menchú's testimony, I am convinced that Stoll is mistaken in his assumption and that, indeed, upon reading Menchú's story, students are likely to have the opposite reaction. North American students do not understand why Rigoberta Menchú does not portray indigenous Guatemalans as more assertive, more ready to fight back, and even more eager to join armed revolutionary movements. Regardless of the degree to which Stoll is correct about the attitudes of Guatemalan peasants (and, he may indeed be quite incorrect, as scholars in this book point out), many teachers report, along with Stacy Schlau, that

> [w]hat generated the most heated debate (with many quite vocal students arguing against my position) was the notion, to which many firmly held for at least the first two-thirds of the book and several classes, that Quiché parents and elders were teaching indigenous children resignation and thereby contributed in a very real sense to their oppression. After all, doesn't telling infants that they are going to suffer throughout their lives condemn them to that suffering? (180)

Andrea Smith describes working hard to help her students understand the reluctance of the Quiché to fight back.

> As we read and discussed, the student reactions seemed to evolve, and I noticed many were getting angry at the Indians for, as they saw it, not sticking up for themselves. My students had a difficult time understanding why the native people seemed, as they saw it, "unable to help themselves." One student questioned, "Why do the Indians continue to live in shacks with no walls or floors?" Stephanie [coteaching with Smith] and I began to turn their questions around, "Why would they live like that?" We trusted that the students could find answers to their own questions, and, as a class, we began to question everything Rigoberta and the Indians did. We tried to think about the situation from the viewpoint of the Quiché. In this way we found that students could better understand Rigoberta's situation and empathize with her struggle.[9]

In a move typical of teachers of Menchú's testimonial, Andrea Smith uses the reluctance of the Quiché to engage in violence to help American students gain a perspective on the violence in the media and in their own communities:

> Students were glad to see the title of this chapter [Self-Defense in the Village]. Now they thought they'd finally see a little action by the good guys. But, it ended up that the students just laughed. Living in 1998 as sophomores in a high school where two guns have already been confiscated this year and fights are an everyday occurrence, Rigoberta's methods of self-defense seemed like child's play.
> "Why don't they use guns?"
> "Why don't they use guns?" I threw back.
> "Because they don't have any and can't afford any."
> "Why else? How many in this class would feel comfortable using a gun?" Only a few raised their hands and we began a discussion of how guns are viewed within the value system of the Quiché culture. (Ibid.)

By reading Rigoberta Menchú's testimony, students may come to understand more clearly why revolutionary movements exist and why Guatemalans, for instance, might join such movements, yet one reason this testimony is effective with North American students is that Menchú carefully describes her decision not to join her sisters in the armed struggle, insisting instead that "the whole truth" is not found in Marxism and stressing the importance of the Bible and her Christian faith as aids in her struggle.

Gerald Graff has urged us to "teach the conflicts,"[10] and the conflicts between representations of violence that our students are normally exposed to and that they encounter when reading *I, Rigoberta Menchú* are just one of the many important conflicts Menchú's testimony can lead them to explore. There may be classrooms where reading David Stoll's book along with Menchú's testimonial might be a relevant inquiry; advanced courses specifically focused on revolutionary movements in Latin America might be truly engaged by the devil's advocate position that Stoll assumes.[11] Yet, exploring the interpretive point he wishes to make about indigenous participation in guerrilla movements is likely to distract from the main issues that arise in most classrooms. For teachers who want to explore the topic of "political correctness" and/or the supposed domination of the academy by liberal scholars, it seems to me that there are other books with a wider frame of reference that might raise the issues or stimulate a broader discussion in more effective ways.

The extensive and inflated press that Stoll's book has received is another matter and, of course, it would be easy to introduce a copy of the *New York Times* article or a similar piece into a classroom reading of Menchú's testimonial. Stephen Benz has commented:

> It was interesting to me as we edited the book *[Teaching and Testimony]* to note how many teachers in different disciplines had struggled with students who just couldn't accept Rigoberta's story. Stoll seems to be the apotheosis of the response—and no doubt many of those students will take comfort in his arguments. We as teachers need to take advantage of the situation by bringing Stoll into the classroom and subjecting his argument to scrutiny—doing unto his tale what he wants to do to Rigoberta's. One advantage of this is that in contesting Stoll we will not seem to be directly "attacking" those students who struggle with Rigoberta's story—which is an uncomfortable pedagogical position to be in.
> (E-mail correspondence, March 1999)

Bringing a copy of the *New York Times* article or portions of Stoll's book into class should also be accompanied by responding pieces, perhaps chapters of this volume. Given the controversy, it would certainly be wise for teachers to at least read Stoll's book–as well as this volume—so that they are well informed about the controversy and can direct students to more information when the topic arises.

The needs, purposes, and contexts for teaching Rigoberta Menchú's testimony are diverse and widely varied. Central to them is addressing American ignorance and misunderstanding about Guatemala, Latin America, the third world, and contemporary Native Americans. Exploring distortions, stereotypes, and gaps in American news reporting is also a vital part of teaching Menchú's testimonial. Yet it also seems to me that there are many more effective ways to address these questions than to involve students in a reading of Stoll's research or the controversy it generated. Most teachers who carefully examine Rigoberta Menchú's testimonial will not, and should not, feel obligated to include Stoll's research or the publicity it has generated in their classrooms.

Testimony and Respect

> "This is my testimony," Menchú declares in the text's opening lines, "I didn't learn it from a book." The case for her readers is different, given our good fortune. We are to learn it from a book.
> —John Willinsky (in Carey-Webb and Benz, *Teaching and Testimony*, 331)

> No one has the right or the authority to deny the pain that her heart has felt and continues to feel.
> —Statement released by the Rigoberta Menchú Tum Foundation, 1999

David Stoll's book has occasioned a variety of ill-informed and vicious attacks by right-wing commentators and created a climate in which teaching Menchú's testimony has become a suspect activity. Advertisements taken out in campus newspapers have publicly accused professors who use her testimony of "perpetuating and defending a fraud." The PBS talk show the *McLaughlin Group* has labeled teachers who use Menchú's testimony "blatant liars." Charles Krauthammer, in an editorial in *Time* magazine (October 4, 1999), called professors who defended

Menchú's version of the events "slavish academics" justifying a "brazen confabulator." And so on. While casting aspersions at Menchú, scholars, and teachers who use her story in the classroom, these attacks do not critically investigate Stoll's claims, consider the complexity of pedagogical issues, or, above all, acknowledge the realities that Rigoberta Menchú's testimony conveys.

Yet, teachers have not taught Menchú's testimony because doing so would be easy or noncontroversial. Indeed, teachers who have brought her testimony into North American classrooms are not seeking easy truths. They have intentionally stepped beyond prepackaged curriculum and the canon of approved literary works. They want to add multiple sources and perspectives to student understanding. Far from being "politically correct," they understand that truth telling may mean challenging complacency and political orthodoxy. Indeed, these are precisely the reasons why teachers have brought Menchú's testimonial into the classroom in the first place. Far from being attacked, their efforts should be lauded and their pedagogy recognized as critical, courageous, and highly ethical.

More than two decades after a twenty-three-year-old Rigoberta Menchú told her story, despite challenges, attacks, and negative publicity, her testimonial remains an excellent, provocative, and most credible classroom resource. It is a work to approach thoughtfully, carefully, and with respect. Joseph Bruchac, an Abenaki poet, storyteller, and teacher of Native American literature, stresses the importance of non-native teachers listening attentively to Native people. Although sensitivity must not silence discussion, Bruchac also advises:

> Much of Native America's traditional culture is living in the strongest sense of that word. Revealing that culture to the uninitiated is sacrilegious. A good teacher of Native American literature needs to know enough to be able to know which works need to be shown special respect. I cannot emphasize that word respect strongly enough. In some cases it may even mean *not* discussing something. This is a hard direction for people with the western mindset to follow, that western mindset which says, "Tell it all, show it all, explain it all." I feel that those with that mindset would be better off avoiding the teaching of Native American literature.[12]

At its best, the teaching of testimony helps students regard the voice of others and honor the way that those others share their reality. An awareness that the most disempowered can speak out may give students hope that their voice, too, might be valuable. Working with blue-collar and small-town students in western Massachusetts, June Kuzmeskus writes:

> I know many of my students struggle with problems that limit their effectiveness as students and truly mar their lives. They confront problems they feel they can't speak of, that compel them, they think, to suffer silently. The courses I teach provide a forum and an academic validation for consideration of a wide range of expression–painful as well as joyful. Within this approach, testimonial literature has value for my students far beyond the classroom. It provides a much needed signal not to give up on themselves or on others. It inspires them to reach out and speak for themselves, to generalize from their own experience. Using testimonial as a model teaches students first to name their hardship, to contextualize it, and then to reach out through their writing to activate themselves and others. In this way, my students begin to reduce their isolation and harness the power inherent in the commonalities and compassion to be found both among their classmates and in the world beyond the school doors. (124)

Sometimes adults can relearn priorities from children. Teachers who work with younger students have a special opportunity to gain from their students' clarity and passion. In particular, two responses to Rigoberta Menchú's testimonial stay with me; both are from high school students. The first is from a ninth grader and the second is a letter to Rigoberta Menchú from a student who is learning Spanish (who wrote in Spanish that is translated here):

> I have been, to put it bluntly, disgusted. What happened to these people—and still is happening—makes me sick. No government anywhere in the world should have the power to do what they did and are doing.[13]

> Rigoberta, su historia me tocó mucho. Su vida era muy difícil y yo creo que ha abierto los ojos de los pueblos. Su historia ha estado una inspiración para mí. Yo pienso que muchas personas en los Estados Unidos dan por supuesto las vidas que ellos tienen. Que ellos no se dan cuenta de que tienen mucho, y otras personas no tienen nada. Nosotros nunca paramos a pensar acerca de esas que sean menos fortunadas. Les toca a unas personas muy fuerte con las cosas que Ud. dice en su libro. Si Ud. puede vencer la adversidad yo puedo manejar todos mis pequeños problemas. Espero que algún día yo esté fuerte como Ud. Yo le admiro muchísimo.—Su amiga.

Rigoberta, your story touched me greatly. Your life was very difficult and I believe that you have opened people's eyes. Your story has been an inspiration to me. I think that many people in the United States take their lives for granted. They don't realize how much they have, and that other people have nothing. We never stop to think about those who are less fortunate. You touch some people very powerfully by the things you say in your book. If you can overcome adversity, I can manage all of my small problems. I wish that someday I could be as strong as you. I admire you very much.—Your friend.[14]

Notes

1. Unless otherwise specified, page numbers refer to Allen Carey-Webb and Stephen Benz, eds. *Teaching and Testimony: Rigoberta Menchú in the North American Classroom* (Albany: State University of New York Press, 1996).

2. Stoll's animus toward Menchú is clearly ideological and may stem from remarks Menchú has made about Christian evangelicals. In an interview granted to Richard Wright in 1990, during a visit to Canada, Menchú raises objections to "a veritable invasion from the fundamentalist sects–evangelicals closely tied to the American right.... They are directly attacking the roots of the Maya" (Wright, *Stolen Continents: The "New World" through Indian Eyes* [Toronto: Penguin, 1992]; quoted in John Willinsky, in Carey-Webb and Benz, *Teaching and Testimony,* 347).

3. Arthur Applebee, "Stability and Change in the High School Canon." *English Journal* 81.5 (November 1992): 27–32.

4. Allen Carey-Webb, Teresa Anderson, Matt Kemp, Jessica Miller, and Andrea Smith, "Testimony from the Classroom: High School Contexts for *I, Rigoberta Menchú,*" in *Latin American Women's Testimonial,* ed. Isabell Dulfano and Linda Maier, forthcoming, under review at University of Arizona Press.

5. Ibid.

6. Ibid.

7. David Stoll, *Rigoberta Menchú and the Story of All Poor Guatemalans* (Boulder, Colo.: Westview Press, 1999), viii.

8. See Rarihokwats, *Guatemala!: The Horror and the Hope* (York, Pa.: Four Arrows, 1982).

9. Carey-Webb et al., "Testimony from the Classroom."

10. Gerald Graff, *Beyond the Culture Wars: How Teaching the Conflicts Can Revitalize American Education* (New York: Norton, 1992).

11. Of course the teaching of Menchú's testimonial does not necessarily depend on its "truth," as Michael Berube points out by apt ironic comparison. "Despite the fact that some of the events narrated in the book are either untrue or impossible to verify, and despite the fact that the author engages in what many historians have found to be whitewashing, self-aggrandizement, and outright falsehood, I think the book remains important to the history of anti-imperialist nationalism in this hemisphere, and I think its considerable intellectual and emotional appeal is not contingent on its status as a factual record. For these reasons I will continue to teach the

autobiography of Benjamin Franklin" (Michael Berube, professor, University of Illinois (posted *Chronicle of Higher Education* bulletin board 1/14, 3:40 P.M., E.S.T.).

12. Joseph Bruchac, "Teaching Native American Literature," in *Rethinking Classrooms: Teaching for Equity and Social Justice* (Milwaukee: Rethinking Schools, 1994), 149.

13. Carey-Webb et al., "Testimony from the Classroom."

14. Ibid.

Between Silence and Lies

Rigoberta Va

Ileana Rodríguez

> It was better to deceive her and tell her that Justino was badly wounded;
> but the truth had already spread, what they had done to Justino was
> something terrible: his body was found in one place and his head in
> another, stuck on a road marker.... They sliced his head off with one
> blow just when he turned his back to them.... And they say that when
> Doña Lupe reached the road where her son lay, she only shut her
> eyes.... That she didn't shed a single tear.... Anyone could say that it
> was hardness of heart, but if you know these people, you know it's not
> that ... It's a way of gaining courage to live what remains of life.[1]

I have been studying the Guatemala highland for some time. I am very
familiar with the area studied by David Stoll located along the Sierra de
los Cuchumatanes. My point of departure was Utatlán, the old capital
city of the Maya-Quiché, a mile or so away from Santa Cruz del Quiché,
the Spanish city where the former Utlatecans were resettled in the first
year of the Spanish Conquest. This is an old Dominican area where Dominican friars established their first haciendas, as they did in Patzizé. It
was from Santa Cruz del Quiché that Fray Bartolomé de Las Casas, in
collaboration with some of the old members of the ruling indigenous
elites, probably the Caweks, organized his first excursions into Alta Verapaz, where some of the indigenous people had fled trying to escape
the Spanish Conquest, and where theater and performance, the first *jue-
gos* and *chirimías,* were used to lure the rebels back into subjection. The
collaboration between the former indigenous elites and the Spaniards
gave rise to a series of land grants and titles that in turn produced a

large bibliography of titles, one of the most famous being that of the Totonicapán. In that area many struggles occurred between Mercedarios, Franciscans, and Dominicans for the possessions of the land, and later on between hacienda grantees and religious orders for the governance of the indigenous people. The thematization of these legal struggles over land titles is revisited by Stoll in his book and taken to the present day where the main protagonists are *hacendados*, Ladinos, indigenous people, and state structures such as the INTA (National Institute for Agrarian Transformation) in its struggle with labor unions like CUC (Committee for Peasant Unity). As an Uspantán human rights activist citation states: "The problem is always that of land."[2]

I have also visited the area by car, driving from Guatemala City via Antigua, the first capital city of the Spanish empire in the Maya-Quiché territory, and then traveled up north via Sololá, another stopping point of the Spanish conqueror Pedro de Alvarado, where he fought the Tzu-tujiles. I have passed by Iximché, or Tecpàn-Guatemala, the old capital of the Maya-Cakchiquel, and then Chichicastenango, one of the most spectacular indigenous markets in Guatemala, with a church in whose atrium we can still witness the burning of copal and in whose aisles we can smell the rose blossoms in homage to the saints that still today hear prayers in indigenous languages. I have been able to experience first-hand the rugged topography described by Pedro de Alvarado and re-peated by all the subsequent bibliographies, including Stoll's: the deep ravines, the impassable abysses unfit for the horses that served as both war machines and farm tractors, slopes that Stoll tells us are cultivated by indigenous people under duress. I have seen indigenous populations walk the roads, and have been able to observe the preservation of the milpa structure of the land in some parts of the steep terrain. I visited Santa Cruz del Quiché with a friend from the MINUGUA (United Nations Verification Commission in Guatemala) that was overseeing the transition from the insurgency into the period of peace. I was in the terrain and I bore witness to the international army that was in Santa Cruz on one of the Sundays when the *guerrilleros* were surrendering their weapons.

On the map that Stoll provides at the beginning of his text, "The Quiché Department and Environs," I can see the little town of Ixcán, where Jesuits and Maryknolls together tried to settle the land and build self-subsistent communities. Ricardo Falla eloquently speaks about the type of agricultural social experiment they attempted to create and what were the results.[3] But all in all, Stoll's area is the environs of the heartland, the place where everything colonial and imperial began, an area well studied by the most outstanding Mayanists such as Las Casas, Ximénez, Remesal, Vásquez, Fuentes y Guzmán, Juarros, Stephens, Tedlock, Carmack, Recinos, Villacorta, Garza, and Friedel.[4] I am sure Goyo Yic, Gaspar Ilóm, and María Tecún, the living characters of Miguel Angel Asturias's *Hombres de maíz* also lived in this area, which forms the lines of Guatemala's hand.[5]

Stoll in Context: Colonial and Postcolonial Bibliographies

The merit of David Stoll's text on Rigoberta Menchú's testimonial is that it is situated within a long bibliographical tradition. This tradition begins with the arrival of Pedro de Alvarado to the same area Stoll is investigating. In Alvarado's attempt to describe his route to Hernán Cortés, he initiates a tradition characterized by obfuscation, approximation, and invention that Maya studies forcefully try to unravel. In the twentieth century, following the tradition of the anonymous *Isagoge* and *Libro Viejo*, Adrián Recinos, together with José Antonio Villacorta, tried to retrace Alvarado's steps not only with the intention of outlining his route with geographical accuracy, but also in order to demonstrate that the area was densely populated.[6] Ruth Bunzel has studied the land-tenure systems in an attempt to understand the survival of the milpas and to further the survival of the social indigenous organization to this day.[7] Other scholars such as Robert Carmack have read the documents in an attempt to reconstruct the social, historical, and cultural dimensions of Maya civilization. W. George Lovell has studied with accuracy the area of the Cuchumatanes.[8] David Freidel, Linda Schele, and Joy Parker have studied Maya cosmology.[9] Denis Tedlock and Barbara Tedlock have studied the languages in order to unravel the meaning of the Maya universe.[10]

Stoll uses this same measure of tedious documentation to prove step-by-step that the testimonial rendered by Rigoberta Menchú to Elisabeth Burgos-Debray is a kind of "red book" or "guerrilla communist manifesto" of the EGP (Guerrilla Army of the Poor), and hence, it does not speak for "all poor Guatemalans." According to Stoll, Rigoberta's testimonial is a manual that demonstrates the manipulation of the indigenous population by Marxist guerrillas. Thus, Stoll's aim falls squarely within bibliographical traditions that try to prove that the testimonials rendered by some members of the indigenous populations are not quite accurate. In the process of writing his book, however, what is most important, and what I want to underscore, is how he repeats a thematics that is five hundred years old and in which he is unable to discern between misunderstandings (that which translations are unable to account for), silences (that which informants are not ready to tell), and lies (that which informants believe the interrogator wants to hear). And although I must credit him with writing with some awareness of this phenomenon, his goal takes him far afield, where I find the second merit of his book, and that is to conversely prove the difficulties of organizing communities in the areas covered by his own research. The kinds of atrocities he recounts are the same as those Rigoberta and her family experienced. Furthermore, Stoll seems to move swiftly and under protection within a hidden geographical zone that was forbidden to most of us, a terrain that would have cost many of us our lives. In this respect, he reminds me of two previous research moments, one represented by the Guatemalan Francisco Antonio de Fuentes y Guzmán, and the other by the French priest Brasseur de Bourbourg.

In my current study of topographies I say that Fuentes y Guzmán, who was close to many conquest-marking events, tells us how he obtains reliable information. First, he has access to *cabildo* archives and the "papers of his elders."[11] As a *corregidor* and war captain of the Totonicapán and Huehuetenango districts (75), he was able to peruse the documents having the exact frozen word of archives (history) at his disposal, hoping that "God will open the roads so that the secrets of some archives that today deny [his] prayers will be open and forthright" (55). In addition, Fuentes y Guzmán is privy to the oral information of his relatives, such as Jacinto del Castillo, his uncle, a provincial of the region, and to Bernal Díaz. He also reads other chronicles such as that of José de Acosta.

His method of knowledge is that of an *oidor,* a hearer, and that of a surveyor, a seer. As a caballero-captain, he enjoys mobility, and can directly inspect the fields—both farmlands and battlefields. However, he confronts the same problems that baffled earlier *oidores.* Once the threatening postures have all been played out, perception itself, seeing and hearing, is invested with an epistemic doubt. As in Matthew Gregory Lewis's appraisal of former slaves in the Caribbean plains, Fuentes y Guzmán cannot discern how much of the telling is mere mimicry, playacting, performance.[12] An infinite process of interpretation ensues, which often regresses to the mere enumeration of sites, people, and habits.[13] In order to distinguish what is accurate from what is not, he measures all informational sources against his ideal of the most reliable informant: a reliable informant is an educated, religious, experienced, Spanish caballero, one firmly and legally instructed by religious people, learned and experienced, or by Christian caballeros of certified credibility. He also tries using his knowledge of Amerindian languages and grammar to trace the etymological roots of words. Although he can trace some etymologies and genealogies with a certain degree of accuracy, he is forever suspicious of "Indians" who, in his opinion, do not entirely tell everything. As Richard Madden said about the Caribbean slaves, "they are addicted to stealing, prone to dissimulation, and inclined to dishonesty," and "unless a negro has an interest in telling the truth, he always lies."[14]

But now, can we ask where doubt comes from? In Fuentes y Guzmán and perhaps in Stoll, it comes from the fact that Amerindians' cultures are still not subdued. Fear props up the military notion of the Amerindian: on the flip side of dumbness lies cunning. The simple ascription of brilliance or idiocy to indigenous groups marks the moments and types of resistance. What is observed as a war stratagem carries into the second moment of resistance: secrecy, guarded counsel, mystery, reunions, the hidden. Here is one example of the battle of Sacatepequez, which Fuentes y Guzmán describes lavishly:

> All among them was meetings, discussions, council, and intrigue, and all doubts on the part of our men; until, arriving at the end of the third day, their secretive and repeated conventicle burst forth in anger. . . . with raucous shouting, they arrived to our first group of guards. . . . fighting like beasts, they had taken the tremor to signify the anger of their god Camanelon . . . appearing very angry and sad because the Sacatepeques faithful had distrusted his power and rendered all his lands to those of Castilla, who came to subdue their freedom. (81)

In the same tradition, in his attempt to counteract Fuentes y Guzmán's indictments, Severo Martínez Pelàez writes his book *La patria del criollo* (The criollo's fatherland) and *Motines de indios* (Indian mutinies), where he writes the indigenous history against the grain of *criollo* historiographies.[15]

Aware of their location between secrets and lies, Mayanist archaeologists and ethnohistorians plainly state that the rendering of Mayan societies by Spanish documents is sketchy. Maya scholars expect little from them.[16] For them, Spanish interest in Mayan societies limited itself to matters of government and the extraction of wealth. Hence it paid attention to political geographies and trade networks—that is, to those institutions that benefited Spanish ends. The net result is the existence of parallel histories, ones that only rarely mention even the existence of the other.[17]

We are destined to remain baffled by these questions. Populations and depopulation, transplantation, and mobilization of populations then follow two necessities: the necessities of war as cultural resistance, and the necessity of secrecy hampering the organization of labor.[18] Reading against the grain of these Hispanic texts, and into the stone documents that form part of the indigenous culture, an opposite tradition is established by anthropological work, which tries to prove cultural continuities and bridge the gap between ancient and modern and postmodern indigenous societies. It is through the studies of sites, agricultural patterns, and religious rituals, as well as by the reading and deciphering of glyphs and the reconstruction of monuments, that anthropologists try to reconstruct a "lost" world.

Without any question, in the confusion created by the narrative intersections of cross-culturation, indigenous documents contribute a consistent obscuring of referents. Doris Sommer has insightfully perceived this moment in her readings and hearing of Rigoberta. Referring to Rigoberta's pauses, she states that they work in two directions because it seems quite clear that Rigoberta's secrets are doubly strategic. They stop avid readers in their appropriative tracks, tracks that threaten to overstep the narrator's authority by assuming that the textual terrain is unobstructed and accessible to their mastery. Also, the secrets serve to whet academic appetites by producing intrigue that can turn into productive, collaborative, political desire.[19]

These strategic secrets can be interpreted according to different epistemological frames as impossibility, unwillingness, or both. It is simple common sense to presume that during the first moments of the Spanish/Maya-Quiché confrontation, it was impossible to fully and competently translate both languages and ways of thinking. It is not hard to imagine either that translating them was intended or desired. Truly, writing indigenous cultures and epistemologies in a precariously known and unmastered Spanish, under the vigilance of authority, is a quite maddening proposition. This situation is repeated today in the case of Rigoberta. Arturo Taracena says that his work on *I, Rigoberta Menchú* was "on the grammatical coherence, everything having to do with syntax, gender, number, and tenses, which Rigoberta did not dominate very well then. The truth is that Rigoberta spoke Spanish very poorly; she was fluent in her expression, but her grammar was very poor."[20] But to the technical impossibility must always be added the indigenous people's unwillingness to speak about themselves, given the overbearing and obscure presence of the threatening Christian (or, in the case of Rigoberta, military) context. Obscurity, or secrecy, then, is simultaneously a technology and its effect; it is a way for indigenous peoples to renegotiate the continuation of their culture by submerging it. Again, if knowledge is power, doesn't the denial of knowledge constitute a counterpower? Can we not say the same about Stoll's gathering of data?

However, in the early indigenous testimonials (as in that of Rigoberta as attested by Arturo Taracena and Elisabeth Burgos-Debray) there are other markers that make their documents appear quite trustworthy. For one, the strong presence of their coerced biculturalism—a reason why it is essential for Stoll to prove Rigoberta's bilingual education. The ambivalent literacy, visible in the enjoining of names that indicate a mixture of words, the misunderstanding of where one word ends and the other begins, as in the *Memorial of Sololá* calling Alvarado Tonatiuh (or Tonadiu) Avilantaro (a combination of Alvarado and Adelantado), gives us access to a world in which at least two epistemes are being interwoven. Important as a sign of defense and preservation is the placing of events within indigenous chronologies such as Day 1, Ganel (February 20, 1524) (Luján 75), the day the Maya-Quichés were destroyed by the Spaniards. In this same order, the presence of indigenous terms such as *calpulli,* and the plotting of indigenous visions and symbols within the indigenous peoples' own core belief system, or in the same sense blending the flying wings of Tecúm with the appearance of a white girl and/or dove that protected Tonadiu, is another telling sign.

The testimonial betrays these doubts of adjacency. What to say and how to say it is the question. A process of second-guessing is being suggested. The Quiché informants must guess what the Spanish compilers

want. They must be careful with their words. Are they to trust these foreigners? What should they keep to themselves, and preserve for their
own self-defense? How do they preserve their culture and simultaneously render a testimonial amenable to the interrogating and prosecut-
ing Christian (or counterinsurgency-induced) epistemes? Assuring these
evangelists that their religious teachings have taken hold is a principal
concern in these narratives, but so is the preservation of what is their
own. The informant's own Maya-Quiché history of resistance and heroism and the Spanish religion are mixed within his own troubled consciousness, all amalgamated with grief. Negotiation and the awareness
of imminent danger are, then, the context of testimonial production.
The lack of language and cultural parameters adds trouble to what is
already an untenable situation, namely, that of what to say and what
not to say, or whether to say simply what they want to hear, to express
oneself properly, or simply to hide it all away. Theories of transculturation must take these dilemmas seriously.

The main tendency of indigenous documents to obscure the referent
(Inga Clendinnen asserts that some passages of the books of Chilam
Balam are totally unintelligible),[21] or our modern incapacity to read
them as they were meant to be read when they were initially encoded
by the culture, is a noticeably common trait that would fit a tradition
equally characterized by encores, that is, a recalcitrant repetition of the
initial events and their reinterpretations. Nevertheless, a caveat is in order.
The Spaniards are establishing a dominant tradition. They had already
conquered and dominated the Mexican highlands, and having covered
the terrain all the way to Yucatán and now the Guatemalan highlands,
their prose is very assertive. It displays a sense of direction and purpose
that is lacking in the indigenous documents, while still being much more
knowledgeable and authoritative with regard to their own matters, which
are obscured. Assertive ignorance and intentional obscurity, then, set
the foundational rhetorical parameters that document the traversed
physical and cultural geographies that plotted the first as well as the last
confrontations.

This tradition is initiated by Don Pedro de Alvarado himself, and by
the Maya-Quiché and Cakchiquel who write the early chronicles and
titles. After them, the territories are physically, politically, historically,
and academically cross-fertilized, and the story is repeated by all the
major Spanish chroniclers, by *criollos,* by independentist and postcolo-

nial historians, until it becomes the province of contemporary fiction in the works of Miguel Ángel Asturias, Luis Cardoza y Aragón, Mario Monteforte Toledo, Arturo Arias, and Mario Roberto Morales, to name just a few. Referring to this enormous confusion, Remesal states:

> Because this matter is so full of random accounts that are so far from giving pleasure in their understanding, with either their substance or their manner, it quite fatigues and exhausts one to read such disordered things, and it is the same to transcribe them from the memoirs or the books of the natives, or from those that the aforementioned authors had written, as it is for the most disconcerted thinking of the world to simply imagine them.[22]

The documents produced at this time burst into the maddening confusion of the aforementioned names. The Spanish phoneticization of Quiché place-names, nouns of habitations, the mandatory political will to rename such places, and the confusion of *pueblos* as peoples with *pueblos* as towns are all traits of the historiographies of confrontation. They correspond to the politics of location, relocation, and the redrawing of jurisdictions. They concern government and are the praxis of wartime conquerors. On the other side of the divide runs a countertradition that reconstructs the destructured sites in accordance with indigenous markers. This heritage brings up the juxtaposition of names in an effort to resituate indigenous and Spanish locations and names adjacently, allowing one to simultaneously read both worlds. What is important about this collective endeavor is the determination to retrieve past cultural topographies, and to thus validate the indigenous civilizations that inhabited these places before the Spaniards came, enabling the circulation of their reconstruction. The availability of different spellings for the names of one and the same sites is, in this regard, very telling of the current struggle for the divisions and retentions of the land. It is also a way of signaling the imposition of the power of both the Spanish and their language, whose phoneticization of indigenous words is endowed to posterity. As an example of the realization of this dilemma, we can quote Quetzil Castañeda, who, in his "Note on Orthography," states:

> I retain the use of multiple spellings of words—such as "Cuculcán," "Kukulcan," and "K'uk'ulkan" for what is more commonly known by the Nahuatl word "Quetzalcoatl," or by the English "Feathered Serpent." These variations are maintained as traces of the writers' political, cultural, ethnic, linguistic, historical, and other locations.[23]

With regard to cultural genealogies, Ximénez tells us that to understand origins and epochs is difficult, because the Maya-Quiché did not take care to indicate time periods. They marked periods by the names of their kings. By inference, Ximénez calculates their origins to around 1054 A.D., giving each one of the kings a period of forty years of government. He informs us that from the time of Balam–Quitzé, and then from his time to the other three kings, they count thirteen generations. When the Spaniards arrived, Tecúm–Tepepul (*amontonada grandeza*/heaped greatness, majesty, boiling like water) was their king. Further on comes Ximénez's list of kings. (The route offered in note 22 follows Tedlock's version of the *Popol Vuh*.)[24] Here we can see how, as J. Hillis Miller states, genealogies, "far from being a somewhat boring series of adventitious 'begats'... have a crucial function. They testify to the continuity of... culture. Its unbroken tradition is demonstrated by the continuity of its bloodlines."[25]

Of Lies and Truths

I could not avoid the localization of Stoll's book within a bibliographical tradition he follows at a moment when the confrontation between the Guatemalan guerrillas and the army reintroduces in the region the thematization of conflict. Specifically, what is it about Rigoberta's testimonial that Stoll wants to straighten out? First and foremost, he wants to speak for those Rigoberta neglects, and those she neglects are the large majority of the indigenous population of the Quiché and its environs who, when interviewed by Stoll, either obscured, cast doubts, or told him the opposite of what Rigoberta states in her testimonial. The question for the reader is to decide who is speaking for all poor people in Guatemala. We must here invoke Foucault's idea of "situated knowledges" and Spivak's injunction on "speaking for" and/or "speaking about" to grant Stoll what he advocates—namely, that he is speaking for, or about, the large majority of the indigenous people of the area—and choose whom to believe.

But now, how does Stoll proceed to prove Rigoberta's lies? He challenges the concrete details of what he believes she is inventing. The most salient inventions are reiterated throughout his text. I want to highlight two of them. The first refers to the death of Rigoberta's family—her brother, father, and mother—which brings Stoll to speak about the land-tenure system of Guatemala in the area of the Cuchumatanes. The second concerns Rigoberta's denial of her schooling. The first observation serves Stoll as the entry point to what is his fundamental argument, and perhaps his weakest point, namely, that rather than holding the government and the army responsible for the Guatemalan holocaust, what is important is to recognize the regional interethnic and family struggles and animosities that Rigoberta ignores or bypasses and that are part and parcel of the cultures of the indigenous peasants in the Guatemalan highlands. In the 1960s, this type of thinking was known as blaming the victim. The second observation serves Stoll to discredit the role of the church in relation to the overall insurgency in Guatemala.

In Stoll's view, Rigoberta altogether eschews the Indian–Indian interaction, which enables him to make a statement on transethnic variables and dilemmas that concern not only ontological identities but also land rights and merchant occupations of the inhabitants of the area. Stoll also holds Rigoberta responsible for neglecting other important variables of analysis such as ignoring the ancestral history narrated by liberals and conservatives, some of which I quoted earlier. On the flip side of his argument is the statement that what he says is true, or at least that his information is more reliable, because he is not associated with any political party (a fact that does not exempt him from partaking of the colonial imaginary). He knows better because, like Fuentes y Guzmán before him, he has had access to archives, books, travel, and conversation and hence his method and understanding of Guatemalan matters is more accurate. Here we have again and again the confrontation between oral and written traditions, and of living versus studying, Foucault's difference between wisdom and knowledge.

All that I have stated here is historical knowledge and puts Stoll in the bibliographical context that entitles him to be part of the field of debate. But where his argument really suffers is in his positioning himself against the guerrillas and their making Rigoberta their instrument. His excellent research and the knowledge he provides about the difficulties of organizing oppositions then lends itself to be read exactly in the same way he reads Rigoberta's testimonial, that is, as an instrument and propaganda on behalf of the other side of the divide. What could have been an excellent scholarly exercise in the unraveling of the difficulties of organizing populations, and even a theoretical position on hegemony and counterhegemony, becomes a piece of propaganda at worst, and at best, a sentimental writing of indigenous misrepresentation of indigenous people. Fortunately for both, prosecutor and accuser, their words fall within a huge bibliographical fund in which, as in the case of Fuentes y Guzmán, the anthropologist is judge and part, and the *oidor* of testimonials, the mediating voice of reason, one who under the pretext of positioning himself in an impartial position, is indeed accusing the other side of telling lies.

Lessons to Draw from Anthropological Research

We must, first of all, be grateful to Stoll for his fieldwork, the piecing together of information that was not possible to collect in times of insurgency and insurrection. When one does not have access to classified documents or cannot move freely within the territories of war, one cannot be absolutely certain of the reading of either side. I am interested in bringing back to the discussion the question of land titles and the play between CUC (Committee for Peasant Unity) and INTA (National Institute for Agrarian Transformation) as a way of debating the difficult question of transethnic relations immersed in the class struggles of colonial and postcolonial societies. This discussion, I would argue, is one of the most important ones for scholars interested in postinsurgency and postcommunist politics, avid to theorize the Restoration.

If Stoll were my only source of knowledge over land-tenure issues in Guatemala, the clearest knowledge he would imprint in my imagination is that the INTA, in spite of all its malfunctioning and corruption, was still the organization set up to settle accounts related to land disputes both among the indigenous families themselves and between what we consider indigenous people, Ladinos, and *hacendados*. In other words, INTA is perhaps a counterinsurgency structure, a means of neutralizing insurgent peasants not yet affiliated with the guerrillas. Knowing from my past readings that the land-tenure system was one of the main offensives launched by colonialism against the ruling Maya elites, and having read the accounts of the partitions and repartitions of land, as well as of the conundrums between a patrilineal ideology for land distribution and the antimercantile notion of partitioning and selling the land, it is easy to understand the difficulties INTA as well as CUC had to deal with—one of them being that of Vicente Menchú. My own take on this is that the discrepancies are between indigenous and capitalist land-tenure systems *tout court*.

On pages 26–27, Stoll narrates Vicente Menchú's troubles with his in-laws over the property of the land. In a typically tangled manner, Stoll's text leaves the reader unclear as to how the dispute between Vicente Menchú and his brother-in-law Antonio Tum Cotojá began, given that what is being litigated is 125 of the 2,753 hectares granted to Vicente. And it is not clear if these 125 hectares belonged to Tum Cotojá or to some Ladino family. What belongs to whom and where is an old question, so old it can be traced back to the *Popol Vuh*. But in addition to the difficulties of knowing in the past what belonged to which ruling elites, or which elites were favored by the Spaniards for collaborating with them, there is now added the discussion of ethnic categories that come to play a great part in this dispute. It is important to distinguish the ontological identities of the contenders because part of the importance of Stoll's and Rigoberta's discussions, as well as the discussion between the guerrilla contenders, is who is who, or rather, in the name of whom each one is speaking for or against.

Uspantán, the region where the Menchú-Tum-Cotojá live, is declared an agricultural frontier. The area is dominated by K'iche', which is the dominant indigenous group, but there are also Ladinos and Ixils who call the K'iche' *ula* (meaning "foreigners from other places"). The problem with this classification of people is that all of them seem to be hyphenated identities because it is very difficult to distinguish between Ladinos and indigenous people, between poverty-stricken peasants and *indios*, between the indigenous bourgeoisie and Ladinos. Here we repeat the same dilemmas of the nineteenth-century Ohioan geographer Geo Squier's classification of people, together with his dictum that when two races mix the most backward cannibalizes the most advanced, and therefore the category of mestizo is of no use; it is better to call them all Indians. However, that is not possible for Stoll, for he is already confronted with the modern insurgent imaginaries that romanticize peasants and make Mayan farmers rooted to the land. Thus mixtures, immigration, frontier agriculture, Ladinos, and Mayas all come to be mixed with German immigrants and the government in a total mélange of categories that, in the best of all cases, leads to a hybridization of methodologies, as Néstor García Canclini would advocate.

In the 1950s, Tax Sol raised very similar questions regarding ethnic identities. His original question concerns the universe scholars are trying to describe both in geographical terms and in types of population. The first question he asks is anthropological: What is the Indian culture? The second relates to the different interests of rural sociologists interested in finding the "major core of interest," "the basic culture of one type of Indian." Or, as he puts it, "how far the things which we can describe apply or do not apply to certain types of rural or *mestizo* cultures? A number of things apply to *Mestizo,* as well as to Indian."[26] Rural mestizos, non-Indian people, might have economic and technological things in common with Indians, but not social organization. Anthropologists are not interested in cities and factories either. Some Indians are not inserted into the market economy, some because they are small groups (e.g., the Lacandones), some because they have an unremarkable homogeneity of production. In some regions there are no markets but there are traders.

The types of criteria chosen, plus the nuances attributed to them, result in delimiting the population to be described within a very narrow geographic circumscription. Who is more Indian, what groups are more or less Ladinized is the question. Sometimes the area is defined by the type of loom used. The distinction between the foot versus the *tum* loom gives geographic precision. Others distinguish by the distribution of the land, such as plantation sites, because there the Indian is enmeshed in a commercial agricultural economy. Still others measure groups by the type of agricultural technology—for example, the digging stick economy.

We can see how the discussion is enmeshed in modernism and how what is found here is arrived at by using different criteria. What is obtained are similarities with other groups or other categories. For instance, when one considers the inhabitants of Panajachel, the fact that they produce almost exclusively for the market and that they do not grow any of the material for it, makes them more similar to specialized farmers in the United States. This exception applies to any other category, for instance, to differentiation between village and *municipio.* Jurisdictional divisions are related to concentration of populations and/or imaginary lines between rural communities, on one side of which there is some kind of labor different from the other. Distinctions are even drawn between landowning and sharecropping, or distinguishing as a milpa not the land but the product: the milpa is turned into corn.

After considering all these matters, it is easy to see why Stoll reads the story of the Menchús as a family feud, which in turn, I say, is immersed in a larger social feud. The larger context is that the Tums and Cotojás had acquired eight hundred hectares of forest as early as 1928 at a place called Laguna Danta while some terrain north of it, a ridge, was also public land. A slice of the ridge had been claimed by Vicente and his group of homesteaders. But there was a disputed boundary. The Tums considered the land on which Vicente had already built his house their own. Antonio Tum and Vicente Menchú were to fight over the property rights to this land.

Stoll's point is that regardless of the historical context or the corruption of the INTA, the romanticism and heroic view of the peasants must be dismantled and it must be recognized that in this particular instance, the feud was between peasants, or between indigenous people. It is not against Ladinos they are fighting, it is among themselves. Although he recognizes part of the land under litigation has also been granted to Ladinos, "the only disputed boundary was at the southeast corner, where a Ladino family claimed a narrow wedge of forty-five hectares that INTA subsequently adjudicated to Vicente" (27) but that the Tums considered to be their own. The corollary is political: (1) it is not true that "indigenous communities are more cohesive than non-indigenous ones"; and (2) it is not true that the peasants' most important conflicts are vertical, with external oppressors, such as plantation owners and state authorities. For Stoll, a heroic view of peasants blinds us to the possibility that they consider their main problem to be one another. It also blinds us to the possibility that "instead of resisting the state, peasants are using it against other members of their own social class" (31). But, it also blinds him, Stoll, to the heavy pressures exerted by the larger social milieu over defenseless peasants.

This is a well-known tactic, that of blaming the victims, that, in addition to revealing the poverty of politics in its commitment to oppression, really contributes little to the understanding of a situation in which popular insurrection, poverty, domination, and the penury of theory all contribute their share. There was nothing to be gained in those days by subtracting the state; but perhaps there is something to be gained now. Can we better explain the old argument on underdevelopment and "premodernity," on backwardness, by attributing the responsibilities to the petty internal struggles of the local alone? Can the truth really be found by researching a field that has been characterized by a millenarian fear imposed by colonialism, in an area where dissimulation and pretense can perhaps be the only way of sparing one's life, where a precarious bilingualism cannot really translate between cultures? Or is it really the point, as I believe it is, to debunk theories of revolution, show us how closely a life can be under surveillance even, or more so, when insurrection is over—a warning against any other text that might succeed the way Rigoberta's did?

Stoll has dedicated many years of his research to convincing us that "[w]e should not suppose that because there was a meeting in Vicente's villa, there was a meeting of minds. It cannot be assumed that guerrillas and villagers were candid about their respective objectives, let alone arrived at a shared understanding of what future cooperation would mean. The creation of a middle ground between two such different groups takes time" (122–23). Some of us keep believing that a meeting of minds is indispensable and that a shared understanding of what future cooperation would mean is a must for the working out of future political strategies. But that group, of which I am a part, is not ready to subtract the global from the local, neither to withdraw the intervention of the army nor to exonerate any of the other interests that have also come to bear on the destinies of the poor in Guatemala. Statism is still the condition of being of nations in their international relations, as is the condition of discipline formation. A North American colleague once told me that all ex-militants would be under surveillance for life because, he wisely warned, what is important during times of stasis is to figure out the new emerging forms of resistance. I find in Stoll's text a vivid example of that dictum. I find the advertisements run by a conservative think tank, the Center for the Study of Popular Culture, based in Los Angeles, in student newspapers at six leading universities attacking professors who have defended Rigoberta Menchú a sample of the same kind of academic counterinsurgency. In the same line of argument we can take Dinesh D'Souza's indictment of Rigoberta's work: "While it would be unrealistic to expect someone who knows little about Indian culture to teach the Upanishads, the Stanford faculty was generally quite happy to teach *I, Rigoberta Menchú,* since the latter represents not the zenith of Third World achievements, but rather, caters to the ideological proclivities of American activists."[27] I find in Stoll's book a clear instance of what good and rigorous research can achieve when one has access to sources that do not belong to the public domain but can be accessed, as in the case of Fuentes y Guzmán, Geo Squire, and John Lloyd Stephens, by being privy to the group in power that holds the keys to *cabildo* archives and the papers of their elders.

Notes

1. Manlio Argueta, *One Day of Life,* trans. Bill Brow (New York: Vintage Books, 1983), 105, 107, 108.

2. David Stoll, *Rigoberta Menchú and the Story of All Poor Guatemalans* (Boulder, Colo.: Westview Press, 1999), 119.

3. Ricardo Falla, *Massacres in the Jungle, Ixcan, Guatemala, 1975–1982* (Boulder, Colo.: Westview Press, 1994).

4. Pedro de Alvarado, "Cartas de relación a Hernando Cortés," in *Inicios del dominio español en Indias,* ed. Jorge Luján Muñoz (Guatemala City: Editorial Universitaria, 1987), 79–98. Robert M. Carmack, *The Quiche Mayas of Utatlán: The Evolution of a Highland Guatemala Kingdom* (Norman: University of Oklahoma Press, 1981); idem, *Quichéan Civilization: The Ethnohistoric, Ethnographic, and Archaeological Sources* (Berkeley: University of California Press, 1973); idem, *Rebels of Highland Guatemala: The Quiche-Mayas of Momostenango* (Norman: University of Oklahoma Press, 1995); Dwight Wallace and Robert Carmack, eds., *Archaeology and Ethnohistory of the Central Quiché* (Institute for Mesoamerican Studies; Albany: State University of New York Press, 1977); Edmundo O'Gorman, ed., Bartolomé de las Casas. *Apologética historia de las Indias* (Mexico City, 1967); Quetzil E. Castañeda, *In the Museum of Maya Culture: Touring Chichén Itzá* (Minneapolis: University of Minnesota Press, 1996); Michael Coe, *The Maya Scribe and His World* (New York: The Grolier Club, 1973); idem, *The Maya* (New York: Thames and Hudson, 1987); John W. Fox, *Quiche Conquest: Centralism and Regionalism in Highland Guatemalan State Development* (Albuquerque: University of New Mexico Press, 1978); Richard G. Fox, ed., *Recapturing Anthropology: Working in the Present* (Santa Fe: School of American Research; distributed by the University of Washington Press, 1991); Francisco Antonio de Fuentes y Guzmán, *Historia de Guatemala o Recordación Florida. Escrita en el siglo XVII por el capitan D. Francisco Antonio de Fuentes y Guzmán, natural, vecino y regidor perpetuo de la ciudad de Guatemala,* ed. Justo Zaragoza (Madrid: Luis Navarro, 1883); Domingo Juarros, *A Statistical and Commercial History of the Kingdom of Guatemala, in Spanish America,* trans. John Baily (London, 1825); Adrián Recinos, ed. and trans., "Los Popol Vuh o Popolhuum míticos, históricos y proféticos," in *Literatura Maya,* ed. Mercedes de la Garza (Caracas: Ayacucho, 1992); Antonio de Remesal, *Historia General de las Indias Occidentales, y particular de la governación de Chiapa y Guatemala (1619)* (Guatemala City: Tipografía Nacional, 1932); Linda Schele and Freidel David, *A Forest of Kings: The Untold Story of the Ancient Maya,* color photographs by Justin Kerr (New York: Morrow, 1990); David A. Freidel, Linda Schele, and Joy Parker, *Maya Cosmos: Three Thousand Years on the Shaman's Path,* photographs by Justin Kerr and MacDuff Everton (New York: Morrow, 1993); Francisco Ximénez, *Las historias del origen de los indios de esta provincia de Guatemala, traducidas de la lengua Quiché al castellano para más comodidad de los ministros del S. evangelio* (Vienna: Gerold e Hijo, 1857); Alonso de Zorita, *Los Señores de la Nueva España* (Mexico City: UNAM, 1963).

5. Miguel Ángel Asturias, *Men of Maize,* trans. Gerald Martin (New York: Delacorte Press, 1975).

6. C. Villacorta and J. Antonio, *Prehistoria e historia antigua de Guatemala* (Guatemala: Tiopgrafía Nacional, 1938); Anonymous, *Libro Viejo de la Fundación de Guatemala y papeles relativos a D. Pedro de Alvarado,* Prólogo de Jorge García

Granados (Guatemala: Sociedad de Geografía e Historia, 1934); *Isagoge histórica apologética de las Indias Occidentales y especial de la Provincia de San Vicente de Chiapa y Guatemala,* Prólogo de J. Fernando Juárez Muñoz (Guatemala City: Sociedad de Geografía e Historia, 1935).

7. Ruth Leah Bunzel, *Chichicastenango: A Guatemalan Village* (New York: AMS Press, 1986).

8. W. George Lovell, *Conquest and Survival in Colonial Guatemala: A Historical Geography of the Cuchumatan Highlands, 1500–1821* (Montreal: McGill-Queen's University Press, 1992).

9. Freidel, Schele, and Parker, *Maya Cosmos.*

10. Barbara Tedlock, *Time and the Highland Maya* (Albuquerque: University of New Mexico Press, 1982); Dennis Tedlock, *Popol Vuh: The Definitive Edition of the Mayan Book of the Dawn of Life and the Glories of Gods and Kings* (New York: Simon and Schuster, 1996); idem, *Breath on the Mirror: Mythic Voices and Visions of the Living Maya* (San Francisco: HarperCollins, 1993); idem, "Hearing a Voice in an Ancient Text: Quiché Maya Poetics in Performance," in *Native American Discourse: Poetics and Rhetoric,* ed. Joel Sherzer and Anthony C. Woodbury (Cambridge: Cambridge University Press, 1987).

11. Fuentes y Guzmán, *Historia de Guatemala,* 11.

12. Matthew Gregory Lewis, *Journal of a West Indian Proprietor* (1834) (London: John Murray; New York: Negro University Press, 1969).

13. Antonio Cornejo Polar, *Escribir en el aire. Ensayo sobre la heterogeneidad sociocultural en las literaturas andinas* (Lima: Editorial Horizonte, 1994).

14. R. R. Madden, *Travel in the East: A Twelve Months Residence in the West Indies, during the Transition from Slavery to Apprenticeship; with Incidental Notices of the State of Society, Prospects, and Natural Resources of Jamaica and Other Islands* (Westport, Conn.: Negro University Press, 1970), 104, 129.

15. Severo Martínez Peláez, *La patria del criollo. Ensayo de interpretación de la realidad colonial guatemalteca* (San José: Editorial Universitaria Centroamericana, 1981); idem, *Motines de Indios* (Guatemala City: Ediciones en Marcha, 1991).

16. See, for instance, Carmack, *The Quiche Mayas of Utatlán* and *Rebels of Highland Guatemala;* Wallace and Carmack, *Archaeology and Ethnohistory of the Central Quiché.*

17. One example of this is Anonymous, *Libro Viejo,* but also the works of all the Spanish friars, particularly Vásquez and Remesal.

18. Robert Carmack tells us that although the Quichés had developed a civic-religious hierarchy that gave them some negotiating power, by the middle of the eighteenth century they had become thoroughly peasantized. Ximénez informs us that the population was dispersed widely over the land, "rarely forming towns; rather [the people lived] in hamlets *[parajes],* where the land was good, generally in low places and canyons; there the family or clan [chinamital] lived, not together, but each one in his milpa" (Ximénez, *Las historias del origen de los indios,* 12). The most important economic activities, cattle and sheep raising, were in the hands of Spaniards, mestizos, or "Ladinos." Cattle often broke into the natives' fields, and haciendas had the reputation of being havens for mestizo thieves, who carried off the few sheep owned by native peasants, as Cortés y Larraz's narrative informs us (*Descripción geográfico-moral de la Diócesis de Goathemala hecha par su arzobispo, el Illmo. Sor. Don Pedro Cortés y Larraz del Consejo de S.M. en el Tiempo que la vis-*

itó, y fue desde el día 3 de Noviembre de 1768 hasta el día 1.o de Julio de 1769, desde el día 22 de Noviembre de 1769 hasta de día 9 de Febrero de 1770, y desde el día 6 de Junio de 1770 hasta de día 20 de Agosto del dho. 1770; prólogo del licenciado Adrián Recinos [Guatemala City: Sociedad de Geografía e Historia de Guatemala, 1958]). The indigenous population lived in rural settlements. Their agricultural economic activity supplied food to the haciendas, and as late as 1830 towns such as Antigua still received food from the Quiché. Haciendas gave little in return. By the beginning of the twentieth century, then, the lands of pre-Hispanic Utatlán had been subdivided into nine towns: Santa Cruz del Quiché, San Sebastián Lemoa, Chichicastenango, San Pedro Jocopilas, San Antonio Ilotenango, Patzité, Chinique, Chiché, and Santa María Chiquimula. Despite the incredible persistence of old territorial divisions, the resemblances between Quiché territory in 1900 and what it had been in 1524 were becoming remote. This sums up the fate of the Utatlán community after the Conquest.

19. Georg M. Gugelberger, ed., *The Real Thing: Testimonial Discourse and Latin America* (Durham, N.C.: Duke University Press, 1996), 140.

20. "Arturo Taracena Breaks His Silence," interview by Luis Aceituno, trans. Jill Robbins. E-mail from Juan Carlos Escobedo.

21. Inga Clendinnen, *Ambivalent Conquest: Maya and Spaniards in Yucatan, 1517–1570* (New York: Cambridge University Press, 1987).

22. Remesal, *Historia General de las Indias Occidentales,* 302. Unless otherwise indicated, the translation of quotes is by Derek Petrey.

23. Castañeda, *In the Museum of Maya Culture,* ix.

24. According to Denis Tedlock, there are three groups listed, the Lord Quiché (Not Right Now and Noble Lord); the Cauecs (Jaguar Quitze and Noble Two); the Great House (Jaguar Night and Noble Acutec). Don Juan de Rojas and Don Juan Cortés are the sons of Black Butterfly and Tepepul. So these are the generations, the sequences of lordships for the Keeper of the Mat and Keeper of the Reception House Mat, the lords who have led the Cauecs of Quiché (Tedlock, *Popol Vuh*).

25. J. Hillis Miller, *Topographies* (Stanford, Calif.: Stanford University Press, 1995), 330.

26. Sol Tax, *Heritage of Conquest: The Ethnology of Middle America* (Glencoe, Ill.: Free Press, 1952), 66.

27. Dinesh D'Souza, *Illiberal Education: The Politics of Race and Sex on Campus* (New York: Vintage Books, 1992), 74.

Menchú after Stoll and the Truth Commission

Mario Roberto Morales

> . . . as any true born Guatemalan . . . I confuse reality with words.
> —Miguel Ángel Asturias (440)

> Not even Mr. Stoll's book says I'm a liar.
> —Rigoberta Menchú (in Aznárez)

> The tragedies that befell families like the Menchús are undeniable.
> How these were understood by the revolutionary movement, its
> foreign supporters, and human rights activists is another matter.
> —David Stoll (xii)

When the *New York Times* corroborated some of David Stoll's findings in his book *Rigoberta Menchú and the Story of All Poor Guatemalans,* editorialists in Latin America and Spain attacked him as an agent of the CIA and the Guatemalan army.[1]

In the United States, academics produced a wide array of justifications for the factual problems that Stoll cataloged in *I, Rigoberta Menchú.* Rigoberta's defenders argued that *testimonio* is not constrained by the need to be factual, especially in view of the justness of Menchú's cause, which was to draw the world's attention to the massive killings that the Guatemalan army committed in the 1980s in its war against the Guatemalan National Revolutionary Unity (URNG). Arguments regarding postmodernist relativism about truth and veracity were also used.[2]

In Latin America the principle that "the best defense is a good offense" characterized all these passionate defenses and attacks, polarizing the diatribe—which is what the inevitable intellectual debate became— whereas in the United States the tirade turned into a new battle in the ongoing cultural war between leftist and rightist scholars about the sub- altern subject and his/her struggles. It also reactivated the ongoing cul- tural war in the academic left over the issues related to political correct- ness, identity politics, and the use of the victimization of the Indians to avoid the academic debate that, as part of this cultural war, ironically deals with the validity of certain veracity and truth standards. Besides the argument of postmodernist relativism regarding historical veracity, the academic left adhered to the "conspiracy theory"—launched by the Menchú Tum Foundation, to which, interestingly enough, veracity and truth seemed to be very important and not precisely in a postmodern relativist mode.[3] As "the real thing," and it was immediately supported by organizations under the influence of URNG.[4] Supposedly, this con- spiracy was being orchestrated by powerful sectors of the world's right wing to delegitimize the credibility of the indigenous populations, espe- cially in the wake of the final report of the truth commission (Comisión del Esclarecimiento Histórico, CEH), established by the peace accords signed by the guerrillas and the government in December 1996.[5] This particular element in the general accusation proved to be superfluous because it was easy to suppose that, in view of the fact that the final re- port of the truth commission (of about three thousand pages) was is- sued a few weeks after the attacks began, the commission's job was al- ready finished when the anti-Stoll crusade began. Therefore, the report could not have been influenced by his findings. This fact leads one to wonder if the reasons for the anger of the academics who defended Menchú by attacking Stoll had to do with the deconstructive effect that they felt on their own personal construct as solidarian intellectuals when their foundation—that is, Menchú's own construct of herself, Guate- mala, and the local guerrilla in her *testimonio*—was reframed and put in a different perspective by Stoll.[6] For her part, Menchú was the first to support the truth commission's final report as soon as it was re- leased on February 25, 1999:

> With deep emotion I affirm that *Guatemala, Memory of Silence* is a
> transcendental document for Guatemalan society, especially for the
> thousands and thousands of victims of the dirty war. It is transcendental
> because it represents an invaluable contribution to the reconstruction

and recuperation of our historical memory; because it contributes to breaking the official history that not only denies and silences the victims but that has been elaborated with the version of the victimizers; because it is a call to conciliation and reconciliation, and because it is a testimony of what can never nor should ever happen again.... It is a document that ... reveals the profound causes and origins of the conflict, as well as its direct and indirect actors. (Fundación Rigoberta Menchú Tum 1999c)

Referring to the important issue of the causes and origins of the armed conflict that Menchú mentions, the report says:

12. The CEH concludes that coincident phenomena such as structural injustice, the closing of political spaces, racism, the enhancement of an excluding and antidemocratic institutionality, and also the refusal to develop substantive reforms that could have reduced the structural conflicts, constitute the factors that determined, in a profound sense, the origin and subsequent outburst of the armed confrontation. (CEH 1999)

Referring to the direct and indirect actors in the conflict that Menchú mentions, the report says:

13. The CEH recognizes that the movement of society and the state toward polarization, militarization, and internal war was not only an effect produced by the unfolding of national history. The cold war also had a special influence.... 14. Anticommunism and the Doctrine of National Security (DSN) were part of the anti-Soviet strategy of the United States in Latin America. In Guatemala these two first had an antireformist sense, then an antidemocratic one and, lastly, a counter-insurgent sense, turned into a criminal one.... 18. The influence of Cuba and its exaltation of the armed struggle also had an influence on these processes in Guatemala and on the rest of the American continent. On this particular issue the CEH concludes that the political, logistic, instructional, and training support that Cuba gave to the Guatemalan insurgency during this period was another important external factor that marked the evolution of the armed conflict.... 22. Even if in the armed conflict the army and the insurgency appear as the more visible actors, the investigation that the CEH undertook has shown the involve-ment of the totality of the state with all its institutions and coactive mechanisms. Also, the responsibility and participation, under different forms, of the economic power sectors, the political parties, the university community, the churches, and other sectors of the civil society was established. 23. Therefore, the CEH concludes that the true explanation of the Guatemalan armed confrontation cannot be reduced to the logic of two armed actors. (CEH 1999)

As we shall see, these conclusions constitute, from now on, an unavoidable reference to foster or conclude the debate that occupies us because they set out important facts that contribute to making clear something that is central to the discussion: the question of the origins of the violence. For his part, Stoll questions Menchú's portrait of the relations between indigenous peasants, Ladinos, and guerrillas, as well as how political violence spread, because he thinks it can be used to justify the appropriation of indigenous people for political projects that are alien to their interests:

> The air of sacrilege about questioning the reliability of *I, Rigoberta Menchú* gives us at least three reasons to do so. The first is what it can tell us about the Guatemalan violence, its popular roots, and how these were mythologized to meet needs for the revolutionary movement and its supporters. The second is to challenge underlying romantic assumptions about indigenous people and guerrilla warfare, for which Rigoberta's people will not be the last to pay dearly. The third is to raise questions about a new standard of truth gaining ground in the humanities and social sciences.
>
> The premise of the new orthodoxy is that Western forms of knowledge, such as the empirical approach adopted here, are fatally compromised by racism and other forms of domination. Responsible scholars must therefore identify with the oppressed, relegating much of what we think we know about them to the dustbin of colonialism. The new basis of authority consists of letting subalterns speak for themselves, agonizing over any hint of complicity with the system that oppresses them, and situating oneself in relation to fashionable theorists. Certainly there is much to be said for listening, but which voices are we supposed to listen to? What I will show in the case of *I, Rigoberta Menchú* is that critical theory can end up revolving around romantic conceptions of indigenous people, mythologies that can be used to sacrifice them for larger causes. (Stoll xv)

So, which voices are we going to listen to? Only Menchú's? Perhaps the argument of authority that is best invoked to diminish the importance of the veracity or falseness of Menchú's account—even if, contrary to her defenders, she seems to be quite concerned about the problem of veracity[7]—is the postmodern claim that the veracity of a fact does not differentiate from its enunciation, that truth is not an essence that precedes its different versions, and that, therefore, personal discourse is the bearer of a truth with which one can or cannot, should or should not be politically in solidarity.[8] According to this logic, what is at stake

is the taking of political positions regarding discourses and their positionality of enunciation. But even if we accept this logic and operate
within its framework, Stoll's findings and their consequences deserve to
be discussed insofar as it was Menchú's discourse that established the
version about Guatemala, its Indian and Ladino populations, and the
revolutionary movement, and that is now in question—especially in light
of the conclusions of the final report of the truth commission—by other
Indian voices: those of Stoll's informants, who, according to this postmodern logic, would have the same right to be heard as Menchú, so as
not to succumb to the mirage of Lacan's Legislator. Besides, let us not
forget that the self-construct of the subject through the word is done in
relation to the mirror that returns the image of the subject's own construct and that allows his/her imagination to objectify his/her subject
condition for the other. Also, that the mirror(s) is (are) the other(s).
Menchú's self-construct was made to incite solidarity, that is, it was made
explicitly for others. And it seems that some of these others now claim
to be better polished mirrors so as to—like Little Red Riding Hood's
wolf—be worthy of the privilege of "better reflecting you," forgetting
that the image that the mirror returns is also the pose that the subject
adopted in front of it to constitute himself or herself as object of knowledge for self and for others.[9] In the face of this, what is the point in constituting oneself as defender of the truth of a version that we already
know is a construct, one version among others? Even (and mainly) if we
accept the validity of a given truth in a given discourse, it is inescapable
to try to establish the social and political functions that that particular
truth has fulfilled, because no doubt it has had concrete consequences.[10]
Comparing Menchú's version of events with others given by indigenous
people cannot be avoided precisely because of her version's deliberate
function of inciting solidarity with a specific cause. I say this as a Guatemalan and a left-wing militant since the mid-1960s, someone who is
interested in establishing the components of the past that marked the
life of his generation and that of other generations of Guatemalans.

Based on his interviews and archival research, Stoll is opening up an
inescapable debate because he defies the usual paradigms in understanding the relationship between the guerrilla avant-gardes and their popular bases. He is also challenging the persistent essentialism that some
intellectuals still construct when dealing with the relationship of indigenous cultures and modernity, forcing them to face the reality that

subaltern agency often fails to fit into fashionable bipolarized notions of cultural resistance and otherness. To assume that it does is to fall into the trap of romanticizing the objects of our solidarity according to our own needs.

Although Stoll does not theorize in terms of subalternity, what he is obviously describing is a multiplicity of subaltern spaces articulated (and hybridized) in many ways with the hegemonic and dominant spaces and processes with which subalternity dialogues and where it confronts itself in many oblique forms. It is all too evident that the fashionable notions of cultural resistance and radical otherness do not correspond with the hybrid agency that the subaltern puts creatively into practice in order to construct his or her own spaces of expression and struggle. The challenges that derive from Stoll's findings, in view of the accusations that befell him of having an alleged rightist ideological and political agenda, as well as dubious intentions in questioning Menchú's version of events, are too great to ignore. Those findings and their consequences (if they are true—and to this day there are no reasons to believe they are not) must at least be examined. Academic analysis is, then, inevitable, and neither diatribe nor ideological preferences nor solidarities nor moralizing accusations can replace it.

With this in mind, and with no intention of taking sides in the "culture war" over the manipulation of Menchú as a symbol, I will now explore the implications of what Stoll's informants have to say for Guatemala's political future. Let us ask, What is it in Stoll's argument that has provoked such intemperate reactions? Let us enumerate the main points of his argument, as well as their gnoseological consequences for the study of *testimonio* as a narrative genre and as political document, their political consequences for the perception of Menchú as a political and ideological figure, and their ideological consequences for the history of the Guatemalan guerrilla movement.

For Stoll (159–66), Menchú's story cannot be the eyewitness account that she claimed it to be because, according to his informants, she spent much of her childhood and adolescence studying in boarding schools with nuns of the Order of the Holy Family (160). That is why she could not have been a political organizer (173–74). Judging from the recollections of family and friends, he thinks it is unlikely that she was a laborer on the plantations of the south coast (24–25), or a maid in an upper-class Ladino household in Guatemala City, as she claimed she was.[11]

When the controversy over Stoll's findings began, Menchú admitted that she had used experiences of other people (other testimonies) to build her story (Fundación Rigoberta Menchú Tum 1999c). If so, then her actual life cannot be the metaphor or metonym for the life of an entire people. Instead, she becomes a skillful storyteller who helped to build international solidarity for the Guatemalan armed struggle, through the construction of a character whose persona incarnated the sufferings of an entire population.

That key passages in the story are fiction, not lived experience, undermines certain assumptions that were common among North American advocates of *testimonio.* Now Menchú can be appreciated as the author of effective oral fictions about atrocities that needed to be denounced. This should also put into question the idea that *testimonio* is a subaltern form of expression distinct from and contrary to literature. Instead, it could be regarded as subaltern literature (or "oraliterature"). If Stoll is right about the actual basis of *I, Rigoberta Menchú,* then *testimonio* benefits as an oral or written narrative genre. Besides, illiterate (oral) subalterns see nothing improper in reinterpreting the personal and collective memories they transmit to others.

It should be obvious that pinning so many political assumptions on one account, as many did on Menchú's, was a risky operation to begin with. Whether or not we welcome Stoll's challenge to rethink this operation, I am afraid that it is an offer we cannot refuse. Based on his informants and archival research in the National Institute for Agrarian Transformation (INTA), Stoll also establishes that Rigoberta's father, Vicente, was enmeshed in a land dispute, not with Ladino landowners, as she had claimed, but with his in-laws, the Tum family (29–40). Nor did these disputes lead him into the struggles of the Committee for Peasant Unity (CUC), of which he seems never to have been a member (89–105). Besides, his death—as well as that of his friends—at the Spanish embassy on January 31, 1980, was the result of an EGP operation that was criminally repressed by the military regime, and in which several peasants (not all) were involved probably without fully realizing what that meant in terms of the plans of the guerrilla organization (71–88). This fact, says Stoll, reframes the figure of Vicente Menchú as the peasant prototype who gains political consciousness and embraces the revolutionary cause, to put him in a perspective that speaks of the forms of manipulation that the EGP (and all the guerrilla organizations) exerted on indigenous peasants—and, I would argue, also of the forms of sub-altern agency that originate in the strategic acceptance of manipulation in order to construct, within it, a margin of subaltern power. It also dis-articulates the notion that the central problem of the Guatemalan Indi-ans was harassment by Ladino landowners who would steal their prop-erties, turning that fact into the main cause of the armed confrontation (8–12, 15–27).

Stoll does not deny the injustice of the land-tenure system in Guate-mala, or the plight of indigenous peasants, but he does question the notion that peasants like Vicente Menchú joined the guerrilla organiza-tions because they had no other way to defend themselves from Ladino landowners.[12] Stoll's analysis of the prewar northern Quiché also chal-lenges the widespread perception in North American academia that Guatemala is a country comparable to apartheid-era South Africa, fa-voring instead an intercultural and interethnic analysis over a multicul-tural one that magnifies cultural differences, turning them into irrec-oncilable contradictions.

The conclusion that Menchú was not the illiterate girl that she claimed to be, and that her father apparently encouraged rather than discouraged her education,[13] bears out the point that hybridization is the norm and not the exception in Guatemala's interethnic relations (Morales 1999a). The fact that Vicente Menchú's land disputes were against Mayan in-laws rather than Ladino plantation owners does not erase the wider class and ethnic conflicts in the Guatemalan countryside. But it does suggest that the insurgent/counterinsurgent dialectic may not have grown out of these in the simple way some scholars have assumed because this was the version that was offered to them by the EGP and by Menchú. Instead, the armed confrontation has to be traced to U.S. intervention in 1954, how this restored the power of the oligarchy, how the avant-gardes of the Ladino left responded to the lack of democracy by imitating the Cuban model, and how the Guatemalan army redefined itself to defeat the new threat.

The details of this history are important because, as early as 1982, some sectors of the armed left, such as the People's Revolutionary Movement-Ixim (MRP-Ixim), were criticizing the avant-gardism of the largest of the three guerrilla organizations grouped in the URNG, the Guerrilla Army of the Poor (EGP).[14] Perhaps without realizing all the implications, the EGP conceived of the indigenous masses of the western highlands as instruments who would be put into violent confrontation with the army, in order to exacerbate repression and raise mass consciousness of the guerrillas as defenders of the people against the state.[15]

The guerrillas lost the war, it should now be obvious, because they could not protect their support base from being annihilated. All of which gives validity to Stoll's point in regard to the immediate origins of the violence. If to all this we add the fact that the truth commission established, as we will see, the same version of events as being true and that the URNG publicly asked for forgiveness from the victims, thus accepting the commission's version,[16] we have the version that Menchú offered in Elisabeth Burgos's book confirming itself as an EGP version, opening the debate about the meaning and the consequences that the suppression of the link between the CUC and the EGP and between Menchú and the EGP (a silence that is evident throughout the book) had for the indigenous population and the continuation of a lost war, up to December 1996.

Judging from Stoll's findings in Uspantán, the violence in this locality did not originate in Indian–Ladino conflict (even though the problems between them provided motives for the combatants), nor did the guerrillas have anything but a transient relationship with local peasants. It was the EGP that began political killing near Menchú's village, by shooting two Ladino farm owners, which then brought the army to the scene. The truth commission corroborates Stoll's scenario as a wider pattern in the conflict:

> 31. During the years of exacerbation of the confrontation (1978–83), with the widening of the base of support and action range of the guerrillas, in several regions of the country, the army identified the Mayas as sympathizers of the guerrillas. On some occasions this identification came about because of their support of the insurgent groups, as well as preinsurrectional conditions in limited areas of the interior. However, the CEH has managed to pinpoint the fact that, in the majority of cases, the identification between the Mayan communities and the insurgency was intentionally exaggerated by the state, which, on the basis of traditional racist prejudices, instrumentalized this identification to eliminate present and future possibilities that the population would help or join any insurgent project.... 32. The consequence of this manipulation, widely documented by the CEH, was the massive and indiscriminate aggression against the communities, regardless of their real involvement with the guerrillas and of their civilian, noncombatant condition....

34. The CEH has established that the guerrillas applied a tactic of "armed propaganda" and temporary occupation of towns, in order to gain partisans or demonstrate force; but when they withdrew, they left the communities helpless and vulnerable. In many cases, these communities were later attacked by the army, with many people killed among the civilian population, especially Mayas. In some of them that were examined by the CEH, entire villages were wiped out by state military forces a few days after the withdrawal of the insurgent groups that had occupied them. In these cases, even recognizing the army as the single entity responsible for the massive violations, the CEH is convinced that the actions of the guerrillas played a role in the unchaining of these events. (CEH)

Stoll also shows how Menchú's version of events intentionally coincides with the needs of the Guerrilla Army of the Poor, the group whose political apparatus she joined after her parents were killed and the nuns educating her at a boarding school in Chiantla took her to Mexico (167–75). Ironically, by the time her story became famous, the EGP had been defeated militarily:

What would her testimony have looked like without a significant amount of reinvention? It would go something like this: Government death squads are on the rampage in some parts of Guatemala, but not in others. One day, a guerrilla column shows up in a village whose most serious conflict is with other peasants. Shortly thereafter, the guerrillas introduce political assassinations to the area, which prompts the army to start kidnapping peasants. When relatives go to Guatemala [City] to protest, fifteen die in the conflagration at the Spanish embassy. Back home, the army kidnaps more villagers. One young woman, who has lost three members of her family while away at boarding school, flees to Mexico. There she joins the revolutionary movement, returns to Guatemala as an organizer, and starts telling her story to the world.

This would have been a fascinating story, but not a very useful one for the Guerrilla Army of the Poor. . . . Rigoberta's mentors probably advised her to broaden her story, to make it more typical of the oppression of Guatemalan peasants. Even without instructions, however, the discrepancies between EGP teachings and her own circumstances could encourage a neophyte to omit inconvenient features of her life and add others. According to the sociolinguist Charlotte Linde, anyone put to the task of telling a life story struggles to maintain coherent principles of causality and continuity. That is, tellers of life stories tend to downplay the incoherence, accident, discontinuity, and doubt that characterize actual lived experience, because these detract from the sense of purpose and agency that audiences expect narrators to demonstrate. In

Rigoberta's case, she achieved coherence by omitting features of the situation that contradicted the ideology of her new organization, then substituting appropriate revolutionary themes. Since she was very new to the movement, during a period in which it seemed to offer a solution to Guatemala's crisis, there is no need to question her good intentions. All she had to believe was that revolutionary portrayals of the oppression of *campesinos* were more typical than the experiences of her own land-wealthy village, a lesson that would have been underlined by the sudden, shocking manhunt of her family. (Stoll 192–93)

It is in this sense, according to Stoll, that *I, Rigoberta Menchú* served the purpose of attracting international support for the guerrilla (273–83). Maybe the EGP did not know that it was already defeated, Stoll concedes. He is also careful to leave room for Menchú as a narrator in her own right, on the margins of the EGP, as well as of her interlocutor and editor Elisabeth Burgos-Debray.[17] However, he is not aware that, as far back as 1982, the EGP's defeat had been analyzed by the MRP-Ixim, which exhorted the rest of the guerrilla movement to come together and stop the chaotic retreat to reorganize under a single military and political command.[18] This is to say that the defeat was well acknowledged on the left by 1982 and that, therefore, at least the leadership of the EGP should have been aware of it.

The fact that Menchú's account reflects the needs of a guerrilla organization suggests that the subaltern discourses and their political agency should not be read from a binary perspective, that is, the assumption that they are enunciated from a locus of absolute otherness. Instead, it should be recognized that subaltern discourse is often solicited and elicited by dominators who wish to instrumentalize the subaltern's political potential and also to identify with its discourse to solve their own internal conflicts (e.g., Lacan's construct of the other). As anybody with experience on the left can testify, subalterns like Menchú (and also Ladino subalterns) must adjust their discourse to the interest of their interlocutors in order to meet their own material and ideological needs.[19] Another disruption of binary thinking in Menchú's case is that, since she cannot be considered the illiterate girl she claimed to be, the myth of radical cultural otherness does not stand up before the multiple hybrid forms in which the subaltern expresses herself in the dominant codes.

All this leads us to conclude that the locus of enunciation of the subaltern is, in our case, the diglossic *mestizaje* characteristic of our cultures, and not the multiculturalist divisionism based on the magnification of the cultural differences that certain scholars seek to impose on us, as part of the distortion of our image that they reflect back to us with their mirrors. In other words, what all this suggests is that third-world subalterns constitute a much wider conglomerate than the one formed by the subjects and discourses chosen by first-world academics to meet their own spiritual needs, one that often sees itself contradicted by real events.

Even if Menchú's *testimonio* unintentionally resuscitated a defeated guerrilla force, thus prolonging the suffering of victims, I do not see the need to waste time issuing condemnations, rationales, or apologies. Joining the insurgent left in the Guatemala of the 1980s was hardly a crime, as confirmed by the report of the truth commission. Rather, this should be a moment for a reflection by the left on its legacy and its possibilities for urgent renewal, given that the atrocities committed by the URNG, even though to a much lesser degree than the ones committed by the army, cannot be overlooked, excused, or justified from any point of view.[20]

The Central American *testimonios* of the 1980s were generally linked with leftist avant-gardisms. That is why reading them as discourses that form part of the imaginary of that political force is not misleading. What is misleading is postulating them as the expression of a radical otherness that denies the cultural, political, and ideological hybridizations and *mestizajes* that constitute the core of the subaltern discourse, which needs to articulate itself with the dominant imaginary so as to achieve its effectiveness.

John Beverley situates *testimonio* as a possible counterpoint for avant-gardist discourse:

> *Testimonio* was intimately linked to international solidarity networks in support of revolutionary movements or struggles around human rights, apartheid, democratization; but it was also a way of testing the contradictions and limits of revolutionary and reformist projects still structured in part around elite assumptions about the role of cultural and political vanguards. In the context of redemocratization and cultural and media globalization, *testimonio* loses its special aesthetic and ideological power and runs the risk of becoming a new form of *costumbrismo,* the Spanish term for "'local-color' writing." (139)

In contrast, Stoll affirms what has always constituted common knowledge in the Guatemalan left: that Menchú's *testimonio* expresses the vision and the version of the revolutionary avant-garde as constructed by the EGP.[21] To what extent her account puts to the test or supports the revolutionary avant-gardism, and to what extent her power of agency relates to the EGP's ideology, are the issues that could be discussed now, in the light of the conclusions of the truth commission's report. These lines seek to contribute to that analysis, assuming that Menchú's leftist militancy was something not only explicable but coherent given the historical circumstances that determined her decision. Whether we agree or not with what the EGP did and did not do is a different matter and must be framed within the Guatemalan debate about the left.

Should anyone doubt Stoll's argument that some scholars have constructed the subaltern to satisfy their own spiritual needs (231–47), the proof lies in the witch hunt that the *New York Times* coverage unleashed. How else to explain the ad hominem attacks heaped on Stoll by academics who had yet to read his book? If this was Stoll's main objective, to demonstrate the self-serving idolatry at work in scholarly solidarity toward the subaltern considered as an abstract otherness, no doubt he achieved it.[22] But what do his findings mean for Guatemala and our immediate political future? Is he just another scholar appropriating our tribulations for internal debates in North American academia? Whether or not this is the case, it is important to analyze the polarized perceptions of Guatemala in North American academia because we have so few means to contest them and sooner or later these perceptions colonize our own academic work and political action. Even if we rightly condemn the appropriation of our contradictions for the North American "culture wars," we have to contribute to these debates to prevent them from serving careerist ends and perverting images of ourselves in scholarship that will affect how we view ourselves for generations to come.[23]

In view of the truth commission's report, it is obvious that the avant-gardism of the Guatemalan left still needs to be critiqued.[24] Stoll's argument challenges us to do that, even if we do not agree with him.[25] My own conviction, which I think is borne out by the truth commission, is that the armed struggle was a justified response by a sector of society to the strangulation of possibilities for legal political struggle. This is not the same as insisting that the armed struggle was a response by "the people," still less of the indigenous people.[26] Even though the truth commission found that the URNG (and especially the EGP) shared responsibility for massacres of indigenous people, less often by direct authorship than by militarizing civilians and provoking the enemy, I do not think that the revolutionary effort was in vain. The point is not to condemn Menchú and to praise Stoll, or vice versa. Instead, we need to settle accounts with a history in which, as the truth commission says, we are all responsible by commission or omission, even though I do not think we are all responsible in equal terms.[27]

Instead of engaging in diatribe, we should instead contribute to the encounter of Guatemala with her own image, reflected in her own mirrors, an image devoid of paternalistic idealizations that serve only to feed intellectual narcissism and quiet the prick of bad conscience. If we are going to see ourselves in a mirror, let it be—remembering Martí— our own mirror. If others want to reflect us, let us take care that the others' reflection does not replace our own because that will serve their needs rather than ours.[28]

No doubt, after Stoll and the truth commission, Menchú will never be the same. She has been humanized. I believe that she as well as her *testimonio* have gained a great deal thanks to Stoll's deconstruction of the myth. I also believe that the debate will benefit the left, in the United States as well as in Guatemala, by retiring certain kinds of idealism that have outlived their usefulness. Academics must accept indigenous peoples as human beings with all the contradictions that the rest of us face, not elevate them to the illusory stature of myth. The ex-guerrilla leadership must assume responsibility for the consequences of its manipulation of the masses by stimulating the debate about the left in the light of the report of the truth commission. Menchú must assume responsibility for having offered a version of events that fitted the needs of the EGP and its erroneous conception of the role of the popular masses in a war, and not elude her responsibility by victimizing herself as the object of an international conspiracy. As for the North American, European, Latin American, and Guatemalan intellectuals whose cult of the subaltern satisfies their ideological expectations and identity needs, they will have to learn that much of what they hear from the subaltern is an ad hoc discursive construct, not completely dissimilar from what this enigmatic subject offers to tourists visiting his or her environment.[29] They will also have to learn that it is worth the effort to study the subaltern discourse from the perspective of the multiple possibilities of agency that this subject is capable of displaying when dealing with the reality of

discursive domination and hegemony of which the solidarian intellectuals form part, and that these forms of agency do not simply resolve in
the binary notions of cultural resistance, otherness, and cultural difference that the dominant rhetoric so cherishes because they simplify its
subject of study.

If this debate serves some purpose, it will be to rehumanize an idealized subaltern subject. This poses major new responsibilities for representatives of the subaltern such as Menchú and for intellectuals who
want to support them. Instead of wasting time with more recriminations,
we should congratulate each other for embarking on a difficult, new stage
in political debate.

Notes

1. These passionate attacks all had a common denominator: their authors had
not read Stoll's book when they wrote them and their arguments were ad hominem,
seeking to delegitimize Stoll as a racist and a rightist. This was done through an intense bombardment of confusing accusations, expressions of paranoia, inaccuracies, and insults that annulled the possibility of academic and political discussion.
The articles containing such attacks were by Liano, Galeano, Arias, Ramírez, Montero, Vázquez, and others. In an article published on January 25, 1999, I intervened
by proposing that the attackers read Stoll's book in order to refute his arguments in
a proper manner, given the fact that it was obvious that they had not (Morales 1999b).
For their part, the Menchú Foundation and the New Guatemala Democratic Front
issued communiqués in which they spoke about a right-wing conspiracy to delegitimize Menchú and all the indigenous peoples of the world. This "conspiracy theory"
was soon disseminated and taken as a basis for justifying personal attacks against
Stoll. The Guatemalan right reacted by accusing Menchú of being what it had always said she was: a liar. And the leftist sympathizers of Menchú reacted paranoically,
voicing another U.S. attack against popular interests in Guatemala and Latin America. Irresponsible opinionatedness substituted for direct knowledge and academic
discussion, and the old left/right bitterness experienced a sudden revival, positing
the issue in the old binary fashion: she was a liar versus he was a CIA agent.

2. See, for example, Grandin y Goldman. Robin Wilson's article contains a series
of opinions of North American academics that, on the one hand, attack Menchú
from the right (D'Souza, Horowitz) and, on the other, defend her by attacking Stoll
from the left, arguing that veracity in her account of events is not very important
compared to what she represents. We find quite a contrast in Diane Nelson's serene
opinion: "I kind of wish she had done what we wish Clinton had done" (15). At the
beginning of his article, Wilson had quoted Gene Bell-Villada as saying: "Many scholars have accused Mr. Stoll of conducting a 'Kenneth Starr-style' investigation" (14).
This interesting and immediate "translation" of the problem into North American
cultural codes (Clinton was being acquitted in the Monica Lewinsky scandal) illustrates the way in which the issues that emerge in the realm of third-world subalter-

nity are transformed into battles of campus cultural wars, as a necessary step toward positing what will become the accepted truths or lies about a given object of study in the hegemonic academia.

3. "It is worrisome to realize that in many circles of power in the world the perception of Indigenous peoples as obstacles for the stability of the dominant order and as a potential danger due to the accumulation of discontent and frustrations, augments. It would seem as if, with the ending of the Cold War, some people would need to find new enemies to prolong the confrontation.

"In this scenario, the attacks to which we are referring today widen their significance and seek to put into question not only this or that *testimonio,* but the truth about the colonial history that all the States in the world acknowledged in appointing Rigoberta Menchú as a Good Will Ambassador for the International Year of Indigenous Peoples, and bury in oblivion the acquired compromises" (Fundación Rigoberta Menchú Tum 1999a).

4. "It is a curious thing that a book of little transcendence in itself [Stoll's book] had been magnified by a series of articles in the *New York Times.* It is pertinent, then, to ask who is behind this campaign of attempting to diminish [Menchú's] prestige" *(Boletín Internacional del Frente Democrático Nueva Guatemala).*

5. "What I worry about is that this controversy may be used to undermine the findings of the truth commission and deflect attention away from attempts to reform the army" (Kay B. Warren, in Wilson).

6. "It is therefore readily conceivable how this aggressivity may respond to any intervention which, by denouncing the imaginary intentions of the discourse, dismantles the object constructed by the subject to satisfy them" (Lacan, 12).

7. "Rigoberta Menchú admitted this Thursday that she mixed the testimonies of other victims of the Guatemalan civil war with her autobiographical account in the book that helped her win the Nobel Peace Prize. 'The book that is being questioned is a document that mixes my own personal testimonies with other testimonies about what occurred in Guatemala,' said Menchú at a press conference in New York" (Fundación Rigoberta Menchú Tum 1999b).

8. "Any statement of authority has no other guarantees than its very enunciation, and it is pointless for it to seek another signifier, which could not appear outside this locus in any way. Which is what I mean when I say that no metalanguage can be spoken, or, more aphoristically, that there is no Other of the Other. And when the Legislator (he who claims to lay down the Law) presents himself to fill the gap, he does so as an imposter" (Jacques Lacan, *Écrits: A Selection,* trans. Alan Sheridan [New York: Norton, 1977], 310–11; qtd. in Beverley 136).

9. "Does the subject not become engaged in an ever-growing dispossession of that being of his, concerning which—by dint of sincere portraits which leave its idea no less incoherent, of rectifications which do not succeed in freeing its essence, of stays and defenses which do not prevent his statue from tottering, of narcissistic embraces which become like a puff of air in animating it—he ends up by recognizing that this being has never been anything more than his construct in the Imaginary and that this construct disappoints all his certitudes? For in this labor which he undertakes to reconstruct this construct *for another,* he finds again the fundamental alienation which made him construct it *like another one,* and which has always destined it to be stripped from him *by another.* . . . even if the subject were to reintroduce its form into his discourse to the point of reconstituting the preparatory

image through which the subject makes himself an object by striking a pose before the mirror, he could not possibly be satisfied with it, since even he achieved his most perfect likeness in that image, it would still be the *jouissance* of the other that he would cause to be recognized in it. This is the reason why there is no reply which is adequate to this discourse, for the subject will consider as a takedown every Word participating in his mistake" (Lacan 11–12).

10. "Even if it communicates nothing, the discourse represents the existence of communication; even if it denies the obvious, it affirms that the Word constitutes the Truth; even if it is destined to deceive, here the discourse speculates on faith in testimony.

"Moreover, it is the analyst who knows better than anyone else that the question is to understand which 'part' of this speech carries the significative term" (Lacan 13).

11. "The narrator of *I, Rigoberta Menchú* is widely remembered, but not as a catechist or organizer. In a peasant society ruled by elders, where girls reaching puberty are kept under close watch, it would be very unusual for a person of her age and gender to play the leadership role she describes. She did stand out from other Mayan girls in one respect. Although Rigoberta has often said that she grew up monolingual and illiterate, this is not how she is remembered in Uspantán. What distinguished her was that Catholic nuns took her away to boarding school. Not only is this no secret in Uspantán, but anyone who remembers Rigoberta at all remembers that she left Uspantán for her education, which is held in such high esteem that some think she went as far as San Carlos University" (Stoll 159).

12. "The peasants of *I, Rigoberta Menchú* have been pushed to the wall by plantation owners and soldiers hunting down dissidents. Her village has little choice but to organize for self-defense and look to the guerrillas for help. The insurgency therefore springs from the most basic needs of peasants, for their land.... These were not the prewar conditions I heard about in my interviews with nearby Ixils. Certainly they were living under military dictatorship, some Ladinos had evil reputations, and at least a few Ixils were eager to become guerrillas at an early date. But this was not a population that could defend itself only by force. Instead, Ixils were learning to use local elections and the courts. The 1960s and 1970s were for them, as for many Guatemalan peasants, an era of modest gains. The first armed groups in their accounts were usually guerrillas, whom many blamed for the subsequent arrival of soldiers. Army kidnappings began not in reaction to peaceful efforts by Ixils to improve their lot but to guerrilla organizing and ambushes. If anyone ignited political violence in Ixil country, it was the Guerrilla Army of the Poor. Only then had the security forces militarized the area and turned it into a killing ground.

"Had nearby Uspantán been different? Or was *I, Rigoberta Menchú* voicing a rationale for insurgency that did not really come from peasants, that instead came from someone claiming to speak for them?" (Stoll 9).

13. "Rigoberta tells how her village sent away two government teachers, to prevent them from alienating the children with a Ladino education, and how her father refused to send her to school. What I heard in Uspantán was rather different. Like many village leaders, Vicente Menchú appreciated the value of education and tried to obtain it for his children. At the end of the 1970s, a government teacher worked in Chimel until the violence forced her to leave" (ibid., 159–60).

14. The flyers and pamphlets containing this critique are called *Ixim* and *Estrella popular revolucionaria*. They were written, printed and distributed in Managua be-

tween 1983 and 1989, with the exception of the "Documento azul Ixim," which was written in 1982 and printed in 1983 in Costa Rica.

15. The militaristic mentality of the guerrilla leader is suggested by the interviews that Marta Harnecker conducted with EGP commander in chief Ricardo Ramírez and other URNG leaders in the early 1980s (1983a, 15–101; 1983b, 95–175).

16. "'With profound pain and humility we ask forgiveness to the memory of the victims of the armed conflict, to their families, and to the communities that could have suffered irreparable losses, injustices, or offenses resulting from any kind of excesses or mistakes.' These were some of the first words of Jorge Ismael Soto, known during the armed confrontation as Pablo Monsanto, when he read a document issued by the Guatemalan National Revolutionary Unity (URNG), in which it stated its position on the data that appeared in the report of the truth commission (CEH), in which the ex-guerrilla is incriminated in violent acts against the population" (Pacheco).

17. "If Rigoberta's denial of Spanish and literacy was a preemptive defense of her authenticity, brought on by racist assumptions she was encountering, then the obsessive quality of these denials suggests that she was not just doing it for her listeners. She also could have been doing it for herself. The noble savage was invented by Europeans, but it has been taken to heart by many an indigenous intellectual seeking to join the wider world on equal terms. Rigoberta would be far from being the first Indian who went off to school and the city, who collided with discrimination, and who responded by idealizing her origin as a Rousseauian idyll. It takes time to learn that claims to innocence only encourage paternalism" (Stoll 195).

18. See *Ixim* and *Estrella popular revolucionaria* (note 14 above).

19. In the 1980s, I myself had to undertake the task of coming to the United States to visit groups of university professors and also a few churches, with the objective of creating some resonance for the actions of the revolutionary group to which I belonged. My discourse was carefully designed by my comrades and me so as to express what liberal professors and Christian parishioners would want to hear.

20. "15.... the forces of the state and connected paramilitary groups were responsible for 93 percent of the violations documented by the CEH, including 92 percent of the arbitrary executions and 91 percent of the forced disappearances.... 21. Among the cases registered by the CEH, the insurgent groups produced 3 percent of the violations of human rights and acts of violence on men, women, and children, including 5 percent of the arbitrary executions and 2 percent of the forced disappearances" (CEH).

21. I tried to prove the same point in Morales 1999a, chapter 2.

22. "Under the influence of postmodernism (which has undermined confidence in a single set of facts) and identity politics (which demands acceptance of claims to victimhood), scholars are increasingly hesitant to challenge certain kinds of rhetoric. They do not want to be accused of 'blaming the victim'—an all-purpose, preemptive indictment, like 'racism,' which has been very effective in suppressing unwelcome information and replacing it with defensive theorizing. In the case of Guatemala, I was to avoid focusing on how peasants contribute to their poverty by having large families, or how the guerrillas triggered political killings in some locales, or how the Left is out of touch with the people it wants to represent. At bottom, I was to avoid challenging the Left's claim to speak for victims" (Stoll 244).

23. "Obviously, Rigoberta is a legitimate Mayan voice. So are all the young Mayas who want to move to Los Angeles or Houston. So is the man with a large family who owns three worn-out acres and wants me to buy him a chain saw so he can cut down the last forest more quickly. Any of these people can be picked out to make misleading generalizations about Mayas. But I doubt that the man who wants the chain saw will be invited to multicultural universities anytime soon. Until he does, books like *I, Rigoberta Menchú* will be exalted because they tell many academics what they want to hear. Such works provide rebels in far-off places, into whom careerists can project their fantasies of rebellion. The simplistic images of innocence, oppression, and defiance can be used to construct mythologies of purity for academic factions claiming moral authority on the grounds that they identify with the oppressed. But icons have their cost. What makes *I, Rigoberta Menchú* so attractive in universities is what makes it misleading about the struggle for survival in Guatemala. We think we are getting closer to understanding Guatemalan peasants when actually we are being borne away by the mystification wrapped up in an iconic figure" (ibid., 247).

24. "35. In the face of the scorched-earth operations and the massacres, that corresponded to a strategy and to a systematic planification by the army, the guerrilla failed to protect the population that had sympathized with its purposes or had supported it. This incapacity provoked in these sectors a widespread feeling of abandonment, deception and rejection" (CEH).

25. "Facing the limitations of *I, Rigoberta Menchú* will, I hope, help the Latin American Left and its foreign supporters escape from the captivity of Guevarismo. At bottom rural guerrilla strategies are an urban romance, a myth propounded by middle-class radicals who dream of finding true solidarity in the countryside. The injustices that induce some peasants to join guerrilla organizations are all too real; physical confrontation may be inevitable; but the kind of armed struggle envisioned by guerrilla organizations is not. For the better part of four decades, a misguided belief in the moral purity of total rejection, of refusing to compromise with the system and seeking to overthrow it by force has had profound consequences for the entire political scene. It has strengthened rationales for repression, poisoned other political possibilities that might have been more successful, and repeatedly been fatal for the Left itself, by dismaying lower-class constituents and guaranteeing a crushing response from the state. It is time to face the fact that guerrilla strategies are far more likely to kill the Left than build it" (Stoll 282).

26. "17. The Guatemalan insurgency, on its part, emerged as the response of a sector of the population in view of the diverse structural problems of the country" (CEH).

27. For a personal view of the armed struggle regarding indigenous peoples, see Morales 1994; and for a personal experience regarding the URNG's conduction of the war, see Morales 1998.

28. "This is an amazing and embarrassing discussion. Is it a paroxysm of White liberal guilt that is causing so many presumably intelligent people to tie themselves up in such knots? If Menchú lied, she lied. If she intended her book to be taken as factual truth, it was a lie (apparently); if she was telling a story, as story-tellers have for millennia, and the tale was mistaken for factual truth, then lots of people ought to feel silly. This is a simple issue. There is no need to obscure it with blather about

'telling her truth.' Regardless, as several have pointed out, the horrors of what has gone on in Central America need addressing, and if her book helps do that, more power to it. But present it as what it is: A work intended to stir people to action, not a factual account" (Jeffrey).

29. "The successful tourism product is, therefore, an interpretation of the local, historical experience insofar as it can be related to, and incorporated in, the historical experience of the visitor. Thus a successful foreign heritage tourism industry is dependent not on the sale of the heritage of the destination country to visitors from the consumer country but, on the contrary, on the resale in a different guise of the consumers' own heritage in an unexpected context within the destination country" (Ashworth 24).

Bibliography

Arias, Arturo. 1999. "Más sobre las memorias de Rigoberta Menchú." *El Periódico* (Guatemala City), January 17.

Ashworth, G. J. 1994. "From History to Heritage, from Heritage to Identity: In Search of Concepts and Models." In *Tourism, Culture and Identity in the New Europe*, ed. G. J. Ashworth and P. J. Larkham. London and New York: Routledge. 13–29.

Asturias, Miguel Ángel. 1988. *París 1924–1933. Periodismo y creación literaria.* Edición crítica. Ed. Amos Segala. Paris: ALLCA.

Aznárez, Juan Jesús. 1999. "Los que me atacan humillan a las víctimas" (entrevista a Rigoberta Menchú). *El País,* January 24, 6–7.

Beverley, John. "The Real Thing." *Modern Language Quarterly* 57.2 (1996): 129–39.

Boletín Internacional del Frente Democrático Nueva Guatemala. 1999. Guatemala City, February 8.

Burgos-Debray, Elisabeth. 1984. *Me llamo Rigoberta Menchú.* Havana: Casa de las Américas.

CEH (Comisión del Esclarecimiento Histórico). 1999. *Guatemala: Memoria del silencio.* "Conclusiones," <http://hrdata.aaas.org/ceh/report/spanish/concl.html>, February 28.

Fundación Rigoberta Menchú Tum. 1999a. "Rigoberta Menchú Tum: una verdad que desafió al futuro." Mexico City, January.

———. 1999b. "Rigoberta Menchú admite que usó *testimonios* ajenos en su libro," Guatemala City, February 12.

———. 1999c. "Comunicado de prensa [sobre *Guatemala, memoria del silencio*]." Guatemala City, February 26.

Galeano, Eduardo. 1999. "Disparen sobre Rigoberta." Montevideo, IPS, E-mail de Fundación Rigoberta Menchú Tum. January 15.

Grandin, Greg and Francisco Goldman. 1999. "Bitter Fruit for Rigoberta." *Nation,* February 8.

Harnecker, Marta. 1983a. *Pueblos en armas.* Mexico City: Universidad Autonóma de Guerrero.

———. 1983b. *Punto final. Crear uno, dos, tres Vietnams.* Lima: Verde Olivo.

Jeffrey, H. Joel. "Response, Colloquy." *Chronicle of Higher Education.* //chronicle.com/colloquy/99/Menchú/50.htm.

Lacan, Jacques. 1968. *The Language of the Self.* Trans. Anthony Wilden. Baltimore: Johns Hopkins University Press.

Liano, Dante. 1999. "El antropólogo con la cachucha." *El Periódico* (Guatemala City), January 24.

Menchú, Rigoberta, with Elisabeth Burgos-Debray. 1984. *I, Rigoberta Menchú: An Indian Woman in Guatemala.* Trans. Ann Wright. London: Verso.

Montero, Rosa. 1999. "Ella." *El País* (Madrid), December 4.

Morales, Mario Roberto. 1994. *Señores bajo los árboles.* Guatemala City: Artemis-Edinter. English: *Face of the Earth, Heart of the Sky.* Trans. Edward W. Hood. Tempe, Ariz.: Bilingual Review Press, 2000.

———. 1998. *Los que se fueron por la libre.* México City: Praxis.

———. 1999a. *La articulación de las diferencias o El síndrome de Maximón.* Guatemala City: FLACSO.

———. 1999b. "Leyendo y tomando distancia." *Siglo XXI* (Guatemala), January 25.

Pacheco, Vinicio. 1999. "URNG pide perdón por errores cometidos durante guerra." *Siglo Veintiuno* (Guatemala City), March 16.

Ramírez, Sergio. 1999. "¿Quién le teme a Rigoberta Menchú?" *El Heraldo* (Tegucigalpa), February 4.

Rohter, Larry. 1998. "Nobel Winner Accused of Stretching Truth in Her Autobiography." *New York Times,* December 15.

Stoll, David. 1999. *Rigoberta Menchú and the Story of All Poor Guatemalans.* Boulder, Colo.: Westview Press.

Vázquez Montalbán, M. 1999. "Rigoberta." *El País* (Madrid), January 11.

Wilson, Robin. 1999. "A Challenge to the Veracity of Multicultural Icon." *Chronicle of Higher Education.* January 15, A 14–15.

Truth, Human Rights, and Representation
The Case of Rigoberta Menchú

Victor D. Montejo

The Truth and Testimonies

Despite anthropology's critical view of itself as a discipline, dealing
mainly with the problems of representation and misrepresentation of
indigenous cultures, once again, here we are engaged in the same problem. In terms of the truth, anthropologists have tended to impose their
own views on indigenous people, not respecting the indigenous people's truth in their own terms. It is the practice of anthropologists to
search for the truth, and some expect that it will come in only one version. But with human cultures and behavior the situation is different
and there may be as many interpretations of events and actions as there
are different worldviews. In the case of Rigoberta Menchú, many elements are at play in her testimony: death, memory, the army violence,
fear, leftist ideological conditioning, exile, and so on.

Perhaps the theorists of testimonial literature have pushed us too far
in believing that testimonies are infallible stories or eyewitness accounts.
For this reason some of Menchú's supporters believed that she had told
the absolute truth, and they cannot accept that she has added elements
to her stories to make them more dramatic and appealing to international
solidarity organizations. On the other hand, I recognize the difficulties
of writing and presenting the facts of such a violent and genocidal war
to the general public. For those of us who have written testimonies, it
has been necessary to be in a secure place in exile in order to write these
eyewitness accounts. Here, the protagonist has to rely on his/her memory
in order to recount the events. In this process of forcing the self to relive

those moments of desperation, pain, and death, the mind tries to recall the strongest images of death and destruction experienced collectively. This may explain why Rigoberta Menchú added images of cruelty to her own account that by itself was already so dramatic (e.g., Rigoberta's account of seeing her brother being burned alive). For those who lived those moments of despair and massacres, this is an effort of the part of the unconscious mind to ensure that one's voice is effectively heard— that the voice elicits a strong commitment and solidarity from those who may respond immediately to these human rights abuses. In the case of Rigoberta Menchú, besides these internal and psychological pressures, she had to answer to her editor, Elisabeth Burgos-Debray, and to the guerrilla leaders who approved the final text (see Taracena 1999).

Some of her followers argue that Menchú's authority as a Nobel Prize winner is being undermined as a result of her work being scrutinized or challenged. The problem of isolation that Menchú is currently facing is not because of her book, but because of her lack of presence in Maya communities. Even some of those who worked closely with the popular left and guerrilla organizations now argue that she does not represent them. Everybody agrees that she is an international figure with a limited presence in Maya communities. In other words, her name and image were not well known by the indigenous people in Guatemala.

Despite the criticisms against Menchú in Guatemala, she is still a strong figure who has confronted the Guatemalan government because of its lack of seriousness in developing projects of reparation and implementation of the peace accords. In a recent interview, Menchú said, "I cannot pardon those who killed my parents. To pardon is to know the names of the criminals, to know that they recognize their crimes" (Menchú 1999). Her strong voice on this issue of historical clarification of genocide is important for the future of reparation in the communities massacred during the armed conflict. Meanwhile, the political left is trying to distance itself from her. This distancing by the left will, in the long run, be more beneficial for Menchú, as she will move closer to the general Maya population of Guatemala, not only the most radicalized peasants.

Historically, the work of Menchú and others who write testimonies is very important. Their works resemble those of the Maya who denounced the atrocities of the Conquest during the early sixteenth century. Christopher Lutz and Karen Dakin's book *Nuestro pesar, nuestra aflicción* (1996) contains the testimonies of Maya telling the king of Spain about their suffering under colonial rule:

> Now, you should know that the Auditors came here to the city of Santiago de Guatemala to bring the Audience. They brought us too much suffering. They brought a great affliction to us, those *alcaldes* and councilmen. This is how they forced us to live in slavery. They did not have pity on us. It is in this way that we lived, as slaves. . . . For all this, it is so overwhelming the affliction that they have caused us. (Lutz and Dakin 1996, 5; my translation)

At the same time, Bartolomé de Las Casas wrote to the king of Spain denouncing the crimes and tortures that the Spaniards committed against the Indians. In his *Brief Account of the Destruction of the Indies,* Las Casas mentioned that the Indians were subjected to inhumane treatment by the Spanish lords. Because of these denunciations, Las Casas's account was attacked as a lie, and considered a "black legend." Those who opposed Las Casas called his account an unfounded accusation against the Spaniards, and a major insult to Spain.

The book of Rigoberta Menchú, then, has played an important role in making public the plight of the indigenous people of Guatemala. That is why David Stoll's book has created a fuzzy environment around Menchú's testimony. No doubt the right-wing sectors of Guatemala, especially the army, which was involved in these crimes, may soon consider her story a "black legend" too. Fortunately, the REHMI and truth commission's reports are conclusive proof of such atrocities. Indeed, these reports refer to the massive massacres by the army and the guerrillas as "genocide."

The Maya Situation

The 1970s and 1980s resembled the years of the 1950s with the Arbenz government. Anthropologists John Gillin (1960) and Richard Adams (1960) said that during the Arbenz government, many of the younger and better educated Indians and lower-class Ladinos were drawn first into political activity and then into more "radical" movements. This is what happened to the indigenous population of western Guatemala during the 1980s, with the role of the Committee for Peasant Unity (CUC). This is the historical context in which Rigoberta Menchú played an important organizing role, as stated in her account.

The late 1970s and the 1980s were a very difficult time for the Maya of rural Guatemala. Freedom of speech and the civil rights of Guatemalans were strictly controlled by the successive military governments. The legacy of these years of *la violencia* was silence, fear, and intimidation (Warren 1998). During the violence, it was dangerous to write about these massacres, and I am among the few who wrote testimonies in exile. We had to rely on oral tradition to pass on the information and find mnemonic devices to fix and remember those dates and events that were the most violent in modern Guatemalan history (Montejo 1999). But no attention was paid to other testimonies, because the popular-guerrilla movement decided to promote only one testimony, thus making Menchú the only indigenous voice for the Maya. In this way they consecrated Menchú's testimony as the sole truth to be preached for eliciting international support. Of course, this was not Rigoberta Menchú's fault; she did not say that her account contained the gospel or absolute truth. It was the popular movement, some left-leaning university professors, and international solidarity organizations that themselves made it a sacred text. So when anthropologist David Stoll came out with a devastating deconstruction of the text, they were scandalized. For international solidarity organizations and academics, Stoll committed a sacrilege by questioning Menchú's stories. They have forgotten that all writings are "suspicious" and that they represent the political or ideological conditioning or tendencies of the individual who produces them. Even the Bible has its critics, and this tells us that we must learn to take criticisms constructively.

Let me comment briefly on Menchú's autobiography. To me, the first part of the book, which describes the cultural traditions and ceremonies performed in the villages during birth and infancy, is the most important part of the text. Here it is Rigoberta who speaks with her own voice and knowledge. This is the true Maya aspect of her culture depicted in the book. But when she enters into telling her stories about the plantations, the Maya themselves who have gone there start to feel uneasy with her stories. This is where she began to respond to a different agenda, the revolutionary agenda, which sought to bring and integrate indigenous people into the two major guerrilla fronts in rural Guatemala, the Guerrilla Army of the Poor (EGP) and the Revolutionary Organization of the People in Arms (ORPA). In addition, Menchú provided an oral account to Burgos-Debray, which became a fixed text. The creation of this text brings us to the problems of representation, history, ethnographic authority, military repression, guerrilla warfare, and the truth. Obviously, Menchú was not completely in charge of the representation of the Maya or the description of the events. Her account is controlled by an anthropologist who is an outsider (Burgos-Debray has stated that she had never been in Guatemala). Then we have the problem of history. Who is writing this history? Who decides what is to be said and how? Here we have the leftist view of the history of Guatemala, the revolutionary point of view. With the publication of the book, Menchú's account and painful experience became a political and revolutionary tool. The problem is that Menchú was not in charge of writing her own account, although she may have agreed with the final product.

The book has served its purpose and now we are in the process of revising history. Those who attack David Stoll as the Antichrist of anthropological research are fossilized in time. With the publication of his book, *Rigoberta Menchú and the Story of All Poor Guatemalans,* a firestorm of controversies has been burning in the United States among activists and left-leaning academia. Stoll is being demonized for revealing what he heard among the K'iche' people who are depicted in Rigoberta Menchú's book. Now the debate has turned into Stoll versus Menchú; American anthropologists versus Ladino anthropologists; left-wing versus right-wing intellectuals, and so on. Why is it that Stoll's findings are so cherished by right-wing intellectuals and so damaging to the left and revolutionary supporters? I ask myself, Where are the Maya people in all of this? One side takes Stoll's book as proof that Rigoberta, and by extension the indigenous people, is a liar. The other side believes that *I, Rigoberta Menchú* is a sacred document that does not contain mistakes or distortions. And even if they recognize that Stoll has valid information that supports his claims for such distortions, the left does not want to admit that there are mistakes or problems.

This is a very entertaining debate, but, I would like to remind my colleagues, we are missing something important. Don't we realize that the report of the Commission for Historical Clarification (CEH) has made public the fact that the army committed 93 percent of the massacres and the Guatemalan National Revolutionary Unity (URNG) 3 percent, that both armed groups did damage to indigenous communities, and that Maya now need to reconstruct their lives by trying to remove themselves from those who brought the guns and did the killing? The Maya now want to remember the last words of Monsignor Juan Gerardi, who called for peace and justice in the report *Guatemala: nunca más*. In this cry for justice we can also hear the voices of the thousands killed in this war. The problem that we are witnessing in this debate is internationalist and leftist revolutionary nostalgia; they do not want to let their baby, the revolution, go. They hoped to free the oppressed and have a free Guatemala, but in the process they too became part of the problem that they were struggling to solve.

I, Rigoberta Menchú, the Book

I will now focus on the construction of the book *I, Rigoberta Menchú* edited by Elisabeth Burgos-Debray. The problems in this book appear right at the start. I am talking about the original Spanish version, because the English edition has been slightly changed. The original title of the book was *Me llamo Rigoberta Menchú y así me nació la conciencia* (My name is Rigoberta Menchú and this is how my consciousness was born). This title is very expressive of revolutionary slogans, because here she talks about revolutionary consciousness, *conciencia de lucha*, as if the Maya were not conscious of their situation but passive and opposed to change, as Marxist thought would assert. Appropriately, the title was changed in the English translation to *I, Rigoberta Menchú: An Indian Woman in Guatemala*. Also, in the original version, the guerrilla movement and the CUC as one of its civilian fronts included a pamphlet as an appendix to the book. This does not appear in the English versions of the book. Now, we know that the book was processed by Burgos-Debray and revised by guerrilla leaders before its publication, to make sure that it said what they wanted people to hear, according to Arturo Taracena's interview. The issue of representation, then, becomes problematic. According to Kay Warren, "questioning the politics of who speaks for whom will always be important for insiders and outsiders alike. It raises the issue of representation in both senses: who claims the authority to craft representations of ongoing social and political realities and who gains the position to represent others in public affairs?" (1998, 20).

So the problem of representation is evident in Menchú's book. I agree with Stoll that not all Maya sided with the guerrilla movement as it is portrayed here. The participation of indigenous people varied from place

to place or region to region. Also, those who had some political education were involved in events promoted by the CUC to raise consciousness. The majority did not care about the revolution and they were even
afraid of both armed groups. I have written about the history of these
conflicting relationships between the army and the guerrillas, as the war
took its toll on indigenous people (Montejo 1999). Rigoberta Menchú
and her family, like thousands more, are definitely victims of the army.
Perhaps we could say that the guerrillas too kept Menchú tied to their
agendas as a result of the death of most of her family members. So, what
is the problem here? One of the problems is making a static icon of
Rigoberta Menchú. The political and academic left has singled out Rigoberta Menchú as the only voice for the Maya movement, and that is
why they are now afraid that the extreme right might destroy the movement by discrediting her. But the Maya movement is not only represented by the popular movement, which is guerrilla-oriented. This difference is what the left and right often confuse. First, the Maya movement
referred to in this debate is not necessarily the popular left movement
championed by Rigoberta Menchú. We all know that the guerrilla leaders did not want to hear about Maya culture and its diversity as a positive contribution to the guerrilla struggle. Too many languages, too many
forms or expressions of Maya culture were seen as obstacles to the guerrilla movement. That is why the Maya culturalist movement worked pa-
tiently to promote Maya culture, while the left promoted revolution and
armed struggle with no interest in Maya culture.

Second, it has always been a strategy of the Left to have a unified controlled voice or spokesperson. This was the role of Rigoberta Menchú
in the popular movement, which is now called the Maya movement. This
guerrilla strategy has been a danger to the real Maya movement. If you
have one voice and if that voice is not free to say things unless approved
by partisan interests, then it becomes ineffective. This is what happened to
Rigoberta Menchú. The popular movement and the guerrilla movement
wanted international solidarity support and created one voice, which
became the only voice for all the Maya. The extreme right understands
this strategy, so it is now focusing its efforts on undermining that one
voice and discrediting the Maya movement. It is, then, very important
to recognize the complexity of the Maya movement. "In the post-Cold
War era, with the transition to civilian governments and the signing of

the peace accords, it is particularly important to hear other voices and grammars of dissent" (Warren 1998, 117).

Much like the Zapatista uprising in Chiapas, the Menchú case is a cyberspace intellectual war in which some speak in desperation to "protect" Menchú while condemning Stoll. It seems that those who promoted the guerrilla war internationally are now without much to do, and this is the opportunity to keep fighting and firing from their computers. They are not really interested in the problems that Maya are facing now in Guatemala. For the Maya, the ex-guerrillas and the government are seen as political tricksters who have been deceiving the people.

The Maya want to be in charge of their projects and now are struggling to make the Guatemalan government comply with the peace accords and the reparation recommendations of the CEH. The Menchú–Stoll controversy is only entertainment for academics and politicians who want to accuse each other or themselves of what they have failed to do, namely, to work with indigenous people.

The Menchú–Stoll Controversy

The responses to Stoll's book have been diverse, ranging from right-wing approbation to leftist accusations that Stoll is working for the CIA. In between are the Maya people that both camps seem to dismiss without care or consideration. They tend to forget that there is a Maya movement directed by the Maya and that it is represented by multiple voices. As I mentioned, the left has glorified an individual to the point of apotheosis. On the other side of the camp are those who consider Stoll's book as an open door to dismissing Menchú's arduous work for human rights, accusing her of being a "shameless liar" and a "Marxist terrorist" (Horowitz 1999). Eileen Mulhare has said that the grouping of people who have externalized their opinions with anger have not read Stoll's book carefully, or they have only a one-sided view of the Guatemalan situation. As a Maya and an anthropologist who suffered the violence that scholars here are disputing as an academic pastime, I believe that Maya self-criticism is important at this point. Good-hearted left-oriented anthropologists have been defending Menchú's book, but in the meantime she has tried to distance herself from it.

Here we have foreign anthropologists speaking for Menchú and for the Maya. To engage in this kind of debate is to distance ourselves from the reality that indigenous people are living. We know that they suffered the most, and that because of their ethnicity they were targeted for destruction. And we are aware that no one is being prosecuted for these criminal actions. In fact, there is no reparation project in place to heal the wounds of the survivors of this armed conflict.

Now is the right time to focus on these pressing issues for the Maya. We should insist on the implementation of the peace accords. We must teach human rights in our universities. We should help the Maya, and not just the politicized sectors, in this process of reparation necessary for healing the wounds of thirty-six years of war and destruction of Maya cultures. We should spend our energy on initiatives that will support the Maya movement. We have to see this Menchú–Stoll debate, as a problem not of the integrity of Menchú, but of the revolutionary movement and its relationship with indigenous people. It is unfortunate that Menchú started too late to remove herself from the guerrilla conditioning, because in the countryside, indigenous people still identify Menchú with the guerrillas and that is why they doubt her leadership.

The concern of many is that Stoll's book will have a negative impact on the Maya movement. This may not happen, because the current Maya movement does not rest on one individual. Just think of the four hundred or so Maya organizations struggling today to express their disagreements with the two major players of the armed conflict, the army and the URNG.

Meanwhile, the Menchú–Stoll controversy has been followed by scholars and intellectuals in the Americas and Europe. One of these is the Uruguayan writer Eduardo Galeano. In his article "Let's shoot Rigoberta," which appeared in *La Jornada* (January 1, 1999), he responded to David Stoll's book: "Lying that she witnessed her brother's being burned to death is insignificant," adding that "it is one of the hairs in the soup." The major problem, according to Galeano, is that "these people delegitimize the indigenous movement of resistance" by calling Menchú a liar. Galeano is right that people may dismiss the effort of the Maya to continue their struggle against racist discrimination and violence, but this does not delegitimize the movement. Rigoberta Menchú represented only one sector of the indigenous movement, the so-called popular movement. The Maya movement is very complex and now it has given rise to the Pan-Maya movement, which is focusing on culture and identity as major sources for its revival. Now we can argue that there are multiple voices supporting the Maya movement, and Rigoberta's is just one of them. Galeano also questions Stoll's ethics by pointing out his links to the army. Galeano wonders what documents and archives Stoll investigated. The army archives? But by reading Stoll's book we can find out that indeed the colonization of the national lands in northern Guatemala was common during the 1960s and 1970s, and Stoll makes reference to the records in the archives of the National Institute for Agrarian Transformation (INTA).

Among the North American anthropologists who responded to Galeano's article is the anthropologist Eileen Mulhare. She says that Galeano did not read Stoll's book before giving his statements against the findings presented in the book. Mulhare tried to represent the middle ground and includes the criticism of Dante Liano, who argues that Stoll "came to Guatemala to study us as insects." That's right, this is the traditional critique of anthropology as a colonialist discipline. Mulhare defends anthropologists by stating that thanks to foreign anthropologists the world knows more about the current life of the Maya. This is true, but Mulhare forgot to add that archaeology has fossilized the modern Maya while giving life to the ancient past as reconstructed by the archaeologists to attract tourists. The anthropologist's role is to write about Maya culture and then what? Little has changed in the oppression of indigenous people, even if foreign and Ladino anthropologists have been studying them for a century. But Mulhare gets into difficulty with the Guatemalan Ladino academy when she states, "Those who have the tradition of studying them [the Maya] as 'insects' are the Guatemalan Ladino scholars."

Obviously, this accusation against Ladino anthropologists is false. It is fair to say that the Ladino academics have few opportunities for funding to carry out research. On the other hand, foreign anthropologists have studied Maya culture for one purpose: to write dissertations and to get good-paying jobs at prestigious universities. But, let us not forget that, as in the case of the Ladinos, some foreign anthropologists, including Mulhare, have worked for human rights issues also, and have produced books denouncing the genocide suffered by indigenous people (Manz 1988; Falla 1994). Mulhare mentions the volume edited by Robert Carmack, *Harvest of Violence*. In this book, David Stoll also wrote an article denouncing the role of Protestantism and the CIA in helping the army to repress the indigenous population.

Eileen Mulhare makes reference to the current dialogue between foreign anthropologists and indigenous people. But there are very few indigenous scholars who are also writing about their own cultures, and this has to increase. The truth is that there are North American people that are helping indigenous people in their struggle for their rights and self-determination. I agree with Mulhare on certain points, but her statement that the life history of Menchú is mythical does not convey a full appreciation of the situation. Menchú did suffer greatly and the death of all of her family is not a myth.

Then Mulhare's critique of Ladino anthropology brought another dimension to the debate. A Guatemalan anthropologist, Carlos René García Escobar, at the Centro de Estudios Folklóricos of the University of San Carlos, circulated an angry attack on foreign anthropologists in his article "Antropólogos gringos vs. antropólogos chapines." This article shifted the debate from Stoll versus Menchú to American versus Guatemalan anthropologists.

García Escobar argues that Mulhare attacked and made incorrect references to Ladino academics in Guatemala. He said that she is wrong because she does not know them and their intellectual background. He argued that Mulhare is wrong on several issues. First, "It is not true that only the gringo anthropologists consult the Maya and live with them." Then he said that Ladinos have lived with the Indians and they do not have the difficulties that foreigners have in reaching and living with them; that

> foreign anthropologists have penetrated our territories to obtain information and inform their institutions while obtaining a Ph.D. at their universities. They serve as spies or secret agents providing information, free or paid by the institutions where they work. As tourists, they also plunder the national heritage, be it by buying or stealing archaeological objects and smuggling them out of our country. (García Escobar)

Is this accusation against foreign anthropologists fair? To me, both groups, Ladino anthropologists and foreigners, have a fundamental problem here. In his statement, García Escobar indicates that the Ladinos see Maya culture and people as objects or separate entities that have to be studied by anthropologists, whether they be national or foreign. It seems that he is trying to argue that Ladino anthropologists have more control and "ownership" of indigenous cultures than foreigners. Thus, there is no difference in the conceptualization of indigenous people from that of foreigners, who see them as "informants" and creatures to be studied. Both groups, I believe, obtain their degrees by studying indigenous people. In this same paragraph he stated that U.S. anthropologists are disguised agents who supply information to their institutions. We may think of CIA agents in this case. Certainly, some are involved in intelligence gathering, while others are just anthropologists studying Maya culture. Once again, we see that some Guatemalans, such as army intelligence officers, are on the CIA payroll to gather information.

García Escobar is right when he says that during the revolutionary government of Jacobo Arbenz Guzmán, there were efforts to improve the life of indigenous people, but the intervention by the CIA in overthrowing the Arbenz government placed in power Ladino authorities who became worse tyrants against the indigenous people, and eventually maintained the structure that precipitated the civil war that lasted since the early 1960s. I recognize the frustration of García Escobar, but to compare the University of San Carlos with foreign universities does not fix the problem. It is better to focus on the systematic development of curriculum in the national universities as a starting point, in collaboration with foreign universities.

The Extreme Right and Left Positions

Of course Stoll's book has already fueled fierce attacks against Rigoberta Menchú. The director of the right-wing Center for the Study of Popular Culture based in Los Angeles has placed advertisements in campus newspapers calling Rigoberta Menchú a "Marxist terrorist." The extreme interpretations of Stoll's book are dangerous for indigenous and minority people on campuses. Any kind of revindicating struggle will be dismissed as "terrorism," and they will accuse professors and students who sympathize with third-world struggles of being terrorists. David Horowitz, president of the center, asks the question: "Why are they teaching something that is patently false and intellectually dishonest?" Responses like this are problematic for Menchú's integrity. Most of these right-wing people do not bother to learn about the historical subjugation of indigenous people in the Americas. For this reason, Stoll's book furnishes ammunition to those who hate dealing with the truth and the sources of misery that affect the life of those about whom they write. David Stoll argues for a loyalty to the truth and not to a political viewpoint. But unfortunately, there will be multiple readings and meanings pulled out of his book.

In Guatemala, elite Ladino people who do not want the Maya holocaust to be made public also argue in favor of David Stoll. Alfred Kaltsmith, who was a director of the Foundation for the Aid of Indigenous Peoples (FUNDAPI), and coordinated aid to Maya communities as part of the hideous "guns and beans" program of Ríos Montt, said in an article in *Siglo Veintiuno* (July 11, 1998): "Stoll's book, the product of ten years of careful and extensive research, acquires credibility while Menchú's book loses credibility." For people who worked with Ríos Montt, Stoll's book has come as a delicious aftermath to the conflict. But then, it is truly unfortunate that there are many inconsistencies in Menchú's testimony and that Stoll has decided to chase them down. The winner in all of this turmoil is the Guatemalan army and those who were responsible for committing the massacres reported by the CEH.

A *Los Angeles Times* article, "The Truth Is Enough," represents more impartial reporting, stating:

> Fiction is fiction, there is no way around it, and we now discover that Rigoberta Menchú, the winner of the 1992 Nobel Peace prize, concocted many of the events in the autobiography that brought her fame and adulation. But that does not lessen our need to learn what happened in the bloody war in the highlands of Guatemala during the Central American wars of the 1980s.

I agree. Even if Stoll's new study takes away the merits of Menchú's book as a truthful earwitness account, it should not lead us, according to this columnist, "to reject the book as a pack of lies." And, as all of the Mayanists have argued, the war did occur and the army did commit those horrendous massacres. Menchú had the courage, as did few other Maya, to tell her story and fight against these injustices.

On the other hand, the extreme left has its own arguments against Stoll and in favor of Menchú. César Montes, an ex-guerrilla, tried to justify Menchú's mistakes by using revolutionary arguments. In an article published in *Siglo XXI* he stated:

> Very often we receive information about the death of our brothers clandestinely and in an inexact form. And we transmit the information like this. Not because it is inexact does it become a lie. Perhaps her

brother did not die in the way she described in the book. But the fact is that he was assassinated by the repressive members of the army.

Montes is arguing about something that Stoll already understands. Nobody doubts that Menchú's brother died and that the army is repressive. Stoll explains this, although not forcefully. Then, Montes links her to the guerrillas when he says that "we receive information . . . clandestinely." Menchú's problem is that she had to say this to suit the needs of the revolutionary movement. Montes then says that the efforts of the compiler, Burgos-Debray, may have been to emphasize the suffering of those thousands of Indians who live in extreme misery. Here, he tries to suggest that Burgos-Debray added more than what she was told by Menchú. He also recognizes that Menchú's book was written on the basis of verbal accounts, which were taped and then transcribed, so it cannot be rigorously exact.

Certainly, one may agree with this explanation, that Menchú may have not said everything that is in the book, and that some things may have been added during the editing of the manuscript. This is what I believed personally, but then, she had repeated her stories in other media. She tells the same story of the murder of her brother on TV and in the film *When the Mountains Tremble.* So the story of the death of her brother being burned alive is not Burgos-Debray's fabrication. Stoll is then telling us that in the book there are accounts that did not happen exactly as they are written. Even Rigoberta Menchú admitted in the *New York Times* (December 2, 1999) that she used the experiences and testimonies of others to weave her story.

To me, this is what Stoll is trying to explain to the readers of Menchú's book. He is not denying that the army killed or burned its victims. The army was criminal and genocidal and those responsible should be prosecuted. The problem that he is trying to clarify is that in Rigoberta's account there are pieces that do not fit. This, then, confirms what most Mayanists have argued: that the left created only one voice and obfuscated or dismissed other voices that did not fit their plans or that they could not manipulate and control. The accounts of those Maya who wrote and talked about the violence from their own initiative and convictions were not taken into account. Definitively, this restriction of other voices affected the Maya movement because there were multiple voices denouncing the atrocities, but they were not given attention or importance.

More on the Academic Camp

Because it was an anthropologist who wrote *I, Rigoberta Menchú*, and it is an anthropologist who challenged some facts in it, the book has become a source of entertainment and debate by anthropologists. Some express their views with sobriety and some with anger against David Stoll. I think we should understand the viewpoint of Stoll and his research, even though it may affect the image of Rigoberta Menchú. On the other hand, we are talking about Rigoberta's book and not about her dignity as a person or as a major Maya leader. We know, as suggested by Diane Nelson, that her book is "an explicitly political book, seizing hold of memory in a moment of extreme danger." I would add that the book was also a political propaganda piece forced out of her by the political strategists of the EGP and Burgos-Debray. Perhaps we have to recognize that she too suffered manipulation by the same guerrilla movement that she was supporting.

But Nelson rightfully asks the question of Stoll's undermining Menchú's credibility. "Will it [Stoll's book] support the struggles of indigenous and poor peoples?" Obviously not, this is just another academic work. Although the right wing and the Guatemalan oligarchy are very happy with Stoll's book, the spaces that were open for the implementation of the peace process are now being closed. Even in the United States, Victoria Sanford has indicated that some individuals are already using it to discredit the importance of multicultural education. Jeffrey Hart, a columnist of the Dixon town newspaper, *Independent Voice,* published an article about Rigoberta Menchú's book with the title "A Classic of Lies." This is very unfortunate, because in Guatemala the oligarchy is now accusing Menchú of being an Indian liar, reinforcing the stereotypes imposed on indigenous people.

An article appearing in the *Nation* by Greg Grandin and Francisco Goldman said that Menchú's book was a "piece of wartime propaganda designed not to mislead but rather to capture our attention" (25). I think these two critiques are right on target. The guerrilla movement was more successful with the written word than with its weapons, as it lacked a good understanding of Maya people and their cultures.

David Stoll is free as an anthropologist to write about issues that he thinks are challenging. Similarly, I want to make clear that the role of the guerrillas in fighting the monstrous Guatemalan army is a positive historical event. Many non-Maya as well as Maya gave their lives for this revolutionary ideal, and they must be remembered with pride and honor.

I am not defending Stoll's book either, because he too has many misrepresentations of Menchú and Maya people. He does not really understand what it means to be persecuted by the army and to be in danger of being killed. Stoll also says that Menchú learned Spanish earlier with the nuns, despite her "repeated claim that she never went to school and learned to speak Spanish only recently, *as if this was a point of pride*" (159; my emphasis). Of course this is not a point of pride. She was trying to let people know that she is using the language of the oppressors and that she speaks it with some difficulty. She needed to justify herself to the international community, which was listening to her voice as that of an international spokesperson.

To avoid returning to these heated debates about an individual, it is important that solidarity organizations, scholars, and activists also recognize the contributions of other Maya. We tend to focus only on one voice and that is why people fear that the Maya revitalization movement will be destroyed. It is as if Maya culture were resting on a single pillar. The truth is that thousands of Maya are working to promote their culture and they are not given credit for their contribution. Academia creates icons and talks about one "voice," one representation, and one Maya movement. But the Maya movement has multiple voices, multiple actors, and multiple expressions, so it is difficult to keep up with it.

For this reason, I think it is necessary to have Maya views and self-criticism of the events. It is our fault that others have directed us to violence and have represented us in this struggle. Even in the national dialogue for the peace accords, others represented the Maya. I am sure that those who were named as responsible for the massacres—and not those who were affected by the violence—will be again in charge of projects for reparation. It is time to be more impartial and support the Maya in their efforts to represent themselves. President Arzú has remained silent about the truth commission's report.[1] The government is now saying that it has already done what was needed, so there is no need for reparation. For this reason, those scholars who are engaged in the Stoll–

Menchú controversy should focus their attention on current issues concerning the Maya people. The revitalization of Maya culture requires their support and anthropologists can contribute their knowledge to projects that will benefit the affected communities. Anthropologists have been studying Maya cultures for so long; now let's confirm the usefulness of anthropology.

Generally speaking, *I, Rigoberta Menchú* has fulfilled its mission. But it is still important to use it in the classroom, especially the part that talks about Menchú's K'iche' culture, because this is the culture that she lives and cherishes. For the second part, which is about the guerrilla movement, there are other works that we can use to complement her text, which may be more impartial concerning the roles of the army and the guerrillas. Fortunately, more Maya are writing for themselves, being in control of their own ideas and of what they write. We should be owners of our own voices and thoughts and move away from this intellectual and ideological colonialism that we are still living. Most important, I agree with Paul Sullivan, who wrote in the *UC Mexus News* (winter 1999): "One cannot help but wonder who is being silenced when only certain indigenous voices are enabled by outsiders to speak" (5). This is the case of Rigoberta Menchú, considered by the left to be the "only voice" of the Maya people. In other words, the controversy involving this book falls into what Marcus and Fisher called the "crisis of representation" (1986). On the other hand, Stoll is not that evil person who wants to destroy Menchú for winning the Nobel Peace Prize. He is following the rules of scientific inquiry in which he must test his hypotheses. At the end his work confirms the failure of anthropology, that these anthropological works only fulfill academic curiosity and are irrelevant for indigenous people.

One thing is certain, though: in Guatemala most indigenous people are questioning Menchú's role. By being part of the popular left movement, which gave her her position, the guerrillas have also damaged her image as she now tries to become her own voice. The indigenous people have doubts about her, mainly concerning her links with the guerrillas. Stoll is not the only person who says that the people in her village do not totally support her accounts. This is what Maya women in the K'iche' region say: "She likes the foreigners more than she likes her own people." I think Rigoberta Menchú recognizes this criticism and is now living and sharing with the Maya inside her own country.

Conclusion

Returning to Menchú's autobiography, I truly believe that the first section of the book requires more attention by scholars who use it in their classrooms. The human relationships with the land and issues of respect and child rearing are very important for understanding indigenous cultures. Hopefully, scholars will recognize that we cannot teach Menchú's life story as the sole "truth." The Maya have multiple voices and we must listen to other voices. It has been the tactic of the revolutionary movements to create one voice so that international support hears the same message. They had the ability to neutralize other voices that were not in conformity with the political and military goals of their high command.

A final criticism of Stoll is the use of the photograph of Menchú on the front cover of his book. For those who have books published, we know that the editors and publishers have much to say about the front cover because their interest is to market the product. But this is a demolishing critique against the Nobel laureate, and so it could be considered unethical to use her picture on the cover of the book. First, the context in which she appears in the photograph is a protest of the murder of Bishop Juan Gerardi. Second, the uses of indigenous people to market a product is wrong because it makes them seen as objects to be consumed. Third, by presenting Rigoberta Menchú on the front cover of a book that undermines her credibility is like saying, "Here is the liar I am talking about." This may be one of the readings of Menchú's photograph used in Stoll's book. Stoll may have been unaware of the decision to use Menchú's photograph on the front cover, but if he knew about it, he should have asked that the photograph not be used. It would have been better if Stoll had used one of his own photographs, and changed the title of the book. But here we have the common practice of using indigenous people's images to market ethnographies. This is quite a contradiction because at least, in the first (Spanish) edition, the front cover has a drawing of Rigoberta's face and not a photograph. The same with the English edition of the book, which uses a new drawing of the face of Rigoberta Menchú.

Finally, I would like to address the most current questions of scholars regarding Menchú's book. If *I, Rigoberta Menchú* has problems, how can we now use the book as a college text? This is a legitimate question by those who have used it as a tool to show their students the magnitude of the armed conflict suffered by the Maya and other poor Guatemalans. But if we know that the book has problems, how can we use it as a text? This is what David Stoll was asked during a conference in Berkeley at which I was a participant. Stoll said that he heard someone propose that the best way to teach it is to treat Menchú's biography as an epic novel. It is the truth, but mythologized, or call it a myth-history; we may treat the book as a collection of stories falling into the category of what Miguel Ángel Asturias called magical realism. I think this is a postmodern trick that will push back in time and make unreal the pain and suffering of the Mayans. Thus, it will be easy to forget that the reparation recommended by the truth commission has not yet been carried out. According to the epic approach, we can now read the Menchú book like *El poema de Mío Cid, Roldán,* or even the adventures of Don Quixote. To imagine the recent Guatemalan holocaust as an epic is to remove ourselves from the reality of this genocide that has left two hundred thousand deaths. A problem that is still latent and that remains unresolved.

I think the two books and many more on these issues should be consulted in order to see that history is reconstructed with multiple voices and not by a single voice or truth. This may be one of the messages to be learned if we want to be impartial. Perhaps the left and the right must stop conditioning people to think in black and white, or in binomial appositions, good/bad, left/right. The Maya people and their culture are in the middle of this intellectual debate, which has become highly abstract and removed from current Maya reality.

Note

1. [President Arzú (1995–2000) presided over the signing of the Peace Accords. He was succeeded by Alfonso Portillo (2000–2005).—*Ed.*]

Bibliography

Adams, Richard N. 1960. "Social Change in Guatemala and U.S. Policy." In *Social Change in Latin America Today.* New York: Vintage Books.

Burt, Jo-Marie, and Fred Rosen. 1999. "Truth-Telling and Memory in Postwar Guatemala: An Interview with Rigoberta Menchú." *NACLA: Report on the Americas* 32.5: 6–10.

Falla, Ricardo. 1994. *Massacres in the Jungle: Ixcan, Guatemala, 1975–1982.* Boulder, Colo.: Westview Press.

Galeano, Eduardo. 1999. "Disparen sobre Rigoberta." *La Jornada,* January 16.

García Escobar, Carlos René. 1999. "Antropólogos gringos vs. antropólogos chapines." Distributed via E-mail by aeu@centramerica.com, March 18.

Gillin, John P. 1960. "Some Signposts for Policy." In *Social Change in Latin America Today*. New York: Vintage Books.

Grandin, Greg, and Francisco Goldman. 1999. "Bitter Fruit for Rigoberta." *Nation*, February 8.

Horowitz, David. 1999. "I, Rigoberta Menchú, Liar." *Salon*, http://www.salonmagazine.com/col/horo.

Kaltsmith, Alfred. 1998. "El testimonio de Rigoberta Menchú." *Siglo Veintiuno* (Guatemala), July 12.

Las Casas, Bartolomé de. 1989. *Brevísima relación de la destrucción de las Indias*. Madrid: Ediciones Catedra.

Liano, Dante. 1999. "Respuesta a Stoll." Distributed via E-mail, January 29.

Lutz, Christopher, and Karen Dakin. 1996. *Nuestro pesar, nuestra aflicción*. Mexico City: Universidad Autónoma de México y el Centro de Investigaciones Regionales de Mesoamerica, Guatemala City.

Manz, Beatriz. 1988. *Refugees of a Hidden War: The Aftermath of Counterinsurgency in Guatemala*. Albany: State University of New York Press.

Marcus, George E., and Michael M. Fischer. 1986. *Anthropology as Cultural Critique: An Experimental Moment in the Human Sciences*. Chicago: University of Chicago Press.

Menchú, Rigoberta. 1999. "Menchú no perdona." *Prensa Libre*, April 29.

Menchú, Rigoberta, with Elisabeth Burgos-Debray. 1985. *Me llamo Rigoberta Menchú y así me nació la conciencia*. Mexico City: Siglo XXI.

———. 1996. *I, Rigoberta Menchú: An Indian Woman in Guatemala*. New York: Verso.

Montejo, Victor D. 1987. *Testimony: Death of a Guatemalan Village*. Willimantic, Conn.: Curbstone Press.

———. 1999. *Voices from Exile: Violence and Survival in Modern Maya History*. Norman: University of Oklahoma Press.

Mulhare, Eileen M. 1999. "Respuesta a Galeano." Distributed by E-mail, Colgate University, Hamilton, New York, February 4.

Nelson, Diane. 1999. "Rigoberta Menchú: Is Truth Stranger Than Testimonial?" *Anthropology Newsletter* 40.4.

Sanford, Victoria D. 1999. "Rigoberta Menchú Debate." Distributed via E-mail, February 19.

Smith, Carol, ed. 1990. *Guatemalan Indians and the State: 1540–1988*. Austin: University of Texas Press.

Stoll, David. 1999. *Rigoberta Menchú and the Story of All Poor Guatemalans*. Boulder, Colo.: Westview Press.

Sullivan, Paul. 1999. "Why Are You the Enemy?" (Guest editorial, *UC Mexus News* 36 (winter). Berkeley: University of California Institute for Mexico and the United States.

Taracena, Arturo. 1999. "Arturo Taracena rompe el silencio" (entrevista por Luis Aceituno). *El Periódico*, January 10.

Warren, Kay B. 1998. "Maya Multiculturalism and the Violence of Memories." In *Violence, Political Agency, and the Self*, ed. Veena Das. Berkeley: University of California Press.

———. 1999. "Indigenous Movements and Their Critics." In *Pan-Maya Activism in Guatemala*. Princeton, N.J.: Princeton University Press.

The Battle of Rigoberta

David Stoll

> ... the critics have mixed their scholarly calling with their political beliefs, in the process converting oral literature—the most supple of genres and the most subject to personal invention—into an almost religious canon, bordering on the absolute. By delegitimizing every attempt at critical skepticism, they have obtained a contrary result: the status of the texts, specifically in this case that of Rigoberta Menchú, has actually become fragile, vulnerable to any misstep.
>
> —Elisabeth Burgos (1999, 86)

For many of the contributors to this volume, my decision to publish the problems with a beloved story is hard to fathom. The dismay is not surprising in view of how and why the Nobel laureate told her story and why I decided to challenge it. Rigoberta Menchú was not the first to tell us that the Guatemalan dictatorship of the early 1980s was slaughtering peasants. The story that she told and Elisabeth Burgos turned into a book was instead an answer to the question: Why should we care? About another far-off conflict in which people we don't know are being killed for reasons we don't understand.

The first-person nature of the story provided an immediacy and credibility that no other narrative style would have achieved. That is why the book has been so effective in spreading interest in Guatemala to wider circles, especially in colleges and churches. That is why it could not have been as effective as anything but eyewitness testimony—the kind of account that I demonstrate it was not. How can you question the eyewitness nature of Rigoberta's story without suggesting that she is guilty of a hoax, fraud, or lie? None of these labels is appropriate for a person telling how she lost three members of her family, but that is the implication. Once my book was translated into the column inches of journalism, the issue was the veracity of a Nobel laureate.

Ordinarily, cultural anthropologists such as myself are more interested in perspective than accuracy. That includes autobiographical accounts where partisanship is only to be expected. But in the case of *I, Rigoberta Menchú*, the story has been so appealing to foreigners that it has overshadowed other Mayan perspectives on the violence. I felt obliged to point out gaps between Rigoberta's story and that of neighbors because of the enormous authority that so many readers have attributed to it. If you take the book at face value, as an eyewitness account, you will probably conclude that guerrilla warfare in Guatemala grew out of peasants' need to defend themselves from intolerable conditions.

Because of the different story I heard from many peasants, this is what became the most important issue for me: Was the Guerrilla Army of the Poor (EGP) that Rigoberta joined, and whose version of events she gave us in 1982, an inevitable response by the poor to oppression? Should the conflict be understood primarily in social terms, as the inevitable outcome of centuries of oppression suffered by Guatemala's indigenous population? Or is it better explained on the political level, as the result of particular decisions made by particular groups including the U.S. government, the Guatemalan oligarchy, the Guatemalan army, and the opposition groups that decided to fight back with guerrilla warfare?

The Ixil Mayas whom I interviewed in the late 1980s had been a bastion of the largest of the three guerrilla groups, the EGP. Nearly everyone, including myself, assumed that the guerrillas had been a deeply rooted popular movement. If not, why would the army kill so many people? In the wake of repression, the EGP's support might seem impossible to gauge because survivors would be afraid to discuss it. This has become the most common rejoinder to my argument: that peasants were too repressed to say much about their experiences. Yet many Ixils were willing to acknowledge that they had supported the guerrillas. Some were also rather candid about the atrocities committed by the army, even in the late 1980s and early 1990s when they were still under army occupation.

Typically, Ixils said that the army had done most of the killing but blamed the guerrillas for being the first to show up in uniform with guns. If the EGP was to be believed, the Ixils were so oppressed that they had no choice but to join the insurgency. It is true that they were living under a dictatorship. Most were poor; many had suffered discrimination. When the EGP sent cadres into the area, some Ixils were eager to join. Many more were interested in the revolutionary message, of a Guatemala where they would enjoy the same privileges as wealthy ladinos. But the pre-EGP Ixils were not facing intense repression. Despite patronal backlashes, they were regaining control of local governments from ladinos. Although the region was policed by a dictatorship, it was not militarized, because the army had no reason to be there.

Once the EGP began to assert control, a succession of Ixils told me, they were on the horns of a dilemma. If they cooperated with the guerrillas, the army would kill them in droves. If they cooperated with the army, the guerrillas would kill them more selectively. They were "entre dos fuegos" (between two fires), the peasant expression I turned into the title of my much-excoriated *Between Two Armies in the Ixil Towns of Guatemala* (Stoll 1993). Once the army began to lash back at the guerrillas by punishing nearby civilians, in 1979–82, waves of Ixils joined the less homicidal EGP for protection. You can call this a popular movement if you want, but the connection with prewar political organizing was often weak.

My skepticism about why Ixils supported the guerrillas, and the anger of some of my colleagues that I expressed it, reflect the divide between *indígenas* and ladinos in Guatemalan life. On the national level, the guerrilla movement was a seemingly inevitable response to the 1954 CIA intervention and the right's destruction of democracy. But the leadership of the insurgency was urban and nonindigenous, with little participation by the country's Mayan population. Only in the late 1970s did the guerrillas recruit large numbers of Mayas. The most widely read account of that relationship is *I, Rigoberta Menchú*. So what do my interviews in Rigoberta's hometown tell us about the EGP's popular base there? Did her village join the guerrillas to defend itself from ladino landlords? Did many of her neighbors see the insurgency growing out of their own needs?

As I have often pointed out, oral testimony from a repressed town such as Uspantán could be affected by fear of the army or distrust of myself. That is why I checked what Uspantanos told me against land records and human rights reports. Judging from both kinds of information, the epic struggle against plantation owners in *I, Rigoberta Menchú* was actually an internecine conflict between K'iche' Maya in-laws. The first local political murders were committed by the EGP. These are mere details in terms of who bears responsibility for most of the subsequent killing—the army. But the import of Rigoberta's story is not just a detail, because it turned her family and village into model revolutionaries of the kind desired by the EGP.[1]

Judging from her story, five hundred years of indigenous resistance to colonialism had finally joined the larger revolutionary struggle. She gave foreign readers a firm sense of which side they should be on, even though the divided feelings expressed by Victor Montejo in his less-read testimonio *Death of a Guatemalan Village* (1987) were probably more widespread. Certainly there was Mayan support for the EGP—lots in the Ixil area and some in Rigoberta's *municipio*. But most of it was rather brief, for a year or two, and Rigoberta was telling her story at its apogee. When Rigoberta's story acquired the permanence of a book—not the original purpose of the tape recordings, which were for a magazine interview—it became a rationale for guerrilla warfare that acquired more weight than the many forms of Mayan alienation from this strategy. Over the next decade, as foreign readers fell under the book's spell, it consecrated a brief period of support for the guerrillas at the height of peasant consciousness, the golden age of militancy.

Still, the result was not just an EGP script or fabrication. Even if you object to Rigoberta's approach, her story became a parable about the social context of the violence that is easy to defend as truthful. By claiming to have suffered in ways that she never had herself, Rigoberta turned herself into a symbol for an entire people. By blaming all the violence on the army, she targeted the side that did 93 percent of the killing, according to the UN truth commission.

The main problem with Rigoberta's story is not that she chose to communicate the problems facing Guatemalan Indians by turning herself into a composite Maya, with a wider range of experiences than a single person could have. It is not important if her relatives died a bit differently than she says they did. Even if readers should know that *I, Rigoberta Menchú* is not a literal account of her life, it is not hard to defend her narrative strategy because her most important claim is true—the Guatemalan army was indeed slaughtering defenseless villagers. In a crisis situation, Rigoberta was dramatizing herself the way a Hollywood scriptwriter might, to stir an audience and move it to care about far-off victims.

What mattered most in 1982 was orchestrating international pressure against the Guatemalan army to stop the killing.

That said, there is a problem with Rigoberta's story. Arguably it was not a major problem in the early 1980s, when the killing was at its peak and what mattered most was drawing attention to a human rights emergency. But now that truth commissions are delivering reports, what may have been a secondary issue is no longer so. I refer to the social background of the killing, including how it spread to previously quiet areas. If you interpret Rigoberta's story as the eyewitness account that it claims to be, you will conclude that the rebel movement grew out of the basic needs of her people, which is not what many of them have to say about it.

My books are controversial because they take the intense localism that many anthropologists have found in rural Guatemala, then use it to challenge the assumption that the insurgency of the late 1970s and early 1980s was an inevitable Mayan reaction to oppression. That Mayas had very mixed feelings about the guerrillas is not a discovery made by myself.[2] Although the EGP was stronger in Rigoberta's region of the Sierra Cuchumatanes than in most others, a string of ethnographers (Davis 1988, 24–26; Watanabe 1992, 179–83; Kobrak 1997, 113; Montejo 1999, 63–65) have had doubts about the depth of its support, as have Yvon Le Bot (1995) and Carol Smith. Because Smith misconstrues my argument, let me quote some of her previous writings on the subject:

1. Did support for the insurgency spring from the steady immiseration of the poor? "Obviously, then," she concluded from her surveys of the prewar peasant economy, "it is incorrect to describe as general a pattern of increasing impoverishment of peasant communities in this period [to 1978], though one could point to increasing penetration of market relations into the fiber of indigenous society.... Both individuals and communities generally reported a much lower dependence on plantation income than was formerly the case.... there was no general trend toward increasing dependence on plantation wages, no general impoverishment, relatively little internal class polarization, and much less destruction of indigenous community organization than would be expected from the usual accounts of the period (Smith 1984, 212–16, for case studies, see Falla 1980 and Brintnall 1979)." No one denies that most Mayas were poor, that some welcomed the guerrillas, and that more joined the insurgency to protect themselves from repression. However, the tapestry of conditions that Mayas faced was not compatible with the ideo-

logical justification for the high cost of armed struggle, that the Mayas were being impoverished en masse.

2. Was the insurgency a last resort for peasants who had no other way to defend themselves? The last-resort paradigm fits some local situations, but more broadly it is not compatible with what we know about the origins of the Maya movement, which is led by people who are taking advantage of expanding opportunities. Nor is the last-resort paradigm compatible with the Maya movement's critique of the guerrillas as well as the army: that both sides imposed the war on Mayas. If the insurgency was an inevitable response to oppression, then ladino-led guerrilla organizations would not be guilty of imposing it. Here is what Smith had to say just as I was finishing *Between Two Armies:* "The guerrilla insurgency of the 1980s, in which many Maya participated, was not the kind of resistance described above—limited in goals, leaderless, localized. There was a clear strata of leaders, most of them middle- or even upper-class Ladinos, who had little experience with Maya culture or people.... From interviews with guerrilla leaders, as well as their own accounts, it seems fairly clear that they chose to recruit in the Maya area; Mayas did not seek out Ladino leaders for their own insurgency" (Smith 1991, 32).

3. Should blame for starting the violence be laid exclusively at the door of the Guatemalan army? Here I must repeat what so many peasants told me: although the army did most of the killing, it was often the guerrillas who were the first to visit their villages, as part of their announced strategy of spreading the war to new areas. Returning to Smith: "Both [Mario] Payeras [of the EGP] and Gaspar Ilóm of the Revolutionary Organization of the People in Arms (ORPA) have discussed how difficult it was to enlist Maya, but how recruitment snowballed after army repression began. It is now widely recognized that many Maya joined the insurgency *after* they were attacked by the army for merely living in places the guerrillas visited. For these people, following the guerrillas into the montaña was little more than an act of self-preservation. We do not yet know what revolution meant to those who joined the insurgency as voluntary participants, since Maya accounts of the 1980s are mainly those of victims rather than rebels" (1991; 32).[3]

Contrary to Smith, our colleague Paul Kobrak (1997) was not the first to point out that "we're caught in the crossfire" rhetoric was a protective response to army repression. "Because so much coercion and concealment is involved in this kind of warfare," I noted in *Between Two Armies,* "how can we be sure that statements of neutrality or alignment with the army are anything but tactical, James Scott's 'public transcript' as opposed to a 'hidden transcript' of support for the guerrillas? . . . At the most public level, that is, face to face with the army, Ixils mimic its rhetoric, as when civil patrollers volunteer that 'we're protecting our communities from the subversives.' Almost as public, that is, offered to just about anyone except perhaps an army officer, are protective statements of neutrality such as 'we're between two fires.' This is the safest possible presentation of self, the least compromising in many situations where one's interlocutor is not clearly marked politically. Needless to say, sharper feelings operate below the surface. . . . it was not hard to elicit frank descriptions of how the army imposed itself in the early 1980s, and few or none could be said to share the army's point of view. Even ex-army sergeants, civil patrol leaders, and military commissioners recounted their experiences from the in-between position of the beleaguered civilian" (Stoll 1993, 125, 139)."

Like Victor Montejo, Duncan Earle, and Mario Roberto Morales, Kay Warren appreciates the importance of debating the painful issues I raise. Was the "just war" of the disenfranchised Guatemalan left also a just war for the Mayan population that paid so much of the price? Does an anthropologist have a duty to report the kind of information that I discovered? I'm flattered by Warren's suggestion that *Rigoberta Menchú and the Story of All Poor Guatemalans* is an experimental ethnography. She is right that I adopted some of the conventions of the exposé genre, and her juxtaposition of it with the testimonial approach is interesting. However, she minimizes the defensive attitude about Rigoberta that more than a few Guatemala scholars have shown. If the essays from our colleagues Smith, George Lovell, and Christopher Lutz are not sufficient evidence, compare some of Warren's interpretations of what I wrote with what I actually wrote. Any reader of my two books about northern Quiché can verify that (1) I do not accuse Rigoberta of fraud; (2) I do not neglect the scholarly literature on Mayan communities; (3) I am not trying to discredit popular opposition to state violence; and (4) I have no objection to reading testimonial literature as a mediation between individual and collective veracities.

Far from seeking to discredit *I, Rigoberta Menchú* or testimonial literature, my book insists on interpreting it on the multiple levels that its significance requires. Comparing Rigoberta's story with those of her neighbors did not lead me down the "unitary path" that Warren decries. Instead, it led directly into the "contested interpretations in the past and their political stakes in the present" that she prefers. Listening to a wider range of Mayas has always been my explicit agenda. That my book was not a complete failure in contested interpretation is demonstrated by Mary Louise Pratt's complaint that I afflicted her with a "whirlwind of voices, details, innuendos, questions, possibilities, and judgments."

How could a scholar like Pratt, who has spent her career stirring up whirlwinds of contestation, find it tedious to listen to conflicting versions of events from Rigoberta's neighbors? How could some of the other scholars in this collection use the language of multicultural inclusiveness to belittle new information that enriches the study of a widely assigned book? For scholars not enmeshed in Latin America, the most astonishing feature of the controversy is how reexamining a life story could arouse so many furious objections. One reason is that, as a symbol for indigenous people and human rights victims, Rigoberta invokes the certainty-generating symbolism of martyrdom.[4] Yet no credible party questions the Guatemalan state's responsiblity for most of the victims, least of all myself.

At issue in this collection is not my scholarship. My findings about the Maya–guerrilla relationship are corroborated by an array of sources. At issue is sacrilege, which I committed by questioning a revered figure. To borrow a term from Michael Ignatieff (1999), Rigoberta's story was a moral narrative that simplified the complexities of the Guatemalan conflict in order to engage foreign sympathies. By describing how Rigoberta's neighbors recalled the war differently than she portrayed it in 1982, I disrupted a story line that activists have used to build interest in Guatemala since the early 1980s. That is why I provoked the moral dualism that still underpins much thinking about Guatemala and manifests itself in this collection in a series of non sequiturs. Criticizing the guerrilla agenda hardly means portraying Mayas as being incapable of successful collective action (Beverley) or lacking agency (Warren). Challenging Rigoberta's version of events does not mean "disassociat[ing]" myself from the army's many victims (Ferman). Paying attention to conflicts within indigenous communities is not diverting attention from state violence (Sommer) or "blaming the victims" (Rodríguez). Showing how Mayas used neutralist rhetoric to drop out of the conflict, long before the army and the guerrillas signed a peace agreement in 1996, hardly perpetuated the dualistic logic of the cold war (Ferman). Instead, I put the violence into more local context than moral dualism can accommodate.

Mary Louise Pratt is tempted to reduce my book to the culture wars over multiculturalism. However, my critique of *I, Rigoberta Menchú* will not be a "triumph ... for the political right" unless instructors make it so, by trying to stifle the questions it raises. As an anthropologist, I support efforts to diversify the curriculum like the one that Pratt helped lead at Stanford University. She may be right that I have made it harder to use *I, Rigoberta Menchú* for certain kinds of consciousness-raising. But I doubt that it will disappear from many classrooms, reading lists, and libraries: too many instructors and administrators have come to its defense, for good reasons as well as bad. If anything, the controversy has made the book a better assignment for teaching constructed history, that is, how a memoir can be both partial and true. A few students may ask, Why are you assigning us a hoax? Should you still be wondering how to explain why *I, Rigoberta Menchú* is not a hoax, read my book.

Several contributors decry my campaign against Rigoberta, so I should remind them how it began. From 1990 to 1995 my campaign against Rigoberta consisted of four academic talks (for a Berkeley panel, a Stanford brown-bag, a department lecture in New York, and a guest lecture in Florida), for a cumulative audience of about one hundred people. The other part of my campaign against Rigoberta consisted of two testimonio scholars, John Beverley (1993, 1996) and Marc Zimmerman (1995), deciding to publish their responses to a twelve-page talkscript that I had unwisely sent one of them. My first publication on Rigoberta was several years later (Stoll 1997).

At the 1991 meetings of the Latin American Studies Association (LASA) it was Beverley, not myself, who decided that it was time to debate one of my first conclusions—that Rigoberta had not witnessed her brother burn to death as described in *I, Rigoberta Menchú*. Whether she had was significant to Beverley because he had defined testimonio as a first-person narrative by a person who is a protagonist or witness. If he was right about his definition and if I was right about Rigoberta not being a witness, then the most widely read testimonio was not a testimonio.

This was indeed a problem, which Beverley and his colleagues solved by redefining the genre (Gugelberger 1996, 1999).

However, they also began to attack my still-unpublished inquiry into *I, Rigoberta Menchú*. They doubted that I had found serious problems with the 1982 story, but if I had these were of small consequence because it was a work of literature transcending mere factuality. Yet they continued to insist on a rather literal interpretation. Alternative versions that I brought back were just a "he said, she said" problem between Rigoberta and a suspect anthropologist. Although they wanted her testimony to be accepted as reliable, they were reluctant to see it compared to other forms of evidence, an attitude that continues to run through their defense of the book.[5] Now I am guilty of "the prose of counterinsurgency," according to Beverley, and to publish what Rigoberta's neighbors say is to return her to the status of a native informant.

In this collection, only Mario Roberto Morales, Daphne Patai, Victor Montejo and Duncan Earle deal with my argument about why Rigoberta became a quasi-religious figure for many foreign scholars and activists.[6] In debates over the insurgency and the Maya movement, she closes the gap between ethnography and destiny—that is, between what we can reasonably establish about Mayan peasants and how many of us wish to see them, as a revolutionary subject that it is our duty to vindicate. Behind complaints about my "journalistic" methodology (that is, I interview and quote Mayas) is discomfort with the many who are not living up to our hopes for them. The discomfort has generated various rationales for protecting Rigoberta's 1982 story from contradiction by other survivors:

1. The repression argument is that most Mayas have been too repressed to be quoted reliably on how they feel. No doubt some are; others are not. The generalization that Mayas have been "silenced" means that what they have to say can be ignored if it does not fit their presumed place in history.

2. The collective-memory argument is that Rigoberta's portrayal of Mayan experiences is so representative that differences between what she and her neighbors say must be insignificant. Unfortunately, collective-memory claims tend to assume what needs to be demonstrated. What about Rigoberta's story is widely shared with other Mayas and what is not? George Lovell and Christopher Lutz seem reluctant to factor in Rigo-

berta's affiliation with the EGP, but the need is obvious to Mayas who feel that it manipulated them.

3. The helpless-relativism argument is that there is no reliable way to evaluate the discrepancies between Rigoberta and that of other survivors. To do so therefore falls into what Doris Sommer calls "the nefarious game of judging." But if everyone has the right to a preferred truth, how do we refute the Guatemalan army's version of events? If scholars like ourselves do not have the authority to evaluate contradictory versions of events, how can outsiders intervene in human rights cases?

In practice, scholars who recur to these arguments want accountability for the Guatemalan army and literary license for Rigoberta. Yet the laureate received the Nobel Peace Prize for her work as an indigenous human rights activist, not as an author. She and her editor Elisabeth Burgos-Debray were trying to persuade readers to stop massacres, not to create world literature. That they managed to do both is a huge accomplishment, but not one that can protect Rigoberta from obvious questions. The right to compare narratives about the violence cannot be confined to scholars with advanced training in literary theory. Human rights activists cannot hold the Guatemalan army to a factual standard while making excuses for the most widely read book about the conflict.

I would like to thank Arturo Arias for putting together this collection, as well as the contributors for taking the time to respond to my work. It is an honor to be the subject of a book, and I am sorry that the occasion requires me to point out its limitations. One is that few of the editorialists reprinted here had read *Rigoberta Menchú and the Story of All Poor Guatemalans* before they damned or praised it.[7] In particular, I should respond to an accusation that cannot be answered simply by referring readers to my book. It is that I "entered war zones in the friendly embrace of the army, interrogating—excuse me, 'interviewing' informants in the presence of armed soldiers." The author of this statement was the editor of this collection (Arias 1999). "It would be interesting to know," Dante Liano asked about the same time, "if the Guatemalan army opened its archives to the North American." Without further evidence, the novelist Eduardo Galeano and the Mayan educator Demetrio Cojtí turned Liano's rhetorical question into affirmations that the army had given me access to archives that it denied to the UN-sponsored truth commission. Via the essay by Ileana Rodríguez, this groundless accusation has become scholarship in a refereed volume published by the University of Minnesota Press.[8]

It is not hard to see how some of the recrimination could have been avoided. In the realm of might-have-been, there could have been a less injured response to my first presentations to small academic gatherings a decade ago. Some of the contributors to this volume do not grasp that much of the scandal is over their own phobic reactions. The result was to discourage communication, convince me to undertake a major research effort, and encourage Rigoberta to think that she would never have to face certain facts about her life. It is much easier to defend the story that Rigoberta told in 1982 than some of the arguments in this collection. Like a Bill Clinton scandal, the denials and cover-ups are more consequential than the original transgression. Why didn't someone persuade her to preempt my findings with a well-timed statement? She was already preparing a new book about herself (Menchú 1998) with the help of Dante Liano. Supposedly it was going to set the record straight. That is why I sent her a complete draft of my book in June 1997, to spell out what she would have to deal with. The only response was a delivery receipt from the post office.

When the scandal broke, Rigoberta countered that challenges to her story were an attempt to discredit all victims of the violence (Burt and Rosen 1999). Except for a few admissions in press conferences, this was her main response, and it was a popular one with many of her supporters, who decided that questioning her 1982 story was tantamount to defending the Guatemalan army. In the national press the bulk of the editorializing was against me, not her, with the implication that there was no need for Guatemalans to read my work.[9] To make sure that they will not have the chance, some of Rigoberta's supporters pressured the Mayan publishing house Editorial Cholsamaj into killing its Spanish edition of my Ixil book.

Many have asked why I published the Rigoberta book just before the report of the truth commission—was I trying to discredit it? My book appeared when it did because it took two years and more than thirty queries to find a publisher, even in the North American academic presses. Finding a publisher for the Spanish translation has been impossible.[10] For some of the contributors to this volume, there never has been a good time to compare Rigoberta's story with that of her neighbors, and there probably never will be. Had I agreed to talk to the New York Times in

October 1990, I would be responsible for adding to the backlash against political correctness. Two years later, had I not declined comment to Tim Golden of the *Times,* I would have been guilty of discrediting the Nobel award. Had I published my findings prior to the signing of the peace agreement, I would have deflected international pressure on the Guatemalan army. Now that the reports of the two truth commissions are being digested, I am sabotaging them. If I waited longer, I would be distracting attention from the latest human rights trial or wrecking Rigoberta's bid to become president of Guatemala.

Fortunately, the controversy over my book did not divert attention from army atrocities or shatter the human rights consensus. The *New York Times* soon devoted more column inches to the truth report and a massacre exhumation than it did to Rigoberta's veracity. The indictment against the army does not depend on a story that was told eighteen years ago. Exhumation teams are digging up more evidence every month. In May 1999 the U.S. government released documents in which the army listed how it disposed of 183 kidnapping victims. Soon Rigoberta persuaded a Spanish court to indict General Efraín Ríos Montt and two other former Guatemalan dictators for genocide, terrorism, and torture.

Of the possible costs of my book, the one I take most seriously is that of depriving Mayas and other Guatemalans of a national hero. Until the press reaction to my book, I could not be sure that there would be much wounded feeling because Rigoberta had become so unpopular with her allies in the Maya movement and on the left. By the late 1990s it took some effort to hear anything but complaints about her, usually for being peremptory and unreliable. Perhaps because she receives such an uncritical reception abroad, she still spends much of her time there and is often criticized for failing to recommit herself to Guatemala (Zarembo 1999). Significantly, however, the criticism focuses on Rigoberta as a person, not as a symbol for victims of the violence. The reaction against my unread book helped her overcome some of the enmities she faces, but the relief is probably only temporary. As Diane Nelson (1999, 170–205) has pointed out, jokes about the laureate condense the ambivalence of Guatemalans over their ethnic, gender, and national identities. Feelings about her have become barometric.

There is no need to apologize for Rigoberta's stature. Nobel Peace prizes are not a reward for personal virtue. You get one because it serves a larger purpose in the opinion of the Norwegian social democrats on the Nobel committee. Once that is understood, it was clearly a good idea to give Rigoberta the 1992 prize, regardless of what you think about the guerrilla movement. Internationally, the prize increased pressure on the Guatemalan power structure to make concessions to a rather weak opposition. Even now, the upper class has to face the fact that the Guatemalan with the most name recognition in the world is a Mayan woman from a peasant village. At least in human rights symbolism, the first is last, and the last is first. The award told the upper class that it could not regain international respect without acknowledging the rights of the poorest Guatemalans.

Unfortunately, some of the assumptions behind Rigoberta's fame have narrowed the range of what can be said without causing offense. When the army's crimes bestowed moral authority on the guerrilla coalition, the latter's claim to represent the rural population became difficult for the domestic and international left to question. It seemed too close to betraying the victims. Once it was hard to debate the assumptions behind the revolutionary thinking of the early 1980s, much of what Mayas had to say became suspect.

Not enough thought has been given to the Guatemalan left's dependence on international support. Much of Rigoberta's career can be attributed to the weakness of what she represents at home. While the Guatemalan left finds itself with moral high ground, potent symbols, sympathetic foreigners, and urban-based structures for channeling foreign donations, it does not have enough local organization and interest from the people it wants to represent. Entire careers, organizations, and funding plans have been predicated on "Guatemala heart of darkness" imagery that has a basis in history but may have more appeal in foreign foundations than in villages.

Even popular support for the reforms envisioned by the peace process is less than might be hoped. In May 1999, much of the left's potential constituency failed to vote for constitutional changes required by the peace agreement, with the result that these were defeated. In the November 1999 presidential election, the URNG-backed left coalition placed a respectable but distant third (12 percent) behind the ruling conservative party (30 percent) and the right-wing populist party (48 percent) of Efraín Ríos Montt, the evangelical dictator who defeated the guerrilla movement in 1982–83. The left's electoral weakness is part of the legacy of repression, and its support could grow quickly. But the vote for Ríos is not just a function of intimidation. Even though Rigoberta has enough evidence to try him in a Spanish court, he is a surprisingly popular politician. For too many Guatemalans, including Catholics and Mayas, the man responsible for the peak of army massacres stands for law and order.

Using *I, Rigoberta Menchú* to canonize the revolutionary political claims of the early 1980s does not leave enough room for how many victims of the violence feel about it. If the story told in Paris remains sacrosanct, it will perpetuate a colonialism of images in which one person is held to be the indispensable intermediary between Mayas and the international community. Within Guatemala, Mayan intellectuals know that they do not have to fall into line behind a single leader; why do they still think they must on the international level? Perhaps this is what Rigoberta's foreign admirers have unwittingly communicated.

The most constructive suggestion in the controversy over my book has been made by the anthropologist Gary Gossen (1999). In the Mexican state of Chiapas, according to Gossen, Mayas are reading *I, Rigoberta Menchú* as a charter text, one that speaks to their identity as a people even though, strictly speaking, it is not about them. This is also how many Mayas in Guatemala hear the laureate's story. Because of the almost biblical power of the narrative, about a village girl who loses her parents to the army, flees abroad, tells the world what happened, and returns home in triumph, one woman's story becomes the story of a people.

Maybe it is time to liberate *I, Rigoberta Menchú* from the category of testimonio, which by its very name will continue to arouse expectations of eyewitness truth that this particular example cannot withstand. Let us instead think about Gossen's suggestion to teach Rigoberta's story as an epic. And not just for Mayas, as no small number of ladinos also identify with it. According to Gossen, epic narrative is about a time of tribulation; has a basis in historical fact; is told from a very partisan point of view; yet becomes a charter for a broader identity. An epic is, by the nature of its appeal, more or less beyond refutation for those who find it meaningful. But that does not mean that we should avoid historical exegesis of it. If *I, Rigoberta Menchú* is becoming national scripture for Mayas and other Guatemalans, that is all the more reason for scholars to be producing the historical criticism for which they will be asking us.

Notes

1. Since several contributors defer to the Nobel laureate's January 1999 declarations, as reprinted in this volume, I should make a few clarifications:

    1. At the Colegio Belga, Rigoberta was indeed in a work-study program. According to relatives, schoolmates, and teachers, she also attended two other Catholic boarding schools and the public elementary school in Uspantán, which enabled her to reach eighth grade.
    2. Her mother's family, the Tums of Laguna Danta, indeed sold the claim they were disputing with Vicente Menchú to a ladino. However, the sale occurred five years after his death. For the three decades prior to Vicente's death, according to relatives, neighbors, and land records, he disputed land with his K'iche' in-laws.
    3. Could Rigoberta have heard from her mother the story about her brother Petrocinio being burned to death? When Rigoberta's parents protested the death of their son in January 1980, their delegation told the press what the Chajules told me: that the seven captives from Uspantán had been shot.
    4. Yes, Rigoberta had two brothers named Nicolás. According to relatives, the first died as a small child, long before she was born; the second lives in Uspantán. The inference that the still-living second Nicolás proves that there never was an earlier Nicolás is wrong and regrettable. It appeared in the *New York Times,* not in my book.

2. In this collection, Duncan Earle's experience in southern Quiché suggests just how slender a guerrilla presence could trigger army reprisals. Both sides had tremendous incentives to exaggerate Mayan support for the insurgency. Victor Montejo explains why Rigoberta's international success was a mixed blessing for the Maya movement. While it increased awareness of the Mayas as a living people, it also validated the guerrilla movement's claim on the Mayas as a loyal but suppressed constituency. In the same vein, I wish Mario Roberto Morales had shared with us his memoir of how he came to be a member of MRP-Ixim, the dissident guerrilla group that was repressed by the URNG as well as the army (Morales 1998). As a militant from the 1960s to the 1980s, a period in which Guatemala went from annual political killings in the hundreds to annual political killings in the tens of thousands, Morales understands how Guevarista youth gave the Guatemalan right more excuses for escalating repression.

3. For other points that should be made, see my response in the November 1999 issue of *Latin American Perspectives.*

4. Doris Sommer: "bearing witness has been a sacred responsibility throughout Christianity, which is why witnesses are martyrs etymologically and historically. . . . The double challenge for this Christian leader, as new and as beleaguered as Christ's first witnesses, is to serve truth in ways that make a difference in the world" (in this volume).

5. For other approaches to testimonio, see Ochando Aymerich 1998 and Burgos 1999.

6. "Certainly Rigoberta was a representative of her people, but hiding behind that was a more partisan role, as a representative of the revolutionary movement, and hiding behind that was an even more unsettling possibility: that she represented

the audiences whose assumptions about indígenas she mirrored so effectively. I believe this is why it was so indecent for me to question her claims. Exposing problems in Rigoberta's story was to expose how supporters have subliminally used it to clothe their own contradictions, in a Durkheimian case of society worshiping itself" (Stoll 1999, 246).

7. Other collections of essays on the controversy include the October–December 1999 issue of *Human Rights Review* (www.transactionpub.com, with essays by Daphne Patai, Joan Bamberger, Brian Haley, Daniel Levine, and Luis Roniger); the November 1999 issue of *Latin American Perspectives* (with essays by Carol Smith, Norma Chinchilla, Victoria Sanford, Georg Gugelberger, Elisabeth Burgos, and myself); and the April 1999 and January 2000 issue of *Lateral* (www.lateral-ed.es, with essays by Carmen Ochando, Elisabeth Burgos, Yvon Le Bot, and myself). Other reviews and commentaries have been published by Roger Lancaster (*NACLA Report on the Americas,* May–June 1999, responding to interviews with Rigoberta and myself in the March–April 1999 issue); Peter Canby (*New York Review of Books,* April 8, 1999); Charles Lane (*New Republic,* March 8, 1999); Ilan Stavans (*Times Literary Supplement,* April 23, 1999); Richard Gott (*London Review of Books,* May 27, 1999); and Hal Cohen (*Lingua Franca,* July–August 1999, with my response September–October 1999).

8. Liano's suspicions had been aroused by the fact that (1) I had consulted the public land records for Rigoberta's village, and (2) the records were housed in an archive at the government titling agency. Like other researchers who worked in militarized areas during the late 1980s (Zur 1997; Carlsen 1997; Green 1999), I dealt with the army only when required, which in my case was seldom. One reason I chose to work in Ixil country was that its contingent of foreign aid volunteers had the effect of lowering my profile. In Uspantán I never had to deal with the military personnel because the area was no longer garrisoned by the time I did most of my work there, in 1993–95. If I had approached peasants through the army, they would not have told me about the crimes that it committed and I could not have quoted them the way I do.

This is not the first occasion in which Arias and Liano have been quick to launch allegations. In November 1998 they accused Ann Wright, the English translator for both Rigoberta's books, of "intellectual theft" and "piracy" because Liano and coeditor Gianni Minà failed to appear in the acknowledgments for the English edition of *Crossing Borders* (E-mail circulated by Marc Zimmerman, October 17, 1998). According to Wright, she translated everything she was given and never received the from matter from the Menchú Foundation or the Spanish publisher who sold the English-language rights. Since the two editions were prepared concurrently, Wright was not working from the book in Spanish (E-mail, October 21, 1998).

9. "I found three main kinds of reactions," a researcher visiting Guatemala in mid-1999 told me: "apathy (mostly Maya); different sorts of conspiracy theories—the U.S. government paid you, etc. (mostly middle-class supporters, both ladino and Maya); and agreement (vindictive agreement from some and terse, regretful agreement from others). Is this similar to what you found? I would say half of the people I asked had barely heard about Menchú, let alone know anything about her story. The only people I met who had read at least part of your work were reporters."

10. Because *Between Two Armies* and *Story of All Poor Guatemalans* would otherwise be unavailable in Spanish, I have put both translations on my Web site at www.middlebury.edu/-dstoll. In 1999, Editorial Abya-Yala of Quito, Ecuador, pub-

lished an edition-in-exile of *Entre Dos Fuegos*, for which I am profoundly grateful. Perhaps it can still be ordered from Abya-Yala via admin-info@abyayala.org.

Bibliography

Arias, Arturo. 1985. "El Movimiento Indígena en Guatemala, 1970–83." In *Movimientos Populares en Centroamérica*, ed. Daniel Camacho. Costa Rica: Ciudad Universitario Rodrigo Facio. 63–119.

——. 1990. "Changing Indian Identity: Guatemala's Violent Transition to Modernity." In *Guatemalan Indians and the State: 1540 to 1988*, ed. C. Smith. Austin: University of Texas Press. 230–57.

——. 1999. "Más sobre las memorias de Rigoberta Menchú." *Guatemala Hoy*, January 18.

Beverley, John. 1993. "El Testimonio en la encrucijada." *Revista Iberoamericana* 59: 484–95.

——. 1996. "The Real Thing." In *The Real Thing: Testimonial Discourse and Latin America*, ed. Georg M. Gugelberger. Durham, N.C.: Duke University Press. 266–86.

Brintnall, Douglas. 1979. *Revolt against the Dead: The Modernization of a Mayan Community in the Highlands of Guatemala*. New York: Gordon and Breach.

Burgos, Elisabeth. 1999. "The Story of a Testimonio" and "Testimonio and Transmission." *Latin American Perspectives*. 26.9: 53–63, 86–88.

Burt, Jo-Marie, and Fred Rosen. 1999. "Truth-Telling and Memory in Postwar Guatemala: An Interview with Rigoberta Menchú." *NACLA: Report on the Americas* 32.5: 6–10.

Carey-Webb, Allen, and Stephen Benz, eds. 1996. *Teaching and Testimony: Rigoberta Menchú and the North American Classroom*. Albany: State University of New York Press.

Carlsen, Robert S. 1997. *The War for the Heart and Soul of a Highland Maya Town*. Austin: University of Texas Press.

CEH (Comisión de Esclarecimiento Histórico). 1999. *Guatemala: Memoria del silencio.*

Cushman, Thomas, ed. 1999. "Truth, Fact, and Fiction in the Human Rights Community: Essays in Response to David Stoll's *Rigoberta Menchú and the Story of All Poor Guatemalans*." *Human Rights Review* 1.1: 78–112.

Davis, Shelton. 1988. "Introduction: Sowing the Seeds of Violence." In *Harvest of Violence*, ed. Robert M. Carmack. Norman: University of Oklahoma Press. 3–36.

Falla, Ricardo. 1980. *Quiché rebelde: Estudio de un movimiento de conversión religioso, rebelde a las creencias tradicionales, en San Antonio Ilotenango, Quiché (1948–70)*. Guatemala City: Editorial Universitaria de Guatemala.

Fischer, Edward F., and R. McKenna Brown, eds. 1996. *Maya Cultural Activism in Guatemala*. Austin: University of Texas Press.

Gossen, Gary. 1999. "Rigoberta Menchú and Her Epic Narrative." *Latin American Perspectives* 26.9: 64–69.

Green, Linda. 1999. *Fear as a Way of Life*. New York: Columbia University Press.

Gugelberger, Georg M. 1999. "*Stollwerk* or Bulwark: David Meets Goliath and the Continuation of the Testimonio Debate," *Latin American Perspectives* 26.9: 47–51.

——. 1996. *The Real Thing: Testimonial Discourse and Latin America*. Durham, N.C.: Duke University Press.

Ignatieff, Michael. 1999. "The Stories We Tell: Television and Humanitarian Aid." In *Hard Choices: Moral Dilemmas in Humanitarian Intervention,* ed. Jonathan Moore. Lanham, Md.: Rowman and Littlefield.

Kobrak, Paul. 1997. "Village Troubles: The Civil Patrols in Aguacatán, Guatemala." Ph.D. dissertation, Department of Sociology, University of Michigan.

Le Bot, Yvon. 1995. *La guerra en tierras mayas: Comunidad, violencia y modernidad en Guatemala (1970–1992).* Mexico City: Fondo de Cultura Económica.

Menchú, Rigoberta. 1998. *Rigoberta: La nieta de los Mayas.* Ed. Dante Liano and Gianni Minà. Madrid: El País/Aguilar.

Montejo, Victor. 1987. *Testimony: Death of a Guatemalan Village.* Willimantic, Conn.: Curbstone Press.

———. 1999. *Voices from Exile: Violence and Survival in Modern Maya History.* Norman: University of Oklahoma Press.

Morales, Mario Roberto. 1998. *Los que se fueron por la libre (Historia personal de la lucha armada y la guerra popular).* Mexico City: Editorial Praxis.

Nelson, Diane M. 1999. *A Finger in the Wound: Body Politics in Quincentennial Guatemala.* Berkeley: University of California Press.

Ochando Aymerich, Carmen. 1998. *La memoria en el espejo: Aproximación a la escritura testimonial.* Barcelona: Anthropos Editorial.

Oficina de Derechos Humanos del Arzobispado de Guatemala (ODHA). 1998. *Guatemala nunca más.* Informe Proyecto Interdiocesano de Recuperación de la Memoria Histórica.

Smith, Carol A. 1984. "Local History in Global Context: Social and Economic Transitions in Western Guatemala." *Comparative Studies in Society and History* 26.2: 193–228.

———. 1991. "Maya Nationalism." *Report on the Americas* 25.3: 29–33.

Stoll, David. 1993. *Between Two Armies in the Ixil Towns of Guatemala.* New York: Columbia University Press.

———. 1997. "The Construction of *I, Rigoberta Menchú:* Excerpts from a Work in Progress." *Brick, a Literary Journal* (Toronto) 57 (fall): 31–38.

———. 1998. "Human Rights, Land Conflict, and Memories of the Violence in the Ixil Country of Northern Quiché." In *Guatemala after the Peace Accords,* ed. Rachel Sieder. London: Institute for Latin American Studies.

———. 1999. "Rigoberta Menchú and the Last-Resort Paradigm," *Latin American Perspectives* 26.9: 70–80.

Watanabe, John. 1992. *Maya Saints and Souls in a Changing World,* Austin: University of Texas Press.

Wilson, Richard. 1996. "Introduction" and "Representing Human Rights Violations: Social Contexts and Subjectivities." In *Human Rights, Culture and Context: Anthropological Perspectives,* ed. Richard Wilson. London: Pluto Press. 1–27, 134–60.

Zarembo, Alan. 1999. "Trouble for Rigoberta." *Newsweek International,* June 21.

Zimmerman, Mark. 1995. *Literature and Resistance in Guatemala: Textual Modes and Cultural Politics from El Señor Presidente to Rigoberta Menchú.* 2 vols. Athens: Ohio University Press.

Zur, Judith N. 1997. *Violent Memories: Mayan War Widows.* Boulder, Colo.: HarperCollins.

Contributors

Luis Aceituno is a Guatemalan journalist.

Arturo Arias, Guatemalan by birth and a novelist by trade, is director of Latin American studies at the University of Redlands and a specialist on Guatemalan ethnic issues, a subject central to both his fiction and his academic work. He is the cowriter of the screenplay for the film *El Norte* and the author of several novels, including *Después las bombas* (translated in English as *After the Bombs*), *Cascabel, Itzam Na, Jaguar en Llamas,* and *Los caminos de Paxil;* he was awarded the Casa de las Américas Award and the Anna Seghers Scholarship for two of his novels. He has also published two books of literary criticism, *La identidad de la palabra,* on Guatemalan twentieth-century fiction, and *Gestos ceremoniales,* on contemporary Central American fiction. He recently finished the novel *Sopa de caracol* and the critical edition of Miguel Ángel Asturias's *Mulata de tal.*

Juan Jesús Aznárez is a Spanish journalist.

John Beverley is professor of Spanish and Latin American literature and cultural studies at the University of Pittsburgh. He is a founding member of the Latin American Subaltern Studies Group. His publications include *Del Lazarillo al Sandinismo: Literature and Politics in the Central American Revolutions* (with Marc Zimmerman); *Against Literature* (Minnesota, 1993); *La voz del otro: Testimonio, subalternidad y verdad narrativa* (with

Hugo Achugar); *The Postmodernism Debate in Latin America* (with José Oviedo and Michael Aronna); and *Subalternity and Representation: Arguments in Cultural Theory*. His much-anthologized essay "The Margin at the Center: On Testimonio" (1989) was influential in the literary canonization of *I, Rigoberta Menchú*. He is the "literary theorist" referred to by David Stoll in his book on Menchú Tum who made public Stoll's critique of Menchú at a session of the 1991 convention of the Latin American Studies Association. He is currently working on a book about Miami.

Allen Carey-Webb is associate professor of English at Western Michigan University. He is the author of *Making Subject(s): Literature and the Emergence of National Identity* and the forthcoming *Literature and Lives: Toward a Response-based, Cultural Studies Approach to Teaching English in High School and College*. With Stephen Benz, he is coeditor of *Teaching and Testimony: Rigoberta Menchú and the North American Classroom*.

Margarita Carrera is a poet and newspaper columnist.

Duncan Earle is a Fulbright, Rockefeller, and Mellon recipient. Since 1974 he has carried out periodic research in Guatemala and Chiapas, Mexico, with a comparative emphasis on the role of religion in indigenous society, as social and theological systems interact with other ethnicities, religions, and forms of organization and as they affect power relations. He has worked in numerous grassroots community development efforts, with Guatemalan Mayas, Maya refugees, and other people displaced by political strife, and he has written on issues of identity after displacement. He currently lives on the U.S.–Mexico border (an area he also writes about) and is working on a project on current Maya concepts of death and sacred geography.

Carolina Escobar Sarti is a Guatemalan journalist.

Claudia Ferman is professor of Latin American literature, culture, and film at the University of Richmond. She is the author of *Política y posmodernidad: Hacia una lectura de la anti-modernidad en Latinoamérica*, which won the Letras de Oro award, and *The Postmodern in Latin and Latino American Cultural Narratives: Collected Essays and Interviews*. Her current research projects include a book manuscript, "Nomadic Writings: The Post-National Landscape and the Production of Culture."

Dina Fernández García is a Guatemalan journalist.

Eduardo Galeano, a Uruguayan writer and journalist, is the author of several works, including *Days and Nights of Love and War, The Book of Embraces,* and the highly acclaimed *Memory of Fire* trilogy.

Dante Liano is a Guatemalan novelist and professor at the University of Milan. He is the editor, with Gianni Minà, of Rigoberta Menchú's second book, *Crossing Borders.*

W. George Lovell is professor of geography at Queen's University in Canada. He first went to Guatemala in 1974 and has been a regular visitor since. His research interests, which in 1995 earned him the Carl O. Sauer Distinguished Scholarship Award from the Conference of Latin Americanist Geographers, focus primarily but not exclusively on the colonial period. He is the author of *A Beauty That Hurts: Life and Death in Guatemala,* and, with Christopher H. Lutz, his scholarly partner for two decades, the coauthor of *Demography and Empire: A Guide to the Population History of Spanish Central America, 1500–1821.*

Christopher H. Lutz has researched and written about colonial Guatemalan history for thirty years. In 1978 he was one of the cofounders of the Centro de Investigaciones Regionales de Mesoamérica (CIRMA), based in Antigua, Guatemala. He has written extensively on ethnic relations and population change in colonial Guatemala and the rest of Spanish Central America. He is the author of *Santiago de Guatemala, 1541–1773: City, Caste, and the Colonial Experience,* the coauthor (with his frequent collaborator, W. George Lovell) of *Demography and Empire: A Guide to the Population History of Spanish Central America, 1500–1821,* and coeditor (with Karen Dakin) of *Nuestro pesar, nuestra aflicción/tunetuliniliz, tucucuca: Memorias en lengua náhuatl enviadas a Felipe II por indígenas del valle de Guatemala hacia 1572.* In 1998 he was awarded the Orden de los Cinco Volcanes (Order of the Five Volcanoes) by the Guatemalan Ministry of Foreign Relations in recognition of his publications on Central America, especially Guatemala.

Octavio Martí is the Paris correspondent of *El País*.

Victor D. Montejo is a Maya anthropologist and author who had to leave Guatemala during the early 1980s. He has taught at Bucknell University and the University of Montana in Missoula and he is now associate professor and chair of the Department of Native American Studies at the University of California, Davis. He has authored several books, including *Testimony: Death of a Guatemalan Village; The Bird Who Cleans the World and Other Mayan Fables; Sculpted Stones; Las Aventuras de Mister Puttison entre los Mayas; Voices from Exile: Violence and Survival in Modern Maya History;* and *Popol Vuh: A Sacred Book of the Maya* (a version for young readers).

Rosa Montero is a Spanish writer and journalist.

Mario Roberto Morales is a Guatemalan novelist, academic, and journalist. He has published five novels, two books of essays, and poetry. He is a columnist for *Diario Siglo Veintiuno* in Guatemala and teaches Latin American literature at the University of Northern Iowa. He has actively participated in the interethnic debate in Guatemala since 1992. He was a left-wing militant in Guatemala from 1966 to 1991.

Jorge Palmieri is a Guatemalan journalist.

Daphne Patai teaches in the Department of Spanish and Portuguese at the University of Massachusetts at Amherst. She has written and edited ten books, including *Brazilian Women Speak: Contemporary Life Stories; Women's Words: The Feminist Practice of Oral History* (with Sherna Berger Gluck); *Professing Feminism: Cautionary Tales from the Strange World of Women's Studies* (with Noretta Koertge); and, most recently, *Heterophobia: Sexual Harassment and the Future of Feminism.* She has written extensively on problems in higher education.

Mary Louise Pratt is Olive H. Palmer Professor of Humanities at Stanford University, where she teaches in the departments of Spanish and Portuguese and comparative literature. A native Canadian, she is the author of *Imperial Eyes: Travel Writing and Transculturation* and coauthor of *Women, Culture, and Politics in Latin America.* She has written many essays on literature and politics, and is currently completing a study of gender and citizenship in the work of Latin American women writers and intellectuals.

Danilo Rodríguez is a Guatemalan political commentator.

Ileana Rodríguez is professor of Latin American culture at The Ohio State University. Nicaraguan by birth, she is the author of *Women, Guerrillas, and Love: Understanding War in Central America* and *House, Garden, Nation: Space, Gender, and Ethnicity in Post-Colonial Latin American Literatures by Women.* She is currently working on a text on topographies, which covers islands, highland, and jungle as three of the most important cultural tropes of the transatlantic imaginary.

Larry Rohter is the *New York Times* correspondent in Latin America.

Jorge Skinner-Kleé is a Guatemalan ex-congressman. He publishes opinion columns regularly in Guatemalan newspapers.

Elzbieta Sklodowska, a native of Poland, is professor of Spanish at Washington University in Saint Louis. She is the author of *La parodia en la nueva novela hispanoamericana; Testimonio hispanoamericano: historia, teoría, poética;* and *Todo ojos, todo oídos: control e insubordinación en la novela hispanoamericana (1895–1935),* as well as numerous articles on Spanish-American narrative and literary theory. She is the recipient of Premio Plural (1984), Premio Discurso Literario (1988), and the NEMLA Foreign Language Book Award (1991).

Carol A. Smith is professor of anthropology at the University of California at Davis. She has carried out more than five years of fieldwork in Guatemala, beginning in 1969. Her primary focus has been the Guatemalan economy and its impact on social relations between Indians and Ladinos in Guatemala; since the 1980s she has also studied politics, gender, and racism. Her best-known work is *Guatemalan Indians and the State, 1540–1988,* which she edited and to which she contributed four articles; she has also published widely in anthropological and Latin American journals.

Doris Sommer is professor of Latin American literature at Harvard University. She is author of, among other works, *Foundational Fictions: The National Romances of Latin America* and *Proceed with Caution When Engaged by Minority Writing in the Americas.*

David Stoll is assistant professor of anthropology at Middlebury College. He is the author of *Between Two Armies in the Ixil Towns of Guatemala, Fishers of Men or Founders of Empire?, Is Latin America Turning Protestant?,* and (with Virginia Garrard Burnett) *Rethinking Protestantism in Latin America.* His research in Guatemala has been sponsored by the National Science Foundation, the Inter-American Foundation, the Organization of American States, the Harry Frank Guggenheim Foundation, and the Woodrow Wilson Center for International Scholars.

Manuel Vásquez Montalbán is a Spanish writer and journalist.

Kay B. Warren is professor of anthropology at Harvard University. She has focused her recent research on multiculturalism and public intellectuals, violence and peace processes, social movements and ethnic nationalism, and transnational identity politics. She currently holds an Abe Fellowship from the Japan Foundation and the SSRC, and serves as the faculty chair of the selection committee for the MacArthur Foundation's Research and Writing Competition on Global Security and Sustainability. Her research on Latin America has been supported by fellowships from the John Simon Guggenheim Foundation, the Institute for Advanced Study, and the Wenner-Gren Foundation, and research grants from Princeton University and Harvard University.

Permissions